Gus Nichols Library

Faulkner University

Donated by

Dan Alexander

WHAT THE BIBLE SAYS ABOUT
CIVIL GOVERNMENT

WHAT THE BIBLE SAYS SERIES

WHAT THE BIBLE SAYS ABOUT
CIVIL GOVERNMENT

Paul T. Butler

College Press Publishing Company, Joplin, Missouri

Copyright © 1990
College Press Publishing Company

Printed and Bound in the
United States of America
All Rights Reserved

Library of Congress Catalog Card Number: 90-80691
International Standard Book Number: 0-89900-266-8

This Book is Dedicated
To

Patricia Ann (nee Uthe) Butler
loved and cherished
daughter-in-law

And

T/Sgt. Larry Lee Lankford, USAF
loved and respected
son-in-law

And

My ancestors and relatives, from the Pilgrims at Plymouth to the American War for Independence, the War Between the States, World Wars I and II, Korea, Vietnam, and other patriotic services,

And To

My Own Comrades in Arms in World War II and
the Korean War
Thousands of whom laid down their lives for
the liberty-loving peoples of the world . . . .

"Greater love has no man than this, that a man lay down his life
for his friends."
(John 15:13)

Table of Contents

DEDICATION 5

INTRODUCTION 9

1. THE ORIGIN OF CIVIL GOVERNMENT 17

2. THE PURPOSE OF CIVIL GOVERNMENT 43

3. THE FORM OF CIVIL GOVERNMENT 109

4. CRIME AND PUNISHMENT 141

5. WAR 215

6. PARTICIPATION OF BELIEVERS 249

7. TAXATION 267

8. PRIVATE OWNERSHIP OF PROPERTY 301

9. PUBLIC WELFARE 339

10. CIVIL DISOBEDIENCE 353

11. INTERNATIONAL RELATIONS 373

12. CHURCH AND STATE 391

EPILOGUE 415

APPENDIX:

THE PROVIDENCE OF GOD IN THE
   COLONIZATION OF AMERICA! 421

BIBLE PREACHER — FORERUNNERS OF FREEDOM 435

AN ASSEMBLY OF DEMIGODS 451

INTRODUCTION

The longer one studies the Bible, the more one realizes how little he knows about it! It is, therefore, with sincerest humility that this author presumes to write a book entitled, *What The Bible Says About* — anything! After one has made an exegesis of every passage in the Bible which explicitly uses the word "government" or "kingdom" or "dominion", one would still wish to deal with the implicit passages. The magnitude of such a task is nearly overwhelming. We shall do our best for now and leave it to other generations to complete what is lacking and revise what is erroneous.

Before proceeding with the main discussion, certain word studies are in order. Actually the reader may be surprised to learn just how few times the word "government" is used in the Bible. The word "civil" is used not at all! The following tabulations of the English Bible are from *The New Strong's Exhaustive Concordance of the Bible*, by Nelson, 1948:

WHAT THE BIBLE SAYS ABOUT CIVIL GOVERNMENT

Number of Times these English Words Appear in the English Bible

Govern/Governor/Government
Old Testament - 57
New Testament - 30

Rule/Ruler
Old Testament - 198
New Testament - 63

King(s)
Old Testament - 2696
New Testament - 119

Kingdom(s)
Old Testament - 239
New Testament - 160

Magistrates(s)
Old Testament - 2
New Testament - 8

Lord
7182 (too often referring to God to be significant in civil government)

Prince(s)
Old Testament - 380
New Testament - 4

Principalities
Old Testament - 1
New Testament - 8

Dominion(s)
Old Testament - 49
New Testament - 12

Actually there are only five times the English word "government(s)" is used as a translation of the original languages of the Bible. The Hebrew word *miserah* is twice translated "government" (Isa. 9:6,7) and the Hebrew word *memeshalah* is once translated "government" (Isa. 22:21, KJV) and "authority" (Isa. 22:21, RSV). The Greek word *kuberneseis* is translated "governments" (I Cor. 12:28, KJV) but translated "authorities" in the RSV.

The English word "government" probably originates from the Greek word *kubernetes* which was used by the ancient Greeks to designate a steersman, helmsman, or sailing-master (see Acts 27:11, "captain"; Rev. 18:17, "shipmasters"; Ezek. 27:8,27 "pilots" in the LXX). Perhaps the Romans adopted the Greek word and Latinized it into *gubernare*, which also was used to designate one who "steers, guides, controls, governs." The Latin word *gubernare* is from the Latin noun *gubernaculum* meaning,

INTRODUCTION

"a rudder, a helm." The Hebrew word *radah* is used in Genesis 1:26,28 to describe the "dominion" over creation which God gave to Adam. The Hebrew word most often translated "rule, govern, have dominion" is *mashal*. The Greek word most often used in a generic sense is *hegemon* which means "rulers" or "princes." *Hegemon* is used to describe Pontius Pilate, e.g. Matthew 27:2; Luke 20:20 (Tacitus, the Roman historian, also calls Pilate *hegemon* in his Annals, 15:44). Derivatives of this Greek word are *hegeomai* ("a governor," Matt. 2:6; Acts 7:10) and *hegemoneuo* (a verb, meaning, "to lead the way" and is used of Quirinius, governor of Syria, Luke 2:2; and used to describe Pilate, Luke 3:1). The Greek word *hegemonia*, in Luke 3:1, is translated "reign", and is the word from which we get the English word, *hegemony*.

There are numerous other words in both the Hebrew and the Greek which are synonymous with the subject (civil government) under discussion:

Hebrew:
asoh — to make, to exercise; *chabash* — to fasten, to bind; *nachah* — to lead; (all translated, "govern"); *misherah* — to have dominion; *memeshalah* to have power, or command; (all translated, "government"). *mushel* — ruler; *nagiyd* — a chief leader; *pechah* — a governor (Chaldean); *pakad* — to appoint; *aluph* a dignified person with authority; (all translated "governor"); *melech* — "King."

Greek:
exousia — (from *exesti*, "it is lawful") authority; *dunastes* — (from which we get the English word *dynasty*) potentate; *huperoche* — in high position; (all translated "authority"); *hegemon* — governor; *ethnarches* — governor; (all translated "governor"); *basileus* — the generic term for "King," whether human or divine; *archon* — ruler; *kosmokrator* — world-ruler; *politarches* — ruler of a city; (all translated "ruler"); *kratos* — strong, powerful, mighty;

kuriotes — (from *kurios*, "lord") lordship, potentate; (all translated, "dominion").

There is one word in the Old Testament describing an office of civil power unique to the Hebrew civil-religious structure. That word is *shuphtiym* and is the title given to the "Judges" (Othniel, Ehud, Gideon, Sampson, et al.) between Moses and the monarchy.

The great civil potentates mentioned incidentally in the Biblical text (from Egypt, Assyria, Babylon, Persia, Greece, Rome), and the lesser ones, often bear titles and positions for which there were no Hebrew or Greek words so we find Aramaic, Roman, Chaldean, Persian, Egyptian and Greek government titles transliterated into Hebrew and Greek. We find such words as *yakiyra* (Ezra 4:10) translated "noble," *parettemiym* (Esther 6:9) also translated "most noble." Both of these would probably be of Persian derivation.

A number of other words in the Old Testament used to delineate offices and functions of civil government may be found in Daniel 6:1,2. There is *ahashdarpenim*, translated both "satrap" and "prince" (also found in Ezra 8:36 and Esther 8:9); there is *sigenaya*, translated "governors"; *pachevatha*, or "captains"; *dethaberaya*, "judges"; *gedabereys*, "treasurers"; *edareggazerays*, "counsellors"; *tiphetaye*, "sheriffs"; *shiletoney mediynatha*, "rulers of the provinces." In Daniel 6:7 we find the word *sarekaya* translated "presidents." Most of these would be words "borrowed" from the Aramaic or Akkadian languages and transliterated in the Hebrew text.

There is the word *eth-rabeshakeh* or *Rabshakeh*, in Isaiah 36:2ff, which is from *rab*, "chief" and *saki*, "captains", thus a "colonel" or "general." In II Kings 18:17 Sennacherib, king of Assyria, is said to have sent the *Tartan*, the *Rabsaris*, and the *Rabshakeh* with a great army from Lachish to King Hezekiah at Jerusalem. *Rabsaris* is probably the title conferred upon the "chief of the leading men." *Tartan* is a title translated "commander-in-chief" (Isa. 20:1 RSV).

INTRODUCTION

In Genesis 42:6 Joseph is promoted to *shalat*, "governor" but is called *mashal* "ruler" in Genesis 45:26. Joseph was, of course, second ruler to "Pharaoh" who was "king of Egypt." The word *Pharaoh* probably comes from the Egyptian *Pr-o* meaning, "Great house" or "Palace." Originally it made reference to the royal family's residence and later became a title of the ruling monarch of Egypt. In Genesis 40:2,5, Pharaoh is said to have *saryisaryav*, "chief officers", *sar hamashiqum*, "chief of the cupbearers" (also translated "chief of the butlers"), and *sar haaophim*, "chief of the bakers." Nehemiah was the "cupbearer" to Artaxerxes, king of Persia (Neh. 1:11). Cupbearers and bakers may not have been, strictly speaking, officials of civil government but they possessed considerable political "clout." In the book of Job, considered by some to be the oldest book of the Old Testament, we read of Job using the titles, *melech*, "king," and *sar* "prince" (Job 3:14,15). Perhaps the oldest historical reference to a civil governor-of-sorts is in Genesis 10:8-10 where Nimrod is referred to as "the first on earth to be a mighty man." The Hebrew word is *gibbor* and is sometimes translated "hero" or "mighty one." It is also said of Nimrod that the "beginning of his kingdom" (Heb. *memelaketho*, "his kingdom") consisted of three "cities" named "Babel, Erech, and Accad," all of them "in the land of Shinar."

Additional words used for civil government officials in the New Testament may also be found. In Luke 3:1 we find *Kaisaros*, "Caesar," and *tetrarch*, "ruler of a fourth part of a territory." The word *basilikos* in John 4:46 is translated "official" in the RSV, and "nobleman" in the KJV. The titles of officials in government or civil service in the book of Acts provides an interesting and informative survey. Aside from the titles of king, ruler, governor and others already mentioned, we find *asiarch*, "chief officials of Asia" (Acts 19:31); *grammateus*, "town clerk" (Acts 19:35); *anthupato*, "procounsul" (Acts 13:7,8,12; 18:12; 19:38); *strategois* and *praetors*, "magistrates" (Acts 16:20); *archontas* "rulers" (Acts 16:19); *proto tes nesou*, "chief man of the island"

(Publius, Acts 28:7). Then, of course, the two most used words describing officers in the Roman army: *chiliarchos*, "tribune" (Acts 21:31,32,33; 23:17,18,19,22; 24:22,37; 22:24-29; 23:10; and *hekatontarchon*, "centurion" (Acts 22:25,26; 23:17,23; 24:23; 27:1,6,43, etc.). Erastus is called *oikonomos tes poleos* "treasurer of the city" in Romans 16:23. In I Timothy 2:1ff we have the words *basileon*, "kings", and the phrase, *ton en huperechonti*, those in eminence or in authority"; in Titus 3:1, the words *archais*, "rulers," and *exousiais*, "authorities"; in I Peter 2:13-17 the words *basilei huperechonti*, "emperor as supreme" and *hegemosin pempomenois*, "governors as sent . . . ," and Jude 8, *kurioteta*, "authority."

The book of Revelation, written to the seven churches of Asia Minor concerning their great tribulation at the hands of the Roman empire from 100-450 A.D., mentions *basileis* ("kings") and *megistantes* ("great men") and *chiliarchoi* ("generals") (Rev. 6:15; 19:18); it points to ten *basileis* ("kings") in Revelation 17:12.

The apostle Paul sums up all forms of human government in I Corinthians 15:24 when he reveals that history will come to a climactic end as Christ delivers the "kingdom" to God the Father "after destroying every rule and every authority and power." The Greek words in this text are: *arche* "rule," *exousia*, "authority," and *dunamis*, "power."

The Bible is a history of the spiritual redemption of mankind and a promise of the eventual redemption of all creation (Rom. 8:18ff). It is essentially the history of the incarnation of God in Jesus Christ — the preparation for it, the accomplishment of it, and the results of it. The Bible is *not* a history of human ideologies, or of human politics, *except* as they historically and incidentally come into contact with the redemptive program of God, or as they apply theologically to it.

This brief word study, however, indicates that the redemptive kingdom of God, because it is being formed within the milieu of human history, is in constant contact with civil governments.

INTRODUCTION

From the beginning (Genesis) to the end (Revelation) of the Bible, words pertaining to human rulers and earthly kingdoms are found. It is apparent that from the very early times of man's existence until he resides no more upon this planet earth, the church (God's spiritual kingdom) will have to function parallel to and, so far as ethically possible, in relationship to civil governments. It is imperative, therefore, that Christians understand as clearly as possible what the Bible says about civil government.

1

THE ORIGIN OF CIVIL GOVERNMENT

Civil government has its origin from the mind and will of Almighty God. It did not originate in the mind of man. Its divine source is unequivocally stated in the Bible in such places as Romans 13:1-7 and I Peter 2:13-17. Men are the instruments through which God carries out his purposes in civil government, but civil government has its conception with God.

The Holy Spirit of God revealed to the apostle Paul that " . . . there is no authority except from God, and those that exist have been instituted by God" (Rom. 13:1). The Greek adverbial negative, *ou*, is idiomatically in the emphatic position in the foregoing phrase. Literally, the Greek phrase is, *ou gar estin exousia ei me hupo theou*. Literally translated that would read, " . . . no, for there is authority except from God."

Further, the Greek verb, *tetagmenai*, translated "instituted" (RSV) in Romans 13:1, is a perfect tense participle. This participle is from the Greek root word *tasso* which means "arranged, set, appointed, ordered, framed, fixed." The Greek perfect tense means that the action has happened in the past and continues to happen. The participle *tetagmenai* is also in the passive mood. This means that God "ordered and fixed" the principle or axiom of civil government in the past with a continuity to the present, and it was God acting to establish government — not government acting to establish itself. God acted, he did so in the past and he continues to do so in the present, to give birth to human civil government. The concept of civil government for the human race was not initiated out of the exigencies of human trial and error. It was in the mind of God from eternity and revealed to humanity by planting the need for order, law, structure and direction indigenously in the mind of man at creation.

Ordered social structure inheres in the very nature of Almighty God, the Ruler. He makes nothing disordered. When he created the world, he did not create it chaotic (cf. Isa. 45:18,19). He is not a God of confusion (cf. I Cor. 14:33). Created things and created beings were made to follow divine "laws" (cf. Jer. 5:22). God made man a social being. Man was meant to exist companionably, or interpersonally, with other beings of like nature as himself. And since man is a contingent being (dependent) and not omnipotent himself, he is "programmed" to acknowledge his need for government. God, the Creator, planted that "need" within man when he *created* him. Man's contingency and mortality, however, renders him incapable of originating on his own principles or axioms of sufficient wisdom to guide him in civil government. God *revealed* those axioms and guidelines in the "natural revelation" (in "nature," in human conscience, and human capacity to reason) and in his "special revelation" (the propositional revelation in human language which we call the Bible). The social essence of man logically or naturally necessitates control, order, or structure. Man is incapable of existing in absolute freedom. He is finite, not omnipotent or omniscient. His finitude and contingency proposes a necessary regimentation.

THE ORIGIN OF CIVIL GOVERNMENT

The most ancient form of human social relationship, the family — husband and wife and offspring — necessitated governmental structure. Each member of the civil unit called "family" was intended by God to function within a divinely ordained order (see *First Corinthians*, by Butler, pp. 199-208). The first man, Adam, and his wife, Eve, were commanded, "Be fruitful and multiply, and fill the earth and subdue it; and have dominion . . . " (Gen. 1:28). Let the record show that Adam and Eve (and their progeny) have obeyed God in this commandment! We have approximately five billion descendants of these two now alive on this earth! This does not count the billions who have already lived and died on this planet. They did "multiply"! Human multiplication demanded at least one more form of social government to secure the rights of the fundamental unity of humanity (the family) so people might reach the goal their Creator intended when he made them. Dr. C.C. Crawford, in his book, *Commonsense Ethics*, pp. 360-361 declares:

> 11. *Authority in Civil Society*. The Natural Law (and Dr. Crawford means, the Divine Law, as the reader shall see in the following quotation) in ordaining the society and its proper end, thereby ordains the means necessary to the attainment of that end: civil authority is that necessary means. Indeed, without civil authority the state could not exist. *Authority in itself* must be distinguished from the *form of administration* or type of regime. Authority is always present irrespective of the will of man, and cannot be abolished (any more than the law of gravity, or that of valence, for example, can be abrogated by humankind); the essence of authority is immutable. It is evident, from the fact of natural equality, that no human person has any authority *per se* over any other human person. Hence, not having this authority in the first place, that is, *primary* authority, it follows that no man or group of men can delegate authority to any other man or group of men. The people can determine their form of government and elect men to administer it, but they are powerless to *confer* authority on these men for the simple reason that they have no inherent authority to confer. (Nothing plus nothing equals nothing.) Sovereignty is in the people, to be sure, to determine the type of

regime and the personnel of elected officialdom, *but not to confer authority upon those elected to govern.* The Biblical teaching is that *primary* authority comes directly from the Author of Nature, and that it is by His sufferance that the people execise whatever measure of sovereignty they may have. Romans 13:1 — "There is no power but of God, and the powers that be are ordained of God." Authority is moral power, and this moral power carries with it the right to use physical power to maintain order. There are three basic rights of which the Author of Nature (or the Natural Law) is the sole efficient Cause, rights which need to be exercised by any national state: these are *jus puniendi* (the right to punish), the *jus obligandi* (the right to make and bind laws), and *jus belli* (the right to defend itself by war and force). These powers are necessary for any state to attain its natural and proper end. A state without authority is a joke; as a matter of fact it is inconceivable, human character being what it is, subject to every form of selfishness and greed.

Dr. Crawford attributes the primary origin of government to God the Creator. Power is conferred upon the various forms of human government by divine fiat. Any human being who thinks and acts otherwise is self-deceived and is in rebellion against both reason and revelation.

This universe, and every part of it, even language, thought, ideating, or conceptualizing, was created to function within law (government). This is an incontrovertible, irrefutable axiom communicated by both "nature" (the natural revelation) and "revelation" (the propositional revelation — the Bible). Human government is axiomatic. It is an absolute necessity. This is established idealistically, realistically, and pragmatically.

Alexander Campbell, in an essay entitled, "Is Capital Punishment Sanctioned By Divine Authority?" wrote:

> Though neither Caesar nor Napoleon, Nicholas nor Victoria, were, "by the grace of God," king, emperor or queen; still the civil throne, the civil magistrate, and, therefore, civil government, are, by the grace of God, bestowed upon the world. Neither the church nor the world could exist without it. God himself has,

therefore, benevolently ordained magistrates and judges. Men may call them kings, emperors or presidents . . . but they are God's minister, executors of his will and of his vengeance, ordained to wait upon him and to execute his mandates. They are sort of viceroys — viceregents under law to God, and to govern according to his revealed will. The Bible is of right, and it ought to be, just as much a law to kings and governors and presidents, as it is to masters and servants, to husbands and wives, to parents and children. Those magistrates, therefore, who will not be governed and guided by it in the faithful execution of God's laws, God himself, in his own proper person, will judge and punish.

God is the author of law and order. The devil is the author of anarchy and nihilism. The devil is the enemy of government of any kind. He desires the destruction of all law. He is a liar and there is no truth in him at all (John 8:44). He wishes only to "scatter" (Matt. 12:30). He apparently led in the rebellion against God's government when certain angels "did not keep their own position but left their proper dwelling . . . " (Jude 6). The devil was an anarchist and nihilist in the Garden of Eden (Gen. 3:1ff).

Truth and order (government) are mutually dependent. God is the source of both. It is the truth of God that produces order, and it is order that sustains truth. Anything that contradicts the truth of God destroys order. When anarchy or disorder rules there is no way for truth to exist or be sustained. The truth of God is eternal (cf. Psa. 119:80, 160; Isa. 40:8; Matt. 24:35; I Pet. 1:25). That is one of the great consolations in the Bible for the believer faced with what appears at times to be world-wide lawlessness. God will never allow complete disorder to exist in this world. We shall treat this at greater length in later chapters. The scriptures teach emphatically that Jehovah will not allow lawlessness to be enthroned over the whole world. Even in the world of the Old Testament, when Satan's sphere of influence was much wider than at present, Jehovah often used "pagan" governments to bring relative law and order to society (cf. Isa. 10:5-19; 13:1-22; 45:1-25; Jer. 21:8-14; 27:1-15; 29:1-9).

America's "founding fathers" were, for the most part, Christians and God-fearing men (even those classified by some as "Deists") and they strongly believed that government, law and order, had its origin in the Divine Mind. They believed, further, that even when human beings were afforded the very rare privilege of "choosing" or "forming" the system of government by which they would be ruled, such a "choosing" was ordained by Divine Providence and should be constructed according to divinely revealed principles!

John Eidsmoe, in his book, *Christianity and The Constitution*, gives a brief biography of thirteen men he sees as "founding fathers": John Witherspoon, James Madison, George Washington, Alexander Hamilton, John Jay, Gouverneur Morris, Benjamin Franklin, Thomas Jefferson, Samuel Adams, John Adams, Patrick Henry, Roger Sherman, Charles Cotesworth Pinckney. Citing documentary evidence, Eidsmoe proves that eight of these thirteen men were clearly Christians, and the other five certainly believed that God exists and that He is immanently involved in the affairs of men (especially in governments). Everyone of these "founding fathers" believed that human rights and the civil governments which secured them had their origin in Almighty God.

At the close of the American Revolution, George Washington responded to a compliment for his leadership by saying, "the praise is due to the Grand Architect of the Universe; who did not see fit to suffer his Superstructures and justice to be subjected to the ambition of the princes of the World, or to the rod of oppression, in the hands of any power upon Earth." In his first Inaugural Address, Washington said, "No People can be bound to acknowledge and adore the invisible hand, which conducts the Affairs of men more than the People of the United States. Every step, by which they have advanced to the character of an independent nation, seems to have been distinguished by some token of providential agency."

Benjamin Franklin, when the first Constitutional Convention

THE ORIGIN OF CIVIL GOVERNMENT

was on the verge of disintegrating, June 28, 1787, called for prayer to God, saying, "I have lived, Sir, a long time; and the longer I live, the more convincing proofs I see of this truth, that God governs in the affairs of men . . . We have been assured, Sir, in the sacred writings that 'except the Lord build the house, they labor in vain that build it.' I firmly believe this; and I also believe that, without his concurring aid, we shall succeed in this political building no better than the builders of Babel . . . . "

And Thomas Jefferson, while certainly not an orthodox Christian, said, (and these are the words engraved on the Jefferson Memorial) "God who gave us life, gave us liberty at the same time. Can the liberties of a nation be secure when we have removed their only sure basis, a conviction in the minds of the people that those liberties are the gift of God?"

Penetrating insight into sources from which these "founding fathers" of our Republic drew their concepts of government is provided by John Eidsmoe in *Christianity and The Constitution*, p. 51:

> Two professors, Donald S. Lutz and Charles S. Hyneman, have reviewed an estimated 15,000 items, and closely read 2200 books, pamphlets, newspaper articles, and monographs with explicitly political content printed between 1760 and 1805. They reduced this to 916 items, about one-third of all public political writings longer than 2000 words.
>
> From these items, Lutz and Hyneman identified 3154 references to other sources. The source most often cited by the founding fathers was the Bible, which accounted for 34 percent of all citations. The fifth book of the Bible, Deuteronomy, because of its heavy emphasis on biblical law, was referred to frequently.

Eidsmore cites further research showing that of the sources other than the Bible for these "founding fathers" the three most often referred to are Charles Louis Joseph de Secondat, the Baron Montesquieu of France (1689-1755); Sir William Blackstone (1732-1780), English barrister; and John Locke

(1632-1704), the British philosopher and political theorist who inspired a generation of Americans in both politics and religion (including Alexander Campbell).

Montesquieu wrote a work he titled, *The Spirit of Laws*. At the beginning of this treatise he said, "God is related to the universe, as creator and Preserver; the laws by which He created all things are those by which He preserves them." He wrote in the same treatise:

> Particular intelligent beings may have laws of their own making, but they likewise have some which they never made . . . . Before laws were made, there were relations of possible justice. To say that there is nothing just or unjust but what is commanded or forbidden by positive laws, is the same as saying that before the describing of a circle all the radii were not equal."

In other words, Montesquieu's idea of the origin of government was Almighty God. Montesquieu embraced the Christian faith as a Roman Catholic.

Blackstone, in his *Commentaries on the Laws of England*, expressed his firm conviction that all law has its source in God through two instrumentalities:

> *Law of Nature* . . . God, when He created matter, and endued it with a principle of mobility, established certain rules for the perpetual direction of that motion; so, when He created man, and endued him with free will to conduct himself in all parts of life, He laid down certain immutable laws of human nature, whereby that free will is in some degree regulated and restrained, and gave him also the faculty of reason to discover the purport of those laws . . . . This law of nature, being coeval with mankind and dictated by God Himself, is of course superior in obligation to any other. It is binding over all the globe in all countries, and at all times: no human laws are of any validity, if contrary to this . . . .
>
> *Revealed Law* . . . These precepts, when revealed, are found upon comparison to be really a part of the original law of nature . . . But we are not from thence to conclude that the knowledge of these truths was attainable by reason . . . since we

find that, until they were revealed, they were hid from the wisdom of the ages . . . the revealed law is of infinitely more authenticity than . . . the natural law . . . .

Upon these two foundations, the law of nature and the law of revelation, depend all human laws; that is to say, no human law should be suffered to contradict these.

John Locke had a powerful impact on the thinking of the architects of the American Republic, as well as upon the patriarchs of the Restoration Movement. Locke wrote in his, *Of Civil Government, Book Two*:

Human Laws are measures in respect of Men whose Actions they must direct, albeit such measures they are as have also their higher Rules to be measured by, which Rules are two, the Law of God, and the Law of Nature; so that Laws Human must be made according to the general Laws of Nature, and without contradiction to any positive Law of Scripture, otherwise they are ill made.

We wish to cite two more writers who influenced American government through those 18th century founders — Grotius and Pufendorf. Hugo Grotius (1583-1645), famous Dutch lawyer, theologian, statesman and poet, wrote in, *The Rights of War and Peace*:

Among all good men one principle at any rate is established beyond controversy, that if the authorities issue any order that is contrary to the law of nature or to the commandments of God, the order should not be carried out. For when the Apostles said that obedience should be rendered to God rather, than men, they appealed to an infallible rule of action, which is written in the hearts of all men.

And Samuel de Pufendorf (1632-1694), the son of a Lutheran minister, who first studied theology then law, was a diplomat, university professor, and a historian. He was very influential in establishing "international law" as we know it today. He emphasized that God is the Creator of all in, *The Law of Nature and Nations,* and:

> . . . exercises a Sovereignty not only over the whole World, or over mankind in general, but over every Individual Human Person: Whose Knowledge nothing can escape: Who by Virtue of his Imperial Right, hath enjoined Men such certain Duties by Natural Law . . .

These men were only echoing what the apostle Paul wrote in Romans 1:18-20. Almighty God wills social order in a sinful world. God is the author of governmental regimentation. And God has revealed that in the "natural order." The "things that have been made" (Nature) reveal God's wrath against disorder, sin, and wickedness. Nature gives a clearly perceivable message that governments of some form must be instituted among men to check wickedness and suppression of the truth. It is inexcusable for the human race not to perceive that axiom. It is denied and overturned only by deliberately exchanging rational and moral truth for a lie.

> Sovereignty is lordship, lordship is ownership, and ownership is control. If God is absolute Lord, then he has absolute ownership and absolute control over the universe. This is, to say the least, a rather extravagant claim. What ground or basis does God have for his claim to sovereignty? The answer is the fact that he has created all things from nothing. The fact of creation is the ground of divine sovereignty . . . The fact of creation means, of course, that God is the source of all things. "All things originate from God," says Paul (I Cor. 11:12) . . . .
> The fact of creation provides the ground for two elements essential to real sovereignty, namely authority and freedom . . . God's authority, his legitimate and deserved right to absolute Lordship, is his by virtue of creation. God has the right to do with his creation whatever he wishes because he owns it; and he owns it because he created it . . . .
> In this connection, we may note that if there is no Creator-God then there is no authority at all, for there is no other basis

THE ORIGIN OF CIVIL GOVERNMENT

whereby one person may claim the *right* to tell another person what to do, or to do with another person what he thinks best. In an uncreated universe one personal being or group of personal beings may have the *power* to do these things, but not the right. Thus in such a universe absolute individual autonomy would be the only consistent viewpoint. But in a created universe, the Creator — and the Creator alone — has both the power and the right to rule in whatever way he desires. All authority resides ultimately in him. *He may delegate a measure of authority to some of his creatures if he chooses, as he has done to parents in the home, elders in the church, and civil rulers in the state. But such authority is not absolute; it is relative and derived.* (italics ours). "For there is no authority except from God, and those which exist are established by God" (Rom. 13:1). Thus we see how crucila is the divine sovereignty which includes the authority to rule as grounded in the fact of creation. Without this there remain only the chaos and anarchy spawned by a blind commitment to "might makes right." These are the only consistent choices.

God the Ruler, by Jack Cottrell, pp. 269-271, College Press

The *fact of creation* is "written" not only in "nature" (Rom. 1:18ff), it is also written in the existence of human beings (Acts 17:24-31). The existence of God and his sovereignty is further "written in the rocks" (in the evidence of geological catastrophy — the universal flood of Noah's age) (see II Pet. 3:3-7). The fossil record proves that God rules. The only way to deny that is by deliberate, moral choice. No human being can plead ignorance before God by reason of insufficient evidence.

A.H. Strong says in his *Systematic Theology*, "Physical science, in her very use of the word *law* implicitly confesses that a supreme Will has set general rules which control the processes of the universe."

God has also "written" his sovereign rule by moral law upon the inner being (conscience) of every human (Rom. 2:14-16). This, too, is factual, experiential, evidence that God is the source and originator of human government.

The Moral Law as actively considered, that is, as existing in the Mind and Will of the Divine Lawgiver, the Creator, is what is generally designated the Eternal Law. This is the Law which directs the motions of all created existents, both irrational and rational, to their appointed ends in the scheme of things; the Law which constitutes all things to be what they are, including human nature and human relationships. This Eternal Law, looked at passively, is embodied in the nature and relationships of man; in this sense it is called the Natural Moral Law, which is generally defined as "the participation in the Eternal Law by the rational creature." This Eternal Law, manifestly considered, is said to be human reason itself; it is described by Aquinas as "the light of intellect given to us by God, in virtue of which we know what must be done and what must be avoided"; hence the under-current of unanimity among all peoples, prehistoric, primitive and historic, that certain human acts are good, and certain others bad (e.g., murder, incest, perjury, etc.) both for the individual and for society. Thus the Natural Moral Law is rightly defined as a "rule of action, mandatory in form, which reason itself discovers, as having been established by the Author of man's nature and promulgated by being embedded in the nature of man.
Commonsense Ethics, by C.C. Crawford, pp. 248-249, Brown

John Locke, English philosopher, in his treatise, *Of Civil Government* wrote:

The state of nature has a law to govern it, which obliges everyone; and reason, which is that law, teaches all mankind, who will but consult it, that being all equal and independent, no one ought to harm another in his life, health, liberty or possessions . . . . In transgressing the law of nature, the offender declares himself to live by another rule than that of reason and common equity, which is that measure God has set to the actions of men . . . . A criminal, who having renounced reason, the common rule and measure God hath given to mankind, hath, by the unjust violence and slaughter he hath committed on one, declared war against all mankind.

The American Declaration of Independence, conceived first, incidentally, by George Mason in his *Virginia Bill of Rights*, in

THE ORIGIN OF CIVIL GOVERNMENT

May, 1776, and evidently copied by Jefferson, Madison and Franklin in the July 4th, 1776, document, shows that our "founding fathers" were guided by this concept of Almighty God as the sovereign source of human government:

> When in the Course of human events it becomes necessary for one people to dissolve the political bands which have connected them with another, and to assume among the Powers of the earth, the separate and equal station to which the Laws of Nature and of Nature's God entitle them, a decent respect to the opinions of mankind requires that they should declare the causes which impel them to the separation.
>
> We hold these Truths to be self-evident, that all Men are created equal, that they are endowed by their Creator with certain unalienable Rights, that among these are Life, Liberty, and the Pursuit of Happiness — That to secure these Rights, Governments are instituted among Men, deriving their just Powers from the Consent of the Governed . . . .

It is nothing short of shocking and frightening, however, to read from some American jurists, politicians, philosophers and educationalists their militant disdain of these concepts so clearly enunciated by our founding fathers. For example, note what former President of the United States, Woodrow Wilson said in his book, *The New Freedom*, pp. 44-48:

> . . . government . . . falls, not under the theory of the universe, but under the theory of organic life. It is accountable to Darwin, not to Newton. It is modified by its environment, necessitated by its tasks, shaped to its functions by the sheer pressure of life . . . . Living political constitutions must be Darwinian in structure and in practice. Society is a living organism and must obey the laws of Life, not of mechanics; it must develop.
>
> All that progressives ask or desire is permission — in an era when "development," "evolution," is the scientific word — to interpret the Constitution according to the Darwinian principle; . . . .

What Woodrow Wilson was saying directly contradicts the

Declaration of Independence. The Declaration holds there are "certain unalienable Rights . . . " rights that are divine in origin, everlasting and unchangeable. Woodrow Wilson held that those unchangeable rights elucidated in the U.S. Constitution and its amendments (The Bill of Rights) were *not* unchangeable but were to be subjected to the Darwinian principle of evolution. They could be changed, according to Wilson, indeed, they must be changed as truth evolves. The fundamental doctrine of evolutionism is that truth is always changing, always evolving, never eternal. Therefore, Wilson sought to construct human government on the basis of principles and "laws" that were alterable because they had no divine origin.

Another example of this "evolution" of the principles of civil government is the ruling of former Chief Justice of the U.S. Supreme Court, Earl Warren, in the case, *Trop v. Dulles*, 356 U.S. 86. Chief Justice Warren ruled concerning the Eighth Amendment to the U.S. Constitution: " . . . the words of the Amendment are not precise, and . . . their scope is not static . . . . The Amendment must draw its meaning from the *evolving standards of decency that mark the progress of a maturing society*" (italics ours). Other U.S. jurists have since applied the ruling of Warren to the statute concerning capital punishment, declaring it to be "cruel and unusual punishment." Capital punishment for capital crime is a principle and precept whose origin is divine, eternal and unalienable. It is in the Bible (Gen. 9:6; Exod. 21:12; Acts 25:11; Rom. 13:1-7, etc.).

Contrast the foregoing "evolutionists" with this statement of U.S. District Judge Robert N. Wilkin in the *Saturday Review*, April 26, 1958:

> Our most eminent legal historian and philosopher, Roscoe Pound, in a book just recently published, has correctly criticized the all-too-common impression that the "rights of man" were created by famous documents of legal history like Magna Carta, the Bill of Rights, the Declaration of Independence, and the Con-

stitution. Milestones these great charters certainly are, but they did not, and could not, *create* rights. They are, on the contrary, only formal acknowledgments of rights that have always existed by virtue of a Higher Law — what we may term "true" law.

True law exists without legislation. Men did not create it; they were created subject to it. It is law, as was said twenty centuries ago, "which we were not taught, but to which we were made, which we were not trained in but which is ingrained in us." This idea of a universal, "true" law was advanced by the early Greek philosophers. They accepted human nature as a part of universal nature. It followed that the law and justice on which social life and trade depend exist by nature, not by convention or promulgation. The Romans called it *vera lex*, true law, or *ius naturae*, natural law. And their rule over many different countries, and their administration of justice for foreigners in Rome, led to the discovery of law common to different peoples, which they called *ius gentium*. Some jurists and publicists refer to it as "common right and reason" or "equity and good conscience."

True law is necessarily stated in broad and general terms. To apply it to the varying circumstances of life, it must be supplemented and restated more specifically. Its practical application is established first by custom, then by decision (judgment in special cases), and subsequently by promulgation or legislation . . . .

The most important and immediate need (in our time) is that the people and their leaders understand that sovereignty is not in any man or party or nation, but in True Law. That is so because the Creator made the Universe according and subject to law, and endowed mankind with the ability to learn and apply the law.

Another pertinent statement is from the pen of Dorothy L. Sayers in *The Mind of the Maker*, pp. 20-26, Meridian Books, 1956:

There is a universal moral law, as distinct from a moral code, which consists of certain statements of fact about the nature of man, and by behaving in conformity with which, man enjoys his true freedom. This is what the Christian Church calls "the natural law." The more closely the moral code agrees with the natural law, the more it makes for freedom in human behavior; the more widely it departs from the natural law, the more it tends to enslave mankind and to produce the catastrophes called "judgments of God." The universal moral *law* (or natural law of humanity) is discoverable, like any other law of nature, by experience. It cannot be promulgated, it can only be ascertained, *because it is a question not of opinion but of fact* (italics ours). When it has been ascertained, a moral code can be drawn up to direct human behavior and prevent men, as far as possible, from doing violence to their own nature. No code is necessary to control the behavior of matter, since matter is apparently not tempted to contradict its own nature, but obeys the law of its being in perfect freedom. Man, however, does continually suffer this temptation and frequently yields to it. This contradiction within his own nature is peculiar to man, and is called by the Church "sinfulness"; other psychologists have other names for it . . . .Defy the commandments of the natural law, and the race will perish in a few generations; cooperate with them, and the race will flourish for ages to come. That is the fact; whether we like it or not, the universe is made that way. This commandment (Exod. 20:5,6 for example) is interesting because it specifically puts forward the moral *law* as the basis of the moral *code*; *because* God has made the world like this and will not alter it, *therefore*, you must not worship your own fantasies, but pay allegiance to the truth.

Nathaniel Micklem, former Principal of Mansfield College, Oxford, England, wrote in his book, *The Theology of Politics*, p. 60:

The Source of our being and the Artificer of our nature is God Himself. That "law of nature," which, as the Apostle (Paul, in Rom. 2:14-16) held, is written on the hearts even of the heathen, is an expression of the Reason which of itself is a reflection of the wisdom and "eternal law" of God. First, then, comes the "eternal law" of God; second, as reflecting it, the "law of nature," and, third, the customary and statute law of men, which has no validity except as an approximation to the "law of nature."

Experience and conscience both demand that we admit there is a law of higher obligatory power than the law of the state; a law superior to the will of one man, or of a few men, or even of a majority of men. There is a law that must be binding alike on the ruler and on the ruled; otherwise, a human ruler could never do wrong, the majority could never be unjust, and all human rights would be fantasies. The Bible teaches this by precept and gives documentation of human beings, both believers and unbelievers, who have discovered it and admitted it. Government and law have their origin from Jehovah-God.

In Deuteronomy 17:18-20, anticipating the time when Israel would demand a monarchial form of government, God decreed that kings of Israel would not be absolute sovereigns but would be simply administrators of the higher, Divine law, and would, in fact, be subject to the Divine law themselves. David, king of Israel and Psalmist, wrote: "For dominion belongs to the Lord, and he rules over the nations" (Psa. 22:28); and, "For God is the king of all the earth; sing praises with a psalm! God reigns over the nations; God sits on his holy throne" (Psa. 47:7,8). Solomon (king of Israel) wrote of the Wisdom of God, "By me kings reign, and rulers decree what is just; by me princes rule, and nobles govern the earth" (Prov. 8:15,16) and believed what he preached (II Chron. 1:8-10). There was no doubt in David's mind or Solomon's that human government had its origin in Jehovah.

Isaiah the prophet clearly reveals that all human government, even pagan government, originates from and exists by the sovereign authority of Almighty God. The king of Assyria had his throne only by God's permission, his governing powers were used by God for divine purposes, and he was deposed precisely when and how God decreed it (see Isa. 10:5-34; 37:33-38). Isaiah said the same about the king of Babylon (Isa. 13:1-14:32). And Isaiah is even more specific about the government of Persia, calling Cyrus, king of Persia, God's "anointed" (messiah) (Isa. 41:2-4; 44:24-28; 45:1-13).

Jeremiah wrote pointedly that God "plucks up and breaks down" nations and kingdoms and also "builds them up and plants them" (Jer. 18:5-11). And the Lord spoke to Jeremiah plainly about the origin of civil government:

It is I who by my great power and my outstretched arm have made the earth, with the men and animals that are on the earth, and I give it to whomsoever it seems right to me (Jeremiah 27:5).

In this same passage (Jer. 27:1-11), the Lord calls Nebuchadnezzar, a pagan emperor, "My servant . . . ", declaring that the Babylonian king received his governing position and his government by God's sovereign providence.

The Bible goes so far as to represent God as the One who "stirs up the spirits" of heathen rulers to fulfill divine purposes (see II Chron. 36:22,23; Ezra 1:1; Jer. 51:11; Rev. 17:17).

The book of Daniel is our richest source of Biblical revelation showing the acknowledgment of God as the source of and authority over civil government. First, the inspired prophet says: "Blessed be the name of God for ever and ever, to whom belong wisdom and might. He changes times and seasons; he removes kings and sets up kings . . . " (Dan. 2:20,21). Then Daniel records that king Nebuchadnezzar, impressed with the prophet's demonstration of supernatural wisdom, uttered, "Truly, your God is God of gods and Lord of kings, and a revealer of mysteries . . . " (Dan. 2:47). After Nebuchadnezzar witnessed the miraculous salvation from the fiery furnace of the three Hebrew men and the fourth in the furnace, "like a son of the gods", the heathen emperor said: "Blessed be the God of Shadrach, Meshach, and Abednego, who has sent his angel and delivered his servants, who trusted in him, and set at nought the king's command, and yielded up their bodies rather than serve and worship any god except their own God" (Dan. 3:28). Notice, Nebuchadnezzar admitted that the Hebrew God had "set at nought" the machinations of unjust civil government! Next, Nebuchadnezzar prefaces the account of his egoistic dream with the statement: "It has seemed good to me to show the signs and wonders that the Most High God has wrought toward me. How great are his signs, how mighty his wonders! His kingdom is an everlasting kingdom, and his dominion is from generation to generation" (Dan. 4:2,3). In the middle of the account the king relates the message from God's angel: "The sentence is by the decree of the watchers, the decision by the word of the holy ones, to the end that the living may know that the Most High rules the kingdom of men, and gives it to whom he will, and sets over it the lowliest of men" (Dan. 4:17). At the end of the account, the Babylonian despot now humbled and perhaps even a "believer" states:

> At the end of the days I, Nebuchadnezzar, lifted my eyes to heaven, and my reason returned to me, and I blessed the Most High, and praised and honored him who lives for ever; for his dominion and his kingdom endures from generation to generation; all the inhabitants of the earth are accounted as nothing; and he does according to his will in the host of heaven and among the inhabitants of the earth; and none can stay his hand or say to him, "What doest thou?" . . . Now I, Nebuchadnezzar, praise and extol and honor the King of heaven; for all his works are right and his ways are just and those who walk in pride he is able to abase (Dan. 4:34-37).

After king Belshazzar (son or grandson of Nebuchadnezzar) saw the handwriting on the wall, he called for Daniel's "interpretation." Daniel told him: "O king, the Most High God gave Nebuchadnezzar your father kingship and greatness and glory and majesty; and because of the greatness of the glory that he gave him, all peoples, nations, and languages trembled and feared before him . . . But when his heart was lifted up . . . so that he dealt proudly, he was deposed from his kingly throne, and his glory was taken from him . . . until he knew that the Most High God rules over the kingdom of men, and sets over it whom he will . . . And you his son, Belshazzar, have not humbled your heart, though you knew all this . . . but the God in whose hand is your breath . . . you have not honored . . ." (Dan. 5:17-23).

Daniel also documents for all generations of mankind the decree of Darius, king of Persia, who wrote after witnessing Daniel's miraculous deliverance from the lion's den:

I make a decree, that in all my royal dominion men tremble and fear before the God of Daniel, for he is the living God, enduring forever; his kingdom shall never be destroyed, and his dominion shall be to the end. He delivers and rescues, he works signs and wonders in heaven and on earth, he who has saved Daniel from the power of the lions (Dan. 6:26,27).

The rest of the book of Daniel, chapters seven through twelve, is one prophecy after another detailing how God will exert his sovereign, providential creation and administration of succesive human governments (Persian, Greek, Syrian, Ptolemaic, and Roman) (see *Daniel*, Bible Study Textbook, 3rd ed. by Paul T. Butler, College Press).

Daniel is not the final word of the Old Testament on this matter. The "minor" prophet Hosea contributes further to the revelation that God is the source of civil government (Hosea 8:4; 13:11); so does Amos (Amos 1:1-2:16); Jonah's book makes it plain that God expects obedience from even the most heathen of civil governments (Nineveh — Assyria) and honors such obedience when it occurs; Micah pronounces God's judgment upon unjust and wicked civil rulers (Micah 3:1-4; 3:9-11); the book of Nahum is God's wrath predicted against the civil government of Assyria for its arrogance, cruelty and wickedness; Habakkuk is a prediction of God's use of Babylon's civil ruler to execute God's judgment upon Israel-Judah. A search of the Old Testament prophets would uncover some teaching from each of them about civil government.

The New Testament, while not as prolific as the Old, categorically and clearly declares that not only is God the source and origin of civil government, but it also reveals that, since Jesus Christ is co-equal with God (John 1:1-18; Phil. 2:5-11; Col. 1:19; 2:9, etc.), he, too, is the origin of civil government.

Jesus refused to succumb to the lie of the devil when that arch-enemy claimed all the kingdoms of the world had been delivered unto his satanic sovereignty (Luke 4:5-7). Jesus knew who was sovereign over civil governments — God is to be worshiped as Sovereign, not the devil. Jesus taught Simon Peter that he, Jesus, really did not need to pay taxes to civil authorities because he, Jesus, was "prince" over them; but Jesus paid the tax rather than have anyone offended and misunderstand their duty to civil governments (Matt. 17:24-27). Jesus taught that while "Caesar" (civil government) has his place in this world, God is sovereign and must have priority and sovereignty (Matt. 22:15-22). Jesus also taught that God exercises sovereign providence over all civil governments and over history (Matt. 24; Mark. 13; Luke 21). Jesus intended that his apostles believe his sovereignty over all civil situations, whether just or unjust, for when the mob came to arrest Jesus in Gethsemane and the apostles drew their swords, Jesus said: "Put your sword back into its place . . . Do you think that I cannot appeal to my Father, and he will at once send me more than twelve legion of angels . . . ? (Matt. 26:52,53). But the classic statement of Jesus Christ concerning God as the source of civil power came when Pilate, Roman procurator said, "You will not speak to me? Do you not know that I have power to release you, and power to crucify you?" and Jesus answered, "You would have no power over me unless it had been given you from above . . . " (John 19:10,11).

John the Baptist, prophet of God, confronted Herod Antipas, king of the Jews, with God's sovereignty in even the "personal" affairs of civil rulers when he said to Herod about the king's illicit marriage to Herodias (Herod's sister-in-law and niece), "It is not lawful for you to have her" (Matt. 14:4). John told Herod that God's law was higher than any civil rule or ruler. John told other civil servants the same (Luke 3:10-14).

When Peter and John were arraigned before the Jewish civil and religious authorities and charged to stop preaching the resurrection of Christ, their answer was: "Whether it is right in the sight of God to listen to you rather than to God, you must judge; for we cannot but speak of what we have seen and heard" (Acts 4:19). Clearly, the apostles believed civil rulers and governments were to be subservient to the higher laws and commandments of

God and his Son. They expressed this even more firmly when they reported this incident to their friends and joined them in prayer (Acts 4:23-31).

Gamaliel, celebrated Hebrew rabbi of the first century A.D., also believed that all government was from God and was to be subject to God (Acts 5:33-39).

Paul, missionary to the Gentiles, preached this concept before the Greek philosophers at Athens (Acts 17:26); he preached it to the governor Felix (Acts 24:25); he preached it to king Agrippa (Acts 26:27-29).

In the New Testament epistles there are two categorical statements declaring that the principle of civil govenment is ordained, originated and sustained by God. The apostle Paul's statement in Romans 13:1-7 has been analyzed in the opening paragraph of this chapter. The apostle Peter wrote, similarly:

> Be subject for the Lord's sake to every human institution, whether it be to the emperor as supreme, or to governors as sent by him to punish those who do wrong and to praise those who do right. For it is God's will that by doing right you should put to silence the ignorance of foolish men. Live as free men, yet without using your freedom as a pretext for evil; but live as servants of God. Honor all men. Love the brotherhood. Fear God. Honor the emperor (I Pet. 2:13-17).

The Greek verb *hupotagete* (translated "Be subject") is in the imperative mood, meaning it is not simply a suggestion but a command. The Christian is to "be subject" to every human "institution" *"for the Lord's sake."* The Christian obeys civil government (so long as that government does not order the Christian to disobey a clear command of God) in order to glorify the Lord. Just as a Christian glorifies the Lord by worship, stewardship, evangelism, personal holiness, he glorifies the Lord by obeying every human ordinance. The Greek noun *ktisis* (translated "institution") is related to the Greek verb *ktizo* which describes the action of bringing or creating order in the place of disorder. *Ktisis* is translated "ordinance" in the KJV. The idea is that "human institutions" are the Lord's instrument for producing order within human society. Therefore, all men should obey them when they produce an ordered society. Emperors (Gr. *basileis*, "kings") and governors (Gr. *hegemosin* "leaders") are "sent" by God. The Greek participle *pempomenois* is present tense, passive. Emperors and governors are "continually being acted upon by God as he sends them" to accomplish his purpose. God *continues* to send "human institutions" and rulers. Their purpose is to "punish" (Gr. *ekdikesin* "avenge") evildoers (Gr. *kakopoion*) and "praise" (Gr. *epainon*, "strongly praise") welldoers (Gr. *agathopoion*). When civil governments and governors fulfill the purpose for which God sends them, all men, and especially Christians, are to obey them. They are doing God's will. "Human institutions" are God's "embassies" (Gr. *pempomenois*, "ones being sent") in a sin-infested world of disorder to bring order. "Human institutions" are God's "servant" (Gr. *diakonos*, "deacon, minister") to carry out God's will (Rom. 13:4). Next, Peter says, "For it is God's will . . . . " and the Greek phrase reads, *hoti houtos estin to thelema tou theou*, literally, "because so is the will of the God . . . . " The emphasis in the Greek syntax is that Christian submission to human institutions is specifically the will of God. Christians who disobey civil governments which are fulfilling their appointed mission to punish evil and reward good, are disobeying the will of God! Furthermore, Peter says, Christians are to obey in order to "put to silence the ignorance of foolish men." The implication is that disobedience, and even verbal abuse, of properly functioning civil government is done by fools and ignoramuses. Finally, Peter says, "Fear God. Honor the emperor." When Peter wrote that, Nero (profligate, pervert, diabolical) was Roman emperor. Peter certainly does not mean one should merely "honor" the principle of human government. We should "honor" (Gr. *timate*, "pay homage to"; same word is used of "honoring" parents and "honoring" elders) the *office* or *concept* of human rulership so that social order may be maintained.

It is unequivocally the will of God that civil government be instituted. God ordains it and sustains it. Civil rule has its origin in God. Other New Testament passages declare it and/or imply it. Paul states that when the "end comes" (the final resurrection) God's sovereign power will "destroy every rule and every authority and power" (I Cor. 15:24). Human institutions rule only by God's permission. Paul wrote that Christ has been exalted "far above all rule and authority and power and dominion" and that God has "put all things under his feet and has made him the head over all things for the church . . . " (Eph. 1:20-23). Civil government exists under the rule and for the purpose of Christ and his Church. God has highly exalted Jesus Christ, says Paul, so that at his name (under his authority) "every knee should bow, in heaven and on earth and under the earth . . . " (Phil. 2:9-11), and that would include every "human institution" and every human "authority." Colossians 1:15-20, much like Ephesians 1:20-23, reveals that "in him (Christ) all things were created, in heaven and on earth, visible and invisible, whether thrones or dominions or principalities or authorities — all things were created through him and for him." All civil governments and dominions originated with Christ and for Christ and they "hold together" by his sovereign power.

Paul told the young evangelist Timothy that one of the duties of his office was to "urge" godly men and women to prayers of "supplication, intercession and thanksgiving for all men, for kings and all who are in high positions, that we may lead a quite and peaceable life, godly and respectful in every way." God is responsible for the origin of human governments and he holds their workings and their destinies in his hands. He will answer prayers on their behalf (I Tim. 2:1-4). Another duty of the office of Christian evangelists is to "remind them (Christians) to be submissive to rulers and authorities, to be obedient, to be ready for any honest work, to speak evil of no one, to avoid quarreling, to be gentle, and to show perfect courtesy toward all men" (Titus 3:1,2). It is the duty of Christian leaders to exhort the body of believers concerning their responsibility toward civil government because it is ordained by the will of God.

Finally, the entire book of Revelation (and specifically Rev. 1:5; 4:11; 11:15-18; 18:1-24; 19:1-3; 20:1-15) shows that civil governments have their origin from God. The book also teaches that a civil government (in this case the Roman empire) which perverts and prostitutes its divinely decreed purpose — when it rewards evil and punishes good — will be chastened by God and eventually, if it does not repent, destroyed.

> The Lord reigns; let the peoples tremble!
> He sits enthroned upon the cherubim; let the earth quake!
> The Lord is great in Zion; he is exalted over all the peoples.
> Let them praise thy great and terrible name!
> Holy is he!
> Mighty King, lover of justice, thou hast established equity;
>   thou hast executed justice and righteousness in Jacob.
> Extol the Lord our God; worship at his footstool.
> Holy is he! (Psa. 99:1-5).

> The Lord has established his throne in the heavens,
>   and his kingdom rules over all (Psa. 103:19).

> By me kings reign, and rulers decree what is just;
>   by me princes rule, and nobles govern the earth (Prov. 8:15,16).

2

THE PURPOSE OF CIVIL GOVERNMENT

It is not difficult to determine from the Bible what God intends as the primary purpose for human government. Its immediate concern and function is the preservation of social order by restraining and punishing evil behavior and approving good behavior.

> . . . the chief function of government emphasized by Paul in the thirteenth chapter of Romans is the forcible maintenance of law and order, restraining evil deeds and encouraging the good. From the statement that the authority "beareth not the sword in vain" I am compelled to conclude that extreme pacifism is erroneous and anti-scriptural. It has been argued that Paul refers only to internal police power. Such an argument seems unrealistic in view of the historical situation in which Paul wrote . . . .
> *A Systematic Theology of the Christian Religion*, by J. Oliver Buswell, pub. Zondervan, pp. 403, 404

There are other biblically sanctioned functions to be fulfilled by the civil government. One is to be God's "servant for your (both the individual and the society) good." We take this, in light of other scriptures, to mean "public works". The laws God gave the nation Israel through Moses, many of which are specifically mandated for the civil society rather than the religious, confirm this secondary function of the political structure. Civil rulers of the Old and New Testament times were "builders" of fortifications, water reservoirs, houses, storehouses, roads, and other public utilities. A classic example is King Hezekiah's "pool and conduit" by which he "brought water into the city" (II Kings 20:20). These two functions, civil order and civic works, must necessarily be expressed or executed through a multitude of expediencies. We will examine a number of these in later chapters.

Several biblical texts are quoted in succession. They are not in any particular sequence or arrangement. Some of the more pointed and pertinent passages will be analyzed in this chapter.

> Genesis 9:5,6: For your lifeblood I will surely require a reckoning; of every beast I will require it and of man; of every man's brother I will require the life of man. Whoever sheds the blood of man, by man shall his blood be shed; for God made man in his own image.

> Genesis 41:46-49: Joseph was thirty years old when he entered the service of Pharaoh king of Egypt. And Joseph went out from the presence of Pharaoh, and went through all the land of Egypt . . . And Joseph stored up grain in great abundance . . . .

> Exodus 20:12-17: Honor your father and your mother, that your days may be long in the land which the Lord your God gives you. You shall not murder. You shall not commit adultery. You shall not steal. You shall not bear false witness against your neighbor. You shall not covet your neighbor's house; you shall not covet your neighbor's wife, or his manservant, or his maidservant, or his ox, or his ass, or anything that is your neighbor's.

> Exodus 21:12-14: Whoever strikes a man so that he dies shall be put to death. But if he did not lie in wait for him, but God let him fall into his hand, then I will appoint for you a place to which he

may flee. But if a man willfully attacks another to kill him treacherously, you shall take him from my altar, that he may die.

Laws concerning landmarks; testimonies; education; ecology; loaning of money; sexual perversion; help to the poor, widow, orphans, etc.; limits of punishment; divorce; bribery; honesty in business dealings; warfare; censuses; personal liability; restitution; treatment of employees (servants); appointment of and conduct of administrators (judges) (Deut. 16:18-20); setting up of kings (Deut. 17:14-17); duties of rulers (Deut. 17:18-20); extent of punishments to be meted out (eye for eye, etc. Deut. 19:15-21); conscription into armed forces (Num. 1:1ff).

Exodus 18:15-23: And Moses said to his father-in-law, Because the people come to me to inquire of God; when they have a dispute, they come to me and I decide between a man and his neighbor, and I make them know the statutes of God and his decisions . . . Listen now to my voice; I will give you counsel, and God be with you! You shall represent the people before God, and bring their cases to God; and you shall teach them the statutes and the decisions, and make them know the way in which they must walk and what they must do. Moreover choose able men from all the people, such as fear God, men who are trustworthy and who hate a bribe; and place such men over the people as rulers of thousands, of hundreds, of fifties, and of tens. And let them judge the people at all times; every great matter they shall bring to you, but any small matter they shall decide themselves; so it will be easier for you, and they will bear the burden with you. If you do this, and God so commands you, then you will be able to endure, and all this people also will go to their place in peace.

Exodus 22:28: You shall not revile God, nor curse a ruler of your people.

Deuteronomy 17:14-17: When you come to the land which the Lord your God gives you, and you possess it and dwell in it, and then say, I will set a king over me, like all the nations that are round about me; you may indeed set as king over you him whom the Lord your God will choose. One from among your brethren you shall set as king over you; you may not put a foreigner over you, who is not your brother. Only he must not multiply horses for himself, or cause the people to return to Egypt in order to multiply horses, since the Lord has said to you, You shall never return that way again. And he shall not multiply wives for himself, lest his heart turn away; nor shall he greatly multiply for himself silver and gold.

I Samuel 8:10-18: So Samuel told all the words of the Lord to the people who were asking a king from him. He said, These will be the ways of the king who will reign over you: he will take your sons and appoint them to his chariots and to be his horsemen, and to run before his chariots; and he will appoint for himself commanders of thousands and commanders of fifties, and some to plow his ground and to reap his harvest, and to make his implements of war and the equipment of his chariots. He will take your daughters to be perfumers and cooks and bakers. He will take the best of your fields and vineyards and olive orchards and give them to his servants. He will take the tenth of your grain and of your vineyards and give to his officers and to his servants. He will take your menservants and maidservants, and the best of your cattle and your asses, and put them to his work. He will take the tenth of your flocks, and you shall be his slaves. And in that day you will cry out because of your king, whom you have chosen for yourselves; but the Lord will not answer you in that day.

Judges 17:6: In those days there was no king in Israel; every man did what was right in his own eyes.

I Samuel 30:8: And David inquired of the Lord, "Shall I pursue after this band? Shall I overtake them?" He answered him, "Pursue; for you shall surely overtake and shall surely rescue."

Proverbs 17:15: He who justifies the wicked and he who condemns the righteous are both alike an abomination to the Lord.

Proverbs 18:5: It is not good to be partial to a wicked man, or to deprive a righteous man of justice.

Proverbs 24:23-25: These also are sayings of the wise. Partiality in judging is not good. He who says to the wicked, "You are innocent," will be cursed by peoples, abhorred by nations; but those who rebuke the wicked will have delight, and a good blessing will be upon them.

THE PURPOSE OF CIVIL GOVERNMENT

Ecclesiastes 8:11: Because sentence against an evil deed is not executed speedily, the heart of the sons of men is fully set to do evil.

Proverbs 20:2: The dread wrath of a king is like the growling of a lion; he who provokes him to anger forfeits his life.

Proverbs 20:8: A king who sits on the throne of judgment winnows all evil with his eyes.

Proverbs 20:26: A wise king winnows the wicked, and drives the wheel over them.

Proverbs 21:1: The king's heart is a stream of water in the hand of the Lord; he turns it wherever he will.

Proverbs 23:1-3: When you sit down to eat with a ruler, observe carefully who is before you; and put a knife to your throat if you are a man given to appetite. Do not desire his delicacies, for they are deceptive food.

Proverbs 24:23-26: Partiality in judging is not good. He who says to the wicked, "You are innocent," will be cursed by peoples, abhorred by nations; but those who rebuke the wicked will have delight, and a good blessing will be upon them. He who gives a right answer kisses the lips.

Proverbs 25:2-7: It is the glory of God to conceal things, but the glory of kings is to search things out. As the heavens for height, and the earth for depth, so the mind of kings is unsearchable. Take away the dross from the silver, and the smith has material for a vessel; take away the wicked from the presence of the king, and his throne will be established in righteousness. Do not put yourself forward in the king's presence or stand in the place of the great; for it is better to be told, "Come up here," than to be put lower in the presence of the prince.

Proverbs 28:15,16: Like a roaring lion or a charging bear is a wicked ruler over a poor people. A ruler who lacks understanding is a cruel oppressor; but he who hates unjust gain will prolong his days.

Proverbs 29:4: By justice a king gives stability to the land, but one who exacts gifts ruins it.

Proverbs 29:14: If a king judges the poor with equity his throne will be established forever.

Proverbs 29:16: When the wicked are in authority, transgression increases; but the righteous will look upon their downfall.

Proverbs 30:21-23: Under three things the earth trembles; under four it cannot bear up; a slave when he becomes king, and a fool when he is filled with food; an unloved woman when she gets a husband, and a maid when she succeeds her mistress.

Proverbs 31:4-9: It is not for kings, O Lemuel, it is not for kings to drink wine, or for rulers to desire strong drink; lest they drink and forget what has been decreed, and pervert the rights of all the afflicted. Give strong drink to him who is perishing, and wine to those in bitter distress; let them drink and forget their poverty, and remember their misery no more. Open your mouth for the dumb, for the rights of all who are left desolate. Open your mouth, judge righteously, maintain the rights of the poor and needy.

Ecclesiastes 4:13: Better is a poor and wise youth than an old and foolish king, who will no longer take advice, even though he had gone from prison to the throne or in his own kingdom had been born poor.

Ecclesiastes 8:2-5: Keep the king's command, and because of your sacred oath, be not dismayed; go from his presence, do not delay when the matter is unpleasant, for he does whatever he pleases. For the word of the king is supreme, and who may say to him, "What are you doing?" He who obeys a command will meet no harm, and the mind of a wise man will know the time and way.

Ecclesiastes 10:16,17: Woe to you, O land, when your king is a child, and your princes feast in the morning! Happy are you, O land, when your king is the son of free men, and your princes feast at the proper time, for strength, and not for drunkenness!

Isaiah 26:9,10: My soul yearns for thee in the night, my spirit within me earnestly seeks thee. For when thy judgments are in the earth, the inhabitants of the world learn righteousness. If favor is shown to the wicked, he does not learn righteousness . . . and does not see the majesty of the Lord.

Psalm 72:1-16: Give the king thy justice, O God, and thy righteousness to the royal son! May he judge thy people with righteousness, and thy poor with justice! Let the mountains bear prosperity for the people, and the hills, in righteousness! May he defend the cause of the poor of the people, give deliverance to the needy, and crush the oppressor! May he live while the sun endures, and as long as the moon, throughout all generations! May he be like rain that falls on the mown grass, like showers that water the earth. In his days may righteousness flourish, and peace abound, till the moon be no more . . . . For he delivers the needy when he calls, the poor and him who has no helper. He has pity on the weak and the needy, and saves the lives of the needy. From oppression and violence he redeems their life; and precious is their blood in his sight . . . . May there be abundance of grain in the land; on the tops of the mountains may it wave; may its fruit be like Lebanon; and may men blossom forth from the cities like the grass of the field.

II Chronicles 9:8: Blessed be the Lord your God, who has delighted in you and set you on his throne as king for the Lord your God! Because your God loved Israel and would establish them forever, he has made you king over them, that you may execute justice and righteousness.
    (Words of the Queen of Sheba to Solomon)

Micah 3:1: And I said: Hear, you heads of Jacob and rulers of the house of Israel! Is it not for you to know justice? You who hate the good and love the evil, who tear the skin from off my people, and their flesh from off their bones; who eat the flesh of my people, and flay their skin from off them, and break their bones in pieces, and chop them up like meat in a kettle, like flesh in a caldron.

Micah 3:9-11: Hear this, you heads of the house of Jacob and rulers of the house of Israel, who abhor justice and pervert all equity, who build Zion with blood and Jerusalem with wrong. Its heads give judgment for a bribe, its priests teach for hire, its prophets divine for money; yet they lean upon the Lord and say, "Is not the Lord in the midst of us? No evil shall come upon us."

Proverbs 8:15,16: By me kings reign, and rulers decree what is just; by me princes rule, and nobles govern the earth.

Proverbs 14:34: Righteousness exalts a nation, but sin is a reproach to any people.

Proverbs 11:11: By the blessing of the upright a city is exalted, but it is overthrown by the mouth of the wicked.

Proverbs 16:8-15: Better is a little with righteousness than great revenues with injustice. A man's mind plans his way but the Lord directs his steps. Inspired decisions are on the lips of a king; his mouth does not sin in judgment. A just balance and scales are the Lord's; all the weights in the bag are his work. It is an abomination to kings to do evil, for the throne is established by righteousness. Righteous lips are the delight of a king, and he loves him who speaks what is right. A king's wrath is a messenger of death, and a wise man will appease it. In the light of a king's face there is life, and his favor is like the clouds that bring the spring rain.

Proverbs 19:12: A king's wrath is like the growling of a lion, but his favor is like dew upon the grass.

Matthew 20:25-28: But Jesus called them to him and said, You know that the rulers of the Gentiles lord it over them, and their great men exercise authority over them. It shall not be so among you; but whoever would be great among you must be your servant, and whoever would be first among you must be your slave; even as the Son of man came not to be served but to serve, and to give his life as a ransom for many.

Matthew 22:1-7: And again Jesus spoke to them in parables, saying, The kingdom of heaven may be compared to a king who gave a marriage feast for his son, and sent his servants to call those who were invited to the marriage feast; but they would not come. Again he sent other servants saying, Tell those who are invited, Behold, I have made ready my dinner, my oxen and my fat calves are killed, and everything is ready; come to the marriage feast. But they made light of it and went off, one to his farm, another to his business, while the rest seized his servants, treated them shamefully, and killed them. The king was angry and sent his troops and destroyed those murderers and burned their city.

Luke 13:1,2: There were some present at that very time who told him of the Galileans whose blood Pilate had mingled with their sacrifices. And he answered them, Do you think that these Galileans were worse sinners than all the other Galileans, because they suffered thus?"
(This event is recorded, so far as we know, in no other document. Evidently Pilate had to exercise force to squelch something he considered seditious. Jesus, here, forthrightly affirms the right of the civil government to put criminals to death when they are "sinning" against civil order.)

Luke 14:31-33: Or what king, going to encounter another king in war, will not sit down first and take counsel whether he is able with ten thousand to meet him who comes against him with twenty thousand? And if not while the other is yet a great way off, he sends an embassy and asks terms of peace. So therefore, whoever of you does not renounce all that he has cannot be my disciple.

Luke 12:13-15: One of the multitude said to him, Teacher, bid my brother divide the inheritance with me. But he said to him, Man, who made me a judge or divider over you? And he said to them, Take heed, and beware of all covetousness; for a man's life does not consist in the abundance of his possessions.

Acts 16:37-39: But Paul said to them, They have beaten us publicly, uncondemned, men who are Roman citizens, and have thrown us into prison; and do they now cast us out secretly? No! let them come themselves and take us out. The police reported these words to the magistrates, and they were afraid when they heard that they were Roman citizens; so they came and apologized to them. And they took them out and asked them to leave the city.

Acts 18:14-16: But when Paul was about to open his mouth, Gallio said to the Jews, If it were a matter of wrongdoing or vicious crime, I should have reason to bear with you, O Jews; but since it is a matter of questions about words and names and your own law, see to it yourselves; I refuse to be a judge of these things. And he drove them from the tribunal.

Acts 19:38-41: If therefore Demetrius and the craftsmen with him have a complaint against any one, the courts are open, and there are proconsuls; let them bring charges against one another. But if you seek anything further, it shall be settled in the regular assembly. For we are in danger of being charged with rioting today, there being no cause that we can give to justify this commotion. And when he had said this, he dismissed the assembly.

Acts 21:30-36: Then all the city was aroused, and the people ran together; they seized Paul and dragged him out of the temple, and at once the gates were shut. And as they were trying to kill him, word came to the tribune of the cohort that all Jerusalem was in confusion. He at once took soldiers and centurions, and ran down to them; and when they saw the tribune and the soldiers, they stopped beating Paul . . . and as he could not learn the facts because of the uproar, he ordered him to be brought into the barracks. And when he came to the steps, he was actually carried by the soldiers, because of the violence of the crowd . . . .

Acts 22:25-29: But when they had tied him up with the thongs, Paul said to the centurion who was standing by, Is it lawful for you to scourge a man who is a Roman citizen, and uncondemned? When the centurion heard that, he went to the tribune and said to him, What are you about to do? For this man is a Roman citizen. So the tribune came and said to him, Tell me, are you a Roman citizen? And he said, Yes. The tribune answered, I bought this citizenship for a large sum. Paul said, But I was born a citizen. So those who were about to examine him withdrew from him instantly; and the tribune also was afraid, for he realized that Paul was a Roman citizen and that he had bound him.

Acts 23:26-30: Claudius Lysias (the tribune) to his Excellency the governor Felix, greeting. This man was seized by the Jews, and was about to be killed by them, when I came upon them with the soldiers and rescued him, having learned that he was a Roman citizen. And desiring to know the charge on which they accused

THE PURPOSE OF CIVIL GOVERNMENT

him, I brought him down to their council. I found that he was accused about questions of their law, but charged with nothing deserving death or imprisonment. And when it was disclosed to me that there would be a plot against the man, I sent him to you at once, ordering his accusers also to state before you what they have against him.

Acts 25:10-12: But Paul said, I am standing before Caesar's tribunal, where I ought to be tried; to the Jews I have done no wrong, as you know very well. If then I am a wrongdoer, and have committed anything for which I deserve to die, I do not seek to escape death; but if there is nothing in their charges against me, no one can give me up to them. I appeal to Caesar. Then Festus, when he had conferred with his council, answered, You have appealed to Caesar; to Caesar you shall go.

Acts 26:31,32: . . . and when they had withdrawn, they said to one another, This man is doing nothing to deserve death or imprisonment. And Agrippa said to Festus, This man could have been set free if he had not appealed to Caesar.

II Thessalonians 2:3-7: Let no one deceive you in any way; for that day will not come, unless the rebellion comes first, and the man of lawlessness is revealed; the son of perdition, who opposes and exalts himself against every so-called god or object of worship, so that he takes his seat in the temple of God, proclaiming himself to be God. Do you not remember that when I was still with you I told you this? And you know what is restraining him now so that he may be revealed in his time. For the mystery of lawlessness is already at work; only he who now restrains it will do so until he is out of the way.
(Paul is evidently predicting that even in the first century, some person with "religious" power and influence was eager to enthrone himself as a dictator — probably the bishop of Rome — but was being "restrained" at that time by the political power [Roman emperor]. When this "restraining" political power disappeared [ca. 450 A.D.] then the papacy's power is to "restrain" human beings from obtaining dictatorial powers through religion.)

Luke 3:10-14: And the multitudes asked him (John the Baptist), What then shall we do? And he answered them, He who has two coats, let him share with him who has none; and he who has food, let him do likewise. Tax collectors also came to be baptized, and said to him, Teacher, what shall we do? And he said to them, Collect no more than is appointed you. Soldiers also asked him, And we, what shall we do? And he said to them, Rob no one by violence or by false accusation, and be content with your wages.

Acts 17:26: And he made from one every nation of men to live on all the face of the earth, having determined allotted periods and the boundaries of their habitation, that they should seek God, in the hope that they might feel after him and find him.
(Evidently God determined and allotted periods and boundaries of the habitations of mankind when he confounded their languages at the Tower of Babel — that is, God determined they should be nationalities or "nations, . . . tribes and peoples and tongues" — in order that the whole human race might seek its Creator.)

Luke 2:1-5: In those days a decree went out from Caesar Augustus that all the world should be enrolled. This was the first enrollment when Quirinius was governor of Syria. And all went to be enrolled, each to his own city. And Joseph also went up from Galilee, from the city of Nazareth, to Judea, to the city of David, which is called Bethlehem, because he was of the house and lineage of David, to be enrolled with Mary his betrothed, who was with child.

Matthew 17:24-27: When they came to Capernaum, the collectors of the half-shekel tax went up to Peter and said, Does not your teacher pay the tax? He said, Yes. And when he came home, Jesus spoke to him first, saying, What do you think, Simon? From whom do kings of the earth take toll or tribute? From their sons or from others? And when he said, From others, Jesus said to him, Then the sons are free. However, not to give offense to them, go to the sea and cast a hook, and take the first fish that comes up, and when you open its mouth you will find a shekel; take that and give it to them for me and for yourself.

Romans 13:1-7: Let every person be subject to the governing authorities. For there is no authority except from God, and those that exist have been instituted by God. Therefore he who resists the authorities resists what God has appointed, and those who resist will incur judgment. For rulers are not a terror to good conduct, but to bad. Would you have no fear of him who is in authority? Then do what is good, and you will receive his approval, for he is God's servant for your good. But if you do wrong, be afraid, for he does not bear the sword in vain; he is the servant of God to execute his wrath on the wrongdoer. Therefore one must be subject, not only to avoid God's wrath but also for the sake of conscience. For the same reason you also pay taxes, for the authorities are ministers of God, attending to this very thing. Pay all of them their dues, taxes to whom taxes are due, revenue to whom revenue is due, respect to whom respect is due, honor to whom honor is due.

I Peter 2:13-17: Be subject for the Lord's sake to every human institution, whether it be to the emperor as supreme, or to governors as sent by him to punish those who do wrong and to praise those who do right. For it is God's will that by doing right you should put to silence the ignorance of foolish men. Live as free men, yet without using your freedom as a pretext for evil; but live as servants of God. Honor all men. Love the brotherhood. Fear God. Honor the emperor.

I Timothy 2:1-4: First of all, then, I urge that supplications, prayers, intercessions, and thanksgivings be made for all men, for kings and all who are in high positions, that we may lead a quiet and peaceable life, godly and respectful in every way. This is good, and it is acceptable in the sight of God our Savior, who desires all men to be saved and to come to the knowledge of the truth.

I Timothy 1:8-11: Now we know that the law is good, if any one uses it lawfully, understanding this, that the law is not laid down for the just but for the lawless and disobedient, for the ungodly and sinners, for the unholy and profane, for murderers of fathers and murderers of mothers, for manslayers, immoral persons, sodomites, kidnapers, liars, perjurers, and whatever else is contrary to sound doctrine, in accordance with the glorious gospel of the blessed God with which I have been entrusted.

Matthew 22:15-22: Then the Pharisees went and took counsel how to entangle him in his talk. And they sent their disciples to him, along with the Herodians, saying, Teacher, we know that you are true, and teach the way of God truthfully, and care for no man; for you do not regard the position of men. Tell us, then, what you think. Is it lawful to pay taxes to Caesar, or not? But Jesus, aware of their malice, said, Why put me to the test, you hypocrites? Show me the money for the tax. And they brought him a coin. And Jesus said to them, Whose likeness and inscription is this? They said, Caesars. Then he said to them, Render therefore to Caesar the things that are Caesar's, and to God the things that are God's. When they heard it, they marveled; and they left him and went away.

After God destroyed the early anarchistic civilization with a universal flood, he decreed to Noah (the "father" of a new civilization) the institution of human government by "consent of the governed."

> If anyone takes human life, he will be punished. I will punish with death any animal that takes a human life. Man was made like God, so whoever murders a man will himself be killed by his fellowman (Gen. 9:5,6, TEV).

Neither beast nor man is permitted to spill man's blood. God made man in the divine image. Human life is *sacred* to Almighty God. It is inviolable. It is one of the primary, unalienable, human rights. Even a dumb, amoral beast must be executed if it kills a human being (see Exod. 21:28); further, a human being who owns an animal that kills a human — if the owner has been warned — the owner, too, shall be executed (Exod. 21:29). Most certainly, God's covenant with Noah decrees that any human who kills another human (willfully and culpably) must be executed. The critical phrase in the command to Noah is, " . . . of every man's brother I will require the life of man . . . . " The Hebrew word *darash* translated "require" is a legal term (sometimes translated, "demand") (see Deut. 23:21) and means that God is speaking judicially. This is a divinely imposed law for all society. The statement, " . . . of every man's brother . . . "

means that the whole "brotherhood of man" is responsible to establish and execute this law. All humankind is responsible to see that this law is carried out. Government by "consent" of the governed!

The divine authority to execute capital punishment for the crime of murder is delegated to the "brotherhood of man." This being granted, it is therefore right to assume that the "brotherhood of man" is also responsible to establish laws and institutions and invest certain human beings with the authority to carry out this obligation. This fundamental decree to Noah is the basis for all human, civil governance. Government is primarily ordained to guarantee the most fundamental human right — protection of life! Whatever restraints are necessary (and divine revelation decrees that capital punishment is the most prominent restraint necessary) to sustain human life against willfull, premeditated murder must be legislated and enforced.

John Locke (1632-1704), English physician, diplomat, educator and philosopher, devoted and committed Christian, wrote:

> . . . the end of civil society [is] to avoid and remedy those inconveniences of the state of nature which necessarily follow from every man's being judge in his own case, by setting up a known Authority, to which everyone of that society may appeal upon any injury received or controversy that may arise and which everyone of the society ought to obey . . . .
> *Two Treatises of Government, Second Treatise,*
> *VII, 90,* by John Locke

Locke believed the God of the Bible was omnipotent Creator, Author of fundamental unalienable human rights (life, liberty, and property) and that civil governments were ordained primarily for the protection of those rights:

> . . . The state of nature has a law of nature to govern it, which obliges everyone: and Reason, which is that law, teaches all

mankind, who will but consult it, that being all equal and independent, no one ought to harm another in his life, health, liberty, or possessions. For men being all the workmanship of one omnipotent and infinitely wise Maker, all the servants of one sovereign Master, sent into the world by His order, and about His business, they are His property, whose workmanship they are, made to last during His, not one another's pleasure; and being furnished with like faculties, sharing all in one community of nature, there cannot be supposed any such subordination among us that may authorise us to destroy one another, as if we were made for one another's uses, as the inferior ranks of creatures are for ours . . . .
Two Treatises of Government, Second Treatise,
II, 6, by John Locke

Locke, himself a "closet" Puritan, greatly influenced those first Pilgrims and Puritans in England and Holland to seek religious and political freedom on the shores of the new world — America. Thus his biblical concepts of human rights and civil government, passed on to succeeding generations of Americans, became the foundation upon which the Declaration of Independence and the Constitution of the United States (and its initial Amendments) was formed.

While no specific statement or theological concept of civil government is made, the recurring phrase, "These are the sons of . . . in their own lands, each with his own language, by their families, in their nations . . . (Gen. 10:5,20,31,32) strongly implies that God's *purpose* in "confusing" the universal human language of the post-Flood civilization (see Gen. 11:1-9) into many languages was to divide humankind into a more expedient and manageable aggregate of civil government ("families . . . nations"). The purpose of civil government is to *diffuse* humankind over the face of the earth into the "boundaries of their habitation" as Almighty God has determined them (cf. Acts 17:26,27). This multiplication of social structures (human governments) was to *defuse* human pride and arrogance and drive men to "seek God, in the hope that they might find him" instead of themselves! God is not only disinterested in man's intended purpose for some

THE PURPOSE OF CIVIL GOVERNMENT

"United Nations" — he is opposed to it! Man's purpose for a "one-world" government (as evidenced in Genesis 11 and the "universal" empires of Assyria, Egypt, Babylon, Persia, Greece, Rome) is to deify humankind and assert his omnipotence. God's purpose in proliferation of social structures is to call man from pride and arrogance to faith and dependence upon Him.

There are several illustrations of the God-ordained purpose for civil government in the life of the patriarch Abram (Abraham). There is the protection of Abram's life and that of Sara, his wife, by "order" of Pharaoh, king of Egypt (Gen. 12:17-20). There is much the same kind of incident between Abimelech, king of Gerar, and Abraham (Gen. 20:1ff). Evidently, the Lord expected "kings" (patriarchal or tribal leaders) to enforce laws against adultery even in those ancient, less structured societies. And of course, there is the terrible history of Sodom, Gomorrah, and Lot and his family, illustrating the consequences of social and governmental rebellion against the Lord's purpose for government (Genesis 13:13; 18:1-33; 19:1-38). Abraham's nephew, Lot, was probably one of the "officials" of the government of Sodom because he was "sitting in the gate of Sodom" when the destroying angels came to the city. Lot is even called "Judge" by some of the renegades of Sodom (Gen 19:9). But "Judge" Lot was powerless against a society so lawless that mobs were ruling the city.

The most significant incident in Abram's life as a "civil governor" is in the account of the attack upon Sodom and Gomorrah, prior to their destruction, by the "kings of the East" (Chedorlaomer of Elam, et al.). When news came to Abram that these "kings of the East" had attacked the wicked cities of Sodom and Gomorrah, had looted and plundered the cities, had taken Lot and his "goods" and his family, Abram took 318 "trained" warriors of his clan and routed and pursued these armed invaders, looters and kidnappers. Abram defeated them, rescued Lot and his family, and returned the stolen property of the "king of Sodom" (see Gen. 14:1-24). Abram gave a tenth of everything taken from the "kings of the East" to Melchizedek, king of Salem, and high priest of Jehovah God (this would include some of the property of the king of Sodom). And God's great high priest, Melchizedek, *blessed* Abram.

It is hermeneutically proper to conclude from this singular incident in the life of *the* "father of the faithful" (see Rom. 4:1-24; Gal. 3:1-29; Heb. 7:6-10; 11:8-19) that God blesses those who responsibly and actively involve themselves, by force when necessary, in carrying out God's *purposes* for civil government — protection of the human rights to life, liberty and property. While the "king of Sodom" was probably not a person whose character would be admirable, neither privately nor publicly, he still has the God-given right to possess whatever property may have legitimately come his way. Abram restored his property to him and God blessed Abram for doing so.

There are many other implications which may be drawn from this incident but they will be discussed in later chapters. It is sufficient to note here that Melchizedek's blessing upon Abram was, "Blessed be Abram by God Most High, maker of heaven and earth; and blessed be God Most High, who has delivered your enemies into your hand!" (Gen. 14:19). It was God's purpose that divine laws protecting human life and property be upheld and enforced, and God not only blessed Abram for enforcing them, God *assisted* the patriarch-king in his efforts. Any human government desiring the blessings of the Almighty Creator will follow the example of Abram!

The next indication of Divine *purpose* for civil government comes from the history of Joseph, son of Jacob. The story of Joseph is so familiar to anyone who has ever read the Bible, we refrain from repeating it. The account covers 13 chapters which is 26% of the first book of the Bible (Genesis, chapters 37-50). Joseph, sold into servanthood in Egypt by jealous brothers, through providential intervention is elevated to become ruler of Egypt, second only to the Egyptian Pharaoh himself (see Gen. 41:37-49). The unique civil service rendered by Joseph (only because he had the governmental authority to do so) was the salvation of the Egyptian civilization and his own Israelite family from famine and starvation (Gen. 41:53-57). Joseph, himself, was to later say to his own brothers who had wickedly sold him into Egyptian servitude, "As for you, you meant evil against me; but God meant it for good, to bring it about that many people should be kept alive, as they are today" (Gen. 50:20). God means for civil governments to marshall corporate forces necessary and to exercise such powers to provide for the sustenance of "life and limb" (fundamental physical necessities) when the individuals or smaller units of society are incapable of doing so for themselves.

The book of Genesis gives no detailed account of the development of civil government. But the Bible makes no pretense to being a documentation of minute details in the history of man's "doings." The Bible claims to be a record, of sufficient, historical incidents, to prove to any honest-minded reader that God, the Creator, worked out man's redemption by coming to earth in human form in the person of Jesus Christ.

In order for the Creator to work His redemptive program with sinful man, all the while allowing man to exercise freedom of choice, the Creator must provide an environment of some restraint upon the self-destroying wickedness which the creatures (human beings) have chosen. Further, if the Creator is to become Man, Himself, and thrust Himself into this wicked society, establish His redeemed society ("church") composed of human beings, get a hearing for His message, and provide for the ongoing of all this, He must either restrain opposition to His redemptive program by constant divine intervention (constant miracles) or do so by using secondary means. God chose the latter, and he chose civil government as the instrument.

The book of Genesis does provide brief notices of precepts and practices showing the instrumentality of civil government as God used it to begin his work of redeeming those sinful human beings who would believe and obey him. Genesis, book of

"Beginnings", records the beginnings of civil government and its purpose to restrain evil and encourage good so that men may be saved.

Civil government is ordained of God as one of his instruments to bring fallen, sinful human beings to the perfection (goal or purpose) God intended for them when he created them. Man is a social being. He was created to live in societal relationship to other men and women created in the image of their Maker. He was created to be loved and to love and live in personal kinship to his Creator. The late Dr. C.C. Crawford explains the development:

> . . . of social organization (from family to clan, to tribe, to nation, and finally to national state) is clearly marked out in the history of various peoples. This was a perfectly natural development, corresponding to population growth and need. Civil society is necessary to protect the family against invasion of its rights, against aggression upon its order, prosperity and security . . . . The state exists and functions for the family and its individual members, not the family for the state. The state complements the family, thus actualizing and fulfilling man's natural sociality . . . .
>
> The natural sociality of man is actualized perfectly in civil society. (The word "civil" is from the Latin *civis*, "citizen," and *civitas*, "state.") The state is truly an *e pluribus unum* ("one formed of many"). By *perfectly* as used here is meant *completely*, that is, from the *temporal* point of view. (The word has no reference to moral perfection.) Civil society is a perfect society in that its ends are not subordinated to any other society and that it possesses within itself all the necessary means to the attainment of those ends . . . . The state is of itself sufficient to provide the additional means necessary to the general temporal welfare: no other society is required in the temporal order to complement the family . . . . The state functions properly to preserve that order in which men may develop physically, morally, mentally, and spiritually — the fourfold development the ultimate goal of which is the attainment of *wholeness* (completeness) . . . . Thus it will be seen that the state has certain duties to perform . . . . Having duties to perform, the state (society acting through its government) has the right to take whatever means

may be necessary to the performance of its duties, i.e., the right to impose sanctions, the right to levy and collect taxes, the right to conscript men for the common defense, etc. . . . .

The Essential Elements of a State. These are as follows: (1) A territory. Land or territory is necessary to the existence of a state . . . . The state is not something suspended in mid-air or having its existence through some form of psychic union alone. The state is not a mystic super-entity or super-organism floating around in the stratosphere. This is the specious doctrine championed by would-be tyrants eager to seize absolute power . . . . (2) Independence. The idea of subordination of another entity of some kind is foreign to the very concept of the state. (3) Government. In every state some form of government (kind of ruling regime) is necessary, for without the exercise of authority, weak or strong, regardless of its origin, no social group could be organized and held together in effective cooperation with sufficient continuity. Anarchy cannot exist in nature (which is, itself, the rule of law); neither can anarchy co-exist with, or be tolerated by, the state. [Even the law of the jungle is a kind of cause-and-effect order which is maintained by a strange combination of natural affinity (love and care) and sheer brute force] . . . .

The Final Cause of civil society (the state) is the ground of its existence (Its *raison d'etre*). From this ground or end come the rights and duties of citizens, the rights and duties of governments and the justice of all laws. Civil society exists for the attainment of a specific end — the temporal goods of justice, order, peace, posperity, security, etc. Hence civil society has authority for directing cooperation effectively for the attainment of its natural and proper ends . . . .

. . . the state is both negative and positive in its functions. It is negative in that it functions to protect its citizens and to preserve order; it is positive in that it acts, generally speaking, for the common good, the general welfare . . . .The state is a natural society functioning to meet specific temporal needs. Where a multitude of persons live together under law there is need of *peace* (and peace is *order*): preservation of the juridicial order of rights and duties (need for this is shown by the number of persons in our penitentiaries; the anti-social we have with us always), and there is need of prosperity (a modicum of security, economic as well as political, for all, or at least opportunity for all to provide for their own material well-being). No society can afford to allow its

economy to become so maladjusted that hundreds of citizens who are willing to give honest labor cannot find opportunities to make a living for themselves and their families. Hence the proper and proximate end of the state is the temporal good of justice, order, peace, prosperity, etc. Peace is the tranquility of order, resulting from the mutual fulfillment of duties and enjoyment of rights. *Prosperity is not to be identified with paternalism.* It is not the end of the state to act as "papa" to its members; rather, it is the state's function to supply the means by which each member may be able to develop his physical, intellectual, moral and spiritual life, in proportion, of course, to his own ability, initiative, and willingness to work . . . .
Common Sense Ethics, by C.C. Crawford, pp. 350-354

After the book of Genesis, biblical history *focuses* on one theocratic (God-ruled) nation — Israel. Israel was destined to function in the midst of and in relation to other nations and forms of government (see Deut. 4:5-8; Ezek. 5:5ff). While Israel was a theocracy ruled by religious leaders (prophets, judges, priests) such as Moses, Aaron, Joshua, Samuel, etc., and the separation of "church and state" was not as distinct as it would later become, nevertheless, the concepts of separation and limited civil government have their roots even in the Theocracy. The books of the Bible which record the theocratic era (Exodus chapter one through I Samuel chapter 7) indicate these "religious" leaders were also the nation's civil governors.

Moses was called by God to act as both religious and civil leader to deliver this special nation of Israelites from political, social, physical, and spiritual bondage under Egypt (Exod. 2:10). At this point in human history God established another kind of "kingdom" (spiritual) — thus opening the possibility for human beings to chose to live in relationship to *two* kingdoms. There would be the civil "kingdom" and the spiritual "kingdom." We shall discuss the relationship between the civil and spiritual kingdoms ("church and state") in another chapter.

We turn now to precepts and/or practices illustrating the God ordained *purposes* for *civil* government. This will necessitate drawing conclusions from inferences and attempting to separate the "civil" from the "religious" because in the theocracy the two "states" are so closely meshed.

It is clear from the beginning that Moses accepted the responsibility to govern in civil matters as well as in religious matters. When one Israelite had a "dispute" (undoubtedly "civil" disputes) against another, Moses "decided" the issue (Exod. 18:16ff). This is governing. But the disputes were so multitudinous Moses had to organize the mass of individuals into a nation by appointing subordinate "rulers" to assist him in making these civil decisions (Exod. 18:24-27). There were "civil" disputes even in a theocracy, which had to be administered. This is the purpose of civil government.

While some of the laws "of Moses" deal with religion (worship), many of them are laws about human behavior which is necessary to the maintenance of law and order and the protection of unalienable human rights (see Exodus chapters 20-23). Civil government's fundamental purpose is to enforce those laws that are necessary to protect human rights. And while Aaron's involvement with the "golden calf" was religious apostasy, it was at the same time civil insurrection and rebellion against the governing authority of Moses (Exod. 32:23). Moses, at God's direction, employed force to quell the civil rebellion (Exod 32:25ff). This is the purpose of civil government. Individuals cannot be permitted to "break loose" from necessary social restraint.

The books of Leviticus, Numbers and Deuteronomy, dealing primarily with religious observances, contain certain laws which deal with restraints or obligations necessary to the maintenance of civil order (see Lev. 19:1-37; Num. 1:1-54; 35:1-34; Deut. 5:1-33; 19:1-21; 20:1-9; 21:1-23; 22:1-30; 23:1-25; 24:1-22; 27:15-26).

Joshua inherited the religious and civil authority of Moses (Josh. 1:1-18). He was ordered, "be careful to do according to all the law which Moses my servant commanded you . . . " (Josh. 1:7). The people made a covenant with Joshua, "All that you have commanded us we will do . . . whoever rebels against your commandment and disobeys your words, whatever you command him, shall be put to death . . . " (Josh. 1:16-18). This is the purpose of civil government. There can be no ordered society without it.

After Joshua died and the nation of Israel rebelled against God's laws, both religious and civil, God left them to the consequences of their disobedience. They were in a constant state of oppression at the hands of nations and peoples alien to Israel, except for occasional periods of comparative peace and prosperity under the "Judges" (Othniel, Sampson, Gideon, et al). Except for rare individuals, the office of judge was distinctly separate from that of priest. So judges were actually civil rulers and performed the functions of such officials in carrying out the purposes of civil government. They led the nation of Israel in wars against foreign aggression, they executed justice in civil disputes and against crime within the nation of Israel itself, and whatever prosperity the nation may have acquired was generally due to their godly civic leadership. A number of the judges, themselves, succumbed to temptation and were disobedient. But because of the rebelliousness of the Israelites at large, governing the nation was extremely difficult. A spirit of selfishness and wickedness prevailed until anarchy was the rule rather than the exception. The recurring phrase of the book of Judges is: "In those days there was no king in Israel; every man did what was right in his own eyes" (Judges 17:6). We are told that Samuel, the last Judge of Israel, before the monarchial form of civil government was permitted by God, "administered justice to Israel . . . " (I Sam. 7:17). But it was an almost impossible task, evidently requiring so much of Samuel's time he was unable to rear his sons up to administer justice properly (I Sam. 8:4ff) and the people cried out for a different form of civil government — a monarchy.

The period of the Judges graphically illustrates the consequences of civil governors and governments failing to fulfill their divinely ordained *purposes!* When there is no government, no centralized authority, or when such governments as there are do not exercise their obligations to protect the rights of individuals and their social structures, nothing is secure — not human life, not human property (see Judges 6:1-6; 19:22-30). A "vigilante" form of government was often the only way any kind of justice could be counted upon in the days of the Judges (see Judges 20:1-48). But God has never intended that purposes of civil government be fulfilled through mob rule!

When Israel cried for "a king like all the nations" (I Sam. 8:4-9), God told Samuel to warn the people about the social and economic burdens that would fall upon them through a monarchial form of civil government (I Sam. 8:10-18). But the people insisted, naively thinking that somehow having a king would make them "like all the nations" and the king would take care of everything — including fighting their battles for them (I Sam. 8:19-22). But the "government" of any nation ultimately rests upon the *individuals* within that nation. Eventually, it is individuals who must work and make a "government" prosperous; must become policemen and enforce "government" laws; must become soldiers and fight and die for the "government's" freedom; must pay taxes to support those who administer these duties of "governments." "There are no free lunches!"

If civil government is to fulfill its purposes and execute the actions necessary to protect the rights of the individual, some persons, structured by some form of organization, must administer those actions. These "administrators" must be granted by their constituents certain powers or authorities, and remuneration for services rendered.

When Samuel went to anoint Saul the first "king" of Israel, God told Samuel, " . . . and you shall anoint him to be prince over my people Israel. He shall save my people from the hand of the Philistines . . . " (I Sam. 9:16). God's purpose for civil government in the hands of Saul was to "save" the Israelite nation from foreign aggression and oppression by alien Philistines. Samuel wrote in a book "the rights and duties of the kingship" (I

Sam. 10:25) and laid it before the Lord.

Samuel told Israel, and Saul, that they and their king were to obey the same laws (I Sam. 12:14,15). The king was to fulfill the purpose of governing obeying the same law he was appointed to enforce. Saul started well, but he finished in ruin and disgrace. Saul's obsession to rule for personal fame and fortune, rather than service, alienated him from his family, turned him into a would-be murderer, brought disorder and ruin to the nation, and ended with his dishonor and suicide.

David, the "man after God's own heart", ruled the nation well, made human rights secure (except those of Uriah and Bathsheba), caused Israel to prosper financially, but could not rule his own house. One incident in the life of David is sufficient to show that he properly carried out the purposes of civil government. It is David's war and execution of justice upon the marauding Amalekites (I Sam. 30:1-30). It also shows David's sensitivity to justice as he allowed those who stayed "by the baggage" to be remunerated the same as those who engaged in the action (I Sam. 30:21-25). That is the purpose of civil government. To protect the rights of individuals and see that justice is carried out. While the younger David could impartially administer justice for others, in a moment of capitulation to passion, he unjustly took another man's wife (Bathsheba) and wickedly plotted the husband's (Uriah) death to cover up the crime (see II Sam. 11:1ff). David's failure as a civil servant (and a man of God) came largely because he was taking a hiatus from his obligations as a civil ruler (II Sam. 11:1ff).

In his later years David lapsed into a series of governing failures. He slew seven innocent descendants of Saul (II Sam. 21:7); he allowed his own sons to violate civil laws and human rights and go unpunished (II Sam. 13:1-29); his son Absalom led a civil revolt and David seemed unwilling to pursue any organized, civil punishment; and when Absalom died, David grieved so excessively that he all but abdicated his civil responsibilities (II Sam. 18:33-19:8); civil disorder persisted (II Sam.

THE PURPOSE OF CIVIL GOVERNMENT

20); David's last years involved a serious mistake in civil governance when he pridefully "numbered" his military forces (II Sam. 24:3,9; Psa. 30:6). David wrote the seventy-second "Psalm to Solomon" which clearly reveals his concept as to the purpose of civil government — "judge thy people with righteousness, and thy poor with justice . . . prosperity for the people . . . defend the cause of the poor of the people . . . give deliverance to the needy, and crush the oppressor . . . let righteousness flourish . . . peace abound . . . " etc. (see Psa. 72:1-20). But Solomon is the one to whom we are most indebted for elucidation concerning the purpose of civil governors and governments.

Solomon, who wrote most of the Proverbs and the book of Ecclesiastes, furnishes us with succinct wisdom about the purpose of political leadership. The following quotations are from *Good News Bible, Today's English Version*, published by American Bible Society, N.Y.

> The king sits in judgment and knows evil when he sees it (Prov. 20:8, TEV).

> A wise king will find out who is doing wrong, and will punish him without pity (Prov. 20:26, TEV).

> When the king is concerned with justice, the nation will be strong, but when he is only concerned with money, he will ruin his country (Prov. 29:4, TEV).

> Kings cannot tolerate evil, because justice is what makes a government strong. A king wants to hear the truth and will favor those who speak it (Prov. 16:12,13, TEV).

> Why do people commit crimes so readily? Because crime is not punished quickly enough (Eccl. 8:11, TEV).

> Condemning the innocent, or letting the wicked go — both are hateful to the Lord (Prov. 17:15, TEV).

These are the solemn words which King Lemuel's mother said

to him:
> You are my own dear son, the answer to my prayers. What shall I tell you? Don't spend all your energy on sex and all your money on women; they have destroyed kings. Listen, Lemuel, Kings should not drink wine or have a craving for alcohol. When they drink they forget the laws and ignore the rights of people in need. Alcohol is for people who are dying, for those who are in misery. Let them drink and forget their poverty and unhappiness.
>
> Speak up for people who cannot speak for themselves. Protect the rights of all who are helpless. Speak for them and be a righteous judge. Protect the rights of the poor and needy (Prov. 31:1-9, TEV).

The Queen of Sheba heard of Solomon's wisdom and skill as a civil ruler. She did not believe what she heard so she visited Jerusalem to see for herself. She found those governed by Solomon to be prosperous and happy beyond what she had heard! She said, " . . . Because the Lord loved Israel for ever, he has made you king, *that you may execute* (Heb. *asoth*, "to do, make, perform") *justice and righteousness*" (I Kings 10:9). Prosperity and happiness accrues to the nation whose government *does* justice and righteousness.

But, like his father before him, Solomon, in his old age, indulged himself and let the purposes of governing slip into ruin and shame. When Solomon died, his rule passed to Rehoboam, his son. Rehoboam laid upon his constituents an unreasonable tax burden, heavier than that of Solomon. Rehoboam rejected the advice of older and wiser men who counseled him, "If you will be a servant to this people today and serve them, and speak good words to them when you answer them, then they will be your servants forever" (I Kings 12:7). Rehoboam made the mistake of thinking the purpose of government was that the people were to serve the governing authorities rather than the *authorities serving the people!* A revolt ensued, led by Jeroboam, Solomon's "secretary of public works." The nation of Israel was divided into two national entities (Israel — ten tribes to the north; and Judah — two tribes to the south). They had separate religious, political and economic structures. They often fought one another on the battlefield.

What followed was a history of idolatry, carnality, profligacy, war, exploitation, and assassination, due mainly to wicked civil governors (kings, princes, and other civil authorities). With only a few exceptions (an occasional just and righteous ruler), both nations (Israel and Judah) were governed by people who not only rejected Divine purposes for government, they turned their powers of governing upside down and used them for injustice, wickedness, and exploitation.

The consequences of such perversion in the purpose of civil government are vividly portrayed by the prophet Hosea. Hosea was called to preach to the northern kingdom, Israel, in the days of Jeroboam II (790-725 B.C.). Hosea lived through a time of great national wickedness, social injustice, and what was nearly political anarchy. During his lifetime six kings of Israel were assassinated, each by his successor. Hosea characterizes the civil environment of his day:

> Hear the word of the Lord, O people of Israel; for the Lord has a controversy with the inhabitants of the land. There is no faithfulness or kindness, and no knowledge of God in the land; there is swearing, lying, killing, stealing, and committing adultery; they break all bounds and murder follows murder (Hosea 4:1,2).

Hosea clearly documents the cause for this social chaos:

> By their wickedness they make the king glad, and the princes by their treachery. They are all adulterers; they are like a heated oven, whose baker ceases to stir the fire, from the kneading of the dough until it is leavened. On the day of our king the princes became sick with the heat of wine; he stretched out his hand with mockers . . . (Hosea 7:3-5).

The "literary" prophets (Isaiah through Malachi) speak mostly to the issue of civil governors and governments prostituting their

Divine purposes (see Isa. 3:1-15; 10:1-4; 56:10-12; Jer. 5:28; 22:11-30; 34:6-22; Ezek. 28:1-19; 29:1-32:32; Dan. 5:1ff; Hosea 5:1-7:1-7; Amos 6:1-8; Micah 3:9-12; 6:9-7:7; Zeph. 3:1-3, etc.). These prophets were called primarily to focus attention on the future "King of Righteousness" — the Messiah — and the nature of His kingdom. Civil government was secondary in the scope of their message. They saw civil government, even that closely meshed with religion (the theocracy become monarchy) in the Israelite nation, as disastrously inadequate to be the vehicle for the redemption of mankind. Isaiah and Micah make this prominent in their writing.

However, there are a few statements in the prophets in reference to the purposes of civil government. Isaiah makes it clear that "rulers" are to " . . . cease to do evil, learn to do good; seek justice, correct oppression; defend the fatherless, plead for the widow . . . " (Isa. 1:10,17,23). Jeremiah writes:

> And to the house of the king of Judah say, Hear the word of the Lord, O house of David! Thus says the Lord: Execute justice in the morning, and deliver from the hand of the oppressor him who has been robbed, lest my wrath go forth like fire and burn with none to quench it, because of your evil doings (Jer. 21:12).

> Thus says the Lord: Go down to the house of the king of Judah, and speak there this word, and say, Hear the word of the Lord, O King of Judah, who sit on the throne of David, you, and your servants, and your people who enter these gates. Thus says the Lord: Do justice and righteousness, and deliver from the hand of the oppressor him who has been robbed. And do no wrong or violence to the alien, the fatherless, and the widow, nor shed innocent blood in this place (Jer. 22:1-3).

Some of the prophets pointedly called heathen, idolatrous, Gentile governments to account. Daniel, a Jew, served in very high positions of Gentile governments. He told Nebuchadnezzar, king of Babylon:

THE PURPOSE OF CIVIL GOVERNMENT

Therefore, O king, let my counsel be acceptable to you; break off your sins by practicing righteousness, and your inquiries by showing mercy to the oppressed, that there may perhaps be a lengthening of your tranquility (Dan. 4:27).

Daniel also reminded Belshazzar, another ruler of Babylon, that it was his responsibility to learn Almighty God's purposes for civil government from his predecessors (Dan. 5:17-28).

The Lord states his purposes for specific Gentile rulers in such passages as Isaiah 10:5ff; 13:3ff; 44:24-28; Jer. 27:1-15. God pronounces judgment upon specified pagan governments for their perversion of divinely ordained purposes in civil rule: (a) destructive aggression (Amos 1:3-5); (b) kidnapping, hostage-taking, enslavement (Amos 1:6-8); (c) treaty-breaking (Amos 1:9,10); (d) pitilessness and perpetual aggression (Amos 1:11-12); (e) subjugation of other peoples and atrocities (Amos 1:13-15); (f) implaccable malice (Amos 2:1-3); (g) refusing to lend military and other aid to a neighboring state under seige by foreign invaders (Obad. 11-14).

From the preaching of Jonah we infer that God expected the king of Nineveh to lead his subjects in moral reform and acknowledgment of the sovereignty of Jehovah (Jonah 3:6-10). Isaiah counseled the government of Judah to give asylum to the Moabites when they were dispossessed of their land by the king of Babylon (Isa. 16:1-5).

When Habakkuk complained that "destruction and violence are before me; strife and contention arises . . . so the law is slacked and justice never goes forth . . . for the wicked surround the righteous, so justice goes forth perverted" (Hab. 1:3-4), the Lord promised to send Babylon to punish the government of Judah for its perversions of governmental purposes.

Then last, but certainly not least, in the Old Testament, is the intriguing and inspiring story of Esther. Here we see not only a demonstration of courageous application of the true purpose for civil government, but we have evidence that courageous and wise women are capable of turning a massive and complex civil government to proper, divinely-ordained purposes!

Now we come to five of the most important biblical texts concerning the purpose of civil government. They are all in the New Testament. The first text, Matthew 22:15-22, is the statement of Jesus which on the surface is simple but has unfathomable and profound depth: "Render therefore to Caesar the things that are Caesar's, and to God the things that are God's." Here Jesus unequivocally declared there are some human "things" which *belong* to "Caesar" (civil government) and other human "things" which *belong* to God! Men, all men, live in and are obligated to *two* kingdoms. Not all men "render" their obligations to both kingdoms, but that does not relieve them of the obligations. Lord Acton (1836-1904), English moralist, historian and politician, once said: "I fully admit that political Rights proceed directly from religious duties . . . . The nation is responsible to Heaven for the acts of the State." And he also said:

> . . . when Christ said "Render unto Caesar the things that are Caesar's and unto God the things that are God's," He gave to the State a legitimacy it had never before enjoyed, and set bounds to it that had never yet been acknowledged. And He not only delivered the precept but He also forged the instrument to execute it. To limit the power of the State ceased to be the hope of patient, ineffectual philosophers and became the perpetual charge of a universal church.

In other words, Lord Acton recognized the "two-kingdom" concept and that civil kingdoms derive their existence and purposes from God. It is important to note that the Incarnate God, Jesus Christ, in his terse statement, clearly declared at least one purpose or "lawful" function of civil government was to gather taxes. Jesus implied other purposes for civil governments: (a) "exercise authority" (Matt. 20:25-28); (b) make war upon recalcitrants (Matt. 22:1-7; Luke 14:31-33); (c) judge in matters of civil, temporal disputes (Luke 12:13-15); (d) punish civil disorder (Luke 13:1,2).

THE PURPOSE OF CIVIL GOVERNMENT

The next New Testament passage is I Timothy 1:8-11. Paul wrote to the young evangelist, ". . . we know that the law is good, if any one uses it lawfully, understanding this, that the law is not laid down for the just but for the lawless and disobedient . . . ." In other words, if all humankind was *just* (upright, fair, honest, truthful, righteous) there would be no need for *law*. But that is not the case! Therefore, the purpose for law is the *restraint* of the *lawless* and unjust (unfair, dishonest, malicious, violent). Since there is no such thing as law without penalty and no penalty without enforcement, there must be some government whose purpose and function is to enforce the law. T. Robert Ingram gives a unique illustration:

> We may ask the question, "What would you have to do first if you undertook to organize a new club?" Even among children the answer is forthcoming almost at once: "Set up some rules or by-laws." It is so essential and so elementary that we may say it almost without thinking. It is the rules or the laws that mark out the structure or skeleton of any body of people. It is the legal system of any people which identifies a nation or an empire and locates its boundaries. That is not to say, or course, that a nation consists of its law, or that the law gives life and being to a nation. But it is to say that the law establishes a framework or bone structure in a people which gives them shape and individuality and form.
>
> Law in its simplest form is the set of rules which are consented to and imposed upon all members of any group or people, and its purpose is to preserve the existence and identity of the group as a whole. The law sets forth the terms which every individual must observe for the sake of the whole body. *The end and purpose of the law in this world is to protect society as a whole. The law protects the nation or the people from the vagaries of individuals.* Punishment repairs a broken law; it does not protect or control. So-called international law restores order in the family of . . . nations after violations by a single government. Clearly the law giver in any case is the highest authority for any people. The origin of its law is its god. The final authority for our (USA) law is our God. Since we are a people under God's law, we are a people under God, or God's people.

Wherever the emperor is accepted as the source of law, the emperor is also hailed as god. If Der Fuhrer or Il Duce, or The Leader, or the Soviet dictator, gives and enforces the law, he is openly declared to be god. If the final authority is claimed for parliament, parliament usurps the place of Divinity. Such a claim, in fact incited a War of Independence in the American Colonies. But if the final authority is believed to be in the whole people, the *demos*, then the voice of the people is said to be the voice of god and we have set up the tyranny of the mob. So we who are a people whose god is the Father of Jesus Christ, the One who created all things and who redeemed the world, look to Him for our law . . . .

Ours is a Christian civilization. Ours is a Christian nation. Why? Because everyone in it is a Christian? Or even because its leading citizens are Christians? No indeed. We are a Christian people because the laws under which all must live — whether Jew, Moslem, Buddhist, Confucian, or Christian — are the laws which come from God and are enforced upon His authority through the mediation of Jesus Christ. Our laws, like all law, apply to every person alike, whether he be a Christian . . . or an atheist . . . a devout Jew or a . . . Moslem. The laws are the conditions under which all men must live if they propose to remain within a society. They must be applied impersonally and with absolute justice. *Their end is to protect society as a whole and to preserve its basic structure — a Christian republic.* (italics mine).

The World Under God's Law, by T. Robert Ingram, pub. St. Thomas Press, pp. 3,4

Some philosophers (most prominently, Jean Jacques Rousseau — 1712-1778) have declared "man is good by nature." That is, man left to his own instincts and feelings (without education, without social and civil laws or restraints) will behave morally and peacefully. But this is philosophical utopianism. History, from the earliest records until the present, proves otherwise.

Paul wrote to Timothy, "Now we know that the law is good . . . " (I Tim. 1:8). The Greek conjunction *de* used in this phrase ("Now") is to make emphatic the proposition that our

THE PURPOSE OF CIVIL GOVERNMENT

knowledge of the "goodness" of "law" is a *revealed* knowledge. We accept the rule of law because *God has told* us we must have it! Those who rebel against the Bible as God's infallible revelation to man are also in rebellion against the concept that "law" has a good purpose. If rebels are law-abiding at all, it is because they are fearful of being punished and not because they accept law and civil order as revealed and ordained by God for man's "good."

And Paul's statement to Timothy here clearly includes "civil" laws (murderers, kidnappers, perverts, perjurers, etc.) as well as religious. Actually, *all* "law" begins with God, whether reasoned out and legislated by human ingenuity or revealed directly by the Spirit of God. All "good" laws are ultimately "religious" and have their source in the Omniscient Lawgiver, Almighty God. We believe Paul's use of the word "law" in I Timothy 1:8 is, therefore, generic. He is not specifying merely the Law of Moses, although the Law of Moses certainly delinates numerous "civil" laws (restraints and obligations necessary to sustaining social structures in this present world). In this context, "bad" laws are not really laws at all. Any "law" which is contrary to the precepts or principles of the revealed will of the Divine Lawgiver (God) is a "bad" law. A human "law" that deviates from the Bible or reason guided by the Bible, is not "law" but rebellion, sedition, anarchy.

The most important point of Paul's admonition to Timothy (1:8) is that the "law is good" if anyone "uses it lawfully." Clearly, even "good laws" may become "bad" if they are *used unlawfully*. But what does Paul mean here? Is his statement, " . . . the law is good if anyone uses it lawfully" mere redundancy or verbosity or sophistry? No! Everyone knows that "good laws" can be abused and misused and perverted to accomplish "bad" ends. It happens all the time! This is confirmed by both Biblical and secular history from its very beginning. Jesus declared that the Pharisees and priests of his nation were blatantly perverting "good laws" for bad purposes (see Matt. 5:1-48; 12:1-14; 15:1-20; 23:1-39, etc.).

In I Timothy 1:8 the Greek word *nomimous* ("lawfully") is an adverb modifying the verb *chretai* ("uses"). The "law" (both civil and religious) has to be used "lawfully." The same Greek adverb is used in II Timothy 2:5 declaring that athletes do not receive the winner's prize unless they compete according to the *nomimous* ("rules").

Are there "laws" about how to use laws, or "rules" about how to keep the rules? Apparently there are! The Biblical perspective on "law" is that of both *precept* and *principle*. *Precepts* are declarations in human language which clearly and specifically either prohibit certain actions or require certain actions. *Principles* are propositional statements in human language declaring the fundamental concepts or motivations or virtues which are to be the controlling factors in applying or using precepts. A *precept* would be a command to punish — a *principle* would be the application of *justice* to that precept. *Principles* are concepts such as justice, love, truth, sanctity, freedom, dignity, decency, goodness, benevolence, honesty, impartiality, etc. These are the principles by which men are to "lawfully" use the laws (precepts). *Principles* are actually the *source* of precepts! Statutes and edicts prohibiting or obliging specific actions are legislated and enforced to produce the character or virtue necessary to sustain human social structures. Human beings who are not inherently virtuous or principled must be forced to the level of lawfulness necessary for the maintenance of society by regulating their behavior.

Paul does not tell Timothy in this verse (1:8) where men are to find laws about using the law. He *does* indicate, however, in I Timothy 1:11 that "lawful" use of the law is to be "in accordance with the glorious gospel of the blessed God . . . . " In other words, the *principles* by which the *precepts* of both civil and religious law is to be used are revealed in the Bible. We think the words "gospel of the blessed God" include the entire revelation of God (both Old Testament and New Testament). The Bible also teaches that human reason focusing on "nature" (creation) can arrive at certain *principles* to use in "lawfully" applying civil and religious law (Rom. 1:18-32).

THE PURPOSE OF CIVIL GOVERNMENT

The Bible says that civil government is obligated to use the law (all law) "lawfully." The *principles* by which this is done are found in the revealed Word of God, the Bible, and in Nature (creation). Thus law, whether civil or religious, is never an end in itself. Law is not even primarily perfected in human outcomes. Law is an expression of the Divine Personality and is therefore ultimately perfected (has its end or purpose) in Divine outcomes or purposes. That civil governments must consider themselves required to apply the law "in accordance with the glorious gospel of the blessed God" should be no surprise when it is remembered that "there is no authority except from God . . . " and that rulers and governments are "God's servant" for good (Rom. 13:1-7). Using the law "lawfully" can only be done by governments and governors who have surrendered to the sovereignty of the revealed Word of God, the Bible. That is what the Bible says!

> It is through Jesus that all things have been created. It is through Jesus that all things hold together today. It is through Jesus that every area of life, whether private or public, will ultimately be reconciled to God. In the end every knee will bow and every tongue confess that Jesus is Lord.
> From this foundational faith position . . . [we] understand the state to be created by God in Jesus Christ and to possess a "moral" character which makes it rightly accountable for its actions. Therefore the state by its very nature is never neutral in the positions or actions it takes.
> In a pluralistic society the positions the state takes are usually a composite or combination of a great many varying faith positions. (Secularism is as much a faith position as Christianity.) The final position will most likely be a compromise of these many faith positions. Therefore it is extremely misleading and dishonest to speak or act as if the state exists outside the framework of values, faith, and religious commitments, or to think of the state as existing in some sort of neutral or objective plane above and apart from such fundamental considerations. The state as a real, existing entity has a moral and religious nature, real responsibilities, and corresponding accountability.
> . . . the state [must] recognize its position as creature and

not as sovereign, to declare its dependence on God and not its independence, to find knowledge, values, truth, and justice in revelation not in naturalism or secularism, and in so doing to walk humbly before God.
The Christian Statesman, Vol. CXXXI, No. 1,
p. 15, Nov.-Dec., 1987, Beaver Falls, PA

It is important to notice in I Timothy 1:9 that the apostle declares, "the law is not laid down for the just but for the lawless and disobedient." In other words, those who are inherently (by the *new* birth) lawful, i.e., "constrained by the love of Christ" (II Cor. 5:14) and other *principles* of divine revelation do not need law in precept. Precepts, statutes, laws are "laid down" (by divine fiat) for the "lawless and disobedient" (Gr. *anomois* — without-law; *anupotaktois* — insubordinate, refractory, disorderly). Paul then proceeds to list some specific actions designated "lawless" or illegal by the Sovereign Lawgiver. They are:

a. Ungodly (Gr. *asebes*, disregard for the Person of God).
b. Sinners (Gr. *hamartolois*, transgressors of God's revealed will).
c. Unholy (Gr. *anosios*, not separated from worldliness).
d. Profane (Gr. *bebelois*, filthy, vulgar, heathen, obscene).
e. Murderers of fathers (Gr. *patroloais*, patricide)
f. Murderers of mothers (Gr. *metroloais*, matricide)
g. Manslayers (Gr. *androphonois*, manslaughter).
h. Immoral persons (Gr. *pornois*, fornicators, pornographers, adulterers, etc.).
i. Sodomites (Gr. *arsenokoitais*, literally, "male-coitus", homosexuality, or pederasty; same word is used in I Cor. 6:9; could mean child-molesters — especially young boys).
j. Kidnapers (Gr. *andrapodistais*, "man-stealers" — would apply to kidnapping women and children, too).
k. Liars (Gr. *pseustais, pseudos*, fakers, false ones, "con-men").
l. Perjurers (Gr. *epiorkois*, literally, "take an oath against

THE PURPOSE OF CIVIL GOVERNMENT

oneself" or forswear, perjurer, to contradict one's sworn testimony).

m. And whatever else is contrary to sound doctrine (Gr. *hugiainouse didaskalia antikeitai*, literally, "opposing healthful teaching").

In light of modern opinion it is very interesting to learn the Bible teaches that such things as disregard for the Person of God, disobedience to God's will (the Bible), worldliness, obscenity, fornication, pornography, adultery, homosexuality, and lying are *illegal*. The Bible says the law is "laid down" to prohibit these specific actions! Not only so, any government which does not prohibit them is *not* using the law "lawfully"!

Perhaps we should end the discussion of this text by noting that while there are certain *principles* (concepts) by which *precepts* (statutes, edicts) are to be "used lawfully", even the *principles* must be defined and categorized by revealed truth (the Bible). Love, truth, justice, freedom, etc. are *not* self-defining. Neither is any human being or group of human beings capable of giving absolute, inviolate, infallible definitions of these principles. We must look to the Bible as the final, authoritative, infallible source and guide for definitions and precedents of "lawful" principles. In other words, all human governments are bound to seek revealed truth (the Bible) in order to know how to "use the law lawfully."

A colonial preacher named Jonathan Mayhew, preaching in Boston in 1749, stated:

> . . . it is proper for all who acknowledge the authority of Jesus Christ, and the inspiration of His apostles, to endeavor to understand what is in fact the doctrine which they have delivered concerning this matter (that is, temporal government). It is the duty of Christian magistrates to inform themselves what it is which their religion teaches concerning the nature and design of their office. And it is equally the duty of all Christian people to inform themselves what it is which their religion teaches concerning that subjection which they owe to the higher powers . . . .

The Greek word *antikeitai* in I Timothy 1:10, is translated "contrary." Literally, it would be "anti-laid-down" or "against what is laid down." We should understand Paul to be saying that *anything* which is anti-Biblical in the "laws" of men (civil or religious) or in the "use" of those laws is wrong. That which is contrary to the Bible in civil or religious matters is opposed to the revealed will of Almighty God and the "unalienable rights" of mankind.

Clearly, the Bible says a major purpose of civil government is to "use the law lawfully." And that means according to the precepts and principles "laid down" in God's word, the Bible. But how many Christians know this is what the Bible says? How many would believe and act upon it if they knew it? It is time for all Christians to know it and work to make it a reality in every civil government!

We come now to the third important scriptural statement about the *purpose* of civil government. Paul wrote to Timothy: "First of all, then, I urge that supplications, prayers, intercessions, and thanksgivings be made for all men, for kings and all who are in high positions, that we may lead a quiet and peaceable life, godly and respectful in every way. This is good, and it is acceptable in the sight of God our Savior, who desires all men to be saved and to come to the knowledge of the truth" (I Tim. 2:1-4). This is an apostle's instruction to an evangelist, a preacher, that he should involve himself, at least in prayer, in matters of civil government.

We may correctly infer from this passage that God's desire for the human race is "law and order" in "every way." We may also infer that while all men are generally responsible to see that life's circumstances are "quiet and peaceable" (Rom. 12:18), it is specifically the responsibility of "kings and all who are in high positions"! This is one of the major *purposes* of civil government.

We note first that "urge" may not be strong enough to translate the Greek word *parakalo* used by Paul. *Parakalo* is a present active indicative verb most often translated, "I am exhorting." Second, the Greek particle *oun*, meaning "therefore," or "then", indicates that the "exhortation" to follow is in order to accomplish what has been said earlier — "lawful use of the law." Third, the Greek adverb *proton* ("first of all," or "firstly") modifies the verb *parakalo*, indicating the "exhortation" about praying for all men and their governmental leaders so that a quiet and peaceable life may ensue is of *primary* importance. It would indicate that in order to have civil authorities who will "use the law lawfully" to bring "tranquility and peace" evangelists must teach Christians to pray for these authorities. And this is of *first importance*! Fourth, the Greek preposition *huper* translated "for" is emphatic in signifying that an act is being done with "interest or concern in the subject." It is often translated "on behalf of."

The Greek word *basileon* is the usual word for "king", and *huperoche* literally means, "to be over, to be higher, to be preeminent" and in this context is speaking of people in all kinds of places of civil authority. Christians are to plead with (Gr. *deeseis*, "entreat, supplicate") to humbly kneel before (Gr. *proseuchas*, "pray, do obeisance before"), to intercede (Gr. *enteuxeis*, "to beat a drum for, to implore, to importune") and to give thanks (Gr. *eucharistias*, English eucharist, bless) to the Almighty God with intense interest and concern for kings and all civil authorities. Remember, this is of *first* importance.

And why is it of *first* importance? It is "in order that" (Gr. *hina*) mankind may "lead a quiet and peaceable life, godly and respectable in every way." But there is an even higher purpose for civil government than sustaining "quiet and peace" in human society. The higher purpose is in verses 3 and 4. The "quiet and peaceable life" of man is "good and acceptable in the sight of God." In other words, it pleases God. Nothing can be more important than pleasing God, or doing what God calls "good." Further, it is implied that only when there is civil "quite and peace" can men be "saved and brought to the knowledge of the truth." In other words, the gospel cannot be preached or taught and men will not be saved when nations or the world is in a state of anarchy, strife, and criminal disorder. God wants order and tranquility in human society, and he has ordained human governments and governors for that responsibility. It is the purpose of government to "use the law lawfully" to produce and sustain a peaceful (Gr. *eremon*, peaceful; related to the Greek word *eirene* from which the English words, Irene, irenic) and quiet (Gr. *heschion*, inner tranquility, secure) life. In addition, civil order is to be maintained by civil government so that human life may be lived in *godliness* (Gr. *eusebeia*, in well regard for the Person of God, in piety) and in all *respectfulness* (Gr. *semnoteti*, honorableness, dignity, gravity, seriousness). Indeed, the civil government must maintain order so that citizens may live seriously, and with dignity! The civil government is to so govern that frivolity, irresponsibility, indecency, and impropriety does not hinder the peace, inner security, piety, and dignity of its citizens.

Few people know this! Few Christians, even, know it! But there are many examples and exhortations in the Bible that this is one of the *purposes* of civil government. Paul, even as he was on trial before the governor Felix, "argued about justice and self-control and future judgment" (Acts 24:25). Paul did *more* than pray about the responsibility of governors — he lectured them at every opportunity. Darius the Persian king ordered those who were opposing God's people in their return to Judea from exile to not only support the Jews with money, but to "pray for the life of the king and his sons" (Ezra 6:10). God, though the prophet Jeremiah, told the Jews going into exile in Babylon to " . . . seek the welfare of the city where I have sent you into exile, and pray to the Lord on its behalf, for in its welfare you will find your welfare" (Jer. 29:7ff). Do not forget, "By justice a king gives stability to the land . . . " (Prov. 29:4).

There are many examples in the Old Testament of governments and rulers who contributed to frivolity, irresponsibility, and indecency rather than prohibiting it. In addition to many of the wicked kings of Israel, there is Belshazzar with his drunken orgy (Dan. 5:1ff) and Ahasuerus' indecencies and improprieties (Esther

THE PURPOSE OF CIVIL GOVERNMENT

1:1ff). History, ancient and modern, seems to be a never ending documentation that governments and civil authorities have almost all (with only a few exceptions) defaulted in varying degrees on this Biblical purpose for civil government. Most human governments make more contributions to frivolity, indecency, irresponsibility and impropriety than they do to prohibiting it. It takes very strong, principled, courageous, impartial civil authorities and a principled and cooperative citizenry to fulfill this obligation. It would demand spiritually-oriented leaders and citizens to carry through because it involves the never-ceasing struggle of the flesh against the spirit (see Gal. 5:17; Rom. 7:15-23; 8:5-8; James 4:1; I Pet. 2:11). It takes civil leaders and citizen supporters who are truly Christian.

It is significant that Paul said prayers must be offered for "kings and authorities" so that men might " . . . come to the knowledge of the truth." Where there is no order, no peace and security — where there is no check upon flippancy, silliness, indecency, irresponsibility — there can be no serious discovery of the truth. Truth is purchased only through seriousness, integrity, wholesomeness, and order. Even an austere, dictatorial government, if it keeps indecency and impropriety in check, is better than one that is corrupt, lascivious, loose and irresponsible. Truth has more opportunity to be discovered and promulgated in a dictatorial government than in one that is irresponsible, indecent and indifferent. History has also demonstrated this. The Israelites found this to be the case and so did the early Christians.

Whatever it takes, civil governments and governors are responsible to see that society is "quiet and peaceable . . . godly and respectful" in every way. These are the principles which must be present in the civil society for man's salvation and knowledge of the truth. Governments must therefore enact laws and enforce laws "lawfully" to accomplish this. Those who do not are standing in opposition to God.

Positive (statutory) law is needed to provide what are called *tertiary principles. E.g., primary principles* of the Natural Moral Law are such as the following: Good ought to be done, and evil avoided (that is, regardless of the setting in which the words "good" and "evil" are used); social order must be maintained; the law-abiding must be protected against the lawless; crime must be punished, injustice must be prevented, one should do as he would be done by, etc. *Secondary principles* of the Moral Law are such as are embodied, for example, in the Ten Commandments: Do not commit murder, Do not lie, Do not steal, etc. *Tertiary* principles are those which derive from the primary and secondary principles, such as mentioned above, traffic regulations to protect man's right to life, etc. Tertiary principles, of necessity, are clarified by positive or civil law.

Law that is manifestly contrary to the Eternal Law is no law at all; no one on earth is bound by such a law as, "Do not worship God." Law which places burdens on men to satisfy the stupidity, cupidity, or ambition of an individual, a group or a majority; is simply not valid . . . .

Common Sense Ethics, ibid, p. 272

Actually, the essential function of civil government is that of enacting the enforcing *tertiary* (third level) law. God Almighty has revealed the *primary* and *secondary* principles (laws) by which civil societies are to exist. God has mandated civil governments the responsibility for the next level of law — *tertiary*. Tertiary laws, enacted and enforced according to Divine principles, may differ slightly from one culture or nation to another. There are geographical, historical, anthropological, and technological differences which may require varying applications or statutory modifications in different locales. But the primary and secondary principles remain the same. And all human governments are responsible to see that those Eternal Laws are kept for the benefit of truth. That is the main purpose of government. Governments that will not acknowledge or act in accordance with this purpose displease God and come under his judgments.

The right to resist unlawful authority, as set forth in the part of the Declaration (of Independence) which says "That whenever any

Form of Government becomes destructive of these ends, it is the Right of the People to alter or to abolish it," identifies a higher law of God to which man's laws must conform. Unless a person recognizes some form of supreme law by which man's laws must be judged, there is no basis for believing in any form of disobedience, or that any human law or act of government is unjust.

Christianity and the Constitution by John Eidsmoe, pub. Baker, p. 363

The fourth significant statement in the New Testament about civil government is I Peter 2:13-17:

Be subject for the Lord's sake to every human institution, whether it be to the emperor as supreme, or to governors as sent by him to punish those who do wrong and to praise those who do right. For it is God's will that by doing right you should put to silence the ignorance of foolish men. Live as free men, yet without using your freedom as a pretext for evil; but live as servants of God. Honor all men. Love the brotherhood. Fear God. Honor the emperor.

Peter wrote this sometime between 58-61 A.D. The infamous Nero ruled the Roman empire from 54-68 A.D. It is of great moment that Christians would be commanded by a Jewish apostle to be submissive "to the emperor as supreme," and to "honor the emperor" when that emperor was Nero Claudius Caesar Germanicus! The first years of Nero's reign were peaceful and indicative that such peacefulness might continue. Nero boasted that not a single person had been unjustly executed throughout his vast empire. Nero's private life was extremely lascivous and scandalous. He indulged himself in gluttony, homosexuality, incest, murder, adultery, fraud, exploitation and expropriation of the property of others.

While it is quite true that a Christian is obligated to disobey any order of civil government which would disobey God, it is also quite true that every Christian is obligated to obey *all* civil rulers and governments when those governments are carrying out their God-ordained purposes no matter how corrupt the private lives of the officials are!

> As Christianity spread in the pagan world, it owed much to that order of justice which Roman rule secured. However harsh and defective that order might be, it was better far than anarchy . . . . Not law but love was the principle of the Christian life, but that did not free believers from their obligation to the State, unless these were in direct contradiction to their fidelity to God.
> *The Christian Way,* by Sydney Cave, Pub PLI, p. 236

It will be instructive to look at a number of the words of this text in the original language. *Hupotagete* is in the imperative mood (meaning a command, not merely a suggestion) and is a basic military term meaning, "to put yourself under another's command; to rank under; to submit to." "Submit yourselves" is the NASV translation. *Pase* means "all, every, the whole." *Anthropine* is from *anthropos* and means "human, man-made." And *ktisei* is the noun form of the Greek verb *ktizo* which means to "create, institute, establish, found, call into being out of disorder." The phrase, *dia ton kurion*, is translated "for the Lord's sake"; the preposition *dia* and the accusative (objective) case of the article *ton* make it *emphatic* that being "subject to every human establishment" is for the Lord's sake. Any disobedience to civil authority or human establishment is a very serious matter and is to be taken up only when obeying would *clearly* violate a higher matter of the Lord's will.

Peter uses the common Greek word *basilei* for "king" (KJV), translated "emperor" in the RSV. Since there is no article in connection with *basilei* it would properly be translated "whether to a king . . .", i.e., he means Christians are to be subject to the *principle* of civil rulership. So Peter was not saying Christians had to "honor" a specific emperor (such as Nero) *personally*, but that they must submit to the honor, the authority and purpose of civil government in *principle* (and practice). The *basilei* (emperor) is *huperechonti* ("supreme", lit. "held above all"), and is, along with *hegemosin* (territorial rulers) "sent" (Gr. *pempomenois*, different from *apostolos*) for the sake of, or, "on the cause of" (Gr. *di' autou*, preposition *dia* with genitive singular pronoun *autou*, "on account of him") the Lord! In other words, emperors and territorial rulers are "sent on the cause of the Lord."

And what is the Lord's cause for civil rulers? Peter says it is "for justice upon evildoers and praise upon welldoers." The Greek word *ekdikesin* is a compound word — the preposition *ek* "upon" and *dike* is translated, "right, justice, judicial punishment, vengeance, sentence of punishment, judgment (II Thess. 1:9; Jude 7, Acts 25:15). Personified, the word *dike* became *Nemesis* and *Poena* (English, penal) in Greek mythology. "Justice" seems to be personified by the inhabitants of Malta (see Acts 28:4). The Greek word *epainon* is translated "praise" here; in II Corinthians 8:18 it is translated, "famous"; in Romans 13:3, "approval"; in I Corinthians 4:5, "commendation." The Lord sends civil rulers (and governments) to judge, avenge, and punish those who do "evil" and to approve, commend, praise, and even make famous, those who do "good."

In summary, then, the *purpose* of civil government as revealed through Christ's apostle, Peter, is to establish itself for the *restraint of wrong* and the *rewarding of right* for its constituency (citizens). The citizenry is to submit to any government functioning according to this direction regardless of the *personal* idiosyncracies or *personal* life of one of its officials. Of course, when a civil official's *personal* life becomes illegal, he is to be apprehended, judged and punished according to the requirement of the law the same as any other citizen. And, when a civil official's *personal* life occasions his "unlawful use of the law" toward any citizen, that is, if he orders a citizen to do onything in disobedience to God's higher law (e.g. Acts 4:19,20; 5:29, etc.), the civil official must be disobeyed (and summarily removed from office if he continues his blasphemy). Civil officials must rule justly:

> The Spirit of the Lord speaks by me, his word is upon my tongue. The God of Israel has spoken, the Rock of Israel has said to me: When one rules justly over men, ruling in the fear of God, he dawns on them like the morning light, like the sun shining forth upon a cloudless morning, like rain that makes grass to sprout from the earth (II Sam. 23:2-4).

Such were the "last words" of David, a king "after God's own heart" and one who, though his personal life left a few things to be desired, ruled mercifully but justly. All human rulers are sinners. They all make mistakes in their administration of civil government as well as in their personal lives. But if they are basically just, fair, firm, and repent of any injustices (as David did) they may commit, they are to be submitted to for the sake of the Lord.

Peter goes on to say it is God's *will* that Christians submit to civil rulers as they administer justice. Christian citizens who obey God's will in this matter are giving Christian testimony to the glory of God. They are also "putting to silence" (Gr. *phimoun*, "muzzling", I Cor. 9:9) the "ignorance" (Gr. *agnosian* "agnosticism, no-knowledge") of "foolish" (Gr. *aphronon*, "irrationality, stupidity, senselessness, unintelligence") men. In other words, those who disobey the justice civil rulers are mandated to execute as the cause of the Lord are irrational, stupid, senseless and unintelligent! That sounds like a characterization of animals — not people. And that is actually how Peter characterizes those who "despise authority" in his second epistle (see II Pet. 2:10-16)! One of the *purposes* of civil government is to try to force people to be civil; to make people behave like human beings rather than animals! Remember our prior discussion of Paul's statement to Timothy, " . . . the law is not laid down for the just but for the lawless and disobedient . . . ." Peter warns that while Christians are "free" (from the law, because they are "just" by a new nature), they are not to use their freedom as a "pretext" (Gr. *epikalumma*, "cloak, coat, covering") for evil. In this context, evil would certainly include disobedience to civil authority. The servant of God will also be "servant" (in submission to) civil authority. The servant of God will also be "servant" (in submission to) civil government. The Christianity which disobeys duly constituted and lawfully administered government, whether liked or not, is only a *pretended* Christianity! Christians are to "honor" (Gr. *timesate*, aorist imperative — a sharp, definite command) *all* men. It was a reality that most Jews, at that time, refused to "honor" (venerate, respect, value) any Gentile, let alone a Gentile ruler. But Christians must place the proper value on all men. Christians must evaluate all men as Christ does (see II Cor. 5:16ff). We must "love the brotherhood" (Gr. *adelphoteta*, "the band of brothers", i.e. Christians). We must fear God. And we must "honor" (Gr. *timate*, aorist imperative, sharp, definite command, again) the emperor. Christians must evaluate the principle of "emperor" or civil government in the same way Christ evalutes it! The Christian religion is inexorably tied to politics! The two cannot be separated! Christians are to evaluate and practice their politics, not according to how they feel or even according to what they want, but according to the teaching of the word of God! When civil government is clearly disobeying the principles or precepts taught in the word of God, a Christian's obligation is to verbally and actively attempt to bring his government to repent and conform to the Bible. When a government continues to disobey God and orders that a citizen, too, is to disobey God, the Christian's obligation is to obey God, protest, and, if the occasion requires, forcibly resist that civil government, being willing to suffer the consequences for what is right (see I Pet. 2:18-22; 4:12-19). That is what Peter (and others) did. About 1750, Jonathan Mayhew of Boston, an American colonial preacher said:

> It is blasphemy to call tyrants and oppressors God's ministers . . . . When [magistrates] rob and ruin the public, instead of being guardians of its peace and welfare, they immediately cease to be the ordinance and ministers of God, and no more

deserve that glorious character than common pirates and highwaymen . . . . "

Fifteen years later he said:

> The king is as much bound by his oath not to infringe the legal right of the people, as the people are bound to yield subjection to him. From whence it follows that as soon as the prince sets himself up above the law, he loses the king in the tyrant. He does, to all intents and purposes, unking himself by acting out of and beyond that sphere which the constitution allows him to move in, and in such cases he has no more right to be obeyed than any inferior officer who acts beyond his commission. The subject's obligation to allegiance then ceases, of course, and to resist him is no more rebellion than to resist any foreign invader . . . it is making use of the means, and the only means, which God has put into their power for mutual and self-defense.
> *The Light and The Glory*, by Peter Marshall and David Manuel, pub. Revell, pp. 264,265

So this is what Americans did. When King George III and the British government used force to deny American citizens their unalienable human rights, disobeying God's word and English law itself, Americans resisted. The "American Revolution" was *not* a revolution at all. It was not designed to overthrow a government's "lawful use of the law" — it was entered into as a *resistance* against *unlawful* use of the law. It was a war of resistance against aggression and invasion of human rights.

> I believe that is a misnomer (American Revolution). The American "Revolution" was not a revolution at all; it was a war for independence. That's not just word-playing; there's a vital difference. The American colonies were a continent to themselves, they were an ocean away from England, they had their own colonial governments, and with the exception of Georgia and possibly New York they had received no financial assistance from England.
> Furthermore, they had every legal right to break away from

THE PURPOSE OF CIVIL GOVERNMENT

England. For in asserting its authority over the colonies, England sought to deny to the colonists many basic rights which were not only God-given but which had been expressly recognized by the English Crown when King John signed the Magna Carta in 1215 A.D. and by Parliament when it passed the Petition of Right in 1628 and the English Bill of Rights in 1689. The English government went far beyond its authority when it tried to force its will upon the colonists . . . when the Crown granted the initial charters to the colonies, the Crown gave the colonies full legislative authority . . . . Furthermore, Parliament was to have representatives from all areas over which it exercised jurisdiction. The colonies had no representatives in Parliament . . . the king had gone far beyond whatever limited authority he had over the colonies, for he tried to violate basic rights which the Crown had recognized as belonging to Englishmen in the Magna Carta . . . . British authority . . . evaporated on December 22, 1775, when Parliament . . . passed the Prohibitory Act which removed the colonies from the king's protection and declared that they were to be treated as foreign enemies.

Our founding fathers, then, were not rebels or anarchists. They strongly believed in the divine institution of government, but they also believed government must be founded upon the law of God rather than the caprice of man. Their colonial governments were the true authority in their territories, and the colonies had a moral and legal right to be independent. At Independence Hall on July 4, 1776, they did not rebel against England; they simply declared that which was already an established fact — their independence. The War for Independence took place because the English government refused to recognize the colonies' rightful claim to independence. It was really a war of foreign (British) aggression.

God and Caesar, by John Eidsmoe, pub.
Crossway Books, pp. 33,34,35

Unequivocally, I Peter 2:13-17 declares that the purpose of civil government is to punish those who do wrong and to praise those who do right. That is God's will, and God's revealed will is to be the touchstone of evaluating any and all human institutions (establishments, governments). If *any* civil authority meets the scrutiny of God's revealed will for government, it is to be respected, obeyed, and prayed for. If it does not — if it should reward those who do wrong and/or punish those who do right — it is to be resisted, as peaceably as possible (Rom. 12:18), but with force if necessary. And this is true on an international level as well as a national level. No human government is above and beyond the law of God. And no human being is obligated to submit to any government which refuses to punish wrong or refuses to reward right.

Finally, in considering what the Bible says about the *purpose* of civil government, we will look at the most significant scriptural statement of all, Romans 13:1-7, RSV:

> Let every person be subject to the governing authorities. For there is no authority except from God, and those that exist have been instituted by God. Therefore he who resists the authorities resists what God has appointed, and those who resist will incur judgment. For rulers are not a terror to good conduct, but to bad. Would you have no fear of him who is in authority? Then do what is good, and you will receive his approval, for he is God's servant for your good. But if you do wrong, be afraid, for he does not bear the sword in vain; he is the servant of God to execute his wrath on the wrongdoer. Therefore one must be subject, not only to avoid God's wrath but also for the sake of conscience. For the same reason you also pay taxes, for the authorities are ministers of God, attending to this very thing. Pay all of them their dues, taxes to whom taxes are due, revenue to whom revenue is due, respect to whom respect is due, honor to whom honor is due (Rom. 13:1-7, RSV).

We have discussed this passage earlier in the chapter, "The Origin of Civil Government." It reaffirms that "every Person" is to be in subjection to governing authorities. Whatever the *purpose* of civil government, it is for *every* person, not a minority and not a majority, but for all. Paul wrote his epistle to the Romans about 57-58 A.D. Nero had already been emperor for four years. The Roman empire had brought tranquility and security to the volatile territory the Romans called "Asia" (including Asia Minor, Syria,

Arabia, Palestine). Rome brought a stability and liberty to those territories that none of their own governments had ever been able to produce. So Paul was exhorting these Roman Christians that regardless of how profligate Nero might be in his *personal* life, so long as he and his government "executed the wrath of God on wrong doers" they were to be obeyed.

Paul uses the Greek words *exousiais huperexousiais;* they are translated, "governing authorities." Literally they would be, "authorities, those who are held above or over or superior." Like Peter (I Pet. 2:13-17) Paul is not ordering subjection merely to political officials. He intends that Christians (and all mankind, for that matter) subject themselves to all "human institutions" within the social fabric which are necessary for ordered living. This would include familial structures, educational establishments, business-vocational structures, even avocational-recreational structures. Peter made it plain when he said, "Be subject for the Lord's sake to *every human institution* . . . . " The family, the school, the workplace, the playground, must each have an hierarcy of authority which must be obeyed if order is to be accomplished. Without order, confusion reigns (I Cor. 14:40). Without order goals and purposes are not attained in any social unit.

Paul deals with the *purpose* of civil government in Romans 13:3-6. There are at least five purposes served by civil government according to Paul in this passage:

a. "Terror to bad conduct"
b. "Praise to good conduct"
c. "Execute the wrath of God on wrongdoers"
d. "Good conscience"
e. "Minister of God, attending to" all the above.

The English word "terror" is a translation of the Greek word *phobos.* In verse 3 Paul's use means, "the causing of fear." Men may theorize all they want, but God's word plainly says civil government's *first* obligation is as a *deterrent* (by causing *fear*) against bad conduct. Since God's word is always right, and always practical, all the alleged statistics and nice-sounding sophistries quoted against capital punishment for capital crimes are irrelevant! We shall deal with the subject of capital punishment at greater length in another chapter. Here, the inspired apostle declares unequivocally, " . . . he does not bear the sword in vain." And "sword" is not being used metaphorically to describe any punishment less than *capital* punishment! The Greek word *phobos* ("fear") or a derivative is used *five times* in Romans 13:1-7.

If human governments and rulers are to fulfill their God-appointed purpose to strike *fear* into the minds and hearts of criminals who commit any and all crimes against social order, they must be supported in laws and punishments commensurate to the seriousness of the criminal acts. Justice, that which is equal, that which is proportionate, is both bibically mandated and "naturally" (i.e., rationally) demanded. Justice brought to bear upon bad conduct *will* act as a deterrent to some. Isaiah said it clearly:

> For when thy judgments are in the earth, the inhabitants of the world learn righteousness. If favor is shown to the wicked, he does not learn righteousness; in the land of uprightness he deals perversely and does not see the majesty of the Lord (Isa. 26:9,10).

Solomon also:

> Because sentence against an evil deed is not executed speedily, the heart of the sons of men is fully set to do evil (Eccl. 8:11).

> Kings cannot tolerate evil, because justice is what makes a government strong (Prov. 29:4, TEV).

The English word "conduct" in verse 3 is a translation of the Greek word *ergo*, most often translated "work." In verse 5 the Greek word *prassonti* (related to *pragma*) is translated "doer."

Civil government deals with deeds — actions. The reader should have noticed by now that in every scripture cited there is *not* the slightest indication that the purpose of civil government is to suppress belief or thinking. Prohibiting the *verbal* expression of beliefs or ideas is *not* (with a few exceptions) civil government's purpose. However, if any belief or idea is *acted* out and the action is categorically unlawful (according to God's laws and man's laws), civil government must act to prohibit it and, through threat of punishment, deter others from so acting. Of course, it is *reasonable* and wise to refrain from verbal expression of beliefs and ideas that would violate divine and human law and possibly incite unlawful actions. But civil government has no mandate from the Bible to prohibit verbal expression except in the cases of perjury, libel, treason, and perhaps verbal expressions inimical to the public safety, e.g., shouting "fire" in a crowded theater when there is no fire. Any kind of lying or misrepresentation of truth which would be used to exploit or endanger a citizen should be classified as "wrongdoing." And one of the basic purposes of civil government is to *frighten* people against wrongdoing.

> A king's wrath is like the growling of a lion, but his favor is like dew upon the grass (Prov. 19:12).
>
> The dread wrath of a king is like the growling of a lion; he who provokes him to anger forfeits his life (Prov. 20:2).
>
> A king's wrath is a messenger of death, and a wise man will appease it (Prov. 16:14).

If the law of God is given to *deter* men from unrighteousness, certainly the laws of men which are to have their origin in God's law should serve the same purpose:

> And the Lord commanded us to do all these statutes, to fear the Lord our God, for our good always, that he might preserve us alive, as at this day. And it will be righteousness for us, if we are

careful to do all this commandment before the Lord our God, as he has commanded us. (Deut. 6:24,25).

Jesus indicated that the punishments administered by civil rulers were to serve as *deterrents:*

> There were some present at that very time who told him of the Galileans whose blood Pilate had mingled with their sacrifices. And he answered them, Do you think that these Galileans were worse sinners than all the other Galileans, because they suffered thus? I tell you, No; but unless you repent you will all likewise perish (Luke 13:1-3).

There are numerous examples that the *fear* of government's power to punish does *deter* the perpetration of injustice:

> The police reported these words to the magistrates, and they were afraid when they heard that they were Roman citizens . . . (Acts 16:38).

> For we are in danger of being charged with rioting today, there being no cause that we can give to justify this commotion (Acts 19:40).

> So those who were about to examine him withdrew from him instantly; and the tribune also was afraid, for he realized that Paul was a Roman citizen and that he had bound him (Acts 22:29).

Of course, fear of civil government will not deter *every* person from criminal action. Some crimes are committed in the throes of passion while reason has been suspended. Some criminals have persuaded themselves that they will never be apprehended (and some never are). But the most significant reason the *fear* of punishment by civil government does not deter *more* criminal action is we are having *less* punishment of criminals. And the punishments that are being adjuged are far from commensurate with the seriousness of the crimes!

THE PURPOSE OF CIVIL GOVERNMENT

It is civil government's purpose, by divine mandate and biblical example, to make itself "a terror" to bad conduct! Biblically speaking, civil government does not exist to reform criminals. *Government is the servant of Almighty God to deter crime by punishing criminals with punishment commensurate to the crime committed.*

Second, civil government is to give "approval" to those who "do" good. Paul uses the same Greek word Peter uses, *epainon*, but the RSV translates it "praise" in I Peter 2:14 and "approval" in Romans 13:3.

> He who justifies the wicked and he who condemns the righteous are both alike an abomination to the Lord (Prov. 17:15).
>
> . . . those who rebuke the wicked will have delight, and a good blessing will be upon them . . . (Prov. 24:25).
>
> It is the glory of God to conceal things, but the glory of kings is to search things out . . . it is better to be told, Come up here, than to be put lower in the presence of the prince (Prov. 25:2-7).
>
> Give the king thy justice, O God . . . for he delivers the needy when he calls, the poor and him who has no helper. He has pity on the weak and the needy, and saves the lives of the needy. From oppression and violence he redeems their life; and precious is their blood in his sight . . . . (Psa. 72:1-16).
>
> Righteous lips are the delight of a king, and he loves him who speaks what is right . . . . In the light of a king's face there is life, and his favor is like the clouds that bring the spring rain (Prov. 16:8-15).

Civil government exists to "approve" and "praise" good conduct. Since public officials are "God's servant for your (the citizen's) good" it follows unquestionably that civil authorities will make it a practice to "praise" good conduct. Just as being "a terror to bad conduct" should *deter* crime, "praising" good conduct should *promote* civil peace and security. While the civil government could not ethically or legally take over the news media of a nation, it is obligated to do all in its legal power to "praise" good conduct. Apparently everyday acts of good citizenship, deeds of helpfulness, and justice being accomplished does not "sell newspapers" or "pay for TV news-time." A warped public and a greedy, prejudiced news media feeds on and spouts almost always news of "bad conduct." The entertainment media titillates the evil streak in human nature and profits from "showcasing" bad conduct. What is the civil government's role to be in these areas? Government involvement with the press and with public entertainment would, needless to say, have to be carefully legislated, and even more carefully administered. One thing is certain, government is to "praise" and publicly "approve" good that is done. It is in this way "the ignorance of foolish men" is to be "put to silence" (I Pet. 2:15).

There are some graphic biblical examples of civil government (even "heathen" governments) "praising" good conduct:
   a. Joseph's conduct and his subsequent assistance to Pharaoh as he advised him about preparing for a famine was rewarded. "And Pharaoh said to Joseph, Behold, I have set you over all the land of Egypt" (Gen. 41:4ff).
   b. David rewarded those who "stayed with the baggage" in the war against the Amalekites the same as those who fought (I Sam. 21-15). David honored Abner, a general in Saul's army, for the good Abner had rendered as a civil servant (II Sam. 3:31ff). David honored the good Jonathan, Saul's son, had done by rewarding Jonathan's son, Mephibosheth (II Sam. 9:1ff). David publicly honored his "mighty men" who served his civil administration of the kingdom (II Sam. 23:8ff; I Chron. 11:10-41).
   c. Daniel was rewarded for his good deeds by three pagan emperors (perhaps others) — Nebuchadnezzar, Belshazzar, and Darius — Shadrach, Meshach, and Abednego were also rewarded, (see Dan. 2:48,49, 3:30; 5:16;

6:2,3,25,28).
d. Emperor of Persia, Ahasuerus, rewarded both Esther and Mordecai for good deeds (Esther 5:6; 6:1ff; 10:1ff).
e. Although it was quite out of character for Jews to honor Roman government officials, a group did so for a certain centurion in Capernaum because of his good deeds (Luke 7:1-10).

Clearly, in both precept and precedent, the Bible says civil government has as one important purpose the approval of, the praising of, and rewarding of good citizenship. Perhaps if civil governments put more of their resources to work fulfilling this divine mandate there would be less "bad conduct" and more "good conduct."

Third, civil government is to "execute the wrath of God on the wrongdoer." This is basic; it is fundamental; it is the purpose for which civil government is to be most concerned. The apostle Paul has admonished Christians (Rom. 12:14-21) that they are *not*, on an *individual* basis, to "avenge themselves" for any wrong done to them. The Bible, both Old Testament and New Testament, in no way advocates or condones the execution of vengeance for personal wrongs by individuals or groups of individuals. Administration and execution of civil justice is, biblically, the prerogative and jurisdiction of duly constituted civil officials. Ultimately, *all* vengeance is the prerogative of God Almighty. But if humanity is to dwell on this earth in any semblance of tranquillity and order, and the Gospel have opportunity to be proclaimed, Almighty God cannot wait until the final judgment day to execute his wrath on the wrongdoer. So, the individual who has suffered wrong is *not* asked to "leave it to the wrath of God" at the final judgment day. God's wrath upon wrongdoers is in the here-and-now, to be continuously executed by civil government! The admonition to the Christian is: "If possible, so far as it depends upon you, live peaceably with all" (Rom. 12:18) — but when evildoers make it impossible for individuals to live peaceably they are to appeal to, and expect action from, civil governments to execute God's wrath on criminal and anti-social behavior. The division of the Bible text into chapters and verses is unfortunate in many respects. Romans, chapter twelve (12) through fifteen (15) is one unit, one context, and should be read and interpreted as one. Such a contextual understanding would solve the dilemma faced by Christians who know that God's word stands unequivocally for justice and punishment of wrong doing, and are at the same time commanded (e.g. Matt. 5:38-48; Rom. 12:14-21) *not* to avenge themselves. The Christian must *personally* endure persecution and injustices by turning the other cheek and going the second mile. But that is only if there is no just government to which the Christian may appeal for protection from and redress for injustices. That is what Paul is saying in the *unbroken* context of Romans 12:14-13:7.

The Greek word for "sword" *machairan* describes the usual short sword wielded by the Roman soldiers in their warfare and in executing criminals. The apostle plainly says that government officials do not "carry" weapons "in vain" (Gr. *ou gar eike* — "without plan or system; without cause; to no purpose").

Weapons for punishment and/or death administered by duly constituted civil authorities are God-ordained! They are not merely for adornment. The *purpose* for the "sword" (weapon of punishment and death) in the hand of the civil government is to "execute the wrath of God on the wrongdoer."

The RSV translates the Greek word *diakonos*, "servant" where it is used twice in 13:4. *Diakonos* is the word often transliterated "deacon" (see I Tim. 3:8,10; Rom. 16:1). The idea in the Greek word *diakonos* is portraying the "servant" in relationship to his work. Government officials are "servants of God" in the civic workplace. They are not merely civil-servants, but are servants of the Most High God. Their first allegiance should be, therefore, to God. It is Him to whom they will give account for their stewardship. Of all the people in the world who should apprise themselves of what the Bibles says about civil government, it should be civil-servants! If God has given any revelation at all (apart from human reason) as to how He wishes civil government conducted, it will be in the Bible. Civil-servants who ignore the Bible and its clear principles for governing do so at the peril of their eternal salvation. To displease God as a "servant" in civil government is as serious as displeasing God in service to His church on earth. The church on earth is unable to function as God would have it (I Tim. 2:1-4) unless there is a modicum of tranquillity and peace and civil order. It is the divinely-ordained purpose of civil government to insure peace and order. Government service is a stewardship. It has its "pounds" and its "talents" to put to use; what it has comes entirely from God Almighty; how it uses what it has must meet accountability to God's standards (found only in the Bible). Many civil governments and governors "have been weighed in the balances and found wanting" (Dan. 5:24-28). Paul uses the Greek word *leitourgoi* in 13:6, translated "ministers" in the RSV and KJV, probably because it is specifically, "a person of property who performed a public duty or service to the state often at his own expense." This would definitely include Roman senators of the first century who theoretically made and administered much of the Roman law. This text clearly refers to civil governments and their officials.

An important word to analyze here is the Greek word *ekdikos*. It is a compound word. *Dike* is used in the New Testament to mean *vengeance, punishment* (see II Thess. 1:8,9; Jude 7, etc.). The prepositional prefix, *ex* simply intensifies the word and literally would mean, "vengeance down upon." *Ekdikos* is a noun so it is describing "an avenger, one who inflicts punishment." Israelites were not to personally and individually avenge themselves (Lev. 19:18). The RSV translates *ekdikos*, "execute." That is less emotive and a clearer description of the purpose of civil government.

But the Bible says plainly that civil officials are God's servants to "execute" His *wrath* (Gr. *orgen*; English, *orgy, orgasm*) upon those who do wrong. In order for the government to do this, it is commissioned to "bear the sword" (arm itself with weapons of punishment and destruction) *effectively* and "not in vain." The question that must be answered is, what constitutes the "wrath" of God for specific wrongs? We shall deal with that question, to some extent, in later chapters. First, it must be established unequivocally that civil government has as its *primary purpose* the restraint of wrongdoing by "fear" (deterrents) and by "executing God's wrath" (punishment).

> There never has existed for any extended time an extensive society of men wherein someone did not have power to enforce laws. In enforcement, penalties for infractions are necessary. The power of government to take away the life of offenders is an ultimate and necessary instrument for enforcement of civil order.
> *Toward a Biblical View of Civil Government*, by Robert D. Culver, pub. Moody Press, p. 254

We are persuaded that Romans 13:1-7 is divine revelation through the Holy Spirit of God to the apostle Paul. It is not merely the human philosophy or theology of Paul. But Paul was unequivocally prepared to live out (or die by) what he wrote for God here. We need only to refer to his declaration recorded in Acts 25:11; he spoke to Porcius Festus, governor of the Roman province, Judea:

> I am standing before Caesar's tribunal, where I ought to be tried; to the Jews I have done no wrong, as you know very well. If then I am a wrongdoer, and have committed anything for which I deserve to die, I do not seek to escape death; but if there is nothing in their charges against me, no one can give me up to them. I appeal to Caesar.

Paul had written Romans 13:1-7 about four years before his confrontation with Festus. Now he claims he is willing to abide by God's decree that wrongdoers are to be executed *if* found lawfully guilty of a crime deserving death.

> What must not be lost sight of is that unpleasant as is the task of the jailor and the use of the whip, the cell, the noose, the

guillotine, these things stand behind the stability of civilized society, and they stand there necessarily, for God has declared it so, in harmony with reality, rather than with apostate sociological opinion. Government, with its coercive powers is a social necessity, but one determined by the Creator, not by the statistical tables of some university social research staff! No society can successfully vote fines, imprisonment, corporeal and capital punishment away permanently. The society which tries has lost touch with realities of man (his fallen sinful state), realities of the world, and the truth of divine revelation in nature, man's conscience, and the Bible.
Toward a Biblical View of Civil Government, ibid, p. 256

Finally, Paul states that one of the *purposes* for civil government is to provide mankind (especially Christians) an instrument through which to express and act out a good "conscience." The need for lawfulness, even some of the specific actions that are lawful or unlawful, has been "written" on the human conscience universally:

When Gentiles who have not the law do by nature what the law requires, they are a law to themselves, even though they do not have the law. They show that what the law requires is written on their hearts, while their conscience also bears witness and their conflicting thoughts accuse or perhaps excuse them . . . . (Rom. 2:14,15).

The sanctity of human life and property, the necessity of justice and truthfulness, among other "unalienable rights," are principles of "law" written on the universal human conscience. They are, as Immanuel Kant called them, "categorical imperatives." But while they are "imperatives" for the orderly existence of social structure, there are many individuals who, because of sin and selfishness, refuse to obey their consciences. If such persons are never converted and constrained by the love of Christ to evaluate life no longer from a human point of view (see II Cor. 5:14-17), they must be coerced by civil government to obey the divine laws written on their consciences.

> If rulers are a terror to the evil work, then they must be able to recognize evil works . . . men do not need biblical revelation to have, within limits, knowlege of good and evil. The prophets proclaimed the responsibility of heathen magistracies to enforce these universally known standards. Any reading of the classical authors of ancient Greece and Rome will support this. Falling far short of God's glory as the goal of right action, the classical pagan moralists knew a great deal about basic righteousness. Just how pagans of any age know — whether by right reason, natural law, natural light, general revelation, common grace, or whatever — is a matter of some legitimate difference of opinion. It is a fact, nevertheless, that without written standards, there is a divine morality which rulers everywhere know and enforce, and which the public acknowledges in spite of perverse denials among certain members of society. If this were not so, human life as a society could not exist.
> *Toward a Biblical View of Civil Government*, ibid, pp. 252,253

Civil government is God's coercive instrument to force the "lawless and disobedient" to obey the universal conscience. The Christians obeys what is lawful and right, supports justice with his words and actions and taxes, not because he is forced to, but "for the sake of conscience." The Christian knows what is right (including supporting civil government) and does it *because it is right*! This, as we shall discuss later, includes paying taxes, voting (in a nation that allows it), serving in the armed forces when his government calls him to defend against aggressive war upon his own nation or upon a people his nation has a legal treaty to defend. There can be no "conscientious objection" in such instances. The universal human conscience (unless seared by selfishness) declares that international aggression (a form of anarchy) is as wrong as any individual, local, or national crime destructive of social peace and unalienable human rights! The universal human conscience says anarchy must be restrained! This is right. Therefore, the individual who will not verbally and actively participate in civil government's mandate to restrain anarchy, sins against his conscience, sins against humanity, and sins against Almighty God.

There are, no doubt, other scriptural declarations concerning the *purposes* of civil government. Because of the limitations of time and space, we have been selective. We trust our selection has included the most pertinent passages and that the reader will have gained a clear, if limited, concept of the goals and functions of civil government from a biblical perspective. Civil government is, as the scriptures clearly portray, not a panacea for the ultimate cause of social disorder — human sinfulness. It is not God's instrument for attaining Utopia in this life or the next. It is a divine condescension to the fact that some sin and some sinners are incorrigible. Not every human being is going to believe in Jesus Christ and surrender to the loving persuasion of the King of kings. "Narrow and difficult is the way that leads to life, and few there be that find it." But there are a few who will find it, given the opportunity to do so.

In a world where the majority are in rebellion against God and His law, and where it will be that way until the end of time, civil government is ordained of God to "stand in the breach" to punish and thus stem the flood of wrongdoing so that the Gospel can be preached and accepted by a few. Thank God for civil government and those serving in it, who "use the law lawfully." Support it with your taxes and your actions, for the Lord's sake, and for the sake of a good conscience before God.

3

THE FORM OF CIVIL GOVERNMENT

While the Bible dictates no *detailed* form of civil government (with the exception of the Old Testament nation of Israel), there is a definitive form, a divine expectation, outlined there in general terms.

The basis for civil government was laid by God in the original construction of man. Man was created rational, free to choose, and ordered (to function both physically and spiritually according to "law").

God's nature is *order*. In the Old Testament the creation is described as an ordered arrangement. In the Mosaic dispensation a multitude of human actions, both religious and civil, were precisely *ordered* (even to the arrangement of priestly garments and the showbread on the table of the Tabernacle, Exod. 40:23).

Because he is like God, man has a natural love of order. "God is not a God of confusion, but of peace," (I Cor. 14:22). Thus we

have reason to assert that something of voluntary social organization, or government, was inherent in man from the start. There is precedent for it in the Godhead. The three Persons of the Trinity are equal in dignity and power and possess all the divine attributes in perfect degree, yet the Father *sent* the Son; the Spirit *proceeds* from the Father and the Son. The Scriptures display an eternal economy of relationship between the three Persons and distinguish important differences in their relationships to creation and redemption. These are aspects of that love of order in the Godhead which depraved men can not fully root out of their own nature. In his own way, each man on earth has a different place to fill. He does not find it automatically as does an ant or a locust or a coney or a spider. He may have to be assigned it by authority . . . . In a sinless . . . society, assignment of individual social function — baker, carpenter, teacher, etc. — would have always been done well. In any case, organization of society would have been necessary. Even the first pair, before sin's entrance, had relations to each other involving wielding of authority and submission to it in mutual relations.
Toward a Biblical View of Civil Government, by Robert Culver, pub. Baker, pp. 69,70

When God formed the earth and established it, he did not create it chaotic (see Isa. 45:18,19). It was arranged in order. God wants "all things done decently" (Gr. *euschemonos*, by schematic, by blue-print) and *in order* (Gr. *kata taxin*, by military precision-drill) (see I Cor. 14:40). He wants each individual to "order" his life (see Psa. 50:23; Col. 2:5). Order requires form and arrangement.

In 1659, John Eliot, Puritan missionary to the American Indians, wrote a treatise entitled *The Christian Commonwealth: or, The Civil Policy of the Rising Kingdom of Jesus Christ*. The treatise was a plan of government for the Natick Indian community:

> That which the Lord now calleth England to attend is not to search humane Polities and Platformes of Government, contrived by the wisdom of man; but as the Lord hath carried on their works

for them, so they ought to go unto the Lord, and enquire at the Word of his mouth, what Platforme of Government he hath therein commanded; and humble themselves to embrace that as the best, how mean soever it may seem to Humane Wisdom.

There is undoubtedly a form of Civil Government instituted by God himself in the holy Scriptures; whereby any Nation may enjoy the ends and effects of Government in the best manner, were they but persuaded to make trial of it. We should derogate from the sufficiency and perfection of the Scriptures, if we should deny it. The scripture is able thoroughly to furnish the man of God (whether Magistrate in the Commonwealth, or elder in the Church, or any other) unto every good work . . . .

(The) written Word of God is the perfect System or Frame of Laws, to guide all the Moral actions of man, either towards God or man.

The Puritans in America believed that the Scriptures contained the *general principles* of government, including the "Platforme" it should take. They also believed God left it up to men, guided by the Scriptures, to work out the details of applying those general principles to specific situations.

The Pilgrims, before going ashore at Plymouth, signed a covenant for civil government called the "Mayflower Compact" — it speaks of the necessity of "ordering" and "frame" and a "civill body politick" all "in ye name of God":

In ye name of God, Amen. We whose names are underwritten, the loyall subjects of our dread soveraigne Lord, King James, by ye grace of God, of Great Britaine, Franc, & Ireland king, defender of ye faith, &c., having undertaken, for ye glorie of God, and advancemente of ye Christian faith, and honour of our king & countrie, a voyage to plant ye first colonie in ye Northerne parts of Virginia, doe by these presents solemnly & mutually in ye presence of God, and one of another, covenant & combine our selves together into a civill body politick, for our better ordering & preservation & furtherance of ye ends aforesaid; and by ye vertue hearof to enacte, constitute, and frame such just & equall lawes, ordinances, acts, constitutions, & offices, from time to time, as shall be thought most meete & convenient for ye generall good of ye Colonie, unto which we promise all due submission and obedience. In witnes whereof we have hereunder subscribed our names at Cap-Codd ye 11. of November, in ye year of ye raigne of our soveraigne lord, King James, of England, France, & Ireland ye eighteenth, and of Scotland ye fiftie fourth, Ano: Dom. 1620.

That there were structures of civil government before the flood can hardly be denied. Man was created to "have dominion" (Gen. 1:28; Heb. 2:5-9). "Dominion" in a multiplying human race would necessitate social, civil structure. The first social structure was the human family.

> Sociologists generally agree that there are three *social institutions*, and that they are so called because they have their origin in human needs. These are the family, the state, and the church (or other religious institution) . . . .
> The natural sociality of man is actualized *primarily in domestic society*. (1) Domestic society is necessarily pre-supposed in every other form of society: without the conjugal relation there would be no other form of society that rightly could be called human . . . .
> The natural sociality of man is actualized *imperfectly*, however, in domestic society. (1) By *imperfectly* we mean incompletely . . . (2) Man is first of all a member of a family, and than a member of a state . . . the family is *per se* insufficient to provide for the necessities of the physical, intellectual and moral perfection of the human being. A single family lacks the division of labor essential to the provision of food, shelter and clothing that it needs; and certainly it cannot provide for its needs in the field of education, art, science, business and industry . . . (3) Again, the family is *per se* insufficient to protect its rights, to defend itself against attacks upon its peace and prosperity. It has to rely upon the state for this necessary protection . . . The state arises naturally from the insufficiency of the family as such to provide for the common good ("general welfare").
> *Common Sense Ethics*, by C.C. Crawford, pub. Wm. C. Brown Book Co., pp. 332,333

It would not have been long after creation and the Garden of

THE FORM OF CIVIL GOVERNMENT

Eden that the multiplication of mankind would have necessitated some form of "state" government. Its earliest structure was undoubtedly patriarchial. "Families" then "clans" and then "tribes" would have been the order. The oldest living male of a "tribe" would have been the leader, constantly struggling to sustain by tribal warfare whatever powers he needed to preserve the "tribe."

Cain built a city (Gen. 4:17). Archaeological excavations show the presence of villages and city life in the very early period.

> During recent years excavations have been made of an ancient city in Mesopotamia a few miles north of Nineveh at a site called Arpachiys. Here was found one of the earliest evidences of village life, dated by the excavators to 4000 B.C. or a little before.
> *Archaeology and Bible History*, by Joseph P. Free, pub. Scripture Press, p. 37

Archaeologists have found evidence of extensive "tribal" societies and their "organized" living sites. The Bible indicates Jubal, a member of Cain's family invented musical instruments (Gen. 4:21) and another called Tubal-cain was "an instructor of every artificer in brass and iron" (Gen. 4:22). Archaeological discoveries document the use of smelted metals as early as 4000-3000 B.C. This would require some form of social structure beyond the family.

The Biblical notation that Cain built a city would seem to indicate some *municipal* form of government in the second generation of humankind. Bible scholars have conservatively estimated a population of at least 120,000 within the lifetime of Cain. One commentator, however, doubts that there was any centralized form of human government at all during the pre-Flood era.

> The reference to the city which Cain built possibly suggests that he was trying to defy God's prophecy that he would be a wanderer in the earth. Whatever his intent, the Hebrew verb is indefinite — "was building" — probably suggesting that, though he may have started it, he did not finish it. He moved on after a little

while, perhaps leaving his son Enoch, after whom the city was named, to complete the job and to begin the true Cainite civilization . . . .

During this period from the Fall to the Flood, there seems to have been no organized system of laws or government for controlling human conduct. Although Adam undoubtedly instructed his children . . . there was no human agency ordained to enforce standards of behavior or worship . . . .

There were undoubtedly some, especially in the direct line of patriarchs from Adam to Noah, who heeded Adam's counsel and thus believed and obeyed God's Word. Most people, however, were content to go "in the way of Cain" (Jude 11); and with the creature comforts and advantages accruing from the rapidly developing science and technology of the day, it was not long before "the wickedness of man was great in the earth" (Gen. 6:5). Each man and each clan did whatever they wanted to do, to the extent that their strength and skills permitted. There was nothing to restrain them except, in some cases, the superior strength and skill of others. Thus it was demonstrated long ago that men cannot simply be left to their own devices; laws and governments are absolutely necessary. Consequently, after the Flood, God formally instituted systems of human government among men (Genesis 9:6).

The Genesis Record, by Henry M. Morris, pub. Baker Book House, pp. 144, 148, 149

The commentator cited above also estimates that "by the time of the Deluge, 1656 years after Creation by the Ussher chronology, even using . . . conservative assumptions, the world population would have been at least seven billion people!" The biblical summary of that civilization is:

The Lord saw that the wickedness of man was great in the earth, and that every imagination of the thoughts of his heart was only evil continually. And the Lord was sorry that he had made man on the earth, and it grieved him to his heart. So the Lord said, I will blot out man whom I have created from the face of the ground . . . Now the earth was corrupt in God's sight, and the earth was filled with violence . . . (Gen. 6:5-11).

THE FORM OF CIVIL GOVERNMENT

Before the Flood there was no centralization or recognized structure administered among humankind (except that of the clan or the tribe) for the punishment of crimes against the social order. Perhaps there were patriarchs (heads of families or tribes) who were able to maintain order and restrain total anarchy among their own clans. But there was no authority agreed upon among the roaming and expanding tribes who could restrain evil so the society grew more and more violent and evil. God had to providentially protect Cain from individual "avengers" (Gen. 4:13-16). Lamech boasted that he had slain young men for simply striking him and he would, himself, guarantee a seventy-sevenfold vengeance upon anyone who hurt him in anyway (Gen. 4:23,24). It appears that *each* person, no matter what the "civil" structure, had assumed the authority to act independently of all restraints except those of his own conscience and self-interest. This eventually led to a universal state of violence and anarchy.

Whatever the forms human governments may have taken in pre-flood times they were obliterated by the Creator when he destroyed all the human race except eight persons of one family. It was the very fact that almost total disorder (anarchy and mobocracy) prevailed which prompted God to send the Deluge. God said to Noah, "The end of all flesh is come before me; for the earth is filled with violence through them; and, behold, I will destroy them with the earth" (Gen. 6:13).

The most significant mandate respecting human government is in the form of a *covenant* from Almighty God with the survivors of the Deluge, the family of Noah (see Gen. 9:1-17). This covenant places direct responsibility upon man for a "stewardship" of divine creation and orders mankind to institute *some coercive form* of human government to prevent the anarchy and unchecked evil that brought divine judgment upon the first civilization. There is no indication from this text of any divine commandment or anticipation as to the precise form civil government should take.

Singularly important here is the emphasis on the divine *cove-*

nant. All human governments, all human institutions, no matter what their form, have their *raison d'etre* in this covenant from God. It appears from Biblical history that the Creator permitted *mankind* to develop and improve the particulars of *form* in civil government coincidentally with the gradual revelation of his divine will and its world-wide dissemination through the Gospel of Christ. In other words, the most beneficial forms of human government seem to arise out of cultures and peoples where the Bible and the Gospel of Christ is believed and practiced.

Clearly, there is a *fundamental* profile of divine expectation for human civil government in the Bible. Because of sinful human nature, no civil government has ever fulfilled the divine profile. None ever will! Some fit the basic mold better than others. It is evident that God has granted great latitude in forming the particulars of civil government. This due to human finitude. God does *not* expect any *human* government to fulfill the messianic government profiled in the Scriptures. The *ideal*, messianic government is fulfilled only in the church, over which Jesus Christ alone is Lord. However, God *does* expect conformity to an elemental framework for all civil governments which is outlined in the Bible. That outline appears to contain the following elements:

1. *Covenantal:*

Covenant relationship to Almighty God (discussed already in our chapters on "Origin" and "Purpose") is expected as part of the schematic of human governments (see Gen. 9:1-17; Dan. 2:21; 4:17; I Pet. 2;13-17). God insists (Amos 1:1-2:16) that even the most idolatrous nations are accountable to his fundamental standards for civil government. This is written in the "natural law" and in human conscience (Rom. 1:18-32; 2:12-16) as well as in the Bible.

2. *Nationalistic:*

Sometime after the Deluge "nations" began to form (Gen. 10:32). But then, man attempted to *form* a "one-world" government (Gen. 11:1-9). God intervened, miraculously, demonstrating his opposition. It is clear from Biblical history that

God has determined "one-world" government is *not* his will for the human race (see Deut. 32:8). Although a few "emperors" have tried, and have succeeded temporarily in forging large (but limited) "empires", God predicted through the prophets (especially Daniel and Revelation) that the last such "world empire" would be the Roman "empire" (circa. 100 B.C. — 450 A.D.). Others have tried since (Napoleon, Hitler, et al.) and have validated the prophecies. Christ's church, established during the Roman empire, was to remain the only "universal" kingdom until the return of Christ (see our commentary on Daniel, ch. 2:44-45, etc., College Press). The apostle Paul declared God's will to be *nationalism* (Acts 17:24-28). God has "determined allotted periods and the boundaries of their habitations." Pragmatically, history proves that civil government must be formed on a nationalistic basis. God has distributed varying human genetics, made geographical and climatic differences, thus dispersing the human race into many far-flung corners of the globe. It is logistically and ideologically impossible to construct a "one-world" government that could functionally serve the purposes outlined for civil government in the Bible. In our own lifetime we have seen the evidence of this in the dismantling of the British "empire", the "Yankee, Go home" syndrome, the under-ground resistance to Communist imperialism, the bitter, terroristic fighting between modern Israel and the Palestinians, and even in the tragic war between two Islamic nations — Iraq and Iran. Nationalism is an ongoing fact of history. Every great "world-empire" of the ancient world (Egypt, Assyria, Babylon, Persia, Greece, Rome) and those of more modern times has had to face the stark reality of nationalism as an inevitable enemy of "one-world" government. He has written it in the Bible and in history! He does, of course, want all men to come into the universal kingdom of Christ no matter what their human nationality. Christ's kingom is, even on earth, composed of people from "every tribe, and tongue and people and nation" (see Rev. 7:9-12, etc.). Those in Christ's universal kingdom may be loyal to their national human government so long as their *first* allegiance is to Christ. For the Christian, nationalism must always take second place to obedience to Christ's word. Should the two ever conflict in their demands upon the Christian's allegiance, either in thinking or acting, the Christian must take his stand with Christ and suffer whatever consequences may result from such a stand. Loyalty to one's national government when it does not conflict with clear and unequivocal commandments of Christ has Biblical sanction. It is the right thing to do!

3. *Consent of the Governed:*

Some civil governments do not adhere, in principle, to this Biblical form. In practice, however, all do. For if "the governed" do *not* consent, and if those not consenting are able to muster sufficient force, rebellion, revolution and formation of a different civil structure occurs. Consent of the governed is a condescension from God. That it is Biblical may be demonstrated in a number of examples. The "strife" between the herdsmen of Abram and Lot resulted in Lot separating himself from the patriarchial government under Abram in favor of the suzerainty of the king of Sodom (Gen. 13:1-18). When the Israelites chose to be free of the governmental dominion of Egypt, God intervened providentially and obtained their deliverance (Exodus, chapters 1-13). The Israelites consented to the governance of Joshua (Josh. 1:16-18) and to succeeding "Judges." When the people of Israel became dissatisfied with the administration of Samuel's sons, and asked for a "king like the nations," Saul was anointed King of Israel (I Sam. 8:1-10:27). The elders of Israel, after a long war between the houses of Saul and David, "sought David as king" over them (II Sam. 3:17ff). After David's death, the people of Israel consented to Solomon's rule (I Kings 1:39,40,). With heavy taxation placed upon Israel by Rehoboam (I Kings 12:1ff), the majority of the Israelites consented to be ruled by Jeroboam (I Kings 12:16) and thus the divided kingdom was formed.

Jeremiah delivered God's decree that Jews being exiled from their homeland and divested of their governmental structures should "seek the welfare of the city where I (God) have sent you into exile . . . for in its welfare you will find your welfare" (Jer. 29:7). Most of the Jews complied. Some Jews gave such consent to being governed by their alien hosts, they became "rulers" themselves in governmental structures drastically alien to them (Daniel, Shadrach, Meshach, Abed-nego, Esther, Mordecai, and others).

Of course, a plethora of governmental forms not listed in the Bible existed coincidentally with those which are listed. There were patriarchies, tribes, monarchies, republics (Greece and Rome the most prominent), empires, even alleged "democracies" (Greek). That Almighty God permitted such a diversity of governmental configuration shows that the Biblical principle concerning *form* of government is ideally "by consent of the governed." Thus, even for theocracies and monarchies:

> Throughout the Old Testament people chose kings to rule over Israel: "The men of Israel said to Gideon, Rule thou over us." (Jdgs. 8:22) "The men of Shechem . . . made Abimelech king" (Jdgs. 9:6). "Hushai said unto Absalom, Nay; but whom the Lord, and this people, and all the men of Israel choose, his will I be, and with him will I abide" (II Sam. 16:18). "The people . . . took Azariah . . . and made him king" (II Kings 14:21). God spoke through Moses to "all Israel" (Deut. 5:1) and later God directed the Israelites to choose judges: "Judges and officers shalt thou (speaking to 'all Israel') make thee (again, 'all Israel') in all thy gates, which the Lord thy God giveth thee, throughout thy tribes; and they shall judge the people with just judgment" (Deut. 16:18). These passages indicate that the Jewish kings and judges governed with the consent of the governed, and that the Israelites had some voice in the selection of their leaders.
> *Christianity and the Constitution*, by John Eidsmoe
> pub. Baker, pp. 368,369

4. *Limitation of Powers by Separation of Powers*:

The Lord told Moses: When you come to the land which the

Lord your God gives you, and you possess it and dwell in it, and then say, I will set a king over me, like all the nations that are round about me; you may indeed set as king over you him whom the Lord your God will choose. One from among your brethren you shall set as king over you; you may not put a foreigner over you, who is not your brother . . . And when he sits on the throne of his kingdom, he shall write for himself in a book a copy of this law, from that which is in charge of the Levitical priests; and it shall be with him, and he shall read in it all the days of his life, that he may learn to fear the Lord his God, by keeping all the words of this law and these statutes, and doing them; that his heart may not be lifted up above his brethren, and that he may not turn aside from the commandment, either to the right hand or the left; so that he may continue long in his kingdom, he and his children, in Israel (Deut. 17:14-20).

Granted this Mosaic legislation was for Israel, God's type of the messianic kingdom to be established by Christ (his church). And no human civil government was ever intended to be the anti-type of Israel. However, the Deuteronomy passage *was* intended for a *human* king. It therefore should be applicable to any *human* ruler whether of Israel or not. The principle that all human rulers and governments are to be subsurvient to the "law" of God ("natural," "conscience," "Biblical") is biblical! No monarch, emperor, president, parliament, congress, or politburo is to be *above* the "law." This is what the Bible says. Some rulers and governments have dared to violate that principle but God's word is true and they shall be answerable to the Almighty at the Day of Judgment. The Bible is filled with examples of God's judgment upon rulers and governments who have contravened this principle of the *limitation of power*. The examples begin with "the kings of the East" (Genesis 14:1ff), and Pharaoh (Exodus 1:1ff); they include Saul, king of Israel, many succeeding kings of Israel and Judah, Nebuchadnezzar, Belshazzar, the Syrian king Antiochus IV (see Dan. 11:21-24; 11:36-39), Herod (Matt. 14:1ff), and the Roman emperor ("beast") of Revelation 13:1-18. Others have acknowledged the limits of power and to varying degrees followed such a principle in their governing.

> The authority of the king (of Israel) in matters of state was exercised partly by him in person, partly through his ministers, the "princes" (I Kings 4:2ff). Among these functions are to be classed the communication with subjects and foreign princes and the direction of the taskwork, which was employed for public improvements, partly military, as in the fortification of cities, partly religious, as in the building of the temple. Local affairs had always been left largely to the tribes and their subdivisions, but, with the gradual increase of royal authority, the king sought to exercise it more and more in the conduct of the village communities. Conversely, the "elders of the people," as the (albeit aristocratic) representatives of the communes occasionally had a voice even in larger matters of state.
> *International Standard Bible Encyclopaedia*, art. "Government", Vol. II, pp. 1287-1289, pub. Eerdmans

Numerous examples in the Bible of limited power by separation of powers come to mind. Rehoboam, while he eventually rejected it, sought counsel from the "elders" (I Kings 12:6-11); Ahab's attempt to get Naboth's vineyard was ultimately (for appearances sake, of course) adjudicated by the "elders and the nobles" (I Kings 21:8-14); David was "elected" king by the voice of the people (II Sam. 5:1-5) and David "made a covenant with the elders"; David was returned to his throne after Absalom's rebellion by consent of the people (II Sam. 19:11-15); Jeremiah's trial was called for by the "princes of Judah" (Jer. 26:10ff). The Old Testament prophets are replete with references to "princes" and "elders," "priests" and "prophets" assuming roles of advice and consent to the Israelite monarch. The same is true of incidental references to Gentile kings and emperors (see Esther 1:13ff; 3:1ff; 8:7-17; 10:1-3; Dan. 3:1-3; 5:2; 6:1-5; Isa. 36:1-3; Jonah 3:7, etc.). The political structure of Israel was unique because it was especially chosen by Almighty God to prefigure the spiritual kingdom of the Messiah (the church). At the same time, the very fact that it was not only a human, *national* entity but even more exclusively, a *racial* entity, the fundamentals of its civil-political structure give us an idea of the form of civil government which is pleasing to God.

Limitations and separation of civil powers are exemplified in the Bible as early as Moses' appointment of subordinate "judges" from among the people to assist him in civil leadership (Exodus 18:13ff). It is also evident in the dual-leadership appointment of Moses and Aaron by Jehovah (Numbers, chapter 16-17). The appointment of a judiciary branch of government is mandated in Deuteronomy 17:8-13. Both king and subjects are obligated to keep God's commandments (I Sam. 12:12-25). David conducted his office as king "in covenant" with the elders of the people (I Chron. 11:1-13). David appointed "mighty men" to assist in civil government (I Chron. 11:10ff). David "consulted" his "commanders" (I Chron 13:1ff). David's "commanders" and other governmental assistants are listed (I Chron. 27:1ff; 28:1ff). Amaziah distributed civil powers among assistants (II Chron. 25:5ff). Hezekiah took "counsel" with his "princes" (II Chron. 30:1ff) as did Josiah (II Chron. 34:29). When the Jews returned from the captivities they were ruled by "governors" (Zerubbabel, Ezra 1:8,11; who may be the same person as Sheshbazzar, Ezra 5:14) and "elders" (Ezra 6:7). Ezra was told by Artaxerxes, king of Persia, to "appoint magistrates and judges" who would share civil government with the "governors" (Ezra 7:25ff). Nehemiah shared governance with "nobles and officials" (Neh. 5:6; 5:14ff) and "princes and priests" (Neh. 9:38). Indeed, Solomon, wisest of the wise, wrote, "A nation will fall if it has no guidance. Many advisers mean security" (Prov. 11:14, TEV); and, "Being wise is better than being strong; yes, knowledge is more important than strength. After all, you must make careful plans before you fight a battle, and the more good advice you get, the more likely you are to win" (Prov. 24:5,6, TEV); and "People learn from one another, just as iron sharpens iron" (Prov. 27:17, TEV) (see also Prov. 15:22; 28:18).

An interesting passage is to be found in Isaiah 33:17-22. It is unquestionably messianic. That is, it is a prophecy of the first coming of Christ to establish the messianic kingdom (the church), and that in Christ will be *united* all the fundamental powers of governance. Isaiah 33:22 states:

> For the Lord is our judge, the Lord is our lawgiver, the Lord is our king; he will save us (KJV).

The three fundamental powers of governance, judicial, legislative, and executive, are to be united in the Messiah because he is the Son of God, the Perfect Sovereign. He will be Absolute Sovereign (over those who by faith and repentance choose his rule) and he will not pervert justice or prostitute governance because he is without sin. While Isaiah 33:22 clearly predicts the ideal government, the spiritual government of the Messiah, it certainly is correct that the passage implies a divine will that human governments be structured with a separation of powers.

The Hebrew words in Isaiah 33:22 are: *shophetenu*, "judge"; *mechokekenu*, "lawgiver, legislator"; *malekkenu*, "king." If the *ideal* and *eschatalogical* (final, perfected) government of God (the kingdom of Christ) is structured with "branches" of government, surely the less-than-ideal human governments should be thus structured.

> A balance of powers within each state is desirable. In Isaiah 33:17-22, the now-conventional balanced division of powers is suggested as that of "judge" (judicial), "lawgiver" (legislative), and "king" (executive) . . . The passage does not directly teach balance of powers. Nor do the words judge, lawgiver, and king invariably designate distinct functions. Coming to the passage with knowledge of the customary analysis, the division of powers necessary in government under the condition of sin appears. Under messianic conditions of the coming kingdom of God, they are united. Government always has difficulty in maintaining unity and harmony among these powers.
>   *Toward a Biblical View of Civil Government*, by Robert Culver, pub. Moody Press, p. 104

We have already documented that the Founding Fathers of America's Constitutional Republic were primarily influenced by what the Bible says about civil government. We add here a quotation from the *Federalist Papers* (writing of James Madison and Alexander Hamilton in favor of ratification of the U.S. Constitution):

> It may be a reflection on human nature that such [constitutional separation of powers] devices should be necessary to control the abuses of government. But what is government itself but the greatest of all reflections on human nature? If men were angels, no government would be necessary. If angels were to govern men, neither external nor internal controls on government would be necessary. In framing of a government which is to be administered by men over men, the greatest difficulty lies in this: you must first enable the government to control the governed, and in the next place oblige it to control itself.

The illustrious Scotchman, Presbyterian preacher, Samuel Rutherford (1600-1661), was also influential in forming the thinking of the framers of the U.S. Constitution. Rutherford, in his classic work, *Lex, Rex* (or, *The Law and the Prince*), is unequivocal concerning *limitations* that must be compelled upon human governments and human rulers:

> Rutherford stressed that rulers derive authority from God, as declared in Romans 13:1-4 and other passages of Scripture. But God gives this authority to rulers through the people. The people establish a form of government and choose a particular man to be their ruler. The ruler then acts under the direction of God. Rutherford cited biblical passages to prove his point:
>
> > II Samuel 16:18, "Hushai said to Absalom, Nay, but whom the Lord and the people, and all the men of Israel choose, his will I be, and with him will I abide"; Judges 8:22, "The men of Israel said to Gideon, Rule thou over us"; Judges 9:6, "The men of Shechem made Abimelech king"; II Kings 14:21, "The people made Azariah king"; I Samuel 12:1; II Chronicles 23:3.

The covenant view of government also found secular expression in John Locke's social contract theory — the belief that men in a state of nature formed a government by mutual consent and gave it certain limited authority to act in order to protect their basic rights of life, liberty, and property. Locke, a Puritan by background, based his political theories on Rutherford's *Lex, Rex*.

For Americans the covenant concept finds its ultimate expression in the Preamble to the Constitution: "We the People of the United States, in order to form a more perfect Union . . . do ordain and establish this Constitution for the United States of America."

Calvinists not only believe civil government is ordained and established by God, they also believe that God has given civil government only limited authority. The same power that grants authority to government, also limits that authority . . . .

Rutherford in particular emphasized limited government. The people acting under the will of God, had given the civil government only limited authority, and they had given it conditionally — they reserved the right to terminate their covenant with the ruler if the ruler violated the covenant terms. Consequently the ruler is acting without legitimate authority if he violates the laws of God and nature by suppressing the basic liberties of the people. In such instances he is not to be obeyed. In fact, he is to be resisted. It is the Christian's *duty* to resist — by force if necessary.

Limited government also formed the basis for resistance to British oppression in the War of Independence. The colonists' slogan, "Rebellion against tyrants is obedience to God!" grew from roots firmly planted in Calvinist soil.
Christianity and the Constitution, by John Eidsmoe,
pub. Baker, pp. 24,25

Because the principle of limited powers in civil government is so biblically fundamental, and because Samuel Rutherford had such singular impact in the promotion of it in history, we quote one more writer concerning his *Lex, Rex*:

The governing authorities were concerned about *Lex Rex* because of its attack on the undergirding foundation of seventeenth century political government in Europe — "the divine right of kings." This doctrine held that the king or state ruled as God's appointed regent and this being so, the king's word was law. Placed against this position was Rutherford's assertion that the basic premise of civil government and, therefore, law, must be based on God's Law as given in the Bible. As such, Rutherford argued, all men, even the king are *under* the Law and not above it. This concept was considered political rebellion and punishable as treason.

Rutherford argued that Romans 13 indicates that all power is from God and that government is ordained and instituted by God. The state, however, is to be administered according to the principles of God's Law. Acts of the state which contradicted God's Law were illegitimate and acts of tyranny. Tyranny was defined as ruling without the sanction of God.

Rutherford held that a tyrannical government is always immoral. He said that "a power ethical, politic, or moral, to oppress, is not from God, and is not a power, but a licentious deviation of a power; and is no more from God, but from sinful nature and the old serpent, than a license to sin."

A Christian Manifesto, by Francis A. Schaeffer, pub. Crossway, p. 100

There are different views as to the posture the Christian is to take in the face of "ungodly" government and governors. We shall treat some of those different views in the next chapter. Our point here is to show that *limitation by separation of powers* in human civil government is what the Bible says.

5. Hierarchical:

The word *hierarchy* is from two Greek words, *hieros* (temple, sacred) and *archos* (ruler, rank). It has come to denote, generically, "anything arranged in an order of rank." If there is to be civil government, there must be a hierarchy of authority in some form. Civil government exists only by coercive power. Because of the sinfulness of men that is its mandate from God (Rom. 13:1-7; I Pet. 2:13-17; I Tim. 1:8-11, etc.). Peter writes concerning "the emperor as *supreme*" and Paul says, " . . . the governing *authorities*." God has ordained that civil government be structured upon a hierarchy of "authorities." Some one (or ones) in civil government must be invested with *authority*. Someone (or ones) has to be "in charge." Where there is no hierarchy of authority confusion reigns. When law is not enforced by some authority, moral chaos results. The Bible says so. When "there was no king in Israel; every man did what was right in his own eyes" (Judges 17:6; 18:1; 19:1ff; 21:25). During the days of the Judges, Israel suffered extreme oppression on many occasions because there was only intermittent civil (and spiritual) leadership. God strictly forbids the ruled from cursing the ruler (Exod. 22:28; Acts 23:25). The Bible charges all people, especially Christians, to "be obedient to the governing authorities" and to "every human institution." Authority may be vested specifically in a multitude of individuals or groups by "consent of the governed." That is, God apparently is content to let nations of people exercise some choice in the structure of governmental hierarchy, but ultimately God, himself, has decreed there must be a hierarchy. Historically, both in the Bible and outside the Bible, governmental hierarchies have taken many forms — patriarchal, monarchial, imperial, republican, dictatorial, etc. One thing is certain, unalienable human rights cannot exist when mobocracy or anarchy is the "rule." Classic examples are Paul's experience in the riot at Ephesus (Acts 19:23-41), and the plot against his life at Jerusalem (Acts 23:12-25). Secular history documents this to be an inescapable fact (e.g. the disintegration of the Roman empire, the anarchistic tyranny resulting from the French Revolution, the starvation and chaos during the Bolshevik Revolution, et al.). Social anarchy, however, inevitably creates a vaccum that demands to be filled with order. Some *form* (often tyrannical) of hierarchical authority will *necessarily* issue out of any circumstance where social disorder exists.

> Even the most evil society or the worst government will hold to a basic preservation of life and property. Unfortunately, some good governments do very poorly at it, while some evil dictators do very well. Even the poorest government is a blessing compared to no government at all. Can you imagine what would happen in a society with no one in control? It would instantly self-destruct. If

people had only themselves to protect their lives or property, there would be constant war.
The Christian and Government, Romans 13:1-7, by John MacArthur, pub. Moody Press, p. 40

In essence, there is no such thing as a pure "democracy." Even the angelic community clearly functions through a hierarchy or organization of ranks (see Col. 1:16: 2:15; Jude 9; Rom. 8:38; Eph. 1:21; 3:10; Dan. 10:13). The word "democracy" comes from two Greek words, *demos*, "the people," and *kratein*, "to rule." There has never been a nation where "the people," *en masse*, were their own government. A nation (such as the U.S.A.) with 260 million people could never conduct public meetings to enact laws, administer and execute the laws, adjudicate appeals, assess sentences for violations, and fulfill a multitude of other complicated duties of government. It would be literally impossible. And a *pure* democratic (rule by the people) government for any institution, no matter how small (family, tribe, school, township, city) would also be logistically and practically impossible. There has to be some form of hierarchical authority — some kind of "chain of command." Somewhere, as the late President Harry S. Truman reminded people, "the buck stops." The "buck" has to stop with some person (or representative body of persons) who has final civil authority.

The ancient Greek civilization, as a cursory reference to any modern encyclopedia will reveal, had no pure democracy. Theirs was an aristocratic-democratic-republic. In a limited way the Greek "democracies" were like the government of the United States. But in many ways they were not at all like it. The early Roman Republic was a representative government but its rulers were aristocrats who came to their offices and positions mainly through wealth.

The fear of power so widely and uncritically dispersed led the Puritans to distrust even what is called "majority rule." Unbridled majorities, they believed, were likely to mishandle and even pervert power because majorities are no more possessed of divine wisdom than minorities or monarchies. As Rev. John Cotton (1585-1652), minister of the First Church (Congregational), Boston, wrote:

> Democracy, I do not conceyve that ever God did ordeyne as a fit government eyther for church or commonwealth. If the people be governors, who shall be governed? As for monarchy, and aristocracy, they are both of them clearly approved, and directed in scripture, yet so as referreth the soveraigntie to himselfe, and setteth up Theocracy in both, as the best forme of government in the commonwealth, as well as in the church.

We may disagree with Rev. Cotton that monarchy is "directed" in Scripture, but we must agree with him about the impossibility of a pure democracy for governmental form. We must also agree that God has never specifically ordained domocracy as a form of government. God has never ordained any precise form — only a general form — for human civil government.

While it is true that the United States of America formed its government essentially by a vote of the "people" (although *all* the "people" certainly did not vote), it is *not* a "democracy." The government of the U.S. is founded upon its Constitution. "Representatives" were "chosen" and sent as delegates to the Constitutional Convention in 1787. These delegates (not all present at the final signing) constructed our basic Constitution. That Constitution was declared "in effect" in March, 1789, after nine of the States had ratified it, and was fully ratified (by vote of the "people") by the last of the 13 States, Vermont, in March, 1791. This Constitution provides for its amendment (Article V) by two-thirds vote of both houses of Congress, or by application of the Legislature of two-thirds of the States. It has been amended twenty-five times. But as it now stands, this nation, the United States of America, is a Constitutional Republic. Its laws are enacted by elected representatives; its laws are declared "Constitutional" or not by an appointed-for-life Supreme Court; its chief executive, the President (and the Vice President), although theoretically elected by popular vote of the "people," is in effect "chosen" by the two political parties and presented to the "people" for popular vote. And the system has, on a few occasions, put a man into the office of President who did not get the majority of the popular vote! But even granting that the chief executive is elected by "the people", one must remember that "the people" must elect him in accordance with the Constitution! In other words, Americans have agreed that in their government, the *Constitution* is the *hierarchical* final authority. All citizens and agencies and government officials are subject to the Constitution, including its legislators, its judges, and its chief executive. As a matter of fact, nearly *every* level of civil government in the U.S. is "representative" — not democratic. The legendary Greek philosopher, Aristotle, discussed forms of government in his work entitled: *Politics, Book III*:

Government	True Forms (ruling with a view to the common interest)	Perverted Forms (ruling for the benefit of private interests)
(1) Of the one	royal rule	tyranny
(2) Of the few	aristocracy	oligarchy (usually a plutocracy)
(3) Of the many	constitutional rule	pure democracy (mob rule)

Of these different forms, said Aristotle, royal rule (that of a "benevolent monarch") is probably the most efficient for as long a time at least as the monarch lives; its weakness, however, is in the fact that a succession of benevolent monarchs is too much to expect; history shows that good fathers all too often sire notoriously bad sons. Therefore, on the whole and in the long run, constitutional rule is preferable. This he defines as the rule of the many under a constitution (the organization of powers and offices as determined by law). Every government, Aristotle insists, should be a government under law: "matters are better regulated by laws than by the will of man which is a very unsafe rule"; "the arbitrary power of acting on their own judgment, by rulers, and dispensing with written law, is dangerous"; "whereas the law is passionless, passion must ever sway the heart of man"; "the law is reason unaffected by desire." Pure democracy, a kind of mob rule, says Aristotle, is the least desirable of all forms: this he defines as "a state in which the multitude have power, but supersede the law by their decrees"; the result is that they prostitute liberty into license and precipitate a kind of anarchy. "Such a democracy is fairly open to the objection that it is not a constitution at all; for where the laws have no authority, there is no constitution. The law ought to be supreme over all, and the magistracies should judge of particulars, and only this can be considered a constitution." A citizen Aristotle defines as one who shares in governing and being governed, one who alternates at rule and being ruled. Laws should be changed, of course, when they become obsolete; but frequent and needless changes diminish respect for law in general. (Practically every principle of political science embodied in our Federal Constitution is laid down in Aristotle's *Politics*.) . . .

Pure democracy exists only in cases in which the whole people vote on proposed legislation, determine sanctions, etc. . . . A *representative democracy* is one in which authority is vested in representatives elected by the people at stated intervals; this form of government is usually known as a *republic*. The United States of America is a republic.

Common Sense Ethics, by Dr. C.C. Crawford, pub. Brown Book Co., pp. 359,360

The Bible says civil government must be formulated on some hierarchical system of authority. It does not specify what that system must be. But it does clearly teach that society cannot fulfill the divine purpose without governmental authority:

There is no biblical theory of human political sovereignty — monarchial, aristocratic, plutocratic, democratic, republican, or otherwise. God's is the only sovereignty recognized in the Bible. In biblical doctrine, all political sovereignty is bestowed by God. Biblically speaking, there is no such thing as either popular sovereignty as in Western democracies, or state sovereignty as in the various totalitarian states. The various human methods by which political power is conveyed to magistrates are just that — methods of conveyance only . . . .

. . . government does not have its origin in some primeval social contract among our ancestors . . . neither does it arise out of some immanent force in the world culminating in the state . . . . It has its origin in God's sovereignty. He alone is sovereign, but has delegated the power of civil government to magistrates — the manner of their placement not being specified.
Toward a Biblical View of Civil Government, by Robert Culver, pub. Moody Press, pp. 53,70

6. Moralistic:

God expects a "religious" or moral base for all human government. This is necessary for governments and governors to fulfill their ordained purpose which is to keep evil checked. The human race is fallen from goodness. Mankind in rebellion against its Creator, distrusting the Creator's moral imperatives, is vulnerable to Satan's lies. When man rejects the law of God he is led astray by falsehood into moral anarchy. He makes himself his own god and all his actions become wickedly self-centered. Unwilling to practice divinely revealed goodness through the persuasive grace of God, sinful men must be coerced to behave morally so that an acceptable amount of social order may prevail.

> At the base of every human culture is a shared set of "religious" values that help hold the society together. They are . . . those ideals or things that persons in a culture value most highly, are committed to, and would be willing to die for.
> *The Search for Christian America*, by Noll, Hatch, Marsden, p. 44, pub. Crossway Books

Dr. C.C. Crawford, in his book, *Commonsense Ethics*, expands this anthropological fact when he writes:

Man's moral activity is his quest for Goodness, which is commonly identified with Justice, Order, etc. (1) The fact that all peoples, no matter how primitive their culture, have always been known to make distinctions of some sort between right and wrong, good and bad, in human conduct, can hardly be refuted. Even though anthropologists may designate such distinctions, in their most elementary form, as "customary law," the fact remains nevertheless that the distinctions are made and made universally. Moreover, although different reasons have been assigned for these distinctions, in diverse social structures, and by different systems of ethics, the fact of the universality of such distinctions is historically established. (2) The distinction between right and wrong, good and bad, seems to be a universal judgment of the human race: as one author puts it, "The feeling of obligation is an ineradicable element of our being" . . . . (3) This fundamental distinction between what *ought* or what *ought not* to be done, has been found to be so general that, as we have noted previously, by many philosophers it is designated the Ethical Fact. Moral activity — the quest for Goodness, for the answer to the question, What is the Good Man? — is another manifestation, obviously of the *spirit* that is in man (Gen. 2:7; Job 32:8). (4) Finally, this quest for Goodness, Justice, Order, etc., has been at the root of the progressive development of social and political order in human history, from family to clan, from clan to tribe, from tribe to nation (a people, a specific ethnic group), from nation to national state (characterized by territory, independence, and government).

Man is a being that makes moral choices. That cannot be denied. The crucial issue, then, must focus on the basis or ground of morality. It is evident to any honest human being that he cannot be, himself, the ground of his morality. He must have some base for goodness which is higher, wiser, more enduring than himself. Thus, all human beings and human cultures manifest some "religious" orientation.

The religious consciousness of man has manifested itself in all ages, and among all tribes and peoples, in a great variety of forms (dependent for purity, of course, upon the standard of knowledge by which it was guided) from the crudest animistic beliefs and the ritualistic worship of gods who were but personifications of the

forces of nature up to that *pure love for God and man* which fills the heart of the spiritually-minded person for whom religion is the unbroken communion of the human spirit with the Divine spirit on the basis of the Truth (John 4:24) . . . . It is doubtful indeed that any people ever existed without some consciousness of their human frailty and consequent need of strength to be gotten from a source or sources higher than man himself, and without a sense of moral imperfection, a sense of the need of prayer, and a dim longing for, and expectation of, survival beyond the grave . . . .
Commonsense Ethics, by C.C. Crawford, pub. Brown, p. 123

God has ordained human government as an expedient to restrain the human rebellion that produces social anarchy. Humankind, for the most part, has seen the necessity for some basis of morality besides the mere hierarchical structuring of human beings in some form of government. Thus all civil governments have extolled some form of "religion."

There are only *religions*, and basically two of them. They arise out of man's need to return to God — out of alienation from God to sin. One is the revealed religion of grace; the other is that pervasive natural religion of supposed human merit . . . .

Government always has had a religious foundation. This is because government must always operate with some theory of authority. Another name for authority is sovereignty, or right of rulership.

Many foundational factors go into the structure of a society. Another way of saying this is to assert that every society has many concerns . . . it can also be said truthfully that in all its ethical and judicial aspects at least, and to a high degree in all aspects, a society is the expression of the ultimate concern of its people, especially of its ruling elite. Another name for ultimate concern is religion . . . .
Toward a Biblical View of Civil Government, by Robert D. Culver, pub. Moody Press, pp. 25,52,128

Clearly, all human governments are short of the ideal government which sinful man must have in order that he may be regenerated after the Divine image. The only "government" capable of producing human redemption is that of God's Messiah, Jesus Christ. The love of Christ alone has the constraining (II Cor. 5:14-21) power to rule over man so that man sees everything from the Divine perspective and behaves accordingly. Human governments are (some more than others fundamentally contrapositional to the rule of God.

> Most of the traits of this central "religion" in a culture reflect directly the values that predominate in fallen human nature. So, for instance, one factor that we find holding cultures together everywhere is sinful pride. This pride might be manifested in any one of a number of ways, but among the most common have been tribalism, racism, nationalism, and an inflated loyalty to one's own class or social position. Each is a means of convincing people that they are inherently superior to other peoples and hence that they can treat others as inferiors, even as subhumans worthy of disdain or abuse. Similarly, every human culture is held together by the simple shared values of selfish interest. Putting oneself and one's group first, is in fact, almost the premise on which human governments are based. Other widely held values found in almost every culture are materialism, lust for power, and love of violence. While cultures may be held together also by other values — such as love or respect for elders, respect for law, love of virtue — most of the widely held values related to human nature turn out to be directly antithetical to Christianity.
> *The Search for Christian America*, by Noll, Hatch and Marsden, pub. by Crossway Books, p. 44

However, the fact that human governments are "antithetical" to God does not excuse them from the Biblical imperative that they should be *synthetical* (in sympathy with) to divinely revealed moral guidelines. The Bible speaks clearly on this point. There is sufficient revelation of the Creator and his nature (his wrath against wickedness, his eternality, his power, his deity) in creation that moral deviation and anti-social behavior is inexcusable in individuals and societies. Paul wrote in Romans 1:18-32 that "what can be known about God is plain to them, because God has shown it to them." In the same treatise (Rom. 2:14-16) the apostle writes, "When Gentiles (pagans) who have not the law (the propositional, human-language revelation of God) do by nature what the law requires, they are a law to themselves, even though they do not have the law. They show that what the law requires is written on their hearts, while their conscience also bears witness and their conflicting thoughts accuse or perhaps excuse them . . . . " It is, therefore, a matter of revealed truth that even those without the Bible have a moral base sufficient to carry out the purposes for which God ordained civil government.

Civil governments (which are constituted by people) which do "not honor him as God" and do not "give thanks to him" but "exchange the glory of the immortal God for images" and "exchange the truth about God for a lie" are foolish, futile in their thinking and "darkened." Civil governments which condone and permit "dishonorable" and "unnatural" passions (homosexuality) to be acted out will receive in their own persons "the due penalty of their error" and "deserve to die."

In light of God's revelation of himself in man, his highest act of creation, it is immoral to even think of some basis or religion other than that of the God of the Bible. Paul charged the philosophers of ancient Athens, "Being then God's offspring we ought not to think that the Deity is like gold, or silver, or stone, a representation by the art and imagination of man" (Acts 17:29). Honest reasoning should dictate to individuals and governments that the God to worship does not live in shrines made by man. Human beings and human governments should seek the God who made the world and everything in it as Lord of heaven and earth. God expects that! He expects those who administer human governments to do so as his "servants" responsible to observe the moral guidelines he has revealed in "nature" and in human conscience.

We would expect those who governed and guided God's chosen people, the Israelites, to be called upon to rule from a religious and moral basis of Biblical truth. Some (e.g. Abraham, Joseph, Moses, Joshua, Samuel, David, Solomon,

Jehoshaphat, Hezekiah, et al.) did; others (e.g. Saul, Jeroboam, Ahab, Ahaz, Jeroboam II, Manasseh, et al.) did not. But the Biblical record also declares that God expects all human rulers to govern according to his standards of what is right and just. Those civil governments which did not structure themselves in the moral and religious forms that acknowledged Jehovah were verbally judged and historically destroyed (so far as the Bible details the history of kings and kingdoms).

There are scores of examples that at least a modicum of revealed morality was practiced by some of the heathen empires in Biblical history. We list a few:

a. One of the Pharaohs acted toward Abraham with moral propriety (Gen. 13:17-20).
b. Abimelech, Canaanite king, had moral standards (Gen. 20:1-18; 21:22-34).
c. Joseph's master, Potiphar, acknowledged what was right in Joseph and rewarded it (Gen. 39:1ff).
d. The Egyptian government (while it did not ascertain the truth in the matter) demonstrated scruples against adultery and imprisoned Joseph (Gen. 39:19ff).
e. The Pharaoh contemporary with Joseph acknowledged the justness of Joseph's administration of the famine (Gen. 47-48).
f. When Ahasuerus, emperor of Persia, was given the truth about Haman's plot to commit genocide upon the Jews, he saw that justice was done (Esther 7-8).
g. Even Pontius Pilate declared Jesus innocent some eight times of the false charges of the Jewish rulers, acknowledging the right moral evaluation while lacking the personal character to fulfill his responsibility to it. (John 18-19).
h. Numerous confrontations between the apostle Paul and Roman authorities show the Roman government had been structured on a basic morality which had been "written on their consciences" by Jehovah.

God's expectations for civil governments in the area of religion and morals have never been met. Relatively speaking, some human governments have pleased God more than others. The tragedy of history, however, has been the shocking failure of Israel to govern itself according to the revelation of God. In a number of Biblical passages, Israel is condemned by the prophets of God as being more "heathen" than the heathen (see Amos 3:9-11; Jer. 18:12-16; Jer. 2:10,11; Ezek. 5:5-9). The Old Testament writings of the prophets are also filled with judgments pronounced by God upon Gentile rulers and governments because they failed to think and act according to moral levels within the Divine expectation (Isa. 13-23; Jer. 46-51; Ezek. 27-32; Obad; Amos, 1-2; Jonah; Nahum; Habakkuk; and the book of Revelation).

Two Biblical passages speak with unquestionable precision in this matter. In Daniel, chapter 4, after Nebuchadnezzar's dream of himself as the "tree" whose top reached to heaven, which is then hewn down and "he" is driven to live like an animal, Daniel was called in to interpret the dream. At the conclusion of the interpretation Daniel advised the emperor, "Therefore, O king, let my counsel be acceptable to you; break off your sins by practicing righteousness, and your inquities by showing mercy to the oppressed, that there may perhaps be a lengthening of your tranquility" (Dan. 4:27). Clearly, God expected this heathen ruler to govern from a moral base higher than that which any heathen religion could supply. We might add that Nebuchadnezzar seems to have taken heed to Daniel's message (see Dan. 4:28-37). Furthermore, when Belshazzar, the son or grandson of Nebuchadnezzar, blasphemed Jehovah by drinking from the vessels of the Hebrew temple in honor of idolatrous gods, God's "finger" wrote his doom on the wall of the banquet hall. When Daniel was called upon to "solve Belshazzar's problem" he told the scion of the Babylonian throne that he should have known what Jehovah God expected of him from what had happened to Nebuchadnezzar (Dan. 5:17-22). But, Daniel added, since

Belshazzar had not honored the God in whose hand was his breath, his kingdom was "found wanting" and would be given to the Medes and Persians (Dan. 5:24-28). Those governing authorities who do not learn from history that Jehovah is sovereign and that his moral expectations must be met in government as well as in one's private life, are doomed to repeat the judgments of Jehovah!

The second passage is a record of the confrontation between the apostle Paul and Antonius Claudius Felix, procurator of Judea. Tacitus said of Felix, "he revelled in cruelty and lust, and wielded the power of a king with the mind of a slave." He began his career as procurator of Judea by seducing Drusilla, the sister of Herod Agrippa II, and wife of the king of Emesa, and marrying her. Because she was Jewish he evidently learned much of Jewish life and customs. While he was a moral reprobate, he had enough conscience to be "alarmed" when Paul argued "about justice and self-control and future judgment." But the point is that the apostle's conviction about moral expectations in rulers was so strong he fearlessly demanded it of this ruler before whom he stood as a prisoner.

Finally, the two key passages of the New Testament on civil government (Rom. 13:1-7; I Pet. 2:13-17) unequivocally state that human governments are "to punish those who do wrong and praise those who do right." Those statements from the apostolic pen are divinely revealed and divinely authoritative. The inference seems incontrovertible that civil governments are to find their basis and guidelines for "wrong" and "right" from the divine revelation also. If God is issuing the orders for civil governments to arbitrate and administer "right" and "wrong" in the human arena (in the "kingdom of the world"), then God is the Authority to whom these civil governments must harken for the principles and directions of *what* is "right" and "wrong."

God communicates the grounds and guidelines of right and wrong in his two methods of revelation to the world. The first method of God's revelation is, as Paul writes in Romans 1:18ff, "the things that have been made" ("natural phenomena," history, human conscience). The second method of his revelation is propositional — verbalized in human language through secondary agents, human spokesman (prophets, apostles). This second revelation we call the Bible. Realistically, we may expect few governments and governors to ever make the Bible their "rule of faith and practice" in governance. There may be a very few through the centuries who will make some concessions and exercise government from a general Biblical base. The best the world may hope for is that governments and authorities will apply honest logic and common sense to the divine axiom of the sanctity of life, liberty and property revealed in nature and human conscience, and rule from that moral base. Most human governments operate from a humanistic, relativistic, materialistic and pragmatic base. For most human governments, man is the end — not God. With such a political philosophy, man becomes his own god.

The Bible says human governments are to be structured on the foundation of Biblical religion and morals. The Bible is omnisciently realistic, however, and portrays human history from the Garden of Eden to the Great White Throne of Judgment as never producing such a civil government. God is producing his ultimate moral government under the sovereignty of Jesus Christ over the minds and actions of men and women in the society known as Christ's "church." In the interim, that human government which most nearly structures itself on the religion and moral standards of the Bible will be the most pleasing to God and most useful for his purposes of finishing the redemption of creation.

4

CRIME AND PUNISHMENT

There are three Hebrew words in the Old Testament text sometimes translated in English by the word *crime*: (1) *mishphat*, (see Ezek. 7:23) — most often translated "judgment"; (2) *zimmah* (Job 31:11), translated "heinous crime" and means literally, "an evil scheme" (used in connection with murder, incest, and adultery — see Hosea 6:9; Prov. 10:23; 21:27; Lev. 18:17; 20:14; Job 31:11; Jer. 13:27; Ezra 16:27, etc.); (3) *'asham*, (see Gen. 26:10; Num. 5:7; Prov. 14:9; Jer. 51:5), it means "offence, trespass, fault" and is often translated "guiltiness."

Four Greek words are used to mean "crime" in the New Testament: (1) *aitia* (see Acts 25:18; Matt. 27:34; Mark 15:26; John 18:38; 19:4,6; Acts 13:28; 23:28; 28:18); the word is often translated "charge, fault, cause, case"; (2) *aitioma*, related to the first word, but more implicit (see Acts 25:7) — translated "complaint, charge"; (3) *egklema* (see Acts 23:29; 25:16) also translated "charge, complaint"; (4) *Kategoria, kategoros* and *kategoreo* (two nouns and a verb, from which we get the English words "category" and "categorize"); all have to do with judicial procedure; they are words derived from the Greek word *agora* which means "a place of public speaking", and from the Greek prefix *kata* which means "against" — thus, "a speaking against a person before a public tribunal; this word is the opposite to the Greek word *apologia* which means "a public defense."

A crime is a contravention of the public right; a violation of the natural law or the codified law; all of which subjects the perpetrator to legal punishment. The English word *crime* is derived from the Latin *crimen* which means, "accusation, fault." A crime is an act or omission forbidden by law and punishable upon conviction. People sometimes use the word "crime" to describe any aggravated or gross offence against accepted morality, whether codified as civil law or not. In the Bible "crimes" are regarded as offences against (1) God, or (2) man, or both, but *not*, primarily, as "offences against the state."

The very ideas of crime and punishment are valid only because of the objective existence of the eternal God and the revelation of his divine nature. As Paul put it:

> For the wrath of God is revealed from heaven against all ungodliness and wickedness of men who by their wickedness suppress the truth. For what can be known about God is plain to them, because God has shown it to them. Ever since the creation of the world his invisible nature, namely, his eternal power and deity, has been clearly perceived in the things that have been made (Rom. 1:18-20).

God is just. The Hebrew word for "just" is *tsadaq*. The word is often translated "righteous." God's justice or righteousness is the very essence of his nature.

That God is just is true, analytically, from the definition of his holiness. The Hebrew word *tsaddiq* means "straight," and the Greek word *dikaios* means "upright." Both words express the

CRIME AND PUNISHMENT

justice of a holy God. Justice is the outgoing of God's holiness with reference to moral (or immoral) creatures. If the creature were entirely harmonious with God's holiness, it would follow from God's justice that the creature would be in perfect fellowship with God; but if the creature is, as we know he is, fearfully self-corrupted, it follows that God must be hostile to his corruption. Since the creature is unholy and unjust, it follows that God in His justice must vindicate His holy character and maintain His creation as an expression of that holy character. A holy God if he maintains a creation must maintain a holy creation, and must be hostile to all things in it which are in violation of his own holiness. If there is any difference between right and wrong, God in His righteousness must be hostile to the wrong. This is analytically true. Thus it is evident that the law, "The wages of sin is death" (Rom. 6:23) is logically necessary in consequence of God's holiness . . . .
A Systematic Theology of the Christian Religion, by James Oliver Buswell, Jr., pub. Zondervan, pp I-67,68

It is not our purpose in this volume to make an extended study of the nature and attributes of God. What the Bible says about God's essence and character has been given a thorough and scholarly treatment by Dr. Jack Cottrell, in his three volume work, *What The Bible Says About God (Creator, Ruler, and Redeemer)*, published by College Press, and we heartily recommend that Christians read all three volumes. We do quote from Dr. Cottrell here by way of establishing the ground upon which we shall treat the subject of Crime and Punishment:

That God is righteous means that all his actions conform perfectly to the proper standard or norm. This needs to be very carefully explained, however. It does not mean that there is some Eternal Law existing outside of God to which God himself must give allegiance. All law external to God derives from God; he externalizes it not for his own sake but for the sake of his creatures, that they might have access to the perfect standard for righteousness. For God himself, *his own eternally perfect nature* is the law or norm to which all his actions conform. Clarke puts it well when he says that the righteousness of God means that "God is the eternal Right," that "in him all right is grounded." In other words, "what we name his righteousness is the attitude and work of God as the eternal Right, in his relations with other beings." Berkhof makes this comment: "The fundamental idea of righteousness is that of strict adherence to the law. Among men it presupposes that there is a law to which they must conform. It is sometimes said that we cannot speak of righteousness in God, because there is no law to which He is subject. But though there is no law above God, there is certainly a law in the very nature of God, and this is the highest possible standard, by which all other laws are judged . . . .

Knowing that God is righteous is thus very important to us creatures who are asked to trust him. Because he is righteous, i.e., because he acts with perfect consistency and constancy, especially in keeping his word, we *can* trust him; we *can* rely on him and put our utter confidence in him . . . .
What the Bible Says About God the Redeemer, by Dr. Jack Cottrell, pub. College Press pp. 194-196

Abraham acknowledged, "Shall not the Judge of all the earth do right?" (Gen. 18:25). From beginning to end, the Bible declares God to be Just (Righteous) (see Exod. 9:27; Deut. 32:4; Psa. 37:28; Isa 45:21; 61:8; Neh. 9:33; Hosea 14:9; Zeph. 3:5; Hab. 1:13; Rom. 3:5; Rev. 15:3).

All crime is ultimately against God. Every crime is a rebellion against the absolute holiness of the Creator. Every punishment decreed against crime is ultimately a decree of Almighty God, either administered providentially by God, himself, or by his ordained agency — civil government (institutionalized in the family, the nation and the international community).

Without the objectivity of God's existence and the logical necessity of justice as the essence of his nature there would be no imperative for justice among human beings. Crimes would not be violations of any Absolute Law and punishments, if there could be any justifiable punishments at all, would be entirely relative. Without an Absolute as a final ground, men would inevitably categorize criminal actions from a strictly pragmatic, humanly-autonomous criterion. The most powerful human being (or group of human beings) would determine what was criminal — and that would naturally be whatever was unpleasant or unprofitable for that human being. The determination of punishment for relativistic crimes would also devolve upon the autonomously powerful human beings.

What we are saying is this: justice (punishment of crime) does *not* find its ultimate basis in either individual "human rights" or in "society" — but in God. Crime is what God says it is (either in precept or principle), and punishment is what God says it is (either in precept or principle).

> Unless a person recognizes some form of supreme law by which man's laws must be judged, there is no basis for believing in any form of disobedience, or that any human law or act of government is unjust.
> *Christianity and The Constitution*, by
> John Eidsmoe, pub. Baker, p. 363

In many instances, God has clearly decreed and denominated what is to be counted as criminal action by mankind. In some cases, only general principles are stated (in the Bible) and men are left to define and declare, on the basis of the divine principles or guidelines, what is legal (lawful) or illegal (criminal) — as well as the punishments to be meted out for violations of said determinations.

What must be established, second, is that God has ordained human governments to act coercively, with force, to execute divine wrath upon criminal actions. It is both irrational and unbiblical to insist that human governments carry out their God-ordained purpose of executing God's wrath on wrong without the use of coercion and force. Human governments do not "bear the sword in vain" (Rom. 13:1-7; I Pet. 2:13-17). Some Christians shrink from the idea of the use of force and coercion by civil governments as being contrary to the Bible. What is often not considered is the difference between force and violence. To execute a murderer is not violence when done within the parameters of the revealed will of God — by duly ordained civil authorities acting in harmony with divinely revealed laws. Acting within these parameters human government is trusting justice to be reckoned from an Absolute point of reference from which no injustice will be done.

> Provided that there is a legitimate basis for its use and a vigilant precaution against its overreaction in practice, a qualified use of force is not only necessary but justifiable. Within the Christian framework there is the possibility of truth, justice and authority which are not arbitrary, relativistic or mystifying. Thus an important distinction between force and violence is possible. Force, on the one hand, is the controlling discipline of truth, justice and authority in action. Violence, on the other hand, can come from one of three directions — from the maintenance of authority without a legitimate basis, from the contravention of a legitimate authority or from the injustice of a legitimate authority overreacting as it deals with opposition or violation. Over-reaction in the name of truth too easily becomes the ugly horror of violence once again . . . . Either all force is unmasked as violence (with the consequent chaos of disrespect for all law), or else all violence is masked as force (and there is no redress except by recourse to greater force). The ideal of Justice within law can only be pursued with this distinction kept carefully in mind. Without such a distinction there can be no legitimate justification for authority or discipline of any kind, whether on a parental or on a presidential level. In a fallen world the ideal of legal justice without the exercise of force is naive. Societies need a police force; a man has the right to defend his wife from assault. A feature of any society which can achieve a measure of freedom within form is that responsibility implies discipline. This is true at the various structural levels of society — in the spheres of the state, business, the community, the school, respectively . . . .Of course the mere statement of the ideal of force without violence does not mean that it can be easily or constantly attained. Far from it. But this should not lead to a dilution of the ideal.
> *The Dust of Death*, by Os Guinness, pub. IVP, pp. 177,178

A. REASONS CIVIL GOVERNMENT MUST PUNISH CRIMINALS

1. *To Carry Out Its God-Ordained Mission*: We have discussed this at length in the chapter on Purpose. But it bears repeating. God has "instituted" (Rom. 13:1) and "sent" (I Pet. 2:14) civil governments for the express purpose of "executing divine wrath upon evil doers." That is civil government's main function. It exists for hardly any other purpose. The civil government that does *not punish* criminals is in rebellion against the Almighty. Romans 13:1-7 and I Peter 2:13-17 say nothing about rehabilitating criminals, and certainly nothing about excusing them. Human government is an instrument of God — it exists to serve him.

2. *To Vindicate the Sovereignty and Character of God*: If the wrath of God is revealed from heaven against all unrighteousness of men (Rom. 1:18ff), and if God is in his very essence Justice and Righteousness, that sovereign justness has to be upheld or asserted. God could do that by supernatural intervention every time a crime is committed. He could slay individual criminals or burn up whole cities of criminals (e.g. Sodom and Gomorrah) by direct, miraculous judgments if he should choose to do so. However, the Bible clearly teaches that God chooses in almost all instances (with a few exceptions in Biblical times to give validity to his messengers, the prophets and the apostles), to have his sovereign will against crime upheld and asserted by human beings. This "covenant" from God to man in punishing crime dates as far back as the "rebirth" of the human race when Noah came forth from the ark (Gen. 9:6-9). It predates the Mosaic legislation and is, therefore, not to be restricted to the Israelite theocracy. It is a principle for the whole human race.

God does not administer his justice in time and history by constant supernatural deeds — he does not send angels (with but a few exceptions) — he sends human governments. Man is charged not only with a stewardship of the material creation

(Gen. 1:29,30; 9:1-4), but also with a stewardship of human society (Gen. 9:5,6). "Am I my brother's keeper?" Indeed, in more ways than one! Politicians, governors, rulers and civil workers, will give account of their stewardship just as surely as preachers and elders. It is possible that Hebrews 13:17, "Obey your leaders and submit to them; for they are keeping watch over your souls, as men who will have to give account," applies as much to civil rulers as it does to church elders. Political leaders and government workers will answer to Almighty God for what they have done with the human social order! The Old Testament prophets, John the Baptist, Jesus and the apostles undeniably called civil rulers, both Israelites and Gentiles, to account for their administration of human government.

3. *To Deter Others From Committing Crimes:* It is reasonable, it is a matter of experience, and it is Biblical to expect punishment to be a deterrent against crime. Fear is a viable motivation for producing right behavior. It works because it is true! Paul explicitly named "terror" (Gr. *phobos*, "fear") as an instrumentality of human government in deterring "bad conduct" (Rom. 13:3). Paul also wrote to Timothy, "Now we know that the law is good, if any one uses it lawfully, understanding this, that the law is not laid down for the just but for the lawless and disobedient, for the ungodly and sinners, for the unholy and profane, for murderers of fathers and murderers of mothers, for manslayers, immoral persons, sodomites, kidnappers, liars, perjurers, and whatever else is contrary to sound doctrine . . . " (I Tim. 1:8-10). The very purpose of the law is to produce fear so that such crimes as Paul listed would be deterred. Laws must have penalties to be laws. Penalties must be executed if the law is to be validated. Laws without penalties and punishments are useless. They are nothing more than words on paper. They are worse than useless without penalties. Not only would laws without punishment deter no one, they would actually make the very idea of "law" a mockery.

We are told repeatedly in the Old Testament that the purpose of punishment was that "all Israel shall hear, and fear" (cf. Deut. 13:11; 17:13; 21:21). Isaiah wrote these words:

> My soul yearns for thee in the night, my spirit within me earnestly seeks thee. For when thy judgments are in the earth, the inhabitants of the world learn righteousness. If favor is shown to the wicked, he does not learn righteousness; in the land of uprightness he deals perversely and does not see the majesty of the Lord (Isa. 26:9,10).

The deterrent factor of discipline is assuredly expressed in the well known passage of Hebrews 12:3-11. A number of passages in Proverbs (13:24; 19:18,19; 21:11; 23:13,14, etc.) teach that punishment for crime is to serve as a deterrent, if not for others, certainly for the perpetrator. Hosea depicts God using his punishment of Israel in the captivities as an instrument to "allure" Israel back to him. God says through the prophet that he will make Israel's "Valley of Achor" (Valley of Trouble), a "door of hope" (Hosea 2:14,15).

If God threatened punishment to deter his theocratic people from criminal conduct (see Lev. 26; Amos 3-4; Micah 1-3; Zeph. 1:12-18, etc.) those who are "servants" of God in the arena of civil government could find no better principle by which to govern — especially since they have a clear Biblical mandate to do so (Rom. 13:1-7, etc.)

The Bible gives many examples of governmental leaders practicing this principle. Coercion, force, and fear of punishment by human rulers is actually the only alternative left in maintaining social order when mankind refuses to accept the regenerative power of biblical new-birth. God used the threat of punishment upon Israel and Judah (Isa. 10:5ff; Jer. 27:1ff) to deter them from further crimes — and it worked for some.

In the New Testament we see a number of government officials (both Jewish and Gentile) exercising punishment or the threat of punishment to deter what they ignorantly and wrongfully deem anti-social crimes (John 19:10; Acts 4:13-22; 5;40-42).

We also find some expressing their fear of punishment (Acts 16:27; 16:35-39; 19:35-41; 27:42; Luke 23:40). Proverbs 19:12 and 20:2 tell us that the "dread wrath of the king" is a fearful warning much like that of a "growling lion" so that disorderly and criminal behavior may be deterred.

A significant reason that punishment and fear of punishment does not provide greater deterrence is that punishments are not enacted quickly, impartially, and severely enough (see Eccl.8:2-11; 10:4). The book of Proverbs is widely known for its admonitions about punishment of children as a deterring factor to prevent them from growing up to be adult criminals (Prov. 13:23; 22:15; 23:13,14). Proverbs also declares that the lack of deterring punishment leads to shame (Prov. 29:15). If punishment must sometimes be resorted to as a deterrent in the home, where intimate familial ties usually prevail, how much more must punishment be applied to deter criminal action in civil society where such intimacy does not prevail! And, further, if punishment as a deterrent is mandated for use (in specified cases) even in the earthly existence of the messianic kingdom (the church) how much more in civil societies (see Matt. 18:15-20; Acts 5:7-11; I Cor. 5:1-13; 6:9-11; II Cor. 2:5-11; Gal. 2:11-14; II Thess. 3:6-15; Titus 3:10,11, etc.).

For the Christian, for the Bible-believer, it is beside the point to argue whether punishment deters crime or not. The Bible states that it does and that governing authorities are to act upon that Biblical mandate. It will work because it is true. It has not worked, because it has not been practiced. Of course, only the naive would expect crime to be absolutely deterred by the threat of punishment — it will not, and the Bible realistically teaches that it will not. Only regeneration of the human personality — the new birth — will put an end to crime. But the Bible is realistic enough to teach also that punishment used as a deterrent to crime will be relatively successful — enough so that social order will be maintained and sufficient "peace and tranquillity" will prevail so that some of mankind will be able to come to a knowledge of the truth.

4. *Physical Restraint of Criminals and Crime:* Punishing crime and criminals is plainly necessitated in order to physically, objectively, *stop* crime from recurring. This is done by physically removing the perpetrator (criminal) from an otherwise law-abiding society. There are only two ways by which human governors may physically restrain criminals — execution and incarceration. Incorrigible criminals must either be put to death or imprisoned. We will treat the specific forms of restraint later in this chapter. The Bible clearly advocates the principle of physical restraint as a reason for punishment of criminals. Those who will not be amenable to the laws of social order by reason or persuaded to do so by deterrents, will necessarily need to be physically restrained. Behavior that usurps and sets aside the rules which make it possible for individuals to live in immediate and intimate socialization with others (society) must be prohibited. The criminal actually alienates himself from society by refusing to behave within the compulsory norms of social order. The criminal, in effect, declares war on society. He forfeits his right to be accepted as a member of society. By his criminal activity he is saying that he chooses to live by standards and principles alien to social order. He declares himself in favor of anarchy and disorder. If criminal behavior (robbery, assault, murder, rape, homosexuality, adultery, theft, perjury, treason, etc.) is extrapolated to include every individual in a society — if criminal behavior is the norm — it takes no huge amount of reason and common sense to know that society would self-destruct. Criminal activity must, to the greatest extent possible, be prohibited. This may be accomplished to some degree by punishments which will act to deter some individuals from such activity. But those who commit capital crimes and those who are *incorrigible repeaters* of lesser crimes must be physically removed from the midst of the law-abiding society and executed or imprisoned.

The Bible confirms this principle in numerous places. A recurring phrase in the Mosaic law is, "so you shall purge the evil from the midst of you . . . " (see Deut. 13:5; 17:7; 19:19; 21:21; 22:21; 24:7). Another phrase often repeated is, " . . . the persons that do them shall be cut off from among their people . . ." (see Num. 15:30,32; Lev. 18:29; 20:3). The Mosaic legislation says very little about incarceration. Imprisonment to retain in custody certain violaters or alleged violaters until they could be "tried" and other punishments exacted was occasionally practiced (Lev. 24:12; Num. 15:34; Lev. 25:28; Num. 35:25; Deut. 19:12). But imprisonment as a form of punishment was not practiced by the early Israelites. And many of the heathen cultures incarcerated people only to keep them in custody until disposition of accusations against them were made as the case of Joseph, the baker, and the butler, in Egypt (Gen. 39:20ff). The Mosaic criminal (civil) code legislated principally three forms of punishment: (1) retribution ("an eye for an eye . . . "); (2) restitution; (3) execution (death). Occasionally punishment took the form of ostracism or excommunication (deportation). Later Israelites may have used imprisonment as a method of restraining criminals. Imprisonment as punishment was used by some of the Gentile governments mentioned in the Bible (Babylonians, Persians, Greeks, Romans). Jesus referred to the practice of imprisonment in some of his parables (see Matt. 5:25; Luke 12:58; Matt. 18:30; Matt. 25:36ff). John the Baptist was imprisoned as a punishment (Matt. 4:2; 11:2; 14:3; Mark 6:17,19,22; Luke 3:19,20). Later, he was beheaded. And God himself created the most terrible prison of all — Hell — where impenitent and incorrigible criminals will be incarcerated forever!

5. *To Prevent Private Vengeance:* Society cannot tolerate criminal activity. But neither can social order be maintained when each individual arrogates to himself the authority to prosecute, judge, sentence and execute punishments for crimes against him or others. The structure of human social order must be maintained by administrators (governments and governors) who are as objective and impartial as possible. The passions, sensibilities, and prejudices of victims of criminal acts would make it very prob-

able that the exercise of private vengeance would, in turn victimize innocent people who might have some personal connection to the guilty.

In societies where duly constituted government does not exist or where it exists but does not fulfill its obligations to punish criminal activity, the victim and/or his family or friends will. In such cultures, justice is attempted by personal retaliation. Personal vendettas have been extended through generations of people. The result within such a culture is often civil war and innocent blood-letting. The Bible declares that the guilty criminal, not his innocent family, is to be punished for his crime: "The fathers shall not be put to death for the children, neither shall the children be put to death for the fathers; every man shall be put to death for his own sin" (Deut. 24:16; Ezek. 18:1ff; 33:7ff). The insecurity, injustice and chaos wreaked upon society by private vengeance is recorded in the book of Judges when the phrase is repeated: "Every man did that which was right in his own eyes, for there was no king in Israel in those days." A classic case in point is that of Absalom, David's son, taking personal vengeance upon his brother for crimes against his sister (II Sam. 13:20ff). Terrible consequences for the whole nation of Israel resulted from that incident.

God made provision in the law of Moses, through the "cities of refuge" (Num. 35:25-28), by which private vengeance could be prevented. Gentile societies in ancient times apparently made no such provisions. As a result, private vendettas, family feuds, and vigilante-justice was often perpetrated. While the law of Moses prohibited it, such personal vengeance occurred occasionally in Israel — tribes and families feuding against one another (e.g. Jdgs. 18-21).

6. *To Rehabilitate the Criminal:* There are no specific passages of scripture which state unequivocally that punishment for criminal activity is to rehabilitate the criminal. The inference seems to be that when restitution as a form of punishment for crime or negligence is adjudicated (Exod. 22:1,4; Lev. 6:4,5;

24:21, etc.) it will have some rehabilitative effect on the one punished. Punishment to produce fear and deterrence would, of course, be correlative to rehabilitation. The principle of rehabilitation proposed in Biblical directions for punishing a child (for correction) would seem to apply in the area of criminal justice as well (Prov. 13:24; 22:15; 23:13,13, etc.). The apostle Paul certainly applied the principle of rehabilitation as the purpose for disciplining the immoral man in the church at Corinth (I Cor. 5:1-5).

The obstacles to rehabilitation created by incarcerating criminals guilty of crimes of differing magnitude in one huge and populous penal compound are almost insurmountable. Too often a colony of prisoners becomes little more than a "school" in which criminality in worse forms is learned and practiced. Rehabilitation is *not* the fundamental purpose for the punishment of criminals — the primary purpose for punishment of crime is *justice* and the maintenance of *civil order*. The law of God which is the basis for the laws of man and society must be vindicated (upheld). Society must be protected so that truth and goodness may be proclaimed and practiced. Crime must be prohibited by punishment.

B. PRECAUTIONS TO BE PRACTICED BY CIVIL GOVERNMENTS IN PUNISHMENT OF CRIMINALS

1. *Punish Without Pity:* That does not, at first, sound like a precaution at all. Initially, and on the surface, it sounds extremely cruel and barbaric. But it is what God told the Israelites to do. They were told to "destroy" all the Canaanites "without pity" when God led them into the Promised Land (Deut. 7:16); they were told to execute without pity any fellow Israelite who was guilty of idolatry and who tried to seduce others into idol worship (Deut. 13:6-11); and they were told to administer civil punishments, including death, without pity in cases of severe crimes (see Deut. 19:11-21; 25:12). In fact, the inference in

Deuteronomy 19:21 is that all administration of civil justice — "life for life, eye for eye, tooth for tooth, hand for hand, foot for foot" — is to be done without pity.

The Hebrew word used in the passages cited above is *chus*. It actually means that no mercy is to be shown in the punishments directed. God intended that such crimes as are mentioned were to have unmerciful justice meted out upon them. Justice cannot be tempered with partiality or exoneration of the guilty and still be justice.

The precaution the Israelites were to take was to appoint judges and other administrators of the law who would carry out the punishments of the law without pity. Leniency does not serve justice. When justice is compromised in the civil arena, all the other fibers of moral integrity which hold an orderly civilization together are soon compromised with the result being chaos and anarchy. While the church of God, his redeemed community, is born and sustained by divine mercy, the world of the unredeemed is held together only by the threads of pitiless and impartial justice. Actually, God was able to show mercy unto redemption only when he was able also to execute perfect justice upon sin in his sinless Son (cf. Rom. 3:21-26).

Merciless punishment for civil crimes is intended to serve as a significant deterrent. "Those who remain shall hear, and fear, and shall henceforth commit no more any such evil among you" (Deut. 19:20). A sage once said, "Mercy but murders, pardoning those who kill."

While the Biblical commandment to execute murderers (and others) without pity may sound cruel and barbaric, actually, it is a serious precaution which will lead to a sense of fairness, rightness, and lawfulness in the civil society.

2. *Do Not Delay Justice:* The wise ruler (Solomon) wrote:

> Because sentence against an evil work is not executed speedily, therefore the heart of the sons of men is fully set in them to do evil (Eccl. 8:11).

> There is a vanity which is done upon the earth; that there be just men, unto whom it happeneth according to the work of the wicked; again, there be wicked men, to whom it happeneth according to the work of the righteous: I said that this also is vanity (Eccl. 8:14).

Isaiah, the prophet, spoke to this issue when he wrote (Isa. 26:10):

> If favor is shown to the wicked, he does not learn righteousness; in the land of uprightness he deals perversely and does not see the majesty of the Lord.

The prophet Habakkuk wrote that delayed judgments in his day exacerabated the injustices and increased criminal activity:

> O Lord, how long shall I cry for help, and thou wilt not hear? Or cry to thee "Violence!" and thou wilt not save? Why dost thou make me see wrongs and look upon trouble? Destruction and violence are before me; strife and contention arises. So the law is slacked and justice never goes forth. For the wicked surround the righteous, so justice goes forth perverted . . . .
> Thou who art of purer eyes than to behold evil and canst not look on wrong, why dost thou look on faithless men, and art silent when the wicked swallows up the man more righteous than he? (Hab. 1:2,3,4,13).

It is clear from the instruction in the Mosaic law that justice was to be done swiftly and sentence upon the guilty to be executed without delay (see Deut. 17:10; 19:11-21; 21:18-21; 22:13-21; 22:22; 22:23,24; 25:1-3).

There are Biblical examples which reinforce this principle. David's hesitancy to punish Absalom for his crimes only made Absalom more arrogant and rebellious (II Sam. 13-19). The delayed judgment of God upon Jezebel incited her to more wickedness. The same was true of delayed judgment upon Sodom and Gomorrah. Peter's warning that "scoffers" would intensify their wickedness because of their doubt about final retribution ever becoming a reality (II Pet. 3:3-6) vindicates the principle.

While the American judicial system is probably the best and fairest in history, one of its faults is its tolerance of endless, injudicious, often unethical delays by some defense attorneys in criminal trials. Interminable appeals and judicial reviews of criminal cases already adjudged and thoroughly reviewed accomplish nothing in the interest of justice. They merely add to the burden of the taxpayers and make fair-minded people cynical of the system. The "exclusionary rule" which disallows evidence in court obtained by "strings," phone-taps, etc. has allowed scores of guilty criminals to go free. The pragmatic approach to overcrowded court dockets which allows the practice of "plea-bargaining" lets hundreds of people guilty of serious crimes be assessed much lighter punishment than they deserve. However, Americans must be thankful for the manifold protections guaranteed by its laws and courts.

3. *Guard Against Partiality:* The Old Testament and the New Testament are emphatic about the sin of partiality: Impartial justice is a fundamental dimension of God's own character (Deut. 10:17; Isa. 61:8; Jer. 22:3; Psa. 37:28; 89:14; Micah 6:8):

> You shall not pervert the justice due to your poor in his suit. Keep far from a false charge, and do not slay the innocent and righteous, for I will not acquit the wicked. And you shall take no bribe, for a bribe blinds the officials, and subverts the cause of those who are in the right (Exod. 23:6-8; see also Exod. 23:1-3).

> You shall do no injustice in judgment; you shall not be partial to the poor or defer to the great, but in righteousness shall you judge your neighbor (Lev. 19:15).

> And I charged your judges at that time, "Hear the cases between your brethren, and judge righteously between a man and his brother or the alien that is with him. You shall not be partial in judgment; you shall hear the small and the great alike; you shall

not be afraid of the face of man, for the judgment is God's . . . (Deut. 1:16,17).

You shall appoint judges and officers in all your towns which the Lord your God gives you, according to your tribes; and they shall judge the people with righteous judgment. You shall not pervert justice; you shall not show partiality; and you shall not take a bribe, for a bribe blinds the eyes of the wise and subverts the cause of the righteous. Justice, and only justice, you shall follow, that you may live and inherit the land which the Lord your God gives you (Deut. 16:18-20).

In the presence of God and of Christ Jesus and of the elect angels I charge you to keep these rules without favor, doing nothing from partiality (I Tim. 5:21).

. . . have you not made distinctions among yourselves, and become judges with evil thoughts? (James 2:4).

Almighty God is no respecter of persons, and human civil rulers, judges, and others appointed to administer justice are warned against partiality of any kind (see Deut. 24:17; Psa. 82:2; Prov. 23:23-26; 29:27; 31:4,5; Eccl. 3:16; 5:8; Mal. 2:9; Acts 10:34,35; II Chron. 19:7; Jude 16).

4. *Guard the Concept of Presumption of Innocence:* The Biblical system of justice presumes the accused to be innocent until proven guilty. In other words, the burden of conviction was upon the accusers while the accused was not required to prove himself innocent. Furthermore, at least two witnesses were necessary to establish guilt and secure conviction:

At the mouth of two witnesses, or three witnesses, shall he that is worthy of death be put to death; but at the mouth of one witness he shall not be put to death (Deut. 17:6).

A single witness shall not prevail against a man for any crime or for any wrong in connection with any offense that he has committed; only on the evidence of two witnesses or of three witnesses, shall a charge be sustained (Deut. 19:15).

CRIME AND PUNISHMENT

If any one kills a person, the murderer shall be put to death on the evidence of witnesses; but no person shall be put to death on the testimony of one witness (Num. 35:30).

But if he does not listen, take one or two others along with you, that every word may be confirmed by the evidence of two or three witnesses (Matt. 18:16).

Any charge must be sustained by the evidence of two or three witnesses (II Cor. 13:1).

The Biblical law of presumption of innocence was protected by severe penalties attached to malicious accusation and perjury:

If a malicious witness rises against any man to accuse him of wrongdoing, then both parties to the dispute shall appear before the Lord, before the priests and the judges who are in office in those days; the judges shall inquire diligently, and if the witness is a false witness and has accused his brother falsely, then you shall do to him as he had meant to do to his brother; so you shall purge the evil from the midst of you. And the rest shall hear, and fear, and shall never again commit any such evil among you (Deut. 19:16-20).

You shall not bear false witness against your neighbor (Exod. 23:1-3).

You shall not utter a false report. You shall not join hands with a wicked man, to be a malicious witness. You shall not follow a multitude to do evil; nor shall you bear witness in a suit, turning aside after a multitude, so as to pervert justice; nor shall you be partial to a poor man in his suit (Exod. 23:1-3).

Keep far from a false charge, and do not slay the innocent and righteous, for I will not acquit the wicked. And you shall take no bribe, for a bribe blinds the officials, and subverts the cause of those who are in the right (Exod. 23:7,8).

Anyone refusing to give testimony concerning what he knows about a crime is guilty and must suffer the consequences (Lev.

5:1). Proverbs 6:19; 12:17; 19:9; 24:28; 25:18 all condemn perjury and false accusation (see also Lev. 19:16).

5. *Preserve the Process of Trials by Peers:* Added to the fact that an Israelite was innocent until accused and witnessed against by his peers was the stipulation that those who accused and tried him were also to be the first to carry out the execution of a guilty person's sentence. The man found guilty of blasphemy against God is a case in point:

> And the Lord said to Moses, "Bring out of the camp him who cursed; and let all who heard him lay their hands upon his head, and let all the congregation stone him (Lev. 24:13,14).

And the crime of idolatry was to be tried and punished by one's peers also:

> If your brother, the son of your mother, or your son, or your daughter, or the wife of your bosom. or your friend who is as your own soul, entices you secretly . . . you shall not yield to him or listen to him, nor shall your eye pity him, nor shall you spare him, nor shall you conceal him; but you shall kill him; your hand shall be first against him to put him to death, and afterwards the hand of all the people.
>
> The hand of the witnesses shall be first against him to put him to death, and afterward the hand of all the people. So shall you purge the evil from the midst of you (Deut. 17:7).

6. *Sustain the Principle that the Penalty Must Fit the Crime:* The Bible clearly teaches that laws must be established to deter criminal activity. We have established that. But laws must have penalties to be laws. Sanctions are the only vindication that laws instituted and administered by civil governments have. Without penalties, laws are void.

> *Sanctions* (1) Law must have sanctions, otherwise it is not law; and back of the law there must be legitimate authority (moral

power or *right* to use force) and actual power sufficient to enforce the sanctions. Law is more than mere *wish*; it is more than mere precept which may or may not be heeded. Law carries with it — if it is *law* — its own reward for obedience and its own punishment for disobedience . . . (2) *Purpose of sanctions:* Primarily, *to secure the observance of the law* . . . Secondarily, *to uphold moral order,* or *to restore moral order which has been disturbed* . . . . The function of punishment is first and foremost *vindicatory, that is to secure obedience to the law and hence to make its operation effective: basically to vindicate the ends of justice sought by the will (lawgiver) who ordained it.* Vindication must be distinguished from vengeance: whereas *vengeance* (revenge) is personal and emotional, vindication is impersonal and juridicial. Law that seeks revenge as its object cannot be true law; the very essence of true law is its *vindicatory* character . . . . (3) *Vindicatory sanctions are designed to sustain the majesty of the law, to vindicate the will of the lawgiver (in the fact that his will ordained the law for the good* of his subjects) to restore order that has been broken and hence to reestablish the equilibrium of justice. For example, a hardened criminal machine-guns a man in cold blood, a man who is probably the father of a family. The criminal has taken something out of the totality of being which cannot be restored, namely, the victim's greatest good (his life) and he has, at the same time, robbed the victim's family of their means of material sustenance; hence the state (society acting through its government, the public authority), in order to restore the balance of justice (according to which every person is to receive that which is his *due*), takes the criminal's greatest good (*his* life) in retaliation (reciprocity). Again, man is a person by virtue of the fact that he is a rational being (a fact which remains a fact no matter how irrationally he may act). Hence, by heinous crimes which are offenses against the law of reason, he recedes from — falls far below — the order of reason, and as such a diseased member, he is corruptive of the whole social order of which he is a part, and may be put to death — but only by the public authority — for the common good.
Commonsense Ethics, by C.C. Crawford, pub. Brown, pp. 227,228

Any civil government that does *not* make punishments commensurate with the seriousness of the crimes committed, is an un-

just government. Justice is the administration of law according to the rules of equity. Justice means to see that all citizens receive what is fairly due them — the guaranteeing of unalienable human rights. When one human, without provocation, without reason, takes another person's life (murder), fairness demands that the murderer have his life taken. When one human robs another human of property, fairness demands that the robber pay for the taking of property, either by restitution of the property or some form of payment (unsalaried work, etc.). Justice is poorly served in our modern society when criminals are merely incarcerated and become wards of the taxpayers without making any physical restitution through work or payment. The ideal justice is the restoration of the order (circumstance), as nearly as possible, as it was before the disorder (crime) occurred.

The primary function of civil government is to administer *justice*. When it does not — when it begins to give punishments that do not, as nearly as possible, restore the order that was destroyed by the crime, it has defaulted on its divine reason for existence and ought to be replaced.

> Third, there was a concern that penalty should be adjusted to fit the crime. The quality and form of punishment were, as far as possible, fixed in harmony with the principle that satisfaction was to be rendered for harm done. Guilt and its requital were in some sense to correspond. What the evil man had done, or purposed to do, to another, was to be visited in punishment on his own head.
>
> The so-called *lex talionis*, which required "eye for eye, tooth for tooth" (Exod. 21:23; Lev. 24:17,18; Deut. 9:21), was a vivid expression of this law of proportion. Laws of neighbor nations, frequently designed to discourage theft and assault rather than strictly to vindicate divine righteousness, more often extracted several times more than the strict assessment of guilt required. So, far from teaching cruelty and hate, this formula (Mosaic law) was part of Israel's unique message of mercy, although it did not always prevent miscarriage of justice.
>
> *Toward a Biblical View of Civil Government*, p. 142

Many in modern society object to the penalties set for crimes

CRIME AND PUNISHMENT

in the Mosaic law as "cruel and unusual punishments." But they were neither cruel nor unusual. They were certainly not unreasonable or unfair. They were just.

If any harm follows, then you shall give life for life, eye for eye, tooth for tooth, burn for burn, wound for wound, stripe for stripe (Exod. 21:23).

He who kills a man shall be put to death. He who kills a beast shall make it good, life for life. When a man causes a disfigurement in his neighbor, as he has done it shall be done to him, fracture for fracture, eye for eye, tooth for tooth; as he has disfigured a man, he shall be disfigured (Lev. 24:17-20).

Your eye shall not pity; it shall be life for life, eye for eye, tooth for tooth, hand for hand, foot for foot (Deut. 19:21).

To do any less than is ordained in these Biblical commandments would be less than *fair* (equitable, impartial, unbiased, dispassionate, objective).

Justice has to do with (human) relations to others, and is therefore evaluated on the basis of external acts; that is to say, the Order of Justice is *objective*, not subjective.

The Order of Justice is that arrangement of things as a whole such that each part will receive and have what rightly belongs to it — that which is its due (on the basis of ability and merit). The Order of Justice is based entirely on the natural equality and dignity of human beings as such, as *persons*, and ultimately on the Natural Moral Law which ordains such equality and dignity . . . . Men are endowed *by their Creator* with certain unalienable rights.

The Order of Justice is threefold, on the basis of the relationship between part and part, and between the whole and the parts. (1) *Commutative justice* has reference to the relationship between citizens or persons as individuals; it presupposes equality of persons (before the law, in bargaining power, etc.) and equality of things exchanged. This is the kind of justice that is involved, generally speaking, in the area of civil law, particularly in that of contractual relations. (2) *Distributive* justice takes in the relationship of the whole to each part (of society or the "state" to the individual citizen, e.g., the advantages and burdens of the community as a whole, protection of natural rights, equitable taxation systems, remunerative and vindicatory justice). This is the kind of justice which prevails in the area of what is called criminal law. For example, a man may break into a safe and steal several thousand dollars: he cannot satisfy the demands of justice simply by returning to the legal owner the money he has stolen. That might satisfy the owner's claim but it does not satisfy the demands of the moral law. The thief has not only injured temporarily the legal owner of the money — he has also committed a crime against society, hence he can satisfy the claims of justice fully, only by submitting to the prescribed penalty (which is designed to be both vindicatory and medicinal). (3) *Legal* justice takes in the relation of the part to the whole (of the citizen to the state). It includes all the normal duties of responsible citizenship, such as voting, serving on juries, paying taxes, etc. The end of justice is *objective* right and duty. Cf. the Preamble to our Constitution, "to establish justice." Also the oft-repeated phrase, "peace with justice," or "a just peace."

Commonsense Ethics, pp. 277-278

It is important for Christians to remember that civil justice deals primarily with *objective* fairness (justice). It renders justice on the basis of objective merit. Civil justice is seldom able to deal with justice on a subjective basis. Civil justice cannot usually reward or punish on the basis of motives or assumptions. Civil justice is administered by finite individuals. Only the Infinite God can judge with absoluteness as to motives and purposes. Human beings are capable of not only fooling one another, they are also capable of fooling themselves.

The heart is deceitful above all things, and desperately corrupt; who can understand it? I the Lord search the mind and try the heart, to give to every man according to his ways, according to the fruit of his doings (Jer. 17:9,10).

Civil justice should limit itself as much as possible to rewarding or punishing citizens according to lawful or unlawful *behavior* —

not according to intentions or motives. Of course, even the Bible makes some distinctions between pre-meditated criminal acts and unintentional "accidents." The Bible also distinguishes between guilt by negligence and non-negligence. Surely motive and purpose, responsibility or irresponsibility, should be established if possible when alleged crimes are being adjudicated. Premeditated crime deserves more severe punishment than culpability due to negligence. But for the most part civil government must content itself with rendering justice according to the outward appearance of the case. A classic illustration of the danger of injustice resulting from trying to adjudicate on the basis of subjective evidence is the plethora of appeals in modern criminal cases as "not guilty, by reason of insanity." Psychiatrists and psychologists are paraded before juries testifying of the defendant's inability to have made a moral choice to commit the crime due to "momentary insanity." Reason and common sense dictates that in most of these cases there was not "insanity" — only uncontrolled rage, perhaps frustrated resentment. Only robots commit crimes without having chosen to do so. Perhaps there are degrees of moral maturity or capability in some persons (mentally retarded, etc.) which should alleviate the severity of the punishment, but justice will always be better served if it deals primarily from the posture of objectivity.

7. *Guard Proper Judicial Rules for Evidence:* The God-ordained law of Israel stipulated or implied righteous rules which regulated acceptable and non-acceptable evidence in criminal cases. First, the accused could not be made to incriminate himself. Every accused person had to be incriminated by two or more witnesses whose testimony had to agree. At the trial of Jesus, when the Jewish supreme judge (high priest) questioned Jesus about his disciples and his teaching, Jesus reminded the high priest that a charge should be proved by witnesses and that he should not be required to incriminate himself (John 18:19-21). Second, neither the accused nor witnesses were allowed to be tortured in order to produce testimony. Once

again, Jesus reminded the high priest of this (John 18:22,23). The apostle Paul clarified the same principle (Acts 23:1-5). Third, hearsay evidence was unacceptable. Israelite judges were to "inquire diligently, search out," and determine whether reports were true or not before making judgments (Deut. 13:12-14; 17:2-7), and bearing "false witness" was strictly forbidden (Deut. 19:15-21; Lev. 19:16). Fourth, should a person merely appear to be guilty of a crime, or be accused of a crime which could not be substantiated by *eye-witnesses*, a solemn oath on the part of the accused was sufficient to establish acquittal (see Exod. 22:10,11).

8. *Enact and Enforce Laws to Prohibit Personal Exaction of Justice*: The Bible stands unequivocally against personal retaliation. Jesus made this a fundamental principle for his disciples (Matt. 5:38-42). Paul enunciated the same principle (Rom. 12:14-21) adding that this was the very reason God ordained civil governments (Rom. 13:1-7) — to administer the justice forbidden to the individual. God ordered the Israelites to provide "cities of refuge" for those who became involved in "accidental" crimes or in "acts of God" (Exod. 21:13; Num. 35:10-34; Deut. 19:1-13; Josh. 20:1-9). This was to protect the innocent from "avengers of blood" (those who would take justice into their own hands and exact punishment by the "blood feud").

C. BIBLICAL CRIMES

> . . . it is not possible to transfer Mosaic laws into the civil structure of any state today, owing to their special theocratic character. Yet this does not mean that they have no relevance . . . note how God holds the Canaanite people quite responsible to keep their land free from unrestrained vice. In many respects, Mosaic laws are special enactments for Israel of general divine law applicable everywhere.
> *Toward a Biblical View of Civil Government*, p. 149

It is quite true that some Mosaic legislation (especially religious and ceremonial law) should not be applicable to any secular state of any era. On the other hand, much of the Mosaic law can and indeed should be enacted and enforced in every secular state! The Old Testament prophets explicitly declared the civil governments and governors (kings, princes, emperors) responsible to enforce standards of justice and morality in keeping with the general, fundamental standards revealed in the law of Moses. The reason for this is that these fundamental standards revealed to Moses were also revealed in the "Natural Revelation" (creation and conscience) to the Gentiles. There can be no doubt that biblical revelation concerning crime, public or social morality, and punishment for such are proper guidelines for any and every secular state that exists.

Just as the Bible makes no claim to specify every detail of moral behavior or record all the minutiae of scientific discovery, it makes no claim to be a *complete* codification of civil law. However, just as it *does* claim to give *sufficient* precepts and principles so that mankind may have "all that pertains to life and godliness" (II Pet. 1:3,4, RSV) and that the individual may be "fully qualified and equipped to do every kind of good deed" (II Tim. 3:17, TEV), we are to consider biblical principles and fundamentals in the area of civil law to be sufficient. Civil governments wishing to fulfill their mandate as "servants" of God (Rom. 13:1-7, I Pet. 2:13-17) will apprise themselves of the biblical codification of fundamental crimes and their punishments, and legislate accordingly!

1. *Biblical Capital Crimes*: The word "capital" literally means "head." In jurisprudence it means that a person has committed a crime for which he must forfeit his head. There is anti-social behavior so depraved and destructive of social order that the forfeiture of the life of the criminal is necessary to vindicate the rule of justice and the sustaining of the society. This is not only a matter of divine revelation (Biblical) but it is also a matter of "natural law" found in reason and conscience. Immanuel Kant, the German philosopher proposed that in order to determine

whether a principle or an action was right or wrong one should simply "universalize" it. In other words, to determine the gravity of any anti-social action simply ask, "What if every human being were allowed to take any anti-social action, for any reason or for no reason at all, anytime and everywhere, without suffering a penalty commensurate with the crime?" What would society be like in such circumstances? Would there be any society?

Under the Mosaic law, the crimes that made a person liable to capital punishment (death) were:

a. *Murder*: The Hebrew words used in Exodus 20:13, *lo tiretsaka*, are properly translated "Thou shalt not murder." In Exodus 21:13 which speaks of the execution of a murderer, the Hebrew word used is *yumath* which is often translated "slay" or "to cause to die." All murder is killing, but not all killing is murder! There is a diametrically different morality between murder and capital punishment. The Bible decrees execution (death) without mercy and without the possibility of any kind of ransom (see Num. 35:16-21; Num. 35:29-31; Exod. 21:12,14,23; Deut. 19:11-13; Deut. 5:17

b. *Negligent Homicide*: If a person owned an ox that was known to gore people, and if the owner had been warned but did not confine it and it killed a person, both the ox and the owner were to be stoned to death (Exod. 21:28-31). Connecting Deuteronomy 22:8 with Numbers 35:33 we find another instance of negligent homicide which would deserve the death penalty.

c. *Assassination*: Assassination is murder pre-meditated, by stealth and treachery — usually very violent. It is most often the murder of a civil ruler which makes it extremely destructive of the social order (see Jdgs. 3:20-22; II Sam. 4:5,6,9,10,11,12; I Kings 15:27,28; II Kings 19:37; II Chron. 32:21; Jer. 41:2; Acts 21:38). It must be punished with death upon the perpetrator.

d. *Infanticide*: The killing of babies was punishable by death (Lev. 18:21; 20:1-5).

e. *Rape*: The man who forced himself sexually upon a young woman who was betrothed was to be executed (Deut. 22:25-27).

Punishment by death for rape is called for because of the depraved nature of the perpetrator, because it is a crime so very destructive of the social order, and because it severely traumatizes the victim.

f. *Suicide:* While there is no declaration in the Bible that suicide is a crime, reason would dictate that any pre-meditated, unwarranted taking of human life, whether at the hand of another person or of the person himself, should be classified as murder. Josephus, a Pharisee, well schooled in rabbinical interpretation of the Mosaic law wrote: "Now self-murder is a crime most remote from the common nature of all animals, and an instance of impiety against God our Creator . . . do you not think that God is very angry when a man does injury to that he had bestowed on him? . . . . For from him it is that we have received our being, and we ought to leave it to his disposal to take that being away from us . . . . Accordingly, our laws determine that the bodies of such as kill themselves should be exposed till the sun be set, without burial . . . " (Josephus, Wars, Book III, chap. VIII, para. 5). Of course, the perpetrator of suicide cannot be punished. But if it be classified as "self-murder" should not those remaining alive who may have become willing accomplices in the crime be punished? There are a number of cases of suicide mentioned in the Bible (I Sam. 31:4,5; II Sam. 17:23; I Kings 16:18; Matt. 27:5) and in the Apocrypha (II Macc. 10:13; 14:41-46).

g. *Sodomy and/or Homosexual Behavior:* It is severely condemned in the Bible. It is a crime for which the death penalty is assessed (Lev. 18:22; 20:13; Deut. 23:17,18). Homosexuality is perverse and unnatural. It is declared unlawful and profane (I Tim. 1:8-11). The Old Testament declares it an abomination in the social order. If God intervened directly in history to obliterate societies practicing this perversion (see II Pet. 2:6; Jude 7), surely it should be legislated a crime by civil governments. It is a crime against nature and society. It would inevitably, inexorably result in genocide — destruction of the human race! Homosexuality universalized proves it is perverse, destructive, unreasonable and criminal (see also Rom. 1:26-32; I Cor. 6:9-11; I Tim. 1:8-11). Homosexuality is unequivocally a crime against society! And those charged with "using the law lawfully" (I Tim. 1:8-11), that is civil rulers, should legislate against it as a criminal offense, assessing and executing punishments commensurate with the crime. The criminality and destructiveness of sodomy and homosexuality are graphically documented in the history of Sodom and Gomorrah (Gen. 13:13; 19:5-11) (see also I Kings 14:24; 15:12; 22:46; II Kings 23:7; Job 36:14; Hosea 4:14).

g. *Incest:* Sexual intercourse between immediate and near immediate family members was a crime punishable by death (see Lev. 20:11,12,14; Lev. 18:6-18; Deut. 27:20,23). Sexual intercourse between a man and his mother, stepmother, halfsister, granddaughter, stepsister, aunt, wife of an uncle, daugher-in-law, sister-in-law, stepdaughter, stepgranddaughter, mother-in-law, and most certainly between a man and his own sister and his own daughter (omitted from the Biblical lists as too gross to even consider).

i. *Beastiality:* Human beings who practiced sexual copulation with animals were guilty of a capital crime and sentenced to death (see Exod. 22:19; Lev. 18:23; 20:15,16). It is a crime so perverse that the dumb beast along with the human being was to be executed. It manifests a condition of mind in a human being that is so depraved, so obscene, so utterly unnatural that it is practically beyond any redemming grace whatsoever. Society cannot tolerate it. Practitioners must be exterminated for the safety and salvation of the social order.

j. *Abortion*: The Bible clearly says the taking of human life (except for the punishment of capital crimes, taking life in defensive wars, and accidental deaths) is murder. And the Bible states that the *unborn are persons* (see Psa. 139:13-16; Job 31:15; Isa. 44:24; Jer. 1:5; Amos 1:13; Luke 1:41-44; Gal. 1:15,16). In the passage in Luke 1:41-44 Mary and Elizabeth are speaking of the unborn fetuses then resident in their wombs. Elizabeth refers to Mary's unborn as "My Lord" and tells of her own unborn as "leaping in her womb." Elizabeth's fetus was 6 months old, Mary's just newly conceived. The Greek word used by Luke the physician to describe Elizabeth's fetus is *brephos* ("baby"). This word is used in the New Testament and elsewhere to refer to infants whether born or unborn. This implies that the child does not enter some new level of life at birth but is just as much a baby (a person) before birth as after. To induce the death of an unborn person (a fetus in any stage — from conception to term) is murder. Infanticide at any stage of infancy (born or unborn) is criminal (see Exod. 2;2,3; 20:13; 21:22,23; 23:7; Num. 35:33; Deut. 5:17:27:17,19,25; II Kings 21:6; Prov. 24:11,12; Eccl. 11:5; Jer. 7:31; Matt. 18:10).

The testimony of medical science supports this view in every way. Research within the last two or three decades has given us quite thorough details of fetal development. We know what the baby is like at every stage of growth. The picture is one of an unbroken continuum from conception onward.

At fertilization the single cell is unique and distinct, with its own chromosomal and genetic structure. It is *not* a part of the mother's body. The remarkable thing is that this single cell contains *everything* that the full-grown adult will be . . . . The one-celled person is not qualitatively different from what he will be at twenty-five years of age.
Tough Questions II, by Jack Cottrell, pub. Standard Publishing Co., p. 81

k. *Kidnapping (Manstealing):* "Whoever steals a man, whether he sells him or is found in possession of him, shall be put to death" (Exod. 21:16). In this O.T. passage the Hebrew language uses the two words, *veginev iyish*, "and he who steals a man." In I Timothy 1:10 the word *andrapodistais* is, literally, "foot-man." This Greek word came to mean, "slave-dealer" and, metaphorically, "mansteater." Kidnapping or manstealing is a capital crime, punishable by death (see also Deut. 24:7).

l. *Adultery* (Lev. 20:10; Deut. 22:22); *Unchastity* (fornication before marriage) (Deut. 22:20,21); *Harlotry* (prostitution)

(Gen. 38:24; Lev. 21:9; Deut. 22:21). While modern society for the most part sees these not as "crimes," but as "indiscretions," the Bible sees them as serious crimes against society. First, they are devastating to the home — the indispensable structural unit of society. Second, they are serious breaches of the public trust. Third, they are crimes against persons — exploitations and degradations of personal dignity. They are, in fact, injustices! When punished in the Bible, they were punished with death!

m. *Striking or Reviling a Parent:* Once again, a crime against the fundamental adhesive (the family — the home) of humanity (Exod. 20:12;21:15,17; Lev. 20:9; Deut. 5:16; 21:18-21; 27:16; Prov. 6:20; 19:26; 20:20; 23:22). In the divine order of creation, the parents (especially the father) represent God in the family. The father is charged with the spiritual, moral, physical, and intellectual development of the family. He is to discipline, love, train, supply necessities, and protect what God has intrusted to him — a wife and children. He must be respected and obeyed. Verbal or physical rebellion against this divinely appointed hierarchy is serious enough to God to warrant the death penalty! Rebellion in the home whether by adultery in the parents or disobedience in the children is as treason against the state! It is, in fact, more serious. For the home and society can exist without the state, but society and state cannot exist without the home!

n. *False Testimony (Perjury) in Capital Cases:* "If a malicious witness rises against any man to accuse him of wrongdoing . . . if the witness is a false witness and has accused his brother falsely, then you shall do to him as he had meant to do to his brother . . . it shall be life for life, eye for eye, tooth for tooth . . . " (Deut. 19:16-21; Exod. 23:1-3). Truth-telling is imperative to the maintenance of civil order. Justice can never be accomplished if false testimony is admitted. Perjury in the case of a capital crime would result in the death of an innocent person. Therefore, the perjurer is, in effect, a murderer! His crime is worthy of death.

o. *Treason:* This is a crime sometimes called, "Conspiracy."

While it is not mentioned in the Pentateuch (with the exception of the commandment against cursing the king, Exod. 22:28), treason or conspiracy was almost always punished by death (see I Sam. 15:31; 16:23; 18:9-13; 22:11-19; I Kings 16:8-20; II Kings 21:23-24; Eccl. 10:20; Esther 2:21-23). To "curse" in the Bible means to "call for evil upon someone or call for judgment upon someone." It is verbal sedition. It is the first stage of insurrection.

p. *Breaking and Entering (Night only):* "If a thief is found breaking in, and is struck so that he dies, there shall be no bloodguilt for him . . . " (Exod. 22:2a). This is not exactly capital punishment. It is not a punishment to be administered by civil authorities. However, the crime appears to be serious enough that the homeowner is not held accountable for slaying a thief who breaks into the house at night-time. If a man breaks in during the daytime and his crime is only thievery, he is not to be slain by the homeowner: "but if the sun has risen upon him there shall be bloodguilt for him" (for the homeowner slaying him — Exod. 22:2b).

There are a number of lesser crimes listed in the Pentateuch (as well as in the other books of the Old Testament) which were to receive lesser punishments.

2. *Non-capital crimes*:

a. *Affray (brawling where injury results):* (Exod. 21:18-22; Deut. 25:11,12). Punishment was either payment for medical expenses of the injured and remuneration for loss of time, or when the injury was vicious, maiming was the punishment. The term "miscarriage" in Exodus 21:22 is not in the Hebrew text. It is an *interpretation* of the translators. The original text simply says, "When men strive together and hurt a pregnant woman and her child comes out, and there is no injury," then a fine is imposed. But if there is harm, whether to the mother or the baby, then *lex talionis* ("life for life, eye for eye . . . ") applies. Capital punishment if the child or mother dies!

b. *Assault*: Deliberate attack upon the person of another is a crime punishable by *lex talionis* — retaliation in kind (Lev. 24:19,20).

c. *Breach or Betrayal of Trust*: Breach of contract (failure to pay or hold in secure deposit, etc.) was regarded as a crime. Included in this would be robbery, concealment of stolen goods, and lying about having found that which was lost (Lev. 6:1-7). Removal of landmarks was classified as breach of trust (Deut. 19:14; 27:17; Prov. 22:28; 23:10).

d. *Bribery*: A crime severely condemned, but widely practiced in the later days of the Hebrew monarchy (Exod. 23:8; Deut. 16:19; I Sam. 8:3; II Chron. 19:7; Job 15:34; Psa. 26:10; Prov. 6:35; 17:23; Isa. 1:23; 33:15; Ezek. 22:12; Amos 5:12).

e. *Burglary or Robbery:* As we have already noted under "Breaking and Entering," when the crime was one of violence or one capable of violence (at night), the offender was subject to death at the hands of the victim and the victim was not considered guilty should the robber lose his life (Exod. 22:2a). Otherwise, restitution was assessed.

f. *Cheating or Swindling:* The prohibition is against "unjust weights" or "measures" (Lev. 19:35,36; Deut. 25:13-16). The punishment is not decreed. One would presume it would involve some form of corporeal punishment.

g. *Debt:* Borrowing, *per se*, was not prohibited (except on an international scale, see Deut. 28:12). But to borrow and default on payment was evidently considered to be criminal insolvency or fraud (see Matt. 5:26; 18:28-34). Paul admonishes Christians to live free of indebtedness (Rom. 13:8) and that in a context dealing with one's civic responsibility.

h. *Drunkenness:* The consequences of drunkenness would certainly be criminal. It leads to all manner of henious crimes, including incest (see Gen. 19:30-38). The prophets denounced civil rulers for their drunkenness would cause them to pervert the rights of the afflicted (Prov. 31:4-9). David led Uriah into drunkenness in order to try to hide his adultery with Uriah's wife, Bathsheba (II Sam. 11:13). Ben-hadad's drunknness in the line of duty as a civil officer cost great loss of life to his soldiers and almost his own life (I Kings 20:16-21).

i. *Homicide (Accidental):* Accidental homicide did not incur the death penalty, but it was serious enough to be considered a crime which incurred a form of incarceration (Num. 35:22-28). Should two men be working, or in some other circumstance, and one should be accidentally shoved or thrust-through, or struck with a tool, so that he dies, the other is not guilty of premeditated murder. However the living person who was involved in the accident must flee to a "city of refuge" and remain there until the death of the incumbent high priest. If he does not remain in the "city of refuge" he is subject to death at the hands of the "avenger of blood" (see also Deut. 19:4-10; Exod. 12:13).

j. *Seduction:* The enticement of an unbetrothed virgin to sexual intercourse (Exod. 22:16,17; Deut. 22:28,29). The seducer must marry the woman, or if the father will not give her in marriage, the seducer must pay the woman's dowry to the father.

k. *Slander:* Malicious character assassination was a crime in the Hebrew civil order (Exod. 23:1). When a wife's chastity was slandered the slanderer is to be punished by whipping (Deut. 22:13-19) and by a fine.

k. *Swearing Falsely (Perjury, Lying, etc.) in Non-Capital Cases:* An inexcusable crime even if the false swearing is done to benefit the poor (Exod. 20:16; 23:1-3; Lev. 6:3-5; 19:11,12; Deut. 19:16-21; Jer. 5:2; 7:9; Hosea 10:4; Zech. 5:4).

l. *Theft, Stealing:* (Gen. 44:8; Exod 20:15; 21:16: 22:1-4; Prov. 6:30; Zech. 5:3; Gen. 31:21,26; II Sam. 15:6; 19:3; Prov. 9:17; Matt. 15:19; Mark 7:21; Rev. 9:21). Restitution was the penalty. If the apprehended thief had nothing with which to make restitution, he was sold into indentured servanthood until proper restitution was made.

m. *Negligence Leading to Property Damage or Loss:* (Exod. 22:5-15; Lev. 5:14-6:7; Num. 5:5-8). Full restitution was the punishment.

n. *Usury (Loaning Money for Interest):* This was considered to be a form of exploitation or extortion (Exod. 22:25; Deut. 23:10,21; Deut. 15:7-11; 24:13; Psa. 15:5; 37:21,26; 112:5; Prov. 19:17; Ezek. 18:17; Job 22:6; 24:3,7).

These are not all the crimes listed in the Bible. The Israelites as well as the Gentile societies had a multitude of "common law" crimes codified in their civil systems. "Common law" is that which becomes law through necessity and is established by precedent. One has only to turn to the Jewish Talumd, the Mishnah, the Gemara and the Midrash, to observe the Israelites developing their "common law."

There are laws in the Bible which protect people and property from being victimized and exploited: (1) Property (Deut. 22:1-4; 23:24,25, Exod. 21:33-36; 23:4,5); (2) Environment — Ecology (Deut. 22:6,7; 22:9; 23:12-14); (3) Temporary deferment from Military Service (Deut. 24:5; 20:1-9); (4) Equal Justice for Aliens (Deut. 24:17,18); (5) Protection of Heritage (Deut. 21:15-17; 25:5-10); (6) Protection Against Inhumane Indignities (Deut. 21:22,23); (7) Protection of Bond Servants (Exod. 21:1-11); (8) Protection for Divorced Women (Deut. 23:1-4); (9) Protection Against Excessive Punishment (Deut. 25:1-3); (10) Prevention of Cruelty to Animals (Deut. 25:4); (11) Protection Against Character Assassination (Deut. 22:13-19).

Hammurabi (1628-1686 B.C.) lived some two-hundred years before Moses. Hammurabi made Babylon one of the great cities of the ancient world. He is famous for his "law code." It says, in part, " . . . the savior of his people from distress, who establishes in security their portion in the midst of Babylon . . . that justice might be dealt the orphan and the widow . . . I established law and justice in the language of the land, thereby promoting the welfare of the people." It is now known that his was not the first attempt to systematize the laws of Babylon. Fragments of several previous law codes have been found. But Hammurabi's is the most complete expression of early Babylonian law, and undoubtedly incorporates many laws and customs which go back to far earlier times. The law code itself included nearly 300 paragraphs of legal provisions touching commercial, social, domestic and moral life. There are regulations governing such matters as liability for (and exemption from) military service, control of trade, banking and usury, the responsibility of a man toward his wife and children, including the husband's payment of the wife's debt. Death was the penalty for homicide, theft, adultery, and bearing false witness. Women's rights were safeguarded. Negligence for safety was punished. Perhaps the reason for many similarites between Hammurabi's code and the Mosaic legislation is that there is a common ancestry (Semitic) and that many of the laws of both were already being practiced in the ancient civilizations long before Babylon and Israel (see Gen. 9:6; 12:17-29; 14:13-24; 19:1ff; 38:8; 38:24, etc.). It is further evidence that fundamental divine law is written on the human conscience — it is "Natural Law." Numerous religious laws were codified in the Law of Moses. Violation of some of them required the death penalty: (1) idolatry in any form (Lev. 20:2; Deut. 13:6; 17:2-7); (2) witchcraft and false prophecy (Exod. 22:18; Lev. 20:27; Deut. 13:5; 18:20; I Sam. 28:9); (3) Sabbath-breaking (Exod. 31:14; 35:2; Num. 15:32-36); (4) blasphemy against the Name of God (Lev. 24:14,16,23; I Kings 21:10; Matt. 26:65-66). These were unique to the Israelite community as the "covenant-people" of God and could not be applied in a religiously pluralistic civil society. Some of these are perpetual high crimes against God and when perpetrated by anyone in any age or social unity they will be punished by eternal death.

It is interesting, though, that in many monolithic or dictatorial forms of Gentile government mentioned in the Bible, violation of religious laws also incurred the death penalty (see Dan. 3:1ff; 6:1ff). Since religion is usually the foundation of morality, and morality is the fiber of society, civil laws must be enacted in any society to further the practice of religion, at least by protecting the free exercise thereof. And, further, since morality must be based upon truth, religions that, at least, seek truth must be protected.

177

Religions that pervert human nature that are fraudul, that usurp the laws of civil order must be dealt with accordingly by the civil authority. "Religion" that is behaviorily inimical to civil order cannot be tolerated.

D. BIBLICAL PUNISHMENTS

1. *Capital Punishment:* Punishment by death, lethal execution by the hands of civil authorities, is biblical! In the Old and New Testaments, this is a commandment ordained by God and committed to civil government. Capital punishment (death) for capital crime is not "uncivilized," not "unreasonable," not "cruel," and not "unchristian." Some Christians take a different position:

> The desire for vengeance, for *eye-for-eye* justice, is a principle and a mentality worthy of civilized government and of this body (the U.S. Senate.) — spoken by Senator Mark Hatfield of Oregon in regard to the Senate's passing of a drug bill that legislates capital punishment for drug-related killings. "Liberals from both parties derided the capital punishment as an ineffective vestige of less enlightened times."
> *The Joplin Globe*, Joplin, Missouri, October 14, 1988
>
> An article in *Christian Standard* a few years ago put it this way: "For exactly the same reason that it was wrong for a man to murder, it is wrong for him to be *killed* in the name of the law" . . . .
> One writer for *Christian Standard* expressed this view some years ago: "There is one irrefutable reason against capital punishment. Man cannot give life; therefore, he should not take it away. God says, 'Vengeance belongeth unto me; I will recompense, saith the Lord' " (Romans 12:19, A.S.V.).
> *The Bible Says*, by Jack Cottrell,
> pub. Standard, pp. 54,55

Human life is sacrosanct with God. Human life is so sacred

that even the life of the murderer is to be respected; it is not to be wantonly or ruthlessly taken away. The Lord appointed a sign upon Cain, the first murderer, so that other individuals would not take the law into their own hands and maliciously carry out some personal vendetta by slaying Cain. God said, "If any one slays Cain, vengeance shall be taken on him sevenfold" (Gen. 4:15). Crime is not to be punished by crime; the life of the murderer is not to be taken violently or in thirst for blood. The arrogant boast of Lamech (Gen. 4:24) shows how deeply seated the practice of personal blood-letting had become in the human race. But the pre-flood civilization became so depraved and insensitive to the sanctity of human life that the indictment of God upon it is epitomized by calling it "violent" (Gen. 6:5,11,12). As a result God destroyed the human race with the exception of eight persons.

> It is signal evidence of God's grace that the indictment respecting the depravity of man's heart that "every imagination of the thoughts of his heart was only evil continually" (Gen. 6:5), depravity which filled the earth with violence and therefore with the desecration of life's sanctity, should be given later on as the *reason* why the Lord would not again curse the ground with a flood and destroy all living as he had done (Gen. 8:21). The reason is stated to be that "the imagination of the heart of man is evil from his youth." The import surely is that God's covenant of perpetual forbearance and mercy (Gen. 9:8-17) is necessitated precisely because of the deep-seated and native depravity of man's heart; it is God's grace alone that explains the preservation of man, not any change in the native perversity of the thought of his heart. Symptomatic and confirmatory of this grace of God is the fact that the institutions which guarded and promoted the new order instituted after the flood (the propagation of life — Genesis 9:1-7; the sustenance of life — Genesis 8:22; 9:2b,3; the protection of life — Genesis 9:2a,5,6) are institutions which have as their purpose the maintenance and furtherance of life. The wages of sin is death; the destruction of the flood demonstrated this concretely and conspicuously. After the flood, in accordance with God's covenant and in pursuance of it, the Lord manifested his

grace in making provision for the safeguarding and enhancement of life as the antithesis of death.
Principles of Conduct, by John Murray, pub. Eerdmans, p. 109

God's new civilization, after the flood, would still be, for the most part, insensitive to and unredeemed by the grace of God. If it is not to fall back into implaccable violence and be destroyed as the pre-flood civilization, it must have instituted strong, humanly-administered, sanctions to prevent such violence and anarchy. It hardly needs to be said that modern civilization is equally insensitive to and unredeemed by the grace of God. In fact, it may be more so than some of the pre-diluvian civilizations.

Capital punishment for capital crime (especially murder) is so basic an institution for civilization that God ordered it as a first priority upon Noah's emergence from the ark:

> And surely your blood of your lives will I require; at the hand of every beast will I require it, and at the hand of man; at the hand of every man's brother will I require the life of man. Whoso sheddeth man's blood, by man shall his blood be shed; for in the image of God made he man (Gen. 9:5,6 KJV).

It is important to note that in the original Hebrew language, the word *yod* is in this text; it means literally, "hand." God intended capital punishment to be executed upon murderers by the *hand* of man. God did not intend to intervene providentially or supernaturally to directly administer capital punishment after the flood. Man was delegated authority to act in God's place in this instance. That would be the primary function of civil government (Rom. 13:1-7). It is also important to note that the fundamental reason capital punishment was ordained against murder and the reason man was to administer the punishment is that man is "created in the image of God"! An assault upon man's life is a virtual assault upon the life of God! So depraved is murder, the penalty for it must be nothing less than the crime! Furthermore, since there is certainly no *termination* of the fact that man is made in the image of God (every person born or being born is in His image) the sanctity of life and the sanction against murder (capital punishment) is as true today as it was in the days of Noah. It is a fact that *in no other instance* of biblical jurisprudence is there a penalty inflicted giving for its reason that man is created in the image of God!

Abraham, father of the faithful, pursued the "kings of the East" when they had kidnapped his nephew Lot and his family, and "slaughtered" (Heb. *makkah*, Gen. 14:15,17) some of them. Capital punishment by the hand of the man (Abraham) so often eulogized by the Scriptures as symbolic of the true believer in God (Rom. 4:9-12; Gal. 3:6ff; Heb. 11:13-22; James 2:21-23) should dispel any misgivings Christians might have that God disapproves of capital punishment.

We have listed sixteen crimes for which the nation Israel (according to the Law given by God through angels to Moses) was to exact the death penalty. It will not be necessary here to repeat them or the scripture references. However the clear declaration that capital punishment was to be administered "without pity" (Deut. 19:21), and that there could be "no ransom" accepted (Num. 35:29-31) bears repeating to emphasize that God did not consider it "cruel and unusual punishment," nor did he deem it "uncivilized."

The "cities of refuge" were not for the purpose of giving "sanctuary" or safety to those guilty of murder. They were established so that one who had slain another and whose innocence needed to be established might find *temporary* security from spiteful, personal vendetta by "vigilantes" until he could be brought before the "congregation" for judgment. The Israelite judges were given well-defined criteria by which to decide between accidental homicide and culpable homicide (whether premeditated murder or negligent homicide). If guilty of murder the man was delivered up to the death penalty — if innocent, he was given sanctuary in the city of refuge until the "change of administrations" (see Num. 35:9-28).

We have also noted before that the death penalty was carried out as punishment for capital crimes during the Israelite monarchy. The Old Testament prophets indicate that during the monarchy justice was perverted with ever increasing indifference until the captivities, but this failure does not disavow the biblical mandate already established by the divine law. Solomon wrote in Ecclesiastes 3:1-8:

> To every thing there is a season, and a time to every purpose under the heaven: A time to be born, and a time to die; a time to plant, and a time to pluck up that which is planted; a time to kill, and a time to heal; a time to break down, and a time to build up; a time to weep, and a time to laugh; a time to mourn, and a time to dance; a time to cast away stones, and a time to gather stones together; a time to embrace, and a time to refrain from embracing; a time to get, and a time to lose; a time to keep silence, and a time to speak; a time to love and a time to hate; a time of war, and a time of peace.

God has clearly declared in his revealed word the principles upon which we are to rely for the "time to kill . . . " and the "time to make war . . . " and he expects man to understand his revelation and obey it.

> It is in the light of these principles that we are to view the power of the sword vested in the civil magistrate. It is a strange turn of thought which causes some who espouse an evangelical view of Holy Scripture to fail to appreciate the implications of the biblical teaching that the powers that be are ordained of God to bear the sword and execute wrath upon evildoers (cf. Rom. 13:1-7; I Pet. 2:13-17). It is true, of course, that all punishment is evil; for all punishment is the wages of sin. But it does not follow that the execution of the evil which consists in punishment is *per se* sinful. If this were so then God himself would commit sin in executing wrath, a blasphemous thought.
> *Principles of Conduct*, by John Murray, p. 114

The writer of Hebrews expresses the sentiments of finite mankind when he says, "For the moment all discipline seems painful rather than pleasant; later it yields the peaceful fruit of righteousness to those who have been trained by it" (Heb. 12:11). Capital punishment, even when contemplated for others, does not seem desirable when viewed by the finite and limited perspective of the human mind. But as revealed in the Bible when viewed in the divine perspective which is infinite and unlimited, it yields the peaceful fruit of righteousness to those trained by it!

As Dr. Cottrell points out in his book, *The Bible Says* . . . , Jesus (e.g. the Sermon on the Mount) did not introduce a new system of ethics. He did not come to "destroy the law, but to fulfill it." What Jesus revealed in the Gospels, and what the apostles revealed by His Spirit in the rest of the New Testament, especially about ethics, love, justice, government, is not at all different in spirit or principle from the law of God in the Old Testament. For example, the O.T. Law says, "You shall not hate your brother in your heart, but you shall reason with your neighbor, lest you bear sin because of him. You shall not take vengeance or bear any grudge against the sons of your own people, but you shall love your neighbor as yourself: I am the Lord" (Lev. 19:17,18). Jesus taught no ethic higher than that! His Sermon on the Mount is an admonition for believers to allow the Spirit of God's Law to captivate their thinking and regulate their actions — and to go beyond the pharisaic, hypocritical "letter-of-the-law" mentality. In Jesus' day the "eye for an eye" law was being perverted by many Jews into a mandate for personal revenge but its original intent was for use only by civil judges in executing just and fair punishments. Jesus was actually advocating a return to the original doctrine.

In Jesus' declaration, "Render therefore to Caesar the things that are Caesar's, and to God the things that are God's" (Matt. 22:21) the implication is unequivocal that "Caesar" does have distinct prerogatives and functions which God has authorized.

Later, Pilate judging Jesus, said, "You will not speak to me? Do you not know that I have power to release you, and power to crucify you?" — Jesus granted that Pilate actually had those powers by the will and authority of God as he replied, "You would have no power over me unless it had been given you from above . . . " (John 19:10,11), even though Jesus had been unjustly arraigned.

The penitent thief on the cross, in keeping with the sensitive conscience that characterizes the true believer's acceptance of the demand for justice, said, "Do you not fear God, since you are under the same sentence of condemnation? (death by crucifixion) . . . . And we indeed justly; for we are receiving the due rewards of our deeds; but this man has done nothing wrong" (Luke 23:40,41). His recognition of just retribution for crime is in keeping with the attitude that makes him a proper subject of divine grace as he cries for mercy. But the attitude of the other thief dishonestly railing against justice shows a moral antagonism to the spirit of Christ's kingdom and Paradise.

Captial punishment is to be accepted as a principle by which Christians are to live in this present world. The apostle Paul undeniably lived by this principle for when he was falsely accused by the Jews and was under arrest by Roman officials he declared, "If then I am a wrongdoer, and have committed anything worthy of death, I do not refuse to die" (Acts 25:11). Paul was innocent of any criminal action so he availed himself of his rights as a citizen under Roman law ("appealed to Caesar") and demanded to be tried before the judicial system then in power. Paul knew that if one expected the protections afforded by enforcement of civil law, he must also support the principle that laws without just punishments are no laws! Paul not only preached civil justice (Rom. 13:1-7), he practiced it! There are three points in Paul's statement before Festus: (1) he recognized that there were crimes worthy of death; (2) he declared that he would not resist capital punishment upon himself if he had been guilty of a capital crime; (3) implicit also is his recognition that some authority had the right to execute the death penalty.

The New Testament, in making civil government doctrinally ordained by God (Rom. 13:1-7; I Pet. 2:13-17) ordains in the same passages the doctrine of capital punishment. The Greek words *ekdikos* ("avenger," Rom. 13:4) and *ekdikesin* ("vengeance," I Pet. 2:14) and *ten machairan* ("the sword," Rom. 13:4) plainly indicate that civil authorities were to exercise the use of the sword in carrying out "vengeance" upon evildoers. The use of the word "sword" obviously refers to execution — death (see Matt. 26:52; Acts 12:2; Rev. 13:10). The proper civil magistrate has biblical authority and obligation to inflict death as the penalty for crimes which merit this retribution.

> Nothing shows the moral bankruptcy of a people or of a generation more than disregard for the sanctity of human life. And it is this same atrophy of moral fibre that appears in the plea for the abolition of the death penalty for the crime of murder. It is the sense of this sanctity that constrains the demand for the infliction of this penalty. The deeper our regard for life the firmer will be our hold upon the penal sanction which the violation of that sanctity merits.
> *Principles of Conduct*, by John Murray, p. 122

Many in civil government today, in America as well as in other nations, do not accept the biblical view of capital punishment. Politicians, sociologists, criminologists and even the judiciary are divided on the issue. "Conservatives" generally hold to the biblical view while "liberals" usually oppose it. The "liberal" position is stated succinctly as follows:

> Criminologists today believe that society must protect itself against criminals rather than revenge itself upon them . . . .
> People once considered criminals as sinners who chose to offend against the laws of God and man. But criminologists today regard society itself as in large part responsible for crimes committed against it. Causes of crime include, poverty, undesirable living conditions, and inadequate education. Crime results fundamentally from society's failure to provide a decent life for all the people

and to develop a sense of social responsibility in its citizens . . . .

Criminology is opposed to the death penalty and other forms of cruel and revengeful punishments. Modern criminologists favor applying scientific methods to the study of the causes of crime, and the handling of delinquents and criminals in courts, prisons, and upon their release from prisons . . . .

. . . the best way to protect society is to discover the major causes of criminal behavior. Then, criminologists and other specialists try to rehabilitate the offender so that on release he will be a well-adjusted citizen.

World Book Encyclopedia, Vol. 4, articles on "Crime" and "Criminology," pp. 909-912

This appears to some as the "enlightened" and "civilized" approach to crime. But, (1) it is antiscriptural, and (2) it does not work! There were no prisons in Mosaic Israel and there is no indication in the Law of Moses they were to have any. Occasionally the Law provided for an accused person to be held in "custody" or "in hand" (Lev. 24:12; 25:28; Num. 15:34; 35:25; Deut. 19:12) until judgment could be made and punishment executed. Gentile societies had prisons, of course, but there is no biblical endorsement of incarceration as a form of punishment. Immediate application of punishment, whether retribution (revenge) or restitution (repayment) was the sanctioned biblical practice.

The first prison system in the United States was instituted by the Quakers and it was called the "Walnut Street Jail" in Philadelphia, Pennsylvania. By the year 1790, common law (precedent) had established incarceration as the most used way of punishing criminals. There are approximately 500,000 prisoners in State and Federal prisons in America today, and another 500,000 in County and City Jails. It costs the American taxpayers approximately $18,000 per year per person in prison; that is 18 billion dollars per year! And America has the highest crime rate in the Western world. Incarceration does not work! Prisons are breeding grounds for homosexuality and brutality. Literal "crime schools" operate inside penitentiaries. According to statistics released in 1982, we punish 25 out of every 500 criminals who commit serious crimes. The 25 that are punished are put someplace where they sit for years. Criminals have *more* advocacy for their "rights" by both civil and private authorities than the victims of their crimes have. Those who commit crimes against innocent victims and against society have no "rights" until they have paid for their crimes. Criminals, by acting to violate the laws of society declare themselves, in effect, violently opposed to the only thing that can guarantee rights — the law. They are self-declared insurrectionists. Since by their own declaration they do not wish the rights of law, they should not have those rights! Eighteen billion dollars per year just to maintain one million felons with clothing, food, and housing in a manner that many hard-working law-abiding citizens do not have is not justice. That does not include the tremendous cost of the judicial system afforded them or the psychological trauma and material costs their crimes have caused. These prisoners are contributing nothing productive to the society that is underwriting their subsistence. Such a penal system seems to be an atrocious injustice in itself. Surely a system of punishments closer to the biblical one would be more just.

The objections to capital punishment have all been made and repeated over and over. It is not our purpose to deal with every objection here. We shall consider a few of them. For those whose objections are based on an anti-biblical stance, our resolutions will be unacceptable because we believe the issue must be ultimately settled from a biblically authoritative posture. If the Bible, in both Old and New Testaments, teaches that capital punishment is sanctioned as a mandate for civil government, that settles the issue.

Objection No. 1: The forgiveness Jesus gives and teaches should be followed and criminals should have our forgiveness, not execution. Answers: (1) Jesus earned our forgiveness by his redemptive work and made it provisionally possible in the here-and-now and ultimately possible in the hereafter. Any person, even a murderer, may, upon repentance and acceptance of Christ's New Covenant have the forgiveness of God for the hereafter. But redemption does not relieve us always from the consequences of our sins. A drunk who confesses his sin has no right to expect God to take away his cirrhosis of the liver. The grace of God takes care of the penalty of a man's sin but not always the immediate consequences. If forgiveness of sin meant also the elimination of all its consequences, men would look for more ways to sin in order to "have their cake and eat it too"! (2) Jesus taught no different ethical level than the will of God in the Old Testament. (3) And, for that matter, the faithful of the Old Testament were saved by the grace of God through their faith (Gen. 15:6; Rom. 4:6ff; Heb. 11:6; Gal. 3:8, etc.). If capital punishment was a viable practice then, it is not rescinded by the New Dispensation.

Objection No. 2: The possibility that an innocent person might be executed should make society refuse to practice capital punishment. Answers: (1) The multitudinous checks and balances, the thousands of safety precautions built into our jurisprudence system makes this highly improbable. (2) Doctors, politicians, mechanics, automobile drivers, pharmicists all make mistakes — some of them are fatal mistakes. But no one wants to totally dispense with their contributions to society. (3) All human beings make mistakes, some of them fatal, but that must not cause us to suspend the need for justice and morality to be chosen and practiced.

Objection No. 3: Capital punishment is cruel and inhuman. Answers: (1) This objection completely overlooks the point that the "inhumanity" was the crime and not the punishment. The "inhumanity" is the anti-social, violent murder, perpetrated by the criminal, not the punishment which stops further violence. (2) Execution of a murderer should itself be considered a humane action. It is an extension of mercy to a law-abiding citizenry. To purge from peaceful society the bloodthirsty, calculating, violent murderers of babies, innocent children, women and peaceful men, often murdered by multiples, cannot be inhumane. To simply imprison them briefly and release them on parole to repeat their crimes is inhumane! (3) *Justice* is the prime reason for capital punishment, not reform, not rehabilitation, not restitution (which is impossible for the crime of murder). Since a murderer has taken what can never be restored and no amount of material wealth could be given to equal a human life, the murderer must be brought to justice by the taking of his life. There is nothing inhumane in that.

> There is only one thing that satisfies an offended justice and that is payment of the debt to justice. And the biblical payment for murder is one's life . . . .
>
> The reason why this rationale may sound strange to the modern ear is that the true sense of justice has been obscured. When men no longer believe in God nor in an unchangeable moral law, it follows that no penalty should be incurred for transgressing a law which is not there. Along with this contemporary distortion of justice is an anemic concept of love. A loving God would not punish anyone, it is vainly thought. Hence, it is concluded that a loving parent should not discipline his child. It is little wonder that men do not understand the need for capital punishment; they do not see the need for any kind of punishment. They fail to see that loving parents punish their children (Prov. 13:24) and that a loving God chastises His sons (Heb. 12:5,6). Indeed, almost the converse of the modern mentality is true. The Bible teaches that proper punishment is proof of love. The love is *in* the discipline. The lack of correction is an indication of the lack of true concern for the wayward.
>
> *Ethics: Alternatives and Issues*, by Norman L. Geisler pub. by Zondervan, p. 247

Two more quotations are in order relative to what the Bible says about civil government and capital punishment.

> It seems to me that those who advocate abolition of all capital punishment ignore three vital factors (1) the absolute sovereignty of God as the creator and giver of human existence on earth; (2) the malignancy of sin which left unchecked would destroy the universe; (3) the divinely delegated authority to human society to remove from its fabric those who are incorrigibly devoted to

the destruction of that fabric by acts of violence against the innocent.

It is not the distance from animals but the proximity to God which makes man unique . . . . Man abdicates his responsibility when he gets on the animal level or when he seeks to dethrone God. And he does both when he becomes a wilful and malicious murderer. He attempts to be under what he is over (animal) — and aspires to be over what he is under (God). And it is here that God decrees that man forfeits his right to continue to live with those who remain within the status for which man was made.
Mission Messenger, Vol. 31, August 1969
by Carl Ketcherside, p. 118ff

He (the Christian) has no Biblical authority to tell the state it must renounce the use of force in order to preserve law, or to demand that the law of the state be changed to disarm policemen. This would be to take the "sword" from the magistrate — and the bearing of the sword by the magistrate is recognized and approved by the Word of God.
William LaSor, in *Christianity Today*, January 30, 1970

2. *Forms of Capital Punishment in the Bible:*

a. *Stoning to death:* (see Exod. 19:13; Lev. 20:27; Josh. 7:25; Luke 20:6; Acts 7:58; 14:5; also John 10:31; Lev. 20:2; 24:14-23; Num. 15:32-36; Deut. 13:10; 21:21; 22:21-24; I Kings 21:10; Ezek. 16:40; 23:47; John 11:8). This was the ordinary method of execution. It was efficient, awesome and one in which those who bore witness to the crime would participate (Deut. 13:9; 17:7). The tractate *Sanhedrin* (in the Talmud) directs that the condemned was to be taken to a cliff "the height of two men" and one of his accusers was to throw him down backwards, obviously to stun him by the fall or to break his back; it was only after this that the stones were to be thrown. and the first was to be aimed at his heart. Stunning the prisoner first was undoubtedly to extend him some mercy before the stones fell upon him.

b. *Hanging*: This may not have been a form of execution at all (see Num. 25:4; Deut. 21:23; Gen. 40:22; 41:13; Josh.

8:29; 10:26; II Sam. 4:12; 17:23; 18:10; 21:9; Ezra 6:11; Esther 2:23; 7:10; 9:14; Lam. 5:12; Matt. 27:5; Luke 23:39; Acts 5:30; 10:39; Gal. 3:13). Some of the above references are to crucifixion. The Hebrew word *talah* is most often translated "hang" and means "to dangle or suspend by hanging." In Ezra 6:11 the Hebrew word *macha* is translated "hanged" (KJV); and "impaled" (RSV); *macha* means "to smite together" and therefore should be translated "impaled." "Hanging" which was often done by impaling a corpse already dead was usually done to deter others from committing the same crime (II Sam. 4:12). The person whose body was so exposed was "accursed of God" (Deut. 21:23; Gal. 3:13), and for this reason was not allowed to remain in view overnight (Josh. 8:29; 10:26). Execution by being "dangled" from a gallows was not prescribed for any crime in the Mosaic law. Death by impaling the convicted upon large, upright poles of wood was a favorite method of the Canaanites (II Sam. 21:6-9) and of the Assyrians as the *bas-reliefs* found in the ruins of the Assyrian civilization testify. The Persians also impaled for execution.

c. *Burning*: Before the time of Moses, this was the punishment for sexual unchastity (adultery, fornication, see Gen. 38:24). Burning as a method of execution was also legislated by the Law of Moses (see Lev. 20:14; 21:9). The Lord God used burning as a form of capital punishment (Lev. 10:1-3); Joshua executed Achan and his family by stoning and "burning" (Josh. 7:25). It was practiced by the Gentile civilizations (Dan. 3:6,15,19,20; Judges 14:15; Jer. 29:22; II Macc. 7:5ff). "The lake of fire and brimstone" is God's method of eternal punishment (see Luke 16:19ff; Matt. 25:41; Mark 9:44,45; II Thess. 1:8; II Pet. 3:7,12; Jude 7: Rev. 14:9-11; 20:9,10,14,15,; 21:8).

d. *Sword or Spear (Beheading or Stabbing)*: (see Exod. 19:13; 32:27; Num. 25:7ff; Judges 9:5; I Sam. 15:33; II Sam. 20:22; I Kings 19:1; Jer. 26:23; Matt. 14:8-10). Some of these are cases of assassination, but the *sword* is given to all governments (symbolically) as a instrument of execution (Rom. 13:1-7). The sword was specified in the Mosaic law (and "shot" with an arrow or a spear Exod. 19:13) in rare cases. Ahab's seventy sons were beheaded by command of Jehu (II Kings 10:6-8); John the Baptist was beheaded by order of Herod (Matt. 14:1-8; Mark 6:27); James the apostle was beheaded (Acts 12:2); many of the early Christians martyrs were beheaded (Rev. 20:4). Gentile governments used beheading by the sword as their usual form of capital punishment (Gen. 40:19) for their own citizens; (see also Heb. 12:20; Deut. 13:13-15; Judges 9:5; I Sam. 22:18,18; II Sam. 4:6,7; I Kings 2:25-34; I Kings. 19:1; II Sam. 1:15)

e. *Strangling:* It is not mentioned in the Bible unless I Kings 20:31 implies it. The tractate *Sanhedrin* mentions it as a form of capital punishment for a son who had struck his father and for a "false prophet" — the strangling was done with a garrote. Herod the Great ordered two of his sons strangled to death on suspicion of sediton against his throne (Josephus, Antiq, XVI:11:7). Sometimes the convicted person was immersed in clay or mud, and a cloth was twisted around the neck and drawn in opposite directions by two lictors, so as to take away the breath.

f. *Suffocation:* Also not mentioned except in apocryphal works. This was especially a mode of execution practiced by the Persians and Syrians. A case is described in II Macc. 13:4-8 where Menelaus was fastened to a revolving wheel in a contraption 50 cubits high, filled with ashes, in which he was repeatedly immersed, until death ensued.

g. *Dismemberment unto Death*: "Hacking asunder" is mentioned as a Gentile form of execution (Dan. 2:5; 3:29). It was practiced by the Syrians upon the Jews (II Macc. 7:1ff). See also Matthew 24:51; Luke 12:46. Samuel hewed Agag to pieces with the sword (I Sam. 15:33).

h. *Sawing Asunder*: Hebrews 11:37 describes an ancient form of execution. It could be describing the "threshing of Gilead with threshing sledges of iron" (Amos 1:3). Justin Martyr states that Isaiah the prophet of the Old Testament was "sawn asunder" by Manasseh the king. (See also Prov. 20:26; Isa. 28:27,28; II Sam. 12:31; I Chron. 20:3).

i. *Drowning*: This is not distinctly Jewish in origin even though some Jews apparently practiced it (see Matt. 18:6; Mark 9:24). Josephus records that some Galileans revolted and drowned some of Herod's men (Antiq. XVI; 15:10). Herod the Great had the eighteen-year-old Aristobulus, his brother-in-law drowned because of Herod's paranoia that the young man was after his throne (Josephus, Antiq. XV; 3:3).

j. *Exposure to Wild Beasts*: Daniel was cast into a den of lions for sedition against the law of Darius (Dan. 6). After Daniel's miraculous survival, his enemies (those whose malicious cunning had caused him to break the Persian law) were thrown into the lion's den and were consumed by the lions. Micah figuratively depicts human beings as animals goring others to death (Micah 4:13). Paul talks of being "rescued from the lion's mouth" (II Tim. 4:17) — whether figurative or literal, it shows that such was a form of execution in the biblical civilizations. Paul also claimed to have "fought with wild beasts at Ephesus" (which may also be a figure of speech) (I Cor. 15:32). God himself used wild animals as a form of punishment (execution) upon criminally disobedient people (Lev. 26:22; Deut. 32:24; Jer. 15:3; Ezek. 14:21; II Kings 17:26). The book of Revelation indicates that this was a form of execution by the Romans of the first three centuries (Rev. 6:8). Twenty-four youngsters speaking evilly and disrespectfully toward God's anointed prophet, Elisha, were "torn" by wild bears (II Kings 2:23,24).

k. *Crucifixion*: This method of execution for crimes was not a part of Mosaic legislation. Crucifixion was one of the most cruel and barbarous forms of death known to man. It was practiced, especially in times of war, by the Phoenicians, Carthaginians, Egyptians, and later by the Romans. The gory details of crucifixion are absent from the accounts of Jesus' crucifixion (see Matt. 27:35ff; Mark 15:24ff; Luke 23:33ff; John 19:18ff). Some specifics concerning the torture inflicted upon Jesus *prior* to his crucifixion are recorded. Victims of crucifixion did not generally succumb for two or three days. The physical trauma of being nailed to a wooden cross, bleeding, starvation, infection, exposure to elements and insects, pierced with a spear, "crucifragium" (breaking of the legs), and the psychological trauma, all made death by crucifixion a horror to be feared by the most callous or the most courageous.

1. *Precipitation (Throwing Down from Great Heights)*: (see II Chron. 25:12ff; Luke 4:29). See also II Macc. 6:10; II Kings 8:12; Hosea 10:14; 13:18. On an ancient column of Assurbanipal, an Assyrian emperor, archaeologists found an inscription stating that certain persons were thrown from a great height into a stone quarry landing on sculptured lions and bulls in order that they might be executed. Some Bible commentators believe Oreb and Zeeb (Judges 7:25) were executed by "precipitation."

Some of these methods of capital punishment seem "cruel and unusual." Perhaps they are. Is it any more cruel to execute a criminal by stoning him to death or by casting him down a great height upon stones? Remember, it was the God of omniscience and omnipotence — the God of all mercies — who directed, by divine revelation, that criminals be executed by stoning. Justice, for the criminal, is never pleasant. It is not designed by the all-wise God to be pleasant to the criminal. Capital punishment administered within the principles of jurisprudence (justice) is intended to be quick and final. There is nothing cruel about such an execution. The execution of capital punishment by a drawn out, torturous, malicious, vengeful, painful method is cruel. To eliminate the element of malice and desire to torture, capital punishment for capital crime was forbidden to individuals by God and mandated for systematic civil governments.

U.S. Supreme Court Justice Brennan's opinion (Furman vs. Georgia, 408 U.S. 238,1972) contended that capital punishment is *per se* cruel and unusual punishment and therefore unconstitutional. The U.S. Constitution's Eighth Amendment states: "Excessive bail shall not be required, nor excessives fines imposed, nor cruel and unusual punishments inflicted."

a. The Bible (authored by God's Holy Spirit) does not consider capital punishment "cruel and unusual." That is true of both the Old Testament and the New.

b. "Cruel" must be modified by "unusual." Those who wrote the U.S. Constitution and its "Bill or Rights" (first 10 amendments) knew that death as capital punishment was not *unusual.* They knew history and they knew the Bible. When they wrote the Eighth Amendment there were milleniums of human history plus divine revelation to inform them about capital punishment. Had execution for capital crime been "unusual" they would have specified it as "cruel."

c. The men who wrote the Eighth Amendment were men who had just taken the lives of fellow Englishmen in a bloody war! They had executed people for spying and desertion; they had flogged and imprisoned their own soldiers for disciplinary purposes. How could they have considered execution for capital crime a "cruel and unusual" punishment?

d. The same men who wrote Amendment Eight, also wrote Amendment Five which says, in part: "No person shall be held to answer for a capital, or otherwise infamous crime unless on a presentment or indictment of a grand jury . . . nor shall any person be subject for the same offense to be twice put in *jeopardy of life* or limb; nor shall he be compelled in any criminal case to be a witness against himself, nor be *deprived of life*, liberty, or property, without due process of law . . . " The constitutional fathers believed punishment by death for capital crime was *not* "unusual or cruel"!

Four years after Justice Brennan's opinion, the Supreme Court reviewed the proposition of capital punishment (Gregg vs. Georgia, 428 U.S. 153, 1976) and ruled by a 5-4 majority that execution as capital punishment was constitutional. Many public opinion polls have documented that a large majority of U.S. citizens favor the death penalty. Justice Thurgood Marshall has argued "that public opinion polls and votes of legislators cannot be relied on to ascertain society's standards of decency, because legislators and private citizens do not really comprehend how barbaric capital punishment is." In other words, neither the ordinary citizens nor the Congress of the United States are intelligent enough to know the difference between such principles as decency, justice, cruelty, and barbarism. Apparently the esteemed Justice believes that "wisdom will die" with the Supreme Court's liberal judges (see Job 12:2). Justice Marshall and his minority insist that society has "evolved" to the point where capital punishment is cruel and unusual, and the U.S. Constitution must be "reinterpreted" to correlate to an "evolving" ethic which is more civilized than that of 1787.

> This is not the way the founding fathers viewed constitutional interpretation. They saw the Constitution as the supreme law, and also as a covenant or contract. The Constitution like all legal documents was viewed as a fixed document, to be interpreted according to its plain meaning. And if its meaning was ambiguous as applied to a specific situation, it was to be interpreted according to the intent of those who wrote it, signed it, and ratified it.
> James Madison expressed this view when he wrote, "(If) the sense in which the Constitution was accepted and ratified by the Nation . . . be not the guide in expounding it, there can be no security for a faithful exercise of its powers." His views were echoed by Thomas Jefferson, "The Constitution on which our Union rests, shall be administered by me according to the safe and honest meaning contemplated by the plain understanding of the people of the United States, at the time of its adoption."
>
> *Christianity and the Constitution*, by John Eidsmoe, pub. Baker, p. 392

For the Christian and the Bible-believer, ethics do not evolve — they are absolute and revealed from God. And, it appears, the framers of America's constitution believed in divine absolutes which were applied in the matters of human governance, one of which was capital punishment by death for capital crimes.

In recent decades, some Americans have lobbied vehemently for elimination of the death penalty on the grounds that it is discriminatory against minority races alleging that there are more people from minority races on "death row" than there are white people.

> A majority of the prisoners scheduled to die in the U.S. are white males, 30 to 34 years old, who never married, never went beyond High School and were convicted of murder.
> Two of three of those sentenced to death had a previous felony conviction. One out of nine had killed before.
> Schwarzchild (Henry) agrees that the legal system may not be prejudiced against blacks, but he argues that the economic system is. "The people at the bottom of the social ladder — of whom blacks, of course, are enormously over-represented — obviously are the people who commit violent crimes," he said.
> Interview with Henry Schwarzchild, director of the ACLU Capital Punishment Project in N.Y., *St. Louis Post Dispatch*, Sunday, October 23, 1988

Statistics show that there are approximately 20,000 non-negligent killings in the United States every year. That is a medium-sized city wiped out by homicide every calendar year in this land where a majority of the news media hypocritically bemoans that (because of white collar crimes of public officials) we are a nation where some men see themselves above the law, and at the same time the same media *crusades* (under the guise of news-reporting) against the death penalty! Consistency, thou art a gem!

Capital punishment is biblical; it is rational; it is constitutional. The Bible cannot be altered by human opinion. It is firmly fixed in the heavens (Psa. 119:89; 119:160; Isa. 40:8; Matt. 24:35; I Pet. 1:25). The Bible is God's absolute, perfect, and final revelation to man concerning "all that pertains to life and godliness" (II Pet. 1:3-4) and is able to equip the man of God (including civil rulers) completely, for every good work (II Tim. 3:16,17). The U.S. Constitution is not to be altered by any person or group of persons (including the U.S. Supreme Court) unless amended in due process by vote of the electorate. The U.S. Constitution mandates capital punishment by clear inference, not only in the amendments cited, but in relegating to Congress the power to declare war which is death by execution for capital crime on an international scale. Legislating the specifics for criminal punishments within the nation itself is delegated by the Constitution to each State within the Union. The Constitution *clearly* does *not* delegate the power to legislate to the Supreme Court.

Robert T. Ingram, in his book *The World Under God's Law*, argues the Biblical mandate for capital punishment from the perspective of man's dominion delegated by his Creator. According to Ingram, the sixth commandment of the Decalogue (Ten Commandments, Exod. 20:13) which says, "You shall do no murder" is the "crux of the law." By the sixth commandment, man's station in the hierarchy of Creation is secured, just as God's is legally recognized by the first commandment. All that is right toward God is grounded upon strict, uncompromising observance of the first commandment. In the same way, all that is right toward other human beings is *grounded* upon strict, uncompromising observance of the sixth commandment, "You shall do no murder." Furthermore, in principle this commandment against murder was implicit as long as the human race continues in this world. That God mandated dominion to man is unequivocally stated in Genesis 1:28-30; 9:1-7; Heb. 2:5-9.

The dominion of mankind is maintained, according to Ingram, by preserving the dominion of every single person. Dominion means, among other things, the power to give a name; the responsibility to train and teach those under you: and the power of death. To take away the life of any creature is to exercise the last word in dominion or rule over the creature, except God's which can raise us from the dead. God has required us to exist by giving us existence: no man had any choice in the matter, either as to when and where he would be born, or who would be his parents, or what worldly heritage would be his. But the very *next* ranking power is given into the hands of "every man" (Gen. 9:5,6): the power of death. The combination of physical, mental, and willful powers in every single human being constitutes the power in each one of us to take the life of any other living creature. If, therefore, the *dominion* of man is to be maintained on the earth, then individual men must avenge the death of any other man.

Man, to maintain his dominion, must from time to time prove himself willing and capable to exercise dominion. It is so basic a principle that no person is qualified to discuss matters of government, order, discipline, subordination, or even human relations, who doesn't almost instinctively know it.

It is insufferable that the life of any man shall be taken maliciously and aimlessly by any other creature, including another man. But if it is done, then man, who is the supreme authority (delegated by God) in the world and who must maintain his own dominion, must be the one to take vengeance. Broken laws which usurp the peaceful dominion of man must be repaired.

The power of death is the supreme power of temporal rule; it belongs to God and is delegated to man. Human life has a high price in human civilization. The price is another human life. When a human life can be paid for by a fine, or when it can be paid for by a few years of enforced confinement (even confinement for life), human life is cheapened — man's dominion is usurped.

The rational dominion of man is secure only as long as man exercises the power of death to avenge crimes against his own peace and security under the law of God. The responsibility for the "individuality" of vengeance cannot really be delegated because in the ultimate sense it will always come down to an individual human being — the hangman, the headsman, or the man who pulls the switch on the electric chair. It is true, as God said, "At the hand of every man's brother . . . "God requires the blood of the murderer. God will not do it in this world. He has delegated that dominion to man through civil government.

Man, as an individual, must insist upon death by execution as the penalty for murder, or man rebels and abdicates his divinely ordained dominion! That is the way God has decreed it — whether men like it or not. To do otherwise is to fly in the face of the Creator's omniscience.

2. *Secondary Forms of Punishment*: Punishment, *per se*, was never intended to be pleasant (Heb. 12:11). Punishment is the deliberate infliction of pain. Pain, administered without malice, communicates several desirable principles: (a) reminds individual offenders that "no man is an island" — i.e. everyone must live in a "community." And communal living requires certain norms for behavior. *Punishing abnormal behavior defines normal behavior!* It establishes values. (b) Punishment of uncivil behavior establishes the principle of freedom of choice and responsibility for choices. This, in turn, demonstrates respect for freedom; (c) Punishment communicates that the society believes abnormal behavior can be changed, and it is imperative that the offender choose to make a change. This also communicates that the society believes in the innate dignity of each individual — even offending ones.

Punishment in the Bible is a "last resort" expedient to produce *justice*. If men will not live justly responding with gratitude for the grace of God and with faith in God's faithfulness, then punishment for injustice must be forthcoming. But justice is more than punishment, more than impartiality, more than vindication of the law. Justice is the restoration of the order or well-being that existed before the order was destroyed. That is the meaning of the oft repeated phrase, "law and order." The law and its enforcement are both merely instruments to bring about *justice*.

Justice is present only when human beings are treating one another as God would treat them — honestly, fairly, helpfully, and redemptively. Justice is present when things are right and good. When one human being defrauds another, when one hurts another, when one destroys the well-being or the peace of another justice is *not* present. Justice in the ultimate is only secured by regeneration of the minds and hearts of human beings. Pure justice is only possible in the kingdom of Christ where the rule of love "constrains" citizens to see no one from a human point of view (II Cor. 5:14-17) but from a divine point of view. But some human beings are not constrained by love. Therefore law, including legal actions with punishments for violations, has to be the force which produces some semblance of justice. What is right and honest and helpful for human beings must be produced by coercion when it is not present by faith and love. Justice is the indispensable factor by which human life is sustained on this earth. When a crime is committed, an injustice has always been done. Crimes are committed against individuals — not against institutions. When a house of business or a store is robbed *individuals* are jeopardized. When treason is committed, the lives of *individuals* are jeopardized. When a person is assaulted it is a crime against the person, not a crime against the "state." The Old Testament "civil" laws were designed to protect individuals. They were to produce justice for the victim. What had been disturbed or destroyed in the individual's life was to be made right and restored. That was justice for the real victim. In the Law of Moses, life was more important than property — and people were more important than the punishment to be imposed for crimes committed. It is true, of course, that *ideals* (i.e. liberty, peace, justice, integrity, etc.) are violated when any crime is committed. But ideals are operable only in individuals. Ultimately it is people who are the victims of crime.

There were three fundamental forms of punishment legislated in the Mosaic law (for both civil and religious crimes): capital punishment (execution); corporal punishment (physical punishment short of execution); restitution. We have already discussed capital punishment. Corporal punishment was decreed but probably rarely practiced.

    a. Blinding (Exod. 21:23; Lev. 24:20; Deut. 19:13-20; Jdgs. 16:21; II Kings 25:7; Jer. 52:11; Esther 7:3; I Sam. 11:2).

b. Branding — some think the threat of "burning" was merely "branding" and not execution (Gen. 38:24; Lev. 20:14; 21:9; Isa. 44:5; see also Lev. 19:28; Gal. 6:17).

c. Beating (Deut. 25:2,3; II Cor. 11:24; Exod. 21:25; II Macc. 6:19;30; see also Exod. 5:14-16; Prov. 23:14; Matt. 21:35; Luke 12:45; Mark 13:9; Acts 5:40; 16:37).

d. Braying (Pounding in a Mortar) (Prov. 27:22; II Macc. 6:30) or running over the victim with an iron sledge (II Kings 8:12; 10:32,33; Amos 1:3,4; II Sam. 12:31; I Chron. 20:3).

e. Flaying (mentioned figuratively in Micah 3:2,3). Taking the skin off people in punishment is historically verified as a method of Assyrian punishment.

f. Imprisonment (not used by the early Israelites except to hold the accused in custody to await trial and further disposition). Imprisonment was clearly used by heathen cultures and by the later Israelites. (Gen. 39:20,21; Lev. 24:12; Num. 15:34; Acts 4:2; 12:4; Jdgs. 16:21; Ezra 7:26; Jer. 37:15; Matt. 18:30; Jer. 37:21; 38:6; I Kings 22:27; II Chron. 16:10; Matt. 4:12; Luke 23:19; Jer. 37:16; Zech. 9:11; Acts 16:24; Job 31:18; Psa. 105:18; 107:10; Jer. 40:4).

g. Indignities (various means were used to heap indignities and humiliations upon criminals — usually after they were dead: Josephus Antiq. IV; 8;6; I Kings 14:13; II Kings 9:10; 21:18,26; II Chron. 24:25; Jer. 22:19; Psa. 79:2,3; I Sam. 17:57; 31:9; Josh. 7:15,25; Lev. 20:14; Amos 2:1; II Sam. 4:12; Gen. 40:17-19; Num. 25:4,5; Deut. 21:22,23; Joshua 7:25,26; 8:29; II Sam. 18:17). Indignities such as spitting were assessed as "punishments" (Num. 12:14; Deut. 25:9; Matt. 26:27; Mark 14:65; 15:19; Luke 18:32; Isa. 50:6).

h. Mutilation (Deut. 25:11,12; Jdgs. 1:6,7; II Sam. 4:12; Dan. 2:5; II Macc. 7:1-40; I Sam. 18:27; Ezek. 23:25; II Chron. 33:11; Isa. 37:29; Ezek. 19:4,9; Amos 4:2).

j. Pulling Out the Hair of the Head (Neh. 13:25; Isa. 50:6; II Macc. 7:7; II Sam. 10:4; Job. 30:10; Matt. 27:30; Mark 12:4) and of the Face.

CRIME AND PUNISHMENT

k. Retaliation (Exod. 21:24,25; Lev. 24:19-22; Deut. 19:19; 24:16; Dan. 6:24; I Kings 21:21; II Kings 9:26).

l. Scourging (Jdgs. 8:7,16; I Kings 12:11; see also Job 9:23; Isa. 10:26; 28:15,18; John 2:15; Matt. 10:17; 20:19; Mark 10:34; Luke 18:33; Matt. 23:34; Acts 22:25; Lev. 19:20; Matt. 27:26; Mark 15:15; John 19:1; Heb. 11:36).

m. Slavery (Exod. 22:4; II Sam. 12:31; II Kings 4:1; Neh. 5:5; see also Lev. 25:39-43; Deut. 15:12; Jer. 34:14; Gen. 44:17).

n. Stocks (II Chron 16:10; Jer. 20:2; 27:2; 29:26; see also Job 13:27; 33:11; Prov. 7:22; Acts 16:24). It was a device usually containing five holes for the neck, arms and legs which were sometimes inserted crosswise.

o. Stripes (similar to Beating and Flaying) (Lev. 19:20; Deut. 22:18; 25:3; II Cor. 11:24). It was the most common mode of corporal punishment and the idea of disgrace apparently was not associated with it (see Josephus Antiq. IV; 8:21) (see also Prov. 17:26; 10:13; Jer. 20:2; 37:15; Matt. 5:25; 18:34; Deut. 28:58,59; Psa. 78:38). In later times the adult male was stripped to the waist and in a bending posture lashed to a pillar; a female received the stripes (40 less one) while sitting with head and shoulders bent forward; and a boy was punished with his hands tied behind him. Roman law forbade the whipping of Roman citizens (Acts 16:37; 22:25). Nevertheless it was regarded as a wholesome punishment and is zealously advocated in Proverbs 13:24; 20:30; 23:13,14; Psalm 89:32.

By far the most frequent punishment for non-capital crimes was *restitution*. The victim was to be paid back in full, and in some cases more than in full. Compensation was always to be made to the victim — not to the "state," therefore it is *not* proper to say that *fines* were a method of punishment in Mosaic law.

The kinds of offenses which resulted in restitution included both property offenses (such as theft) and violent crimes (such as battery). Most of Exodus 21-22 is devoted to various cases of restitution. The Mosaic system of restitution was an elaborate one. As far as possible the restoration was to be identical with or comparable with the loss of time or power (Exod. 21:18-36; Lev. 24:18-21; Deut. 19:21). The person who stole an ox and then sold or killed it had to restore fivefold; if it was a live sheep, fourfold. In later history it appears as if sevenfold might be the standard (Prov. 6:31; II Sam. 12:6). If the identical animal which was stolen was restored, another of equal value was all that the law required besides. For breach of trust or for trespass, twenty percent additional to the original sum was demanded (Lev. 6:1-5; Num. 5:5-10). Restitution or "damages" must be paid for destruction by an animal broken loose from its confinement (Exod. 22:5) and when an animal killed a servant, thirty shekels had to be paid to the loser (Exod. 21:32; Deut. 22:19). Compensation was demanded for loss by fire, through negligence, of a standing grain field; or for the loss or damage to a "pledge" (personal property held as security, Exod. 22:5,12). Under Roman law a jailer losing his prisoner was liable to the punishment which was to be inflicted for the crime on which the arrest had been made (Acts 12:19; 16:27). Zacchaeus promised to restore fourfold for any fradulent exactions of which he might be guilty (Luke 19:8). Jesus refers to restitution (Matt. 5:25,26) as a form of punishment.

Restitution as punishment for crime is Biblically sanctioned. Clearly, God prefers restitution above all other methods of punishment as a resolution to crime and injustice. In view of this one wonders why civil governments today claiming "christian" principles for "foundations" are not instituting an expanded program of criminal justice that requires the criminal to make restitution to the victim of his crime. Perhaps this will explain:

> It is surprising to most people that early legal systems which form the foundation of Western law emphasized the need for offenders and their families to settle with victims and their families. The offense was considered principally a violation against the victim and the victim's family. While the common welfare had been breached and the community therefore had an interest and responsibility in seeing that the wrong was addressed and the of-

fender punished, the offense was not considered primarily a crime against the state as it is today.

Old Testament law emphasized that the victim be repaid through restitution.

The Code of Hammurabi (around 1700 B.C.), a collection of Babylonian laws, provided for restitution in the case of property crimes.

The Code of Ur-Nammu, a Sumerian king (around 2050 B.C.), included provisions for restitution even in the case of violent offenses.

In the Code of Lipit-Ishtar (around 1875 B.C.), the king of Isin required restitution when a householder neglected to maintain his property and as a result someone was able to break into the house of a neighbor. He was required to compensate the neighbor for his losses.

The Code of Eshnunna (around 1700 B.C.), a Mesopotamian kingdom, provided for specific compensation when the victim lost his nose, his eye, his ear, or a tooth.

In the ninth book of the Iliad, Homer (around the ninth century B.C.) refers to the practice of victim restitution. Ajax challenges Achilles for not accepting compensation offered by Agamemnon, noting that even the murderer of a brother may, by paying compensation, remain free among his own family.

Roman law also required compensation of the victim. According to the Law of the Twelve Tables (449 B.C.), convicted thieves had to pay double the value of the stolen goods. If the property was discovered hidden in the thief's house, he had to pay three times its value. If he had resisted the house search, or if he had stolen the object using force, he had to pay four times its value.

The Roman historian Tacitus (roughly A.D. 55 to A.D. 117) wrote that among ancient Germanic tribes even murder was punished by paying a fine of cattle and sheep, and that this satisfied the family of the murder victim, since ongoing feuds were destructive of the community.

The earliest surviving collection of Germanic tribal laws is the *Lex Salica*, promulgated by King Clovis soon after his conversion to Christianity in A.D. 496. It includes restitutionary sanctions for offenses ranging from homicides to assaults to theft.

Anglo-Saxon law developed elaborate systems of compensation. Around A.D. 600, Ethelbert, ruler of Kent, issued the Laws of Ethelbert. They contain remarkably detailed restitution schedules, differentiating, for example, the value of the four front teeth from those next to them, and those teeth from all the rest. Each finger (and its fingernail) had a specified value.

In each of these diverse cultures the response to what we now call "crime" was to hold offenders and their families accountable to victims and their families. Crime was understood to be an event involving the parties, as well as their kin, in the context of the community. This reflected a basic understanding that a relationship existed between victims and offenders, and that this relationship needed to be addressed in responding to the wrong. Victims were a key part of the process for pragmatic reasons (they and their families insisted on this), but also for reasons of simple justice — no adequate response to the crime could exclude the victim.

The Norman Conquest of Europe marked the beginning of the end of this approach. When William the Conqueror became king of England, he took title to all land. He then portioned it out to his supporters and to the church. He and his descendants asserted increasing control over the process by which crimes and other judicial matters were disposed of.

But where earlier developments were designed to keep family feuds from tearing apart the community, King William and his descendants were struggling for control of the legal process for the sake of political power. They were replacing local systems of dispute resolution (established by the barons) and were competing with the growing influence of the church over secular matters. The church had issued the Canon Law, which comprehensively regulated every dimension of life. The secular authorities responded to this by creating similar law codes.

A mechanism which the English kings successfully used in this struggle for control was the "king's peace." King Henry I, the son of William the Conqueror, issued the *Leges Henrici* in 1116. These laws established thirty judicial districts throughout the country and gave them jurisdiction over "certain offenses *against the king's peace*, arson, robbery, murder, false coinage, and crimes of violence."

Anything which jeopardized this peace became a subject of the king's jurisdiction. This gave the king control over criminal cases as breaches of that peace. Criminal punishments were no longer viewed primarily as ways of restoring the victims of crime, but instead as means of redressing the "injury" to the king.

The king not only gained power, he also enriched his treasury.

Because of the existing emphasis on compensating victims, the early codes required restitution but confiscated some of the payments for the king's treasury. Over time, the amount confiscated from the victim increased, and eventually restitution was seldom ordered — the defendant was simply fined.

Furthermore, feudal custom held that when a vassal "broke faith" with his ruler, his possessions reverted to the lord — this was called *escheat*.

The Norman word for such a breach of faith was "felony." In England after the Norman Conquest the most serious crimes came to be called felonies because they were considered to be breaches of the fealty owed by all people to the king as guardian of the realm. (The felon's land escheated to his lord, however, and only his chattel to the crown.)

As a result, *the victim had no remedy*. The criminal proceeding generated fines for the king. In felony cases, conviction meant that *all* the offender's property reverted to his lord and to the king. The victim would have no way to recover through civil action against the impoverished offender.

The punishment of crime had become the province of the state. Recovery by the victim was a private matter to be settled in the civil courts. The state's interest in criminal cases was in fixing the responsibility of the offenders and punishing them, not restoring the victims. The role of victims was only to help establish that a wrong had been done.

The "golden age of the victim" — the period when the system of justice emphasized compensation to the victim — had ended. It was replaced with what could be called the "golden age of the state," which continues today. Now the *criminal* justice system emphasizes controlling the injury to the state through various forms of punishment designed to deter, incapacitate or reform criminals. If victims want to recover their losses, they must sue in civil courts.

Crime and Its Victims, by Daniel W. Van Ness,
pub. IVP, pp. 64-68.

Once again what the Bible says about civil government appears to be more reasonable, more just, and more practical than the so-called "enlightened" criminal justice systems of today. Punishment of crimes (except for capital crimes such as murder, etc.) by *restitution* or *recompense* to the individual victims would restore well-being and what is right. That would be justice for the victim as well as for the state. Actually, the "state" receives true and ultimate justice *only* when the individual victim receives it — because the "state" would not exist without its individual citizens.

Restitution would require responsibility from the offender to both the victim and the state. That would restore human dignity to both the offender and the victim, for human dignity is present only where responsibility is accepted and justice is done. Restitution might also produce some rehabilitation in some offenders. But rehabilitation is not the primary purpose of any form of punishment — the restoration of justice (rightness) is. Restitution might serve as a deterrent to crime. Any punishment has some measure of deterrence effectiveness. But, again, restitution's primary function is to restore the factor of justice. Individuals must expect and receive justice if they are to dwell together in a functional, edifying society. Law does not serve society if it does not serve the individual.

The Bible does not equivocate on crime and punishment. It realistically reveals man as not only capable of crime, it documents the commission of numerous crimes — some of them of the most heinous nature. The Bible also clearly prescribes punishment, in principle and specifically, as an obligation of civil government.

Every possible criminal deviation which men may devise is not, of course, catalogued in the Bible. Nor is every acceptable method of punishment codified there. But all the fundamentals and principles of criminality and punishment are revealed so that any civil government desiring to fulfill its "ministry" as Almighty God has ordained it may do so.

We close this chapter with two long quotations — one concerning capital punishment, the other concerning restitution as a form of punishment: Following is the text of a speech made by Mr. Theodore L. Sendak, Attorney General of the state of Indiana, before the Law Enforcement Luncheon Meeting of Officials of Northern Indiana at Wabash, Indiana, May 12, 1971:

The purpose of our system of criminal law is to minimize the quantity of human suffering by maintaining a framework of order and peace. The primary object of the law in this area is to forestall acts of violence or other aggression by which one person inflicts harm on another. To the extent that government fails to do this, the primary function of the state is neglected, and individual suffering is increased.

The question we must ask ourselves about the death penalty is: which of several possible courses of action will serve the true humanitarian purposes of the criminal law? We must weigh the execution of the convicted murderer against the loss of life of his victims and of the possible victims of other potential murderers.

Many factors enter into the perpetuation of crime, some of which are obviously beyond the bounds of social control. And it is true that some murders occur under circumstances which no system of penalties can prevent. Yet the objective, statistical evidence available to all indicates one major factor in the commission of crime is the relative probability of punishment *or* escape. If punishment is certain, the impulse to crime is to some extent checked. If escape seems probable, the criminal impulse has freer reign.

The propaganda drive to abolish capital punishment appears to be a geared part of a general drive toward leniency in the treatment of criminals in our society. Such leniency has had in my opinion, undeniable psychological impact on potential murderers, and has contributed to the upward spiral of the crime rate. There is a striking over-all correlation between the recent decline in the use of the death penalty and the rise in violent crime. Such crime has increased by geometric proportions.

In the first three years of the last decade, the number of executions in the United States was by present standards relatively high. Fifty-six persons were executed in 1960; 42 in 1961; and 47 in 1962. During these same three years the number of people who died violently at the hands of criminals actually declined and the murder rate per 100,000 of population also declined.

Beginning in 1963, however, there was a drop in the number of legal executions, and the graph line of violent crime simultaneously began moving up instead of down. In the following years the number of legal executions has decreased dramatically from one year to the next, until in 1968 there was none at all. But each of these years has seen murders increase sharply both in absolute numbers and as a percentage of population.

In 1964, for example, the number of legal executions dropped to 15. Yet the number of violent deaths moved up from 8,500 to 9,250, and the murder rate per 100,000 went up from 4.5 to 4.8. In 1965 the number of legal executions dropped to seven, while the number of violent deaths increased to 9,850, and the murder rate went to 5.1. Similar decreases in legal executions have occurred in the following years, accompanied by similar increases in the murder rate.

In 1968, with no legal executions at all, the total number who died through criminal violence reached 13,650, while the murder rate climbed to 6.8 per 100,000.

The movement in these figures, with murders increasing as the deterrence of the death penalty diminished, confirms the verdict of ordinary logic: That a relaxation in the severity and certainty of punishment leads only to an increase in crime.

These remarks concern the deterrent effect of the death penalty on those who might commit murder but do not. That is a negative phenomenon which can be inferred both from the record and the assessment of common sense. The repeal of the death penalty would not repeal human nature. To these truisms we may add the fact that there are numerous cases on record in which criminals have escaped the capital penalty for previous murders and gone on to commit others.

Likewise there are numerous cases of prison inmates who have killed guards and other inmates, knowing that the worst punishment they could get would be continued tenancy in the same institution. Opponents of the death penalty ususally resist even life sentences without parole, and the deterrent function of that would be even less effective than capital punishment.

The general growth of violent crime in the past decade is the out cropping of the attitude of permissiveness and leniency going hand in hand with an increase in the rate of victimization. As more and more loopholes have been devised for defendants, the crime rate has increased steeply.

Between 1960 and 1968, the over-all crime rate in America increased 11 times as fast as the rate of population growth — plainly meaning that more and more people are being subjected every day of every year to major personal crimes — murder, rape, assault, kidnapping, armed robbery, etc.

Is a course of action humanitarian which actually encourages a vast and continuing increase in the number of people killed and maimed and otherwise brutalized?

There have been many sentimental journeys into the psychological realm of the criminals who are to be executed; I think there should be more sympathetic concern expressed for the thousands of innocent victims of those criminals.

Opponents of the death penalty may rejoice that in 1968 there were 47 fewer murderers executed in this country than was the case in 1962. But do they say anything of the fact that some 5,250 more innocent persons died by criminal violence in 1968 than was the case in 1962?

In the question of human suffering, this is a staggering loss of more than 5,000 individual innocent lives. What about the human rights and civil rights of the individual victim? Are not those 5,000 persons entitled to the dignity and sacredness of life? Is that a result of which humanitarians can be proud? I think not.

Only misguided emotionalism, and not facts, disputes the truth that the death penalty is a deterrent of capital crime.

Individuals must be held responsible for their individual actions if a free society is to endure.

Ethical Arguments For Analysis, by Baum and Randell, pub. Holt, Rinehart, Winston, pp. 112,113

Our final quotation is an article by Jenkin Lloyd Jones, former editor of the Tulsa, Oklahoma, newspaper, *The Tulsa Tribune*, entitled, "The Pay-Back Crime Code," dated 1971:

Senator Mike Mansfield and Rep. William Green of Pennsylvania have introduced bills in Congress that would appropriate federal money for the relief of the victims of criminals.

The proposed legislation would not only provide funds to victims of crimes under federal jurisdiction, but it would supplement payments which the legislatures of six states have now authorized for the victims of state law infractions.

Crime compensation at taxpayer expense is getting popular. Britain, New Zealand, Sweden and seven Canadian provinces have now enacted such laws.

There is, indeed, little logic in freely spending public money to enable the criminal to perfect his defense, while leaving the bleeding victim to borrow money to overcome his lost earnings and the cost of doctors and hospitals.

But the idea can be improved. It can be improved by going back to the first principle of ancient law — the principle that it is the perpetrator of the crime who has the primary obligation to the victim.

In ancient days the idea of paying damages was not limited to civil law. Hammurabi and Draco understood that a criminal was not merely the enemy of the people as a whole, but was a particular debtor to his victim. Draco provided for fines in oxen, not to be paid to the state, but to the aggrieved party.

A couple of weeks ago Dr. John Kielbauch, prison psychologist, resigned from the Oklahoma Department of Corrections to take a position in the federal penal system. And in departing, he made a few radical suggestions:

It is time, he said, that the man who robs or injures makes direct restitution. To this end, he proposed that the courts determine proper compensation and that the state set up elaborate training programs and prison industries which would enable the prisoner to earn real money in behalf of those he had wronged. Dr. Kielbauch suggests indeterminate sentences, the duration of which would largely depend on the efforts the prisoner would make toward full restitution. He adds that if a prisoner is released or paroled before this restitution is completed, a portion of his outside wages could be deducted.

The trouble with most prison job-training programs, according to Dr. Kielbauch, is that many prisoners associate the training with their punishment. This gives them a negative attitude toward useful work. They develop skills reluctantly and slowly and often turn their backs on them when they hit the street.

If, on the other hand, hard work and the acquisition of marketable trades became their keys to freedom, this might put shop training in a different light.

If a court can decide that the man who suffers a broken arm has $1,000 coming to him from the non-criminal who hit him with his car, why shouldn't the criminal who breaks an arm in a brutal assault also owe the victim $1,000?

And there have been too many cases where robbers who have made big scores have sat out their prison years in the smug confidence that the caches will be waiting for them when they emerge. If full restitutiton is insisted upon the profit vanishes.

Since a law was passed in Michigan making parents financially liable for the depredations of their minor children the incidence of juvenile vandalism in Detroit has turned down remarkably. Parents who were quite casual about scolding in juvenile court began to take a lively interest in the behavior of their young as soon as they received bills from the school board for wrecked classrooms.

Money may be the root of all evil, but the possibilities of using money as a means of discouraging evil have been underexplored in America. The trouble with the bills proposed by Sen. Mansfield and Rep. Green is that they would load upon the blameless taxpayer the indemnity for the victims of crime.

What's wrong with charging the criminal?

Paying one's debt to society would then take on a new and more practical meaning.

And it's about time.

Ethical Arguments For Analysis, by Baum and Randell, pub. Hold, Rinehart, Winston, pp. 112,113

5

WAR

Two Hebrew words are translated "war" (also translated, "fight") in the Old Testament: (1) *lacham*; the verb, appears 171 times in the Old Testament, and appears first in Exodus 1:10; (2) *milechamah*; the noun, appears 315 times in the Old Testament and first appears in Genesis 14:2. The combination of Hebrew words *'aneshey milechamah* is translated "men of war" or "soldiers." In the Greek New Testament five words are used: (1) *polemeo*; a verb meaning, "to fight, to make war (Rev. 12:7; 13:4; 17:14; 19:11; James 4:2 etc.); (2) *strateuo*, a verb used in the middle voice to mean "to make war" (from *stratos*, "an encamped army," II Cor. 10:3; I Tim. 1:18; II Tim. 2:3; Jas. 4:1; I Pet. 2:11); (3) *antistrateuomai*, verb, "to make war against" (Rom. 7:23); (4) *polemos*, a noun, "war" (related to *polemeo*) (I Cor. 14:8; Rev. 9:7,9; 16:14; 20:8; Heb. 11:34; James 4:1; Matt. 24:6; Rev. 11:7); (5) *strateia*, noun, primarily translated "a host" or "an army", the word came to denote "warfare" (II

Cor. 10:4; I Tim. 1:18). The Greek words defined above have been *transliterated* to form our English words *polemics* (in English, "controversy"), and *strategy* (in English, "the science of employing an armed force").

The first war, as such, recorded in the Bible is the one "in the days of Amraphel, king of Shinar, Arioch king of Ellasar, Chedor-laomer king of Elam, and Tidal king of Goiim . . . these kings made war (Hebrew word *milechamah*) with Bera king of Sodom, Birsha king of Gomorrah, Shinab king of Admah, Shemeber king of Zeboiim, and the king of Bela (that is, Zoar)" (Gen. 14:1,2). The same Hebrew word, *milechamah*, is translated "battle" in Genesis 14:8.

From the boasting of Lamech (Gen. 4:23) we may understand that there were "wars" before the Deluge. Certainly if "the wickedness of man was great in the earth, and . . . every imagination of the thoughts of his heart was only evil continually . . . " prior to the Deluge, there must have been much warfare between families (clans) or tribes. That there was "strife" (Heb. *riyv*, "quarreling, disturbance") even between relatives and their clans is demonstrated in the disturbance between Lot's herdsmen and Abraham's (Gen. 13:7,8).

> Every phase of Israel's life, including her warfare, was bound up with her God. War therefore had religious significance. It was customary for priests to accompany Israel's armies into battle (Deut. 20:1-4). Campaigns were begun and engagements entered into with sacrificial rites (I Sam. 7:8-10; 13:9), and after consulting the oracle (Jdgs. 20:18ff; I Sam. 14:37; 23:2; 28:6; 30:8). Prophets were sometimes asked for guidance before a campaign (I Kings 22:5; II Kings 3:11).
>
> The blowing of a trumpet throughout the land announced the call to arms (Jdgs. 3:27; I Sam. 13:3; II Sam. 15:10;), and priests sounded an alarm with trumpets (II Chron. 13:12-16). Weapons included slings, spears, javelins, bows and arrows, swords and battering-rams. Strategical movements included the ambush (Josh. 8:3ff); the raid (I Chron. 14:9); the foray (II Sam. 3:22); and foraging to secure supplies (II Sam. 23:11). Sometimes when

opposing armies were drawn up in battle array, champions from each side fought one another (I Sam. 17). Armies engaged in hand to hand combat. Victorious armies pillaged the camp of the enemy, robbed the dead (Jdgs. 8:24-26; I Sam. 31:9; II Chron. 20:25), and often killed or mutilated prisoners (Josh. 8:23,29; 10:22-27; Jdgs. 1:6), although prisoners were usually sold into slavery. Booty was divided equally between those who had taken part in the battle and those who had been left behind in camp (Num. 31:27; Josh. 22:8; I Sam. 30:24ff), but some of the spoils were reserved for the Levites and for the Lord (Num. 31:28,30).

When a city was besieged, the besiegers cast up huge mounds of earth against the walls from which battering-rams were brought into play against the walls (II Sam. 20:15; Ezek. 4:2). The besieged tried to drive off the enemy by throwing darts and stones and shooting arrows at them from the walls. Captured cities were often completely destroyed, and victory was celebrated with song and dance (Exod. 15:1-21; Jdgs. 5; I Sam. 18:6).

Jesus accepted war as an inevitable part of the present sinful world order (Matt. 24:6), but warned that those that take the sword must perish by it (Matt. 26:52). In the epistles the Christian is said to be a soldier (II Tim. 2:3; I Pet. 2:11). The Apocalypse uses the figure of battle and war to describe the . . . triumph of Christ . . . " (Rev. 16:14-16; 17:14; 19:14).

Zondervan Pictorial Bible Dictionary, Gen. Ed. Merrill C. Tenney, article on "War", pp. 885,886

A. THE ORIGIN OF WAR

1. War began with the *devil* (Rev. 12:7). At some point, because of pride and conceit (I Tim. 3:6,7) the devil, one of God's created beings, and other creatures of the angelic order, all, like man, created with the power of choice, rebelled against the "position" or "place" where God had ordained they should serve (II Pet. 2:4; Jude 6). They were hostile to God and became enemies of the sovereign rule of Jehovah. The devil was a "murderer from the (his) beginning" (John 8:44) — there is no truth in him at all — he is the "father of lies." Since the devil was only a creature, not the Creator, he was defeated and evidently

banished from the presence of God into a "chained" (limited, restricted but not completely) realm of "darkness" where he awaits the execution of "eternal death" (Rev. 20:9,10). In the meantime, the devil goes about tempting and trying to seduce (apparently with much success) mankind to join him in his rebellion against Almighty God. In this effort (which the Bible repeatedly classifies as a spiritual "warfare" Eph. 6:10ff; II Cor. 10:3-5; Gal. 5:16,17; Rom. 7:15-25; 8:5-8, etc.) the devil aims his seduction at the *mind* of man. The battle is there — in thought, in mind, in perspective (see also II Cor. 2:11; 11:3, etc.). His strategy is to seduce man into concentrating his thinking and his desires and his energies on indulging and glorifying the flesh. He tempts man to *get things*, to *glorify himself*, as the sum-total of human existence. The devil began this in the Garden of Eden (Gen. 3:1ff) and he has kept it up for all these millennia (Rom. 8:5-8; I John 2:15-17); he even tried to seduce the Lord Jesus Christ with the "big lie" (Matt. 4:1-11; Luke 4:1-13). The Lord won the victory over the devil by trusting completely in the promise of the Father (John 12:27-32; 16:11; Col. 2:14-18; Rom. 12:1,2, etc.). Jesus has made his victory available to all men by his grace and our faith. But millions, yea, billions, of people are still on the side of the devil in this cosmic war for the human soul either because they have not heard that victory is available, or because they have heard and deliberately rejected it.

2. Mankind, in unbelief, perpetuates this rebellion against God (called *sin* in the Bible). And this constantly results in what the world calls *war*. James gives the clearest explanation of the *cause* of war when he writes:

> What causes wars, and what causes fightings among you? Is it not your passions that are at war in your members? You desire and do not have; so you kill. And you covet and cannot obtain; so you fight and wage war. You do not have, because you do not ask. You ask and do not receive, because you ask wrongly, to spend it on your passions. Unfaithful creatures! Do you not know that

friendship with the world is enmity with God? Therefore whoever wishes to be a friend of the world makes himself an enemy of God (James 4:1-4).

Several interesting Greek words are used by James in this text. The first is *polemoi*, the Greek word (as already discussed) most often used for "war." The next word is *machai*, translated "fightings," probably akin to the Greek word *machaira* translated "sword" (Matt. 26:47,51,52; Luke 21:24; 22:38). The most interesting word in this text, however, is *hedonon* translated "passions"; it is the word from which we get the English word *hedonism*. Hedonism is the "doctrine that pleasure is the sole or chief good in life and that moral duty is fulfilled in the gratification of pleasure-seeking instincts and dispositions." It is in direct opposition to Romans 13:14 — ". . . make no provision for the flesh to gratify its desires" (see also Gal. 5:17,18; I Pet. 2:11). Very clearly, James states that *hedonism* (worldly-mindedness) is the *cause* of war! The desire to gratify fleshly instincts (Gal. 5:19-21) produces war — whether between individuals or nations — and that is the fundamental cause. War is *not* caused by circumstances, but by attitudes! It is *not* poverty or overpopulation or genetic makeup that *causes* war — it is unbelief. The cause of war is in the heart of man. It is caused by the creature's rebellion against God's call for sublimation of the physical and exaltation of the spiritual. Between the "flesh" and the spirit there is constant war (Rom. 7:13-23; 8:5-8) and that internal war in the human rebel inevitably spills over into inter-personal, social and international relationships. War against God causes war against man.

Other scriptures help us understand the causes of war:

1. War, hostility, malice and hatred get into men's hearts (Psa. 55:21; 140:2).
2. Men covet, envy, lust after "tribute" and make war to get what they desire (Psa. 68:30; Micah 2:8; 3:5).

3. War is learned (Isa. 2:4; Micah 4:3); man is not born to be at war.
4. Some men make war their god (Dan. 11:37-39); they worship the power war appears to give them. They love to conquer and dominate (Rev. 6:1-4).
5. There are, of course, times when nations must engage in wars to defend themselves or helpless neighbors who have been attacked without provocation (see Neh. 4:14; Esther 8:11ff; 9:2; II Chron. 20:1ff; I Sam. 30:1ff; Josh. 10:6-11). Such defensive wars are not only justified by Scripture, God apparently condemns any nation that "stands aloof" (Obadiah vv. 11-14) when a neighboring country is being attacked (see also Amos 1:9). But God-fearing men do not start wars.

Wars of aggression are begun by persons, individuals, who are impenitent and unregenerate in their heart. Circumstances permitting, and sufficient wicked-hearted "comrades" available, war-minded individuals grasp as much power as peace-loving (often naive, unprepared, and sometimes pacifistic) people will permit. That is when war starts. A classic case in point is the rebellion of Absalom against his father David (II Sam. 14-18).

It is no coincidence that secular thinking confirms exactly what the Bible says to be the cause of war:

> In modern times no nation or group chooses war if it can get what it wants peacefully. The fighting starts when a nation wants something so badly that it is willing to go to war to get it. Sometimes war results from a disagreement between two nations, and sometimes from a desire for conquest. Some basic causes may be a desire for more land, a desire for more wealth, a desire for more power, or a desire for security.
>
> In a nation disputes are settled in a court, but there has never been an effective law *between countries*. War exists where there is no law.
>
> *World Book Encyclopedia, Vol. 20, article on "War" pp. 20-22, 1964 ed.*

B. THE BIBLICAL PERSPECTIVE ON WAR

God is for peace. His very nature is peace (Rom. 15:33; 16:20; II Cor. 13:11; Phil. 4:9; I Thess. 5:23; Heb. 13:20; Rom. 14:17,19; I Cor. 7:15; 14:33; Eph. 2:14,15,17; Phil. 4:7; Col. 3:15; II Tim. 2:22; Heb. 12:14, etc.). The Bible says that only "peacemakers" shall be called the "sons of God" (Matt. 5:9). *But there are two kinds of peace in the Bible.* There is first the peace which God imputes to us by divine fiat, our justification, reconciliation and salvation. That peace is a result of the breaking down of "hostility" Christ accomplished through his vicarious death and which we appropriate by faith (Eph. 2:11ff). It is not like the "peace of the world" (John 14:27; 16:33). This redemption at work in us through our faith produces a subjective peace that "passes understanding" (Phil. 4:7).

1. When the Bible speaks of "peace" as it relates to civil governments and physical nations (or tribes), it is speaking realistically of a peace that is maintained by the coercive powers of nations and groups of nations in alliance against aggressive, war-making foes. The Bible denounces aggressive war. War is evil. It produces evil, destructive consequences, and never settles any issues permanently. Great masses of innocent people suffer when wars are started. This suffering inevitably passes on to many succeeding generations. The Bible plainly declares that those who deliberately, without just provocation, make aggressive war, will suffer the judgment of Almighty God — it is their "due" (see Amos 1:1-2:3; Isa. 10:15-19; 14:3-27; Jer. 51:1-64; Nahum 1:1-3:19; Rev. 16:4-7; 18:1-24, etc.). God hates war, but the Bible is absolutely *realistic*, and acknowledges that as long as this world exists and there are unregenerate people inhabiting it, there will be wars. Jesus warned his followers to be realistic, too. He said, "There will be wars and rumors of wars" (Matt. 24:4-8). This he said in a context anticipating circumstances which would precede the destruction of Jerusalem and Judasim. But he said it as a warning that Christians should not get the idea that because

the Messiah had come in the flesh and the messianic age was about to be initiated was no reason to expect a war-less society. The risen and enthroned Christ wrote the seven churches of Asia Minor (Revelation) to expect war as a result of Rome's insatiable hunger to "conquer" (Rev. 6:1-4). It would be redundant to cite all the passages in the Old Testament which present the same viewpoint. So, we must mark down first that the biblical perspective on war is candid and realistic. As long as there are unreconciled sinners in the world there will be wars.

2. The biblical perspective on war from the Old Testament, while "theocratic" or theomorphic, it is not exclusively so:

> The Old Testament teaching of aggresive war has encouraged many Christians to engage in armed conflict. These individuals, however, fail to realize that Israel was a theocratic state that went to war at the command of God. In modern times there is no state whose king is God. The Israelites not only fought to take the land according to divine promise, but they also struggled to execute judgment on the wicked people who live there. The reasons for this are cloaked in mystery because it cannot be established historically that the Canaanites were more morally corrupt than other ancient peoples. It is simply stated in the Bible that they were especially deserving of punishment. God used the Israelites to conquer them as he was later to use foreign nations to bring judgment on his own people.
>
> *War, Four Christian Views*, ed. by Robert G. Clouse, pub. IVP, p. 10

The "Canaanites" are found in Egyptian history as early as 1800 B.C. They are earlier than that in Biblical history for they were already in the land of Palestine when Abraham arrived there (approx. 2000 B.C.). "Canaanite" was a term generally applied to a number of people (Amorites, Hittites, Perizzites, Jebusites, etc.) inhabiting Palestine. In Genesis 12:6; 24:3,37; Joshua 3:10 the term "Canaanite" includes the whole pre-Israelite population, even that east of the Jordan River. They were of Semitic stock, and were part of a large migration of Semites (Phoenicians, Amorites, even Chaldeans) from northeast Arabia and Mesopotamia at approximately the same time of Abram's migration from Ur of Chaldea. These peoples (including the Amalekites who dwelt mainly in the Negeb) became nomadic marauding tribes practicing violent aggressive warfare, grossly perverted religious customs, and were generally inhuman. Peter's description of some people as "irrational animals, creatures of instinct, born to be caught and killed . . . " (II Pet. 2:12) would aptly describe the Canaanites. The Lord directed Moses to describe the Canaanites (Lev. 1:1-23) as a people guilty of pervasive incest, homosexuality, beastiality, and continual sacrifice of human beings (in the foundation of every newly built Canaanite home there was entombed the body of a child which had been sacrificed to their gods to ward off "evil spirits").

Canaanites and Amalekites were guilty of unprovoked and unmerciful warfare against neighboring tribes and nations (Gen. 20:11; 21:25; 26:12-22; Exod. 17:8ff; Num. 14:45; Jdgs. 3:13; 6:3,33; 12:15; I Sam. 30:18). There is documentation of the wars, invasions, dispossessions and atrocities which took place in the land of Canaan and its environs *prior* to Israel's entrance (Deut. 2:23-37; 3:1ff). While God put Israel into Canaan for theological and redemptive reasons, at the same time, Israel's "invasion" and her wars with Canaan's inhabitants were defensive (Num. 21:21ff; 31:1ff; 33:50ff) and punitive. There seems to be a long-standing acknowledgment that the Israelites had some civil or judicial claim to the land — Rahab acknowledged it (Josh. 2:8-14).

The warfare to which the Israelites were subjected was also, in the divine purpose, to "discipline" God's people and instill within them a grateful heart (see Deut. 4:32-40; 8:1ff; Jdgs. 3:2). When Israel was forming itself as a nation in the "land of Goshen" (Egypt), the Pharaoh who wanted to enslave them said, "Behold the people of Israel are too many and too mighty for us. Come, let us deal shrewdly with them, lest they multiply and, if war befall us, they join our enemies and fight against us and escape from the land" (Exod. 1:10). So he ordered that all the Hebrews be enslaved and worked (to death) to depopulate them. That did not work so he ordered all Hebrew males to be slain at birth. The Hebrew midwives would not do that. Ultimately, God waged war on Pharaoh with plagues, hardened his heart, and had to deliver Israel from oppression and genocide by miraculously drowning Pharaoh and his pursuing army. Israel, a nation of over one million people, wandered in the Sinai wilderness for 40 years doing battle occasionally in defense against maurading Semitic tribes. They had to have a "homeland." God had already promised Canaan to them (through Abraham). Wherever they went, there was war. Their very presence provoked war. The Hebrews were not, essentially a war-loving people. The Lord would *not* lead them to Canaan "by way of the land of the Philistines, although that was near; for God said, Lest the people repent when they see war, and return to Egypt" (Exod. 13:17). The Lord hardened the hearts of the Canaanites "that they should come against Israel in battle" so that Israel should utterly destroy them (Josh. 11:18-20). Thus, Israel's *warfare* in conquering Canaan, while theomorphic, was *not*, from Israel's perspective, unprovoked aggression. It could be classified from the very first, in a sense, inescapable and defensive.

The New Strong's Exhaustive Concordance of the Bible, by Nelson, 1948, lists the words "War(s), Warring, Warfare" 259 times; the words "Fight, Fighting(s), Fighteth" 113 times; and the words "Battle(s), Battlement" 178 times. Some few of these uses are figurative or illustrative, but for the most part they are used to record or predict actual, physical wars and battles. That is a total usage of 550 times! And, according to the same concordance, the Bible uses the words "peace, peaceable, peaceably, peacemaker" only 541 times! It may surprise even some Bible scholars to know that the Bible uses "war" words more than it uses "peace."

An important point to make about the Old Testament perspective on war is the commandment the Lord gave Israel:

WAR

> When you draw near to a city to fight against it, offer terms of peace to it. And if its answer to you is peace and it opens to you, then all the people who are found in it shall do forced labor for you and shall serve you. But if it makes no peace with you, but makes war against you, then you shall besiege it; and when the Lord your God gives it into your hand you shall put all its males to the sword, but the women and the little ones, the cattle, and everything else in the city, all its spoil, you shall take as booty for yourselves; and you shall enjoy the spoil of your enemies, which the Lord your God has given you (Deut. 20:10-14).

In giving Israel the land of Canaan for theological reasons, the Lord did not sanction atrocities and unwarranted blood-letting. War was only a last resort in his program to put Israel in the land where their ancestors had centuries before dwelt as unwelcome pilgrims and had been exploited by its inhabitants.

There are some reasons for the use of warfare in the installation of the redemptive nation in Canaan. It is not all a mystery. If God was going to put Israel in the land that was given them centuries before he would have to either miraculously remove the belligerent and marauding tribes there, or remove them by human instrumentality. If by the latter, the tribes could either accede peaceably to Israelite occupation or resist by war. War was almost inevitable, given the sinfulness of mankind and its rebellion against Jehovah's redemptive program.

In light of the hundreds of times war is mentioned in the Old Testament, it will be impossible in this work to deal with each one of them. It is our purpose simply to focus on the overriding Biblical perspective on war. On the basis of what we have discussed, clearly, in light of human rebellion and alienation toward divine redemption — as God chooses to work it out within history through human agents — God condescends to warfare to establish and sustain and protect civil and social order. Without order, redemption's work cannot be carried out by human beings. This is graphically illustrated by the experiences of Nehemiah and Ezra when they were sent to restore the commonwealth of Israel.

Ezra was told to establish order by reinstituting laws and punishments (Ezra 7:21-26). Nehemiah had to fight a defensive war to rebuild the walls of Jerusalem (Neh. 4:8,14,21). If the work of redemption is to be made available to mankind, and if human beings (believers) are the only instruments through which that is to be done, someone has to provide as much civil and social order as possible. Realistically, this is going to involve force, coercion, and sometimes war.

The God of Abraham, Isaac and Jacob knew his redemptive program and people would be militantly and violently opposed in Canaan:

> And when you go to war in your land against the adversary who oppresses you, then you shall sound an alarm with the trumpets, that you may be remembered before the Lord your God, and you shall be saved from your enemies (Num. 10:9).

> Then the Lord raised up judges, who saved them out of the power of those who plundered them (Jdgs. 2:16).

> Thus says the Lord, the God of Israel: I led you up from Egypt, and brought you out of the house of bondage; and I delivered you from the hand of the Egyptians, and from the hand of all who oppressed you, and drove them out before you, and gave you their land (Jdgs. 6:8,9).

It is clear, then, God had to institute a military power in Israel to fight preventive and defensive wars (I Sam. 23:1ff; II Sam. 5:19) if some level of order and tranquility was to exist. When Israel was accused of unjustly taking territory, God's "judge" denied it (Jdgs. 11:12ff) and pointed out that three hundred years of possession established ownership rights (Jdgs. 11:26,27).

Whatever God's reason for using military force to take the land of Canaan from the "Canaanites" and allowing Israel to occupy it, whether the foregoing citations justify it from the human perspective or not, God did it and we have no right to question it.

WAR

Inasmuch as war is the inevitable result of a sinful world, there appear to be some concepts and practices in warfare which are sanctioned in the Old Testament:

1. There is no pacifism in the Old Testament. The greatest heroes of the faith were soldiers. Abraham (held up as the "father of the faithful" and a person whose life is to be emulated, Rom. 4; Gal. 3; James 2); Moses; Joshua; and David, the "man after God's own heart" said, "He trains my hands for war" (II Sam. 22:35). All of these are mentioned in Hebrews, chapter 11, as part of the "great cloud of witnesses" urging us to a similar faith.
2. Deceptions and military strategies were used to gain the victories (Josh. 8:1ff). God, himself, even planned and urged such strategy and deception for Joshua in his battle against Ai.
3. Spying and military intelligence gathering was approved (Num. 13:1ff).
4. In war, there is no substitute for victory (II Chron. 16:7ff). Because Israel did not win certain wars decisively and completely, they were told by God, "You have done foolishly in this; for from now on you will have wars." Once a defending nation has decided to go to war, it should resolve to accept nothing less than total victory and unconditional surrender of the aggressor.
5. The "spoils of war" become a "stewardship" to the victor with which he is to do the will of God (Gen. 14:17ff; Deut. 20:14; Num. 31:25ff).
6. Every *able* man should fight to defend against an aggressor (Num. 32:6). It is unconscionable to enjoy the benefits of liberty and peace and be unwilling to fight against aggressors who would take them away.
7. Some are *not* able (Deut. 20:8). The fearful and fainthearted were not conscientious objectors; they were persons whose temperament was such that they simply would not make good soldiers. Their fearfulness would

jeopardize the lives of others fighting alongside them, — they would be poor examples to their comrades and hindrances to good discipline. Some were also exempted for family reasons (Deut. 20:5,7; 24:5) and some were exempted because of other, more important occupations. Should these worry about things "at home" their inattention to the war "at hand" would be dangerous to others.

8. A strong defensive complex (numerical army, weapons, just cause, etc.) deters aggression. This was the situation with Solomon's reign, after David, his father, had built up the military power of Israel. It is also a concept implied in one of Jesus' parables (Luke 11:21,22).

> When a strong man fully armed, guards his own palace, his goods are in peace; but when one stronger than he assails him and overcomes him, he takes away his armor in which he trusted, and divides his spoils.

Granted, this is not primarily about war — it is about the devil. But to illustrate his point, Jesus states a commonly known principle — strength deters aggression — not completely, but acceptably.

9. Refusing to fight against aggression can be a sin against God. The phrase, "Be sure your sin will find you out" (Num. 32:23) *contextually* refers to the sin of refusing to fight against oppressive aggressors.

10. There are certain sanctions allowed in war that cannot be punished in peace-time (I Kings 2:5).

11. The Old Testament (and, in our view, the New Testament) justifies certain "preventive wars." David was sent by the Lord in preventive wars against the Philistines (I Sam. 23:2,4; II Sam. 5:19-25). Francis Bacon said: "There is no question, but a just fear of an imminent danger, though no blow be given, is a lawful cause of war." If self-defense is legitimate at all, then it must be

legitimate to anticipate a deadly or crippling first blow and wage a "preventive war." Severely menacing behavior, depending on its circumstances and extent, is generally accepted as a legitimate basis for initiating an act of self-defense.

3. The Biblical perspective on war in the New Testament leaves us without any details but certainly not without principles by which to make ethical decisions about it. While the major uses of the words, "war" and "battle" and "fight," are symbolic and related to the spiritual struggle the Christian has against the devil and sin, the New Testament does not present an antimilitary, pacifist position.

    a. Jesus realistically acknowledged there would always be "wars and rumors of wars" (Matt. 24:6,7; Mark 13:7,8; Luke 21:9,10).

    b. Jesus acknowledged and approved of the warfare of the Romans against Jerusalem (Matt. 22:1-10; 24:15; Mark 13:14; Luke 21:20).

    c. John the Baptist approved of military occupations (Luke 3:14).

    d. Jesus praised the Roman centurion as having greater faith than any of those in Israel (Matt. 8:10).

    e. Another centurion, a man of great faith, Cornelius was certainly not told that he had to resign his commission with the Roman army to be a Christian and serve the Lord (see Acts 10 and 11).

    f. The attitude of the New Testament toward the military and warfare may be learned by the way military terms are used (see II Tim. 2:3; Eph. 6:10-17; II Cor. 10:3-5; Luke 14:31-33; I Cor. 14:8; I Tim. 1:18; I Pet. 2:11; I Cor. 9:7).

    g. The significance of the centurions and other civil officials commended in the New Testament is that at no time was any of them ever told by Jesus or any man of God that his participation in military service was wrong. People in all other circumstances were told to change their "occupations" and life-style in order to repent, but there is no such requirement for soldiers.

h. Jesus told the disciples to arm themselves with swords (Luke 22:36) for their own protection. Individuals have the right to defend themselves against malicious aggression. Swords are not acceptable in the spiritual struggle, but they are in the physical one. To interpret Jesus' command metaphorically is unacceptable in light of the fact that the disciples obtained two literal swords and Jesus acknowledged two literal swords as being "enough." Peter was not using his sword in the Garden of Gethsemane to defend *himself* but to keep Jesus from going to the cross. That is why Jesus told Peter to put his sword into its sheath.

i. Four passages in the New Testament give unequivocal sanction to the civil use of force, which certainly has to include war, both preventive and defensive. Romans 13:1-7 approves the use of force. And I Tim. 2:1-4 urges prayerful support to civil rulers as peace-keepers. Hebrews 11:32-34 upholds enforcing justice by waging war as an act of faith in God.

j. The book of Revelation acknowledges that the oppressive, blasphemous, murderous Roman empire is to be destroyed by war (Rev. 9:13-21; 16:12-16; 17:15,16; 11:18).

k. Jesus even threatens some of his churches with "war" (Rev. 2:16, 2:23).

l. Paul certainly approved of the Roman military using force to protect his civil rights and his life when it was threatened (Acts 21:31ff; 22:23ff; 23:17ff; 25:11,12; 27:3ff; 27:43).

One thing is certain — God is in control of all history (including wars). All of history will eventually serve (fulfill) the divine goal. "The Most High rules the kingdom of men, and gives it to whom he will" (Dan. 4:25). At various times God clearly ordained the great Babylonian, Medo-Persian, Grecian and Roman governments (Dan. 2,7-12). It is clear that God "gave" dominion and government to these Gentile cultures through *war* (even war upon God's "chosen" people; see Jer. 27:1-22; 29:1-14; Isa. 10:5-27; 44:28; 45:1-13 etc.). God has ordained government (since the fall of man) with a "sword" in its hand to maintain "peace and tranquility." Abraham used it, Moses used it, David used it, and, the Bible points out that many Gentile rulers used it with sanction from God. God approves wars which are for the protection of the peaceful from the aggressor. To disobey government when it is wielding its "sword" to produce "order and tranquility" is to disobey God. Jesus definitely acknowledged there were "things" that "belonged to Caesar" as as "things" that "belonged to God" (Matt. 22:21). He acknowledged Pilate's civil authority (John 19:11). Paul admonishes the Roman Christians to obey civil rules (Rom. 13:1-7), and so does Peter (I Pet. 2:13-17). Paul commanded Timothy to pray and give thanks for civil authorities (I Tim. 2:2) as they carried out their duties to maintain "peace and tranquility." Titus is exhorted, "Remind them (unruly Cretans) to be submissive to rulers and authorities — to be obedient . . . " (Titus 3:1). It would follow from all this that a believer (while some unbelievers may have to be coerced) would willingly be obedient to his government's call to warfare in a cause that is just and proper in restraining aggression.

Ancient philosophers (Plato and Socrates, et al.) argued (from Natural Law) that because one's government has spent years and energies, often at great sacrifice, to maintain peaceful circumstances into which one may be born a citizen, one should be willing to defend one's government against aggression and disruption. Further, what the government had provided by the way of safety, opportunities, and helps to get an education, hold a job, and rear a family should cause such gratitude and obligation that one would be willing to sacrifice greatly, even going to war if necessary, to defend such a government. If one is to accept the privileges and protections of his government, then he has actually and implicitly accepted the "covenant" relationships which bind him to the responsibilities (and penalties) of his government, to obey its laws and even to go to war for it. Thirdly, if anyone does not like his government and does not appreciate what it has done, and feels no obligation to it, he may (especially if he is an American) take up citizenship in some other land, under some other government. In other words, if one is not willing to obey his country, he should find another country he can obey — or be willing to suffer the consequences of disobeying. Finally, without government there would be social chaos. If obedience to government is determined individually or subjectively, then no law would be immune from some citizen's disapproval or disobedience. And it is a greater evil not to resist an evil aggressor than to fight against him. One sage has said, "All that is necessary for evil to triumph is for good men to do nothing."

Wars come! We might even paraphrase Jesus thus: "Woe to the world for wars (temptations) . . . . For it is necessary that wars (temptations) come, but woe to the nation (man) by whom the war (temptation) comes!" (Matt. 18:7) As long as this world stands and there are impenitent sinners in it, there will be wars. Christians (let alone unbelievers) cannot make omniscient or perfect judgments as to the absolute justness of any adversary or any war. It is even questionable as to whether any one nation is ever to be exonerated of some fault in any war. The Christian (as well as the unbeliever) is left to make relative judgments about which side in a war is more on the side of justice and order than the other. That is the kind of world in which we live — those are the kinds of judgments we must make in many areas of life (divorce, civil disputes, personal associations, business or vocational pursuits). For some judgments the Christian has *absolute precepts* (clear commandments) by which he must be guided; in others he has only principles by which he may form a hierarchy of right (lesser of evils). Every war has a relatively just side to it — the defender against the aggressor. Philosophers and theologians have compiled the following categories by which one may declare a war "just":

    1. Just cause. All aggression is condemned; only defensive war is legitimate.
    2. Just intention. The only legitimate intention is to secure a just peace for all involved. Neither revenge nor conquest nor economic gain nor ideological supremacy are justified.
    3. Last resort. War may only be entered upon when all negotiations and compromise have been tried and failed.
    4. Formal declaration. Since the use of military force is the prerogative of governments, not of private individuals, a state of war must be officially declared by the highest authorities.
    5. Limited objectives. If the purpose is peace, then unconditional surrender or the destruction of a nation's economic or political institution is an unwarranted objective.
    6. Proportionate means. The weaponry and the force used should be limited to what is needed to repel the aggression and deter future attacks, that is to say to secure a just peace. Total or unlimited war is ruled out.
    7. Noncombatant immunity. Since war is an official act of government, only those who are officially agents of government may fight, and individuals not actively contributing to the conflict (including POW's and casualties as well as civilian nonparticipants) should be immune from attack.
    War, Four Christian Views, ed. by Robert G. Clouse, pub. IVP, pp. 120,121

    Needless to say, most wars are not fought with close adherence to these principles (U.S. Grant demanded "unconditional surrender" of the Confederate forces in the American Civil War; the Allies demanded the same of the axis powers in World War II; there was certainly a dismantling of axis "political instutions" after WW II). Nevertheless, these principles, when applied, keep wars from exacerbating into international vendettas and pervasive blood-letting. These principles have been arrived at over centuries of analyzing history and the Scriptures. And while the Bible is the final authority for the Christian, and he may question whether all these principles may be substantiated by it, Paul makes it plain that general or "natural" revelation (Romans 1:18ff; 2:12-16) indicates there are some kinds of actions which are "contrary to nature" and all men may be held in obligation to these "natural" moral standards.

Assuredly, not all wars are "just." And the Bible teaches that it is not always right to obey one's government in everything it commands. If the Christian citizen is bound to obey every government command, he may be found supporting an Adolph Hitler or a Joseph Stalin in a war to take the territories of other nations and to slaughter prisoners and conquered peoples who are innocent of wrong doing. There are clear examples of "civil disobedience" in the Bible — both Old and New Testaments. We deal with these in a later chapter. It is wrong to take the life of an innocent human, even if government is "ordained of God" and some government commands it. "Government" is ordained of God to punish those guilty of social disorder and anarchy, but a morally unjustifiable command of any government is never sanctioned by God! Even within a just war, there may be unjust commands given which should be disobeyed. This principle was established in modern times by the Nuremberg trials following World War II, and the U.S. military trials after the Vietnam My Lai incident. No individual member of the armed forces of any country should be excused for engaging in an immoral act or ethical atrocity simply because he has been ordered to do it by his superior officers. Evil is evil whether a government orders it or not. The Bible is clear on the point that one should not always obey government.

This all said and done, however, some wars are just. Total pacifism cannot be justified, either by the Bible or by Natural Law written on the conscience of mankind:

> A nation is required to protect the lives of its citizens; it is not expected to do good to all the world, and those who would demand that it do are not fit citizens. Given a choice of having liberty or death, some would choose the latter, for there are fates worse

than death. Letting it be known that death is not feared if life as one wants it cannot be had, can sometimes be an effective measure of policy. It is sometimes known as calling a bluff. It draws a line, and though the price may be high, in time that line is usually respected. Some may die, even many, but their deaths win worthy goals for their successors. That is sometimes known as laying down one's life for his fellows. It is an act the benefits from which the pacifist is willing to accept without contributing his proportional measure.

Ethical Arguments For Analysis, ed. Baum and Randall, pub. Holt, Rinehart, Winston p. 34

It is significant that while some of the greatest soldiers of history have participated in some of the bloodiest wars of history, they (George Washington, Francis Marion, Robert E. Lee, "Stonewall" Jackson, "Black-Jack" Pershing, Dwight D. Eisenhower, and Douglas MacArthur) have been men of deep Christian convictions and most adamantly against war. We ought also to include the great warriors of the Bible (Abraham, Moses, Joshua, David, Jehoshaphat, Nehemiah et al.) Men of God these were, men of peace, but men who knew that in this world, war is sometimes the only means to a necessary, though temporary, justice.

. . . it seems to me that nothing is more unrealistic in the present state of the world than to say that war must never be used as a means of thwarting wilful and deliberate aggression. This position ignores the fact that God employed war as a judgment upon nations, and even upon Jerusalem (Ezek. 14:21). Surely He was not immoral. This does not mean that God likes war anymore than I like it. I did not punish my children because I derived pleasure from the experience but in order to produce "the fruit of real goodness" in their characters . . . Gen. Sherman said that "War is hell," and I concur, but I do not forget that God also made hell. And it was made as the result of war in heaven! If Michael and his angels had been pacifists, then the devil might have taken heaven over, and if this had happened those who went to heaven would have been in hell . . . . Certainly war is an evil, but it is not necessarily a *sin*. All sin is evil, but not all "evil" is sin. Obviously not every war is justified, but that is not the question . . . it will be necessary for all nations to desist from lifting up the sword against each other, for so long as one learns war with a view to the destruction of others, the others will have to defend themselves . . . God will turn those nations which hate Him and His rule into hell. War is the judgment of God upon such sin here, and hell is the judgment of God upon such sin hereafter. When I assist in the work of rewarding good or in striking terror into the hearts of evil men, I am abiding God's minister to fulfill a responsibility to God.

Mission Messenger, Vol. 31, August 1969, pp. 118ff, pub. Carl Ketcherside

The only conscience a Christian should have against compulsory military service in a world with continued aggressive pressures like ours which demands a ready military establishment as a deterrent, would be if he were a missionary or a minister actively preaching the Gospel. And even then there may come a time when *all* able-bodied men might be needed to hasten the overthrow of evil aggressive forces at work in the world. Moses used the Levites to bear the sword (Exod. 32:25-29; see also Num. 25:7-13). Conscientious objection to war or military service cannot be based on personal desires, but on the direction of God's expressed will and common ("natural") morality in such matters. Romans chapter 13 is a clear expression of God's will for Christians in regard to war and the use of force, if necessary, to check and punish aggression. The Christian has a right to only one conscience — a conscience directed by God. Romans 13:5 states unequivocally, "Therefore one must be subject (to one's government) not only to avoid God's wrath but also for the sake of conscience." People must be forced to do right by laws (conscription/draft) if they will not do right otherwise (I Tim. 1:8ff). This is exactly what government and law is for! Men cannot be left to do what they "feel" is right (especially lawless men). The main function of government is to force the immoral and ungodly to be as moral as is necessary to maintain society. Christians act morally and resist aggression with civil force because their Christian consciences tell them it is right.

> In America, a man stood up in a free pulpit to preach; he quoted detached sentences from the Christ whose hand held the lash when His Father's House was a den of thieves, and whose eyes were often as a flame of fire. The preacher declared that evil, no matter how diabolical, was never to be resisted with any physical weapons. Rhetorically, he asked, "What has a sword ever accomplished worthwhile?"
> In a pew was a worshipper in whose heart was an aching void and in whose home was a Gold Star, speaking of the valor of a young crusader who marched forth with a righteous sword and came not back. At the church door, following the service, that worshipper said to the clergyman: "I can tell you one thing that righteous sword has done."
> "What?" replied the minister.
> Replied the listener with deep feeling: "The sword in the hand of those who have resisted militant evil has given you the right to stand here today and to proclaim your convictions without fear of being liquidated."
> The one who had publicly said that rampant evil was never to be resisted by force paused for a moment and then acknowledged, "I am afraid I cannot refute that."
> There is no refutation in God's world and man's for the flash of a righteous sword!
>
> Dr. Frederick Brown Harris, Chaplain, U.S. Senate, 1943-1969, quoted in *U.S. News and World Report*, October 30, 1972

PEACE

Basically, there are only two Biblical words translated "peace" — one is the Hebrew word *shalom*, which means "peace; completeness; welfare; health; wholeness; well-being." It is used for both physical peace and spiritual peace in the Old Testament — the other is *eirene* in the Greek New Testament, usage and meaning practically the same as *shalom*.

As stated earlier, the Bible says much more about *spiritual peace* than about physical peace. In fact, the Bible teaches that a believer may be in a state of *spiritual* restfulness, contentment and *peace* when all about him there is physical turmoil, war, persecution and tribulation (John 14:27; 16:33; Phil. 4:6,7; Psa. 4:1-8; 23:1ff; 119:165, etc.). This *spiritual peace* is something that comes through *learning* to *trust* God in spite of circumstances (see Phil. 4:8,9; II Cor. 12:10, etc.).

But the Bible does say something about physical peace. Clearly, the Bible obligates civil governments to coercively restrain wickedness and lawlessness so that literal, *physical, peace* may ensue. Paul told Timothy to pray for civil governors and authorities, "that we may lead a quite and *peaceable* (and here the Greek word is *eremon*, "tranquil") life and that the Gospel may be proclaimed throughout the world (I Tim. 2:1-4). That is the plain intent of the admonitions in Romans 13:1-5 and Ezra 6:10.

The Bible is not guilty of naivete. It is realistic about those concepts and practices which do *not* make for physical peace:

1. *Miraculous intervention of God*: God has committed civil government to the job of peace-keeping. He will not intervene and usurp the free choices of mankind. Men must "make" their own physical peace on this earth by accepting and enforcing the "natural laws" of the Creator written in the hearts of men, and through as much exposure as possible to the propositionally revealed will of God in the Bible.

2. *Appeasement*: Sidney Cave, in his book, *The Christian Way*, writes concerning Prime Minister Chamberlain's attempt to appease Adolph Hitler prior to World War II:

> . . . the policy of appeasement before 1939 failed partly because of this myth of the "economic man" (the myth that all men can be "bought off"). What did Hitler care for the economic advantages that were offered to him? It was the domination of the world that he sought, and that domination would have meant the extinction

of freedom and of civil justice. But peace might have been maintained had those who desired peace been strong . . . . Those who seek peace need to have power till all seek peace . . . . If the world is to be saved from war, it will not be because all are wise and good, but because the general will has secured protection for all, and thus made possible a reign of law instead of anarchy . . . (Isa. 26:9,10).

The Bible clearly shows that appeasement of power-hungry tyrants will not keep them from going to war. David tried to appease Saul, but Saul made war against David anyway (I Kings 18-19). David tried to appease Absalom (II Sam. 14:12ff) but Absalom went to war against his father. Ahab's appeasement by letting Benhadad escape free (I Kings 20:30,34) simply postponed war with Syria (I Kings 22:1ff; II Kings 6:24ff). Menahem appeased the Assyrian king Pul (II Kings 15:17-22) but Assyria later took Israel captive. Ahaz appeased Tiglath-Pileser (II Kings 16:7-16) but Assyria invaded Judah and devastated over 40 of her cities in the days of Hezekiah, Ahaz' son. Hezekiah tried to appease the Assyrian king (II Kings 18:13-19:11) but Assyria invaded Judah anyway and besieged Jerusalem (Isa. 36-39). We know this to be true throughout the history of men and nations. Someone has analyzed history and arrived at these startling statistics — only eight percent of the time since the beginnings of recorded history has the world been entirely at peace; in 3521 years, only 286 have been warless; eight thousand treaties have been broken in this time.

3. *Treaties and/or Political Alliances:* Another startling statistic: Since 1919, the nations of Europe have signed more than 200 treaties of peace. Each treaty, simply another scrap of paper, was broken more easily than consummated; from the year 1500 B.C. to A.D. 1860, more than 8000 treaties of peace, meant to remain in force forever, were concluded; the average time they remained in force was two years! Obadiah, the prophet, revealed that the "allies" of Edom had "deceived her" (Obad. v.7) (see also Jer. 30:4; 38:22,23). Tyre violated one of her

treaties and delivered up prisoners to the slave caravans passing through Edom (Amos 1:9). Isaiah warns Judah against making alliances with Egypt against Assyria and Babylon (Isa. 31:1-3). Treaties, whether between only two nations, blocks of nations, or among "United Nations," will not produce peace. God discloses his displeasure against one-world governmental forms in Genesis chapters 10-11. The attempt of ancient empires to consolidate all cultures under one-world government (Babylon, Persia, Greece, Rome) proves that alliances and treaties whether they be coerced or willingly entered will not bring realistic and lasting physical peace. This is documented in the prophecies of the book of Daniel.

4. *Diplomacy and/or Complicity:* While diplomacy should always be the first approach to resolving international disputes, men must be realistic and understand that peace is seldom achieved by diplomacy and never by complicity. Asa, king of Judah, tried complicity with Benhadad (I Kings 15:18-32) but it only provoked more war (II Chron. 16:7-10). Jehoiakim (Eliakim) paid tribute to Pharaoh Necho of Egypt and tried complicity against Babylon (II Kings 23:31-24:19) but brought only war with Babylon. Hezekiah tried complicity with Babylon against Assyria (II Kings 20:12-21; Isa. 39:1-8), but produced later the Babylonian invasion of Judah. Hitler and Joseph Stalin made diplomatic "peace pacts" at the beginning of World War II, but since both were secretly planning duplicity, the "pact" lasted only until Hitler invaded Russia. The United States found that in December, 1941, Japanese diplomats in Washington were *not* trying to arrive at peaceful negotiations, for while they were "negotiating" the Japanese war-lords bombed Pearl Harbor.

5. *Disarmament:* Winston Churchill gave this clever "peace by disarmament" parable:

> Once upon a time all the animals in the zoo decided they would disarm, and they arranged to hold a conference to decide the matter. The rhinoceros said that the use of teeth in war was

barbarous and horrible, and ought strictly to be prohibited by general consent. Horns, which were mainly defensive weapons, would, of course, have to be tolerated. The buffalo, stag, and porcupine said they would vote with the rhino; but the lion and the tiger took a different view. They defended teeth, and even claws, as honorable weapons.

Then the bear spoke. He proposed that both teeth and horns should be banned. It would be quite enough if animals would be allowed to give each other a good hug when they quarreled. No one could object to that. It was so fraternal, and would be a great step toward peace. However, all the other animals were offended with the bear, and they fell into a perfect panic.

Esther, Jewish queen of Persia, found that the "disarmed" Jews living in Persia were destined by Haman to genocide (extermination of the whole race) (Esther 7:4). King Ahasuerus immediately made provision for the Jews to arm and defend themselves against their enemies (Esther 8:11ff). Rabshakeh (Assyrian general) taunted Hezekiah and the citizens of Jerusalem, "Do you think that mere words (diplomacy) are strategy and power for war?" (Isa. 36:5). This general with his powerful army (at least 185,000) bragged about his power and threatened this besieged people (Isa. 36:1-37:38). Unarmed, disarmed, or underarmed, a nation will be prey for the predators of the world. An ancient apocryphal Christian writing says: "Love those that hate you and you will have no enemy." But love does not always overcome enmity, even in personal relationships. Preachers who declare, as pacifists do, that love will melt the hardest heart, show a strange forgetfulness of the incidents of the Gospel story. What of Judas who lived with Jesus and betrayed Him? What of Annas and Caiaphas who became His malignant enemies? There would have been no martyrdoms had Christian love secured immunity from suffering. Before World War I, we were told that no unarmed nation would be attacked and that Denmark thus was safe. It did not prove so. Lack of defenses saved the Danes some suffering, but only at the cost of their liberty and their land being used more quickly as a base against other friendly nations. The Bible realistically declares there are some who will be at peace, physically, only under coercion — by force of arms or power (Deut. 20:10-12; 23:3-6).

Indeed, it is the purview of civil governments to guard the peace of their citizenry. That is their primary function whether it be defense of peace within a nation or defense of its peace against alien forces of war. That is what the Bible says (see Rom. 13:1-7). The writer of Hebrews lists guardianship of civil and physical peace as an act of faith in God:

> . . . who through faith conquered kingdoms, enforced justice, received promises, stopped the mouths of lions, quenched raging fire, escaped the edge of the sword, won strength out of weakness, became mighty in war, put foreign armies to flight . . . (Heb. 11:33,34).

Peace cannot be bought. Hezekiah tried that (II Kings 18:13ff). Those whose "minds are set on the flesh" are hostile to God (Rom. 8:7) and can never be at peace when the flesh is not being fed (Micah 3:5). So long as there are millions and millions with that mind-set, there will be war. Armed force and warfare are the only realistic instruments applicable to that mind-set. It is the greatest of all tragedies that it must be so — but it is nevertheless. Jesus, himself, said absolute truth in the midst of a rebelling and sinful world will mean war:

> Do not think that I have come to bring peace on earth; I have not come to bring peace but a sword . . . (Matt. 10:34; see Luke 12:51).

Peace, worldly peace, comes from strength and power used judiciously by civil governments trying to "do their duties, as God gives them the light to see their duties" (see Josh. 9:15; 10:21; I Sam. 7:14; II Sam. 10:19). Aggressive, predatory nations (or individuals) submit to order and peace only by coercion. That is the only restraint they understand and obey. The Bible demands that law and justice rule in this wicked world. Civil order of law and justice is for the international community as well as the national.

> In an age skeptical of all inherited concepts of law and order, and which wavers between the choice of majority opinion or cynical anarchy, the Church needs nothing less than the authority of the Bible to speak about universally valid standards of justice . . . the Bible unmistakably states the spiritual foundation of the world order. Justice belongs to the very being of God, whose righteousness is the sure source of law . . . . Scripture warns against so fusing and confusing righteousness and love that the dominance of either nullifies the other. The Bible stands sentry against speaking of God's love as the foremost or conditioning divine attribute; it discredits fitting God's justice to love's convenience. Whenever love triumphs at the expense of holiness, whenever love takes priority over righteousness, we have moved outside the scriptural orbit . . . . The plain fact is that in the social order all prattling about love is irrelevant when what is needed is justice. The withholding of justice may be an expression of lovelessness, and the performance of justice may be described as love in action . . . . Nor are they identical in content: love goes beyond justice, although it does not negate it. Sinful men cannot really grasp the true nature of love, therefore, unless they are first taught the responsibility of justice through their common subjection to impartial laws that deal with all human beings alike: indeed, the transmutation of justice can only lead as well to the perversion of love.
> Aspects of Christian Social Ethics, by Carl F.H. Henry, pub. by Eerdmans, pp. 168-171

Justice and peace are inextricably linked. Peace cannot be present where justice is absent. Isaiah wrote:

> Their feet run to evil, and they make haste to shed innocent blood; their thoughts are thoughts of iniquity, desolation and destruction are in their highways. The way of peace they know not, and there is no justice in their paths; they have made their roads crooked, no one who goes in them knows peace. Therefore

justice is far from us, and righteousness does not overtake us . . . we look for justice, but there is none . . . . Justice is turned back, and righteousness stands afar off; for truth has fallen in the public squares, and uprightness cannot enter. Truth is lacking, and he who departs from evil makes himself a prey . . . (Isa. 59:7-15).

The ultimate peace can only come when sinful mankind is reconciled to God through the redemptive grace of Jesus Christ. "For he is our peace, who has . . . broken down the dividing wall of hostility, by abolishing in his flesh the law of commandments and ordinances, that he might create in himself one new man in place of the two, so making peace, and might reconcile us both to God in one body through the cross, thereby bringing the hostility to an end" (Eph. 2:14-16). Only the love of Christ is capable of controlling us (II Cor. 5:14ff) so that we "see" no one any longer from a human (carnal mind-set) point of view. Only then are men able to be at peace with one another. Even great warriors, because they are Christians, have acknowledged this:

> Men since the beginning of time have sought peace. Various methods through the ages have been attempted to devise an international process to prevent or settle disputes between nations. From the very start, workable methods were found insofar as individual citizens were concerned; but the mechanics of an instrumentality of larger international scope have never been successful. Military alliances, balances of power, leagues of nations, all in turn failed, leaving the only path to be by way of the crucible of war. The utter destructiveness of war now blots out this alternative. We have had our last chance. If we will not devise some greater and more equitable system, Armageddon will be at the door. The problem basically is theological and involves a spiritual recrudescence and improvement of human character that will synchronize with our almost matchless advances in science, art, literature, and all material and cultural developments of the past 2000 years. It must be of the spirit if we are to save the flesh. But once war is forced upon us, there is no other alternative than to apply every available means to bring it to a swift end. War's very

object is victory — not prolonged indecision. In war, indeed, there can be no substitute for victory . . . history teaches with unmistakable emphasis that appeasement but begets new and bloodier war. It points to no single instance where the end has justified that means — where appeasement has led to more than a sham peace.
Reminiscences, by General of the Army, Douglas MacArthur, pub. McGraw-Hill, p. 404 (excerpt from Gen. MacArthur's retirement speech before a joint session of the U.S. Congress, 1951).

You are the leaven which binds together the entire fabric of our national system of defense. From your ranks come the great captains who hold the nation's destiny in their hands the moment the war tocsin sounds. The Long Gray Line has never failed us. Were you to do so, a million ghosts in olive drab, in brown khaki, in blue and gray, would rise from their white crosses thundering those magic words — Duty — Honor — Country.

This does not mean that you are war mongers. On the contrary, the soldier, above all other people, prays for peace, for he must suffer and bear the deepest wounds and scars of war. But always in our ears ring the ominous words of Plato, that wisest of all philosophers, "Only the dead have seen the end of war."
Reminiscences, by General Douglas MacArthur, pub. McGraw-Hill pp.425,426 (excerpt from Gen. MacArthur's last speech to the Cadets at West Point, 1962).

In conclusion, it is fair to say the Bible teaches:
1. God does not desire war. His will for all his creatures has always been peace.
2. But God has created his creatures with freedom to make moral choices.
3. Some of his creatures (all mankind — some angels) have chosen to rebel, to be hostile, toward their Creator. This is war!
4. This war against God manifests itself in this world, tragically, through sinful people killing and hurting other people. This is war!
5. But God is in control. No creature will ever dethrone

God. Even in war, God will be the victor — he will be glorified and his purpose will ultimately be served. God uses even the wickedness of men:
a. To punish rebellion
b. To call to repentance
c. To warn the world that judgment is coming
d. To chasten and nourish his covenant people, both in the Old Testament and the New Testament (Deut. 4:32-40; Ezek. 20:1-49; Dan. 11:29-35; 12:1-13; Amos 4:10-12; James 4:1-10; Rev. 12:13-17).

God is not the author of war. But he certainly is the sovereign of war! Neither war in heaven nor war on earth is beyond his control. Everything that is done will ultimately resound to his praise, even war as devastating and horrible as that done *by* the Roman empire and *upon* the Roman empire (see Rev. 15:1-4; 16:5-7; 18:4-8; 18:20-24; 19:1-8; 19:11-21). If men are determined to exchange the truth of God for a lie (and make war) — refuse to have God in their knowledge (and make war), God will give them up to receive in their own persons the due penalty of their error. God has created an eternal prison in which there is constant war (see Rev. 9:1-11; 14:6-11). Those who choose to be at war with God and man will be given their choice for all eternity. Those who choose to be at peace with God and men may, in this life, have to opt for the lesser of two evils, and go to war to defend unalienable human rights of life, liberty and property. That is a reality the Bible acknowledges, ordains, and approves. Those who make a profession (policemen, magistrates, soldiers) of defending with the sword unalienable human rights are "ministers" of God and "peacemakers" in the truest Biblical sense. Those who choose peace and serve peace according to the will of God, will be given, by the grace of God, a life in eternity where nothing but peace (well-being, wholeness, goodness) exists. This state of peace can, and must, exist even now within the kingdom of God (the church). There must be no hostility or rebellion against God or fellow citizens within the church. There must be peace (Eph.

2:11ff). The Christian lives in two kingdoms — the world of unbelief and the church. The constraint that brings peace in the world of unbelief is law and force (I Tim. 1:8-11); in the church it is the love of Christ (II Cor. 5:14-21). *But there is no peace without some constraint! God has created us free to choose our restraint — force or love!*

6

PARTICIPATION OF BELIEVERS

Mark Twain (Samuel Clemens) said something like this: "Politics is like the weather — everybody talks about it but no one does anything about it." Christians are especially reluctant to do much more than vote.

> Christians love to talk about how degenerate society is becoming. They point to immorality in the schools, corruption in the courthouse, crime in the streets. Yet, when an opportunity arises to do something about it, Christians are strangely absent . . . . Until recently at least, evangelical Christians all to often tended to shy away from political participation. Some of this may have been due to apathy, but often there has been a negative undercurrent of thought that Christians shouldn't be involved in anything like politics . . . . There is no biblical support for this idea. Some of the greatest believers in the Bible were kings and judges of Israel. Can you imagine David saying, "No thanks, Samuel, I don't think a believer should be involved in politics"?
> *God and Caesar, Christian Faith & Political Action*,
> by John Eidsmoe, pub. Crossway, p. 10

WHAT THE BIBLE SAYS ABOUT CIVIL GOVERNMENT

The following is a partial list of "believers" who were in one way or another involved in civil government:
1. Melchizedek, king of Salem (Jerusalem), also high priest is given the New Testament as a believer and type of Christ (Heb. 7).
2. Abraham; although only the partiarch of a "clan," he had to make political and civic decisions (Gen. 14).
3. Joseph: second ruler of all Egypt only to Pharaoh (Genesis 37-50).
4. Moses; great emancipator, law-giver, judge (Exod. through Deut.).
5. Joshua; general of the army, judge, pioneer (Joshua).
6. David; general of the army, king, psalmist (I & II Sam.).
7. Solomon; king, scientist, author, international diplomat (I Kings).
8. Asa; king of Judah (I Kings).
9. Jehoshaphat; king of Judah (I Kings).
10. Uzziah; king of Judah (II Kings).
11. Jotham: king of Judah (II Kings).
12. Hezekiah; king of Judah (II Kings).
13. Josiah; King of Judah (II Kings).
14. Isaiah; counselor to Hezekiah, prophet (II Kings; Isaiah).
15. Daniel; very high official in the massive heathen empires of Babylon and Persia (Dan.).
16. Shadrach, Meshach and Abednego; officials in Babylon government (Dan. 2:49).
17. Esther; queen of Persia (Esther 4:14).
18. Mordecai; next in rank to King Ahasuerus of Persia (Esther 10:3).
19. Ezra; organizer of the restored Jewish commonwealth (Ezra 7:21ff).
20. Nehemiah; cup-bearer (a position of great responsibility) to King Artaxerxes of Persia (Neh. 1:11; 2:1) leader of the restored Jews.
21. Zerubbabel; levirate son of Shealtiel, heir to the throne of

David, appointed governor of the restored commonwealth of Judah (Ezra 1:8-11; 5:14; I Chron. 3:19; Zech. 4:6; Hag. 1:1).
22. The centurion of Capernaum, commended by Jesus as having the greatest faith found in all Israel (Matt. 8:5-13).
23. Joanna, the wife of Chuza, Herod's "steward," supported Jesus' ministry (Luke 8:1-3). She participated in politics through her husband's position.
24. Cornelius; the Roman army centurion with great faith (Acts 10:1ff).
25. Sergius Paulus; Roman proconsul of Cyprus, (Acts 13:7-12).
26. The Philippian jailer (Acts 16:25-40).
27. Joseph of Arimathea (Luke 23:50; Matt. 27:57-61; Mark 14:42-47; John 19:38-42), a rich man, on the Jewish high council.
28. Nicodemus (John 3:14), a leading Pharisee, a "ruler of the Jews," a member of the Sanhedrin, stood against the injustice toward Jesus (John 7:25-44), helped with Jesus' burial (John 19:38-42).
29. Erastus; city treasurer of Rome (Romans 16:23; Acts 19:22).
30. Some of the "Praetorian guard" (Phil. 1:13).
31. Some of Caesar's own household (Phil. 4:22).
32. Zacchaeus; the penitent tax collector (Luke 19:1ff).
33. Matthew; the tax collector worthy of being called to the apostleship (Matt. 9:9ff).
34. Jairus; the ruler of the Jews who believed in Jesus (Matt. 9:18-26).
35. Simon; the Zealot also worthy of being called to the apostleship (Luke 6:15).
36. The Nobleman; a believer who was a civil official (John 4:46ff).
37. Lot; "righteous Lot" (II Pet. 2:7) who "sat at the gate" (probably means a civil judge of some sort) of Sodom, and

was "greatly distressed by the licentiousness of the wicked . . . he was vexed in his righteous soul day after day with their lawless deeds."
38. The Lawyer; who was "not far from the kingdom" (Mark 12:28-34).
39. Zenas; the lawyer and co-worker of the apostle Paul (Titus 3:13).
40. Archippus; "our fellow soldier" (probably was in the military) (Philemon 2).

There are surely some names from both the Old Testament and the New not included here. And there must have been literally thousands of other believers, not named in the Bible, who were specifically involved in civil government in those ages. Jesus made much use of the titles and offices of civil service (king, general, nobleman, judge, ruler) in his parables. The list above should be sufficient to indicate that believers from all levels of spiritual growth were involved in many different areas of civil service.

Jeremiah, speaking for God, told the Jews who had been taken into exile by the Babylonians:

> Thus says the Lord of hosts, the God of Israel, to all the exiles whom I have sent into exile from Jerusalem to Babylon; Build houses and live in them; plant gardens and eat their produce. Take wives and have sons and daughters; take wives for your sons, and give your daughters in marriage, that they may bear sons and daughters; multiply there, and do not decrease. But seek the welfare of the city where I have sent you into exile, and pray to the Lord on its behalf, for in its welfare you will find your welfare (Jer. 29:4-7).

Jeremiah uses the Hebrew word *shalom* when he commands the Jews to "seek the *welfare* of their captors. *Shalom* is more than a mere grudging resignation to one's predicament. It requires an attitude that expresses itself in assisting one to find well-being, wholeness and tranquility. In other words, Jehovah commanded the Jews, prisoners of war to the Babylonians, displaced persons, not only to refrain from resisting captivity and displacement, but to actively *seek* the well-being (to assist in building up) of the foreign communities to which they were exiled. In order to do this Jews would have to participate in as much of the *civic* affairs of those communitites in which they lived as they were permitted. Would God want the Christian today, who might find himself exiled from his homeland among foreigners, to do the same? We think so. It is highly significant that the Lord never commanded the Jews to protest, go "underground," escape, or start a revolution against their captors. Of course, for the most part and with but a few exceptions, the Jews were not imprisoned, tortured, or massacred. When that kind of danger arose, the Lord often (but not always) delivered by his providence. But the important point to remember from this text is that God *commanded* civic participation.

Biblical commandment for participation in civil government is to be found as well in the New Testament:

> Therefore one must be subject, not only to avoid God's wrath but also for the sake of conscience. For the same reason you also pay taxes, for the authorities are ministers of God, attending to this very thing. Pay all of them their dues, taxes to whom taxes are due, revenue to whom revenue is due, respect to whom respect is due, honor to whom honor is due (Rom. 13:5-7).

> First of all, then, I urge that supplications, prayers, intercessions, and thanksgivings be made for all men, for kings and all who are in high positions, that we may lead a quiet and peaceable life, godly and respectful in every way (I Tim. 2:1).

While the Biblical commandments do not specify that believers are to seek public office, they certainly demand participation by each individual in respect to promoting justice, paying taxes, and thanksgivings to Almighty God for civil servants. And since participation is required to such extent as the foregoing, the believer could safely assume that participation by entering civil service would not only be acceptable, but desirable as a "ministry" to the Lord.

> There is an old saying: "all that is necessary for evil to triumph is for good men to do nothing." This is precisely where we find ourselves today in the matter of Christian ethics and political morality. For too many political generations too many good men have done nothing.
> Men changed by a confrontation with Christ must build a changed world. Christians must become involved in the processes of transformation in our world, as God leads them. One of the major processes for orderly change is politics — the art and science of government.
> For the Christian to reason that God does not want him in politics because there are too many evil men in government is as insensitive as for a Christian doctor to turn his back on an epidemic because there are too many germs.
> *Facing Your Nation*, ed. by William J. Krutza and Philip P. Di Cicco, pub. Baker, pp. 107,108

It may be that many people do not participate in civil service because as believers they think they must be "separate" (sanctified) from the world. To them, politics, or a job serving one's government, is "worldly." Some have been made to feel repulsed by politics and government because most of the "news" they hear, see, and read focuses on the corruption and wicked behavior of politicians and civil servants; they do not want to "be corrupted." It is true, Christians are not to think of this world as all the world there is. Christians must "set their minds on things above." But that does not mean we are to have our minds so obsessed with heaven that we forget about this world completely. As a matter of fact, no Christian can truly serve God without serving men:

> If any one says, I love God, and hates his brother, he is a liar; for he who does not love his brother whom he has seen, cannot love

God whom he has not seen. And this commandment we have from him, that he who loves God should love his brother also (I John 4:20,21).

Christians who reject participation in civil government, or service in some way through the civic or political processes available to them, are shunning an opportunity to "love their brothers" that cannot be had through the church. And civil service is unequivocally called a "ministry to God" in the Bible. Senator Mark Hatfield of Oregon wrote in his book, *Conflict and Conscience*:

— If everyone in America were just like me what kind of country would this be?
— If everyone took the same interest in government that I do, what kind of government would we have?
— If everyone obeyed the law, including the speed limit, with the same faithfulness that I do, what kind of crime rate would we have?
— If everyone accepted public service or community work with the same attitude that I do, how much would get done for the public good?
— If everyone obeyed his conscience and the spiritual commandments of God with the same faithfulness and courage that I do, what kind of world would this be?

Many people who profess to be strong Bible believers, who insist verbally that all of government is ungodly and that something must be done to "put God back in government," would never think of allowing their names to be put on a ballot to run for public office, or join a patriotic organization, or become a member of a club devoted to civic improvement. They are too busy with heavenly things. Non-involvement is their political posture. It is not enough however to *criticize* the current political scene, or to espouse lofty ideals about how government *should* be, if such attitudes do not impel you to "let your light so shine among men . . . " and actively participate in civic affairs. Christians must "as they have opportunity, do good unto all men" (Gal. 6:10).

That may very well mean becoming specifically involved running for political office or taking up the vocation of civil service in some other area.

In a pluralistic society like America, a politician or other civil servant deals constantly with the hard realities of a world that is mostly unbelieving and not committed to Biblical standards and principles. The best that can often be expected is civic conduct from a basis of "the law of God written on the conscience" (Natural Law). Politics is the art of the possible. Someone has said, "Politics is the art of compromise." But that does not have to mean compromise of the fundamental standards of right and wrong. It usually demands compromise only in the area of opinions or of means (methods). There have been many moral giants who have served in civil government. Biblical history and secular history are records of their service as it pleased God and produced his justice in the earth. We have already called many of the Biblical names to your attention. Daniel is perhaps the most exemplary. Here was a young man with strong faith in God, with clear commitment to practice his religion, who was willing to learn all the "letters and languages of the Chaldeans" (Dan. 1:4), serve as a high official in heathen governments, and be used of God to help perserve the people of God and probably convert at least one heathen emperor (Nebuchadnezzar, see Dan. 4:34-37). He did not compromise his faith or his morals, and served in a government much less God-oriented in its ideology and practice than ours. Daniel was able to "compromise" where possible and be rigid when necessary. It can be done!

In the history of the United States of America there have been many examples of the same kind of civic "ministry." William Bradford, John Witherspoon, George Washington, Alexander Hamilton, John Jay, Gouverneur Morris, Samuel Adams, John Adams, Patrick Henry, Roger Sherman, George Mason, Charles Cotesworth Pinckney — these are all "founding fathers." All these were godly men whose faith in God and reverence for the Bible as the word of God is well documented in their own writings. A long list of succeeding U.S. presidents and other government officials could be given who were godly men. Abraham Lincoln, James A. Garfield (a minister of the Christian Church), Theodore Roosevelt, Herbert Hoover, James Carter, Ronald Reagan, George Bush, and many others.

Some of our greatest military leaders were devout Christians. General Washington, General Francis Marion, General Robert E. Lee, General MacArthur. Twenty-five of our forty-one presidents have worn a United States military uniform. Thousands of other civil officers in America (national, state, local) who are believers have served unheralded, unknown, and often underpaid, to make this nation the best place on earth to be born and to live. Should anyone feel that civic service is not a ministry of God, let that person immigrate to any other nation on earth, take up residence and citizenship. He will soon be longing for the blessings of the United States of America where, for the most part, civil government is still considered a God-ordained stewardship.

It is not biblical and it is not reasonable that Christians should surrender the civil arena to unbelief where morality will inevitably be compromised. We have both biblical commandment and example that the political scene ought to be, and may be, served by believers whose service will not require a compromise of their faith. The weapons of the church in its spiritual warfare are not "carnal" — it is true — but we need to fight with our powerful spiritual weapons in the political arena in order to bring the thoughts of individual civil servants "to captivity unto obedience to Christ" (II Cor. 10:3-5). John the Baptist attempted to do so with Herod; Jesus tried with Pilate (and the Pharisees); Paul tried with Felix and Agrippa and many others. It need not be any different in this century.

Civil service, government service, is not only a necessary fact of this world, and so recognized by the Bible, it is also an *honorable* service and so honored by the Bible (see I Pet. 2:17; Rom. 13:7). Let no Bible believer contradict this for to do so is to "resist God" (Rom. 13:2). The office of civil authority does not, however, arbitrarily sanctify the individual who holds it. Each civil servant (from emperor to cup-bearer) is responsible to consecrate himself to righteousness as a "minster of God." If he does not, he brings disrepute upon the "ministry" of civil service and upon God who ordains it. The concept of civil service is unquestionably a part of God's "good" creation. It deserves "good" people to fulfill it. When these are united, mankind is blessed and the kingdom of God on earth is inevitably extended. May Daniel's, Esther's, Mordecai's, Ezra's and Nehmeiah's tribe increase!

PATRIOTISM

The English word "patriot" has its parallels in French *patriote*, Latin *patriota*, and in Greek *patros*. It means "one who loves his country and zealously supports its authority and interests." Some biblical examples of patriots are:

1. Joseph was patriotic to the extent that although he had become a ruler of Egypt, had married an Egyptian woman, his great desire was that his dead body (bones) be carried by Israelites to the land of Cannan (his homeland) when they left Egypt, to be buried there (see Gen. 50:25; Josh. 24:32). Israelites had to keep his bones in a coffin for 400 years (Gen. 50:22-26; Exod. 13:19) until this could be accomplished.
2. Jacob requested the same patriotic thing (Gen. 49:29-50:14).
3. Moses killed an Egyptian who was abusing one of his countrymen even when Moses was a ruler in Egypt (Exod. 2:11-15). Moses refused to be called Pharaoh's grandson, choosing ill treatment as an Israelite (Heb. 11:23-2).
4. David was a great patriot. He loved Israel and the country with a deep, abiding affection (Psa. 14:7; 25:22; 53;6; 83:1ff; 122:1-9; 136:1-26; 137:1-9). He was so patriotic

(and obedient to God) he would not raise his hand against the anointed king (Saul) or Israel even when Saul was trying to kill him.
5. The Old Testament prophets were patriots who loved their country and the land. Most of them gave their lives trying to save their people from foreign invasion and exile. One has only to read the heart-broken Lamentations of Jeremiah (see Lam. 2:11,13,18; 5:15-18) to hear the cry of a patriot.
6. Naomi longed for her native Israel and was willing to make great sacrifices to return there from Moab (Ruth 1:6ff).
7. Esther, even as a Persian queen, remembered her people and risked her life to save them (Esther 4:14-17). Mordecai also was a Jewish patriot.
8. The Jews of the Maccabean era who "put foreign armies to flight" (Heb. 11:33-38) and suffered tremendous privations for their land are approved of God.
9. The Lord Jesus Christ wept with great sobs over his beloved Jerusalem (Matt. 23:37-39; Luke 19:41).
10. One of Jesus' apostles was Simon the Zealot — most probably a former member of a radically-right group of Jewish patriots, "disciples of the Pharisees" (Matt. 22:15-22).
11. Daniel was patriotically responsible both to his Babylonian and Persian superiors (Dan. 2:37; 4:19; 6:22), and to his own countrymen and homeland (Dan. 1:12-21; 9:3-19).
12. The patriotism of Ezra and Nehemiah stands out like a great light to the world that believers can love, honor and serve their country with God's approval.
13. Paul, the great Jewish apostle to the Gentiles, was loyal to his Jewish culture when it did not interfere with his service to God and man (Acts 16:1-3; 21:39; 22:3; 28:17; Rom. 3:1,2; 9:1-5).
14. Paul wrote that we are to "give thanks for" our rulers (I

Tim. 2:1,2) and to give "respect to whom respect is due, honor to whom honor is due" (Rom. 13:7).
15. Peter wrote, "Honor the emperor" (I Pet. 2:17) which takes some amount of patriotism.

There are undoubtedly many more names from the Bible which might be cited as examples of patriotism. Patriotism would probably be better defined as civic responsibility, for patriotism should not be blindly emotional — it should be rational and moral.

Some Christians are confused about patriotism. Some think Christians have no biblical sanction for loving any country in this world because they are only "citizens of heaven" and pilgrims here. It is true, Christians are citizens of heaven, but they are also citizens of particular nations and cultures while they are in the flesh.

> Why does God want us to be patriotic? I believe God has placed patriotism in men's hearts because God knows a nation cannot survive without it. Patriotism is the bond that unites a nation into one people and holds them together. Patriotism is the spark that makes people willing to place their country above themselves, to sacrifice for their country, even if that sacrifice means their lives. Patriotism is the spirit that gives a special flavor to a nation and which enhances our appreciation for that which is our own. The spirit of patriotism has enabled Americans to unite and struggle through every crisis in our nation's history — until the opinion-makers taught the post-World War II generation that patriotism is neither necessary nor chic.
>
> *God & Caesar*, by John Eidsmore, pp. 40,41 op. cit.

Americans love not only their country (its geographical and topographical features) but its form of government, its liberties, its people and its history. If they did not, they would have no motive for sacrificially defending it against foes whose purposes are to conquer it, change its form of government, take away its liberties, kill many of its people, and plunder its great resources. The true patriot will also actively oppose, through peaceful and biblically-sanctioned means, all immoral and ideological influences practiced and preached by fellow countrymen which would bring about decadence and disorder to one's native land. Thus the prophets of old, the Lord Jesus, and his apostles were true patriots.

But misguided patriotism often produces acute moral blindness. An over-reaching patriotism that vows, "My country, right or wrong . . . " leads to an irrational and dangerous mentality which usually results in disorderly and destructive actions. Roger Thomas, who was then campus minister with Christian Campus House at the University of Missouri in Rolla, gave six fundamental principles which should guide the Christian believer:

> The first truth that must control the Christian view of God and country is the unshakable conviction that *Jehovah God is the absolute sovereign of the universe* . . . . Jehovah is not a local diety whose sole interest is the preservation of one political system . . . .
>
> The second truth is that a Christian's attitude toward his country must be governed by an understanding of the *Lordship* of Jesus Christ . . . . There comes a point when the authority of Caesar must be held in subjection to the claims of the Lord of Glory. When that point is reached, a disciple must choose between obeying God or his country (cf. Acts 4:19). There will be times when it is a Christian's obligation to choose Jesus rather than Caesar . . . . The believer is never free to give unlimited loyalty to his government even in the name of patriotism . . . .
>
> Third, Christian patriotism must always be tempered by the knowledge that *the fellowship of the Spirit* is not limited by national boundaries. Paul's statement in Galatians 3:27,28 makes this unmistakably clear . . . .
>
> The New Testament presents a fourth truth that closely parallels this last one — namely, *the heavenly citizenship of the saints.* "Our commonwealth is in heaven," reads Philippians 3:20. . . . A Christian lives in both time and eternity and must share other men's concern over the problems of this world, but he must never allow these tensions to overshadow his faith and allegiance to Christ. A Christian should exercise responsibility as a

citizen and should show appreciation for the tradition and heritage of his culture; but that appreciation must never be so strong that he forgets how to distinguish his Christian faith from his country's culture . . . .

The fifth truth, one that helps explain God's purpose for governments, is the one most often forgotten — the sinfulness of men. Paul declares in Romans 3:23, "All have sinned and fall short of the glory of God." . . . Sin is not limited to certain tribes, races, or cultures. All have sinned! . . . . Governments exist because God knows that sinful men must have controls or society will degenerate into total chaos . . . . The refusal to acknowledge the sinfulness of men is at the heart of many contemporary political problems. The "liberal" politician whose views are governed by his humanist leaning is convinced that man is inherently good. And so, when much of the money and the well-intended programs end up lining the pockets of those who need it least, everyone asks, "Why?" Jeremiah knew: "The heart is deceitful above all things and desperately corrupt" (Jer. 17:9) . . . . Interestingly enough, the refusal to acknowledge the sinfulness of men is also basic to much "conservative" political theory . . . . Both the liberal who thinks that sinful bureaucrats can solve all the world's problems and the conservative who thinks that individual sinners unrestrained or uninhibited by governmental control will prevent the problems are wrong! Because men are sinful God ordained governments to maintain order and justice. The question may not be how *much* government is good but how *good* is government.

Finally, one last biblical principle must control the Christian response to the God-and-country dilemma — the preeminence of love. The key to Romans 13 is verses 7 and 8, "Pay all of them their dues, taxes to who taxes are due, revenue to whom revenue is due, respect to whom respect is due, honor to whom honor is due. Owe no one anything, except to love one another; for he who loves his neighbor has fulfilled the law."

Facing Your Nation, edited by William J. Krutza and Philip P. Di Cicco, pub. Baker, pp. 78-93

Patriotism is anti-biblical when it places country or culture or race above God or his Word (the Bible). Patriotism is out of control when it will not submit to the revealed guidelines of the Bible and the "natural revelation" of God written upon the hearts and consciences of people (see Rom. 2). One has only to read the Old Testament prophets to gather examples of patriotism gone berserk. A classic example may be found in Jeremiah 26:1-24: Jeremiah is ordered by the Lord to declare the defeat and captivity of his beloved nation, Judah, but the "hotheads" refuse to hear the word of the Lord and declare Jeremiah to be a traitor who ought to be killed. Finally, when Jerusalem was being besieged and burned, a group of "patriots" who refused to accept the word of God from Jeremiah, kidnapped him and took him as a hostage to Egypt, rather than obey God's order to surrender to Nebuchadnezzar (see Jer. 42-43). Jeremiah had warned them long before, "Do not trust in these deceptive words: 'This is the temple of the Lord, the temple of the Lord, the temple of the Lord' " (Jer. 7:4). Clinging to one's culture or nation, or its shrines and institutions when they are clearly disobeying God's revealed word is unacceptable for the believer.

There are many examples of great believers in the Bible who loved their country and their countrymen but whose supreme love for God and his Word compelled them to choose against the wrong in their country in order to be right with God. Moses often had to choose against the majority of the Hebrew people to keep God's commandments; Joshua chose against his countrymen and "served God" (Josh. 24:14,15); Samuel and David had to choose against an ungodly king (Saul), which appeared to some as "unpatriotic"; of course practically all the prophets, from Elijah to Malachi, were accused of being unpatriotic and traitorous (see Isa. 30:1-18; Ezek. 2:1-3:15; 13:1-23; Amos 7:10:17; Micah 3:5). Daniel, a man with two patriotic loyalties (Hebrew and Babylonian), chose to obey God's word against all other loyalties (Dan. 1,5,6). Jesus loved Jerusalem and her people, but he loved God first (Matt. 23:37-39; Luke 29:41-44). Paul was "zealous for the traditions of his fathers" (Gal. 1:14; Phil. 3:4-11) and for his countrymen (Rom. 9:1ff) but he would not let that come above obedience to God's revealed word. Peter and John were loyal, patriotic Hebrews, but they chose to go against their nation's leaders when they were commanded by them to disobey God (Acts 4,5). The Christian must be constantly alert to evaluate the political actions of his country and its leaders, nationally and internationally, in the light of clear biblical teachings and principles. National or cultural patriotism exercised outside the control of God and the Bible inevitably becomes political tyranny. One has only to study the history of the Israelites in the Bible or the great heathen empires in secular history to confirm this.

Clearly, however, Bible believers are not to let patriotism-gone-wrong deter them from active and constant participation in civil government. When the Lord said, "Render unto Caesar the things that are Caesar's; and to God the things that are God's," he said just as much about our duty to our country as about our duty to God. Believers often overlook the importance of political involvement because of the imperative emphasis on their heavenly "citizenship" (see Phil. 3:17; Heb. 11:13-16; 13:14). It is of great significance, however, that the same apostle who wrote the above three statements also constantly affirmed his earthly citizenship all through the book of Acts. He was also the one who told the Roman centurion, "I am from Tarsus in Cilicia, a citizen of no mean city." He was the one who insisted on his rights as a Roman citizen when he was shamefully treated; he was the one who appealed to Caesar for a fair trial when justice seemed to bog down around Jerusalem. The Bible makes it clear, that while the believer's citizenship is ultimately and eternally in heaven, he is also a citizen of the governments of earth — with both their privileges and their responsibilities.

When the Babylonian emperor drove the Israelites into Mesopotamian captivity, they did not forget their homeland. By the waters of Babylon they sat down and wept when they remembered Zion — on the willows there they hung their lyres, and sang patriotically, "If I forget you, O Jerusalem, let my right hand wither!" (Psa. 137).

As Christians we ought to long for the eternal Jerusalem, just as the Israelites longed for the old Jerusalem where their citizenship really was. But shortly after they were taken into captivity, Jeremiah bluntly told them:

> Build houses and live in them; plant gardens and eat their produce . . . seek the welfare of the city where I have sent you into exile, and pray to the Lord for its behalf, for in its welfare you will find your welfare (Jer. 29:5-7).

Most of the Israelites followed the Lord's instructions through Jeremiah. Daniel became a prime minister; Nehemiah became the Persian king's confidant and advisor; Esther became a queen; Mordecai became a high government official. And because these, as well as many others, sought the welfare of Babylon (and later, Persia, Greece, and Rome), the Israelites themselves found their own welfare. Furthermore, a remnant was preserved and reconstituted back in their beloved homeland, from which came the Messiah and Savior of all the world.

In spite of the dangers and complexities of political involvement, the Christian today must realize that "rendering unto Caesar" means more than paying taxes and obeying the laws; it means participating responsibly and knowledgeably in the processes of civil government in every biblically-sanctioned way possible.

7

TAXATION

Some anonymous wag has said, "There are only two things certain in this life — death and taxes!" Other sages have repeated the adage, "There ain't no free lunches!" (meaning any material thing one person may seem to have gotten free of charge, someone else had to work for or pay taxes for). The Bible clearly faces the reality of taxation by civil governments in this world. Biblical sanction for the civil mandate of taxation and the responsibility of human beings to pay taxes is indisputable.

These Hebrew words in the Old Testament text are used for taxation:

1. *erek* — taxation, an estimate (II Kings 23:35)
2. *'arak* — taxes (II Kings 23:35)
3. *nuges* — taxes, oppression (Dan. 11:20)
4. *mas* — tribute (most used word in the Old Testament)
5. *meckes* — a toll, a tax (Num. 31:28,37-41)
6. *middah* — a treasure (Ezra 6:8; Neh. 5:4)

7. *'unesh* — a fine, punishment (II Kings 23:33)
8. *masso'* — a burden, heavy load (II Chron. 17:11)
9. *belu* — (a Chaldean word) — tax (Ezra 4:13,20; 7:24), or custom
10. *ma'esar* — the tithe, ten percent (Lev. 27:30,31,etc)

These Greek words in the New Testament text are used for taxation:
1. *phoros* — (related to the Greek word *phero*, to bring) denotes tribute paid by a subjugated nation (Luke 20:22, 23:2; Rom. 13:6,7).
2. *kensos* — (the word from which Latin and English derive *census*) means a poll tax (Matt. 17:25; 22:17,19; Mark 12:14)
3. *didrachmon* — the half-shekel, is translated *tribute* in Matt. 17:24
4. *telos* — primarily means, an end, a termination; secondary meaning, that which is paid for public *ends* — a toll, tax, custom (Matt. 17:25; Rom. 13:7)
5. *telonion* — denotes a custom-house for the collection of taxes (Matt. 9:9; Mark 2:14; Luke 5:27).

The Greek word in Luke 2:1,3,5, etc., translated "taxed" in KJV is *apographo*. It means, literally, "to write out, to copy, to enroll in a register." It should not be translated "taxed," but either "enrollment" or "census." The enrollment or census was, of course, for the purpose of determining population count in order to collect taxes, but the *apographo* was not the tax itself.

The earliest instance of taxation, perhaps, is that offer of *tribute* made by the king of Sodom to Abram (Gen. 14:21) for services rendered in rescuing the "goods" plundered from Sodom by the unprovoked attack of the "kings of the East" (including the rescue of citizens of Sodom — Lot and his family). Abram had just "tithed" (Heb. *ma'eser*) part of the rescued "goods" to Melchizedek, God's high priest (see also Hebrews 7:1-10). This became the basis upon which God legislated a form of religious taxation to sustain those who rendered religious ser-

TAXATION

vices to others — the Levitical tithes of the Mosaic dispensation. The *principle* that people should be willing to pay (or be "taxed") to sustain those who labor in teaching the truth of God is clearly carried over into the New Testament (see Matt. 10:9-15; I Cor. 9:1-18; II Cor. 12:13; Gal. 6:6; Phil. 4:15-19, etc.).

That exaction of "tribute" was practiced and expected is also exemplified in the account of Jacob's return to his homeland after his exile to Paddan-aram. Jacob evidently expected his brother Esau to demand "tribute" for passage and tenancy upon return to Canaan (see Gen. 32:3-33:11). Jacob called his "tribute" to Esau "a present" (Heb. *minechah*) and hoped to "appease" (Heb. *kapherah phanayv*, lit. "cover the face," sometimes translated, "atone") Esau with it.

The earliest example of *levied taxation* in the Bible is that suggested by Joseph (Gen. 41:33-36) and actually exacted (Gen. 47:24-26) — a twenty percent "social welfare" tax, as it were, on all the people of Egypt. It is significant to notice that the first recorded levying of a "welfare" tax was by a pagan nation — an idolatrous nation! It made no pretense of structuring itself according to the revealed will of the One True God. Yet, God directed Joseph to institute this tax to sustain the civil government of a heathen empire and the truth of God in the messianic nation of Israel was preserved and made available to the world.

The next biblical instance of taxation concerns the nation of Israel. What is called the "tithe" (Heb. *ma'esar*) was, in some cases, actually a tax. One has only to study the case of the Levites in the theocracy (see Lev. 27:30,31; Num. 18:20-24) to observe that they were supported by a tax of one-tenth of all agricultural produce (including animals) from the rest of the Israelite citizenry. In this tax legislation, should a citizen prefer to keep his agricultural produce and give money for the Levites, he was ordered to give one-tenth of what the produce would be worth *plus* he had to *add* "a fifth" (20% of the tithe) to the monetary tax! Levites were consecrated by God to total service of the nation in both religious and civil duties. They could not support themselves by any other occupation. A priest was a Levite, but not all Levites were priests. God levied a tax ("tithe") from the Israelites to support the Levites because they were the nation's civil servants under the theocracy. They served as judges, rulers, policemen (see Exod. 32:21-34), teachers, and workers at civil and religious duties (Num. 7:1-9). The "tithe" had nothing to do with "free-will giving" (See Lev. 23:38; Deut. 16:10; 23:21-23, etc.). The "tithe" was clearly a tax to support the Israelite "system" just like a tax supporting any other form of government (see Mal. 1:8; 3:6-10).

A second tax ("tithe") was the ten percent of produce to be brought at later designated times to the Tabernacle (later to the Temple at Jerusalem) and a sort of "national pot-luck feast" was to be held (see Deut. 12:10,11). It was to be a festival promoting nationalism. It was a civil celebration to bring about national unity. (see Deut. 12:8) and cultivate the social and cultural life of Israel. It was a "patriotic" service paid for by taxes! The times of these "national pot-lucks" were, of course, the great national feast days (Passover, Day of Atonement, Tabernacles, Pentecost, etc.) of the Israelite nation.

A third tax paid by the Israelite was a ten percent ("tithe") "return" paid of all "increase" at the end of every third year for the "needy." It was kind of "welfare" tax (see Deut. 14:28,29). Since this "tithe" was collected every third year it would amount to 3.33 percent per annum. But when we consider the provision of leaving small portions of crops in the fields at harvest-time for the "gleaners," the "welfare" tax comes to more than 3.33 percent (see Lev. 19:9,10).

Thus far we see the Israelite paying as much as 23.33 percent "income taxes" for civil and religious services rendered and for the social welfare of the nation.

Finally, the Israelite paid a "census" or poll tax, sometimes called the "Temple tax" of one-half shekel. In the first century A.D. the half-shekel was worth about half a day's wages (about $13 U.S. minimum wage 1988). It was minor to rich people but critical to most of the people who were poor.

TAXATION

In addition to these taxes ("tithes"), the Israelite was expected to be generous with his possessions and to give "free-will offerings" to the Lord's work and to his neighbors:

> The tithes that are discussed in the Old Testament are not to be considered as free will giving. They have absolutely no parallel to giving in the church. The Old Testament does speak about every man giving as he will in his heart (Exod. 25:2). That refers to gifts offered to the Tabernacle or Temple. But the tithes did not refer to the spontaneous and sacrificial giving of Proverbs 3:9,10 . . . freewill giving is — being generous to God. But people in the Old Testament were required to pay taxes . . . .
> *The Christian and Government*, by John MacArthur, pub. Moody Press, p. 62

The following quotations are concise summaries of what the Bible says about civil government and taxation:

> *TAXES*, charges imposed by governments, either political or ecclesiastical, upon the persons or the properties of their members or subjects. In the nomadic period, taxes were unknown to the Hebrews. Voluntary presents were given to chieftains in return for protection. The conquered Canaanites were forced to render labor (Josh. 16:10; 17:13; Jdgs. 1:28-35). Under the theocracy of Israel every man paid a poll-tax of a half shekel for the support of the tabernacle worship (Exod. 30:13; 38:25,26), and this was the only fixed impost. It was equal for rich and poor (Exod. 30:15). Under the kings, as Samuel had warned the people (I Sam. 8:11-18), heavy taxes were imposed. They amounted to a tithe of the crops and of the flocks besides the forced military and other services which would be imposed. In the days of Solomon, because of his great building program (the magnificent temple,the king's palaces, thousands of stables for chariot-horses, the navy, etc.) the burden of taxes was made so oppressive that the northern tribes rebelled at his death (I Kings 12).
>   During the days of the divided kingdom Menahem (II Kings 15:19,20) bribed the Assyrian king with a thousand talents of silver to support him, and he raised this from the rich men of his kingdom. Similarly Hoshea (II Kings 17:3) paid heavy tribute to

Assyria and on refusing further to pay he lost his kingdom. Later, Pharaoh Necho of Egypt put Judah under heavy tribute, and Jehoiakim oppressively taxed Judah (II Kings 23:33,35). Under the Persian domination, "tribute, custom or toll" (Ezra 4:13) were forms of taxation, though Artaxerxes exempted "priests, Levites," etc. (Ezra 7:23,24). The Ptolemies, the Seleucidae, and later the Romans, all adopted the very cruel but efficient method of "farming out the taxes," each officer extorting more than his share from those under him, and thus adding to the Jewish hatred of the publicans, among whom were at one time Matthew and Zacchaeus, both converts later.

The Zondervan Pictorial Bible Dictionary, gen. ed. Merrill C. Tenney, pub. Zondervan, p. 828

TRIBUTES (Heb. *mas,* forced laborers; *middah,* tribute, toll; Gr. *kensos,* tax, census; *phoros,* tax, burden). The Hebrew word *mas* is incorrectly rendered "tribute," since it means "forced laborers, labor gang." Solomon had a force of taskworkers consisting of 30,000 men, raised by levy upon the people (I Kings 5:13; 9:15,21). David had had a labor gang too (I Kings 4:6; 5:13). Conquered populations were often compelled to render forced labor (Deut. 20:11; Josh 16:10). In New Testament times the *kensos* was an annual tax levied on persons, houses or lands paid to a prince or civil governor on behalf of the Roman treasury. The *phoros* was a tax paid by agriculturists. Customs (*tele*) were collected by the publicans.

The Zondervan Pictorial Bible Dictionary, op. cit. p. 871

CUSTOM, RECEIPT OF (RV "place of toll"), from which Matthew (Levi) was called to follow Christ (Matt. 9:9). In post-exilic days the tribute was usually in terms of a road toll. The Romans imposed tribute or tax upon the Jews as upon all their subjects for the maintenance of their provincial government. Tax collectors or publicans were despised because of their notorious dishonesty and willingness to work for a foreign power.

Zondervan Pictorial Bible Dictionary, op. cit. p. 191

When Jesus was at Jericho, He called Zacchaeus down from a sycamore tree into which he had climbed in order to better see the Lord as He passed by (Luke 19:1-5). Zacchaeus was a publican, or tax-collector; by his own confession (that he would make restoration if he had taken too much) Zacchaeus showed the traits of the tax-collector of ancient times, who extorted all of the money he could from the people. Several papyri have been found concerning the extortions of tax collectors, and they bring vividly to mind the feeling that there must have been against Zacchaeus, as well as against Matthew, who was also a publican (Matt. 9:9).

The need for tax collectors in the ancient world is revealed by the documents which have been excavated in Egypt. The custom house receipts of a town named Socnopaei Nesus show that there was a heavy rate upon both exports and imports, while the individual merchants and tradesman of every kind had to pay heavy taxes. There were taxes on land and farm stock, on goats and pigs, on the temple, and on every item, in fact which was taxable. Evidence of the heavy and widespread taxing program in these ancient documents reminds us that there is nothing new under the sun. The ancients struggled under a twenty percent tax long before the days of the twenty percent deduction of the twentieth century. In Bible times a very heavy force of collectors must have been necessary, and for this reason we are not surprised to encounter tax collectors such as Zacchaeus and Matthew in the New Testament.

Archaeology and Bible History, by Joseph P. Free, pub. Scripture Press, pp. 294,295

The period of the Judges says very little, if anything, about the systematics of taxation in civil government. Apparently the only form of taxation was the giving of "presents" or exacting of "tribute" (see Jdgs. 8:24ff). Judges received nothing more than a share of the "booty" taken in battle. It was a time of disorder and civil chaos. "Every man did that which was right in his own eyes, for there was no king in Israel in those days." We would suppose the Levitical taxes ("tithes") continued in that era.

But when the people demanded that Samuel not perpetuate the civil system of "judgeship" in his sons, but that he anoint for them "a king like the nations" the matter of taxation takes on a much more crucial aspect (I Sam. 8:1-22):

As was to be expected, taxation assumes far greater prominence the moment we cross the threshold of the kingdom . . . the passage (I Sam. 8:10-18) gives us a fairly exhaustive list of royal prerogatives. Aside from various forms of public and private service, the king would *take* (note the word) the best of the vineyards, etc, together with a tenth of the seed and of the flocks. The underlying principle suggested by Samuel's summary and fully exemplified in the actions of Israel's kings, is that the king would take what he needed for his public and private needs from the strength and substance of his people. Constitutional laws regulating the expenditure of public funds and the amount of exactions from the people in taxations seem never to have been contemplated in these early monarchies. The king took what he could get; for constitutional rights has centered from the beginning about the matter of taxation.

International Standard Bible Encyclopedia, Vol. V, article on "Tax, Taxing," by Louis M. Sweet, pub. Eerdmans, pp. 2918,1919

The Israelites cried out to Samuel for justice. Samuel's sons were "perverting justice." But justice in a sinful society must be administered by coercion — and coercion cost. The Israelite wish to be "like the nations" seems also to imply a desire for the "social welfare" they observed in their pagan neighbors. Social welfare administered by the civil state costs — "there are no free lunches." And immediately upon the institution of this restructuring of the Israelite civil system, there was a tax revolt. When Samuel told the people the rights and duties of the kingship (which would include the right to tax) (I Sam. 10:25-27), "some worthless fellows" refused to pay the king his "present" (tax). King Saul, magnanimously (and probably for pragmatic reasons) "held his peace."

During the monarchy there seems to have been various provisions made for exemption from taxes (cf. I Sam. 17:25, etc.). And Samuel wrote in a book (I Sam. 10:25) "the rights and duties of the kingship . . . " so we do have, in effect, a "constitutional" form of civil government in the Israelite monarchy! The king is not totally sovereign. He is subject to the law of God as

Samuel wrote it in a book which was also "told" to the people.

In the time of David taxes would have continued as a civic duty to support the civil state. However, they do not seem to be severe enough to incite civil unrest. That may be due to the constant enrichment of the treasury of Israel by David's many military conquests (II Sam. 8:2,7,8,10,12). But bearable taxation was not the case in Solomon's reign. While Solomon also had a famously-large income (I Kings 10:14-28), his thirst for luxury and public works could be slaked only by massive conscription of taxes (even forced labor by Israelite citizens for the first time I Kings 5:13-17). So Solomon instituted a highly organized and pervasive system of collecting taxes (see I Kings 4:7-19). Since Solomon's reign was one of peace and very little military conquest was made, the burden of income for his indulgences became increased taxation of the citizenry.

When Solomon died and his son Rehoboam inherited the throne, the immediate and urgent demand of the "assembly of Israel" (led by Jeroboam) was:

> Your father made our yoke heavy. Now therefore lighten the hard service of your father and his heavy yoke upon us, and we will serve you (I Kings 12:4).

The elders of Israel who had "stood before Solomon" counseled Rehoboam to accede to the wishes of the people (to lighten the tax burden). But Rehoboam rejected that advise in favor of the prompting of the "young lions" of his own association and decided to "add to their yoke" of taxation and subjugation (I Kings 12:1-15).

A tax revolt (I Kings 12:16ff) resulted and the disastrous division of the chosen people of God into two hateful, spiteful and warring nations. As a consequence the true worship of Jehovah was perverted (eventually in both nations), idolatry and moral decadence became the rule rather than the exception. It ended in the devastation of their homelands and the exile of their peoples in the Assyrian and Babylonian captivities. They were never again the testimony for Jehovah they were in the days of David.

A few references from the Old Testament prophets are sufficient to show that corruption and oppression in taxation was a recurring outrage of the civil leadership against the citizenry of Israel and Judah (see Isa. 3:13-15; Amos 2:6-8; 5:10-13; 7:1; 8:6; Micah 3:1-4; Zeph. 3:1-4). Yet we never read in the Old Testament any precise word from God which would justify a citizen's refusal to pay the taxes or to rise in violent overthrow of the civil government doing the taxing. In the declining and decadent years of the divided kingdoms much of the tax burden was a result of paying forced "tribute" to Mesopotamian overlords (II Kings 15;17-22; 16:5-9; 17:4; 18:13-18; 23:31-35; 24:1-7; II Chron. 36:7, etc.).

The two Israelite nations (first Israel in 722 B.C., and Judah in 606 B.C.) in exile unquestionably paid taxes to their foreign "hosts" (first as captives, and later as adopted sovereigns). This was what they were told to do when Jeremiah (Jer. 29:7) instructed them to "seek the welfare of the city where I have sent you . . . . " A Jew (Daniel) became a chief tax official of the Persian (and probably the Babylonian, earlier) government (Dan. 6:1-5); the Jews who remained in Persia with queen Esther and Mordecai paid taxes to their Persian protectors (Esther 10:1); the Jews who returned to Palestine after the exile paid taxes to Persia (Ezra 4:13); the restored Jews also paid taxes to sustain their new commonwealth (a few being exempted — Ezra 7:21-26). In the days of Nehemiah a tax crisis arose because of the exorbitant demands of the Persian king. The Jewish people newly established in Palestine were mortgaging everything they owned to pay their taxes (Neh. 5:1-31). In addition to the Persian "tribute" they had to pay taxes to support the Jewish governors (Neh. 5:14,15). Because of this heavy taxation the Jews came to feel like "slaves in their own land" (Neh. 9:36,37). But they still laid upon themselves an annual tax of one-third shekel for the Temple and continued to pay taxes ("tithes") to support the Leviticial civil government (Neh. 10:32ff).

Taxes on the biblical scene during the interim between the Old Testament and the New Testament is summarized:

> The Ptolemies, who practically controlled Pal from 301 to 218 BC, do not appear to have been excessive in their demands for tribute (twenty talents for Jews [Ant, XII, iv, 1] seems no great amount), but the custom which they introduced, or at least established, of farming the taxes to the highest bidder, introduced a principle which prevailed through all the subsequent history and was the cause of much popular suffering and discontent. The story of Joseph, the Jewish tax-collector (Ant, XII, iv, 1-5), who was for 23 years farmer-general of taxes and the cause of a "long train of disaster," is peculiarly significant for the student of the NT.
>
> The conquest of Pal by Antiochus the Great (202 BC) brought a certain amount of relief to the "storm-tossed" (Jos) Jews of Pal, as of old the buffer state between contending powers. According to Jos (Ant, XII, iii, 3), Antiochus gave the Jews generous gifts in money, remitted their taxes for three years, and permanently reduced them one-third . . . .
>
> That the Seleucid kings were particularly severe in their exactions is clearly shown in the letter of Demetrius to the Jews, whose favor he was seeking in rivalry with Alexander Balas of Smyrna, the pretender to the Seleucid throne (see I Macc. 10:26-30; 11:34,35; 13:39; 11:28).
>
> In this quoted letter Demetrius promises the following exemptions from (1) "tributes" (*phorioi* — "poll-taxes"); (2) tax on salt; (3) crown taxes (*stephanoi* — "crowns of gold" or their equivalents); (4) the tribute of one-third of the seed; (5) another of one-half of the fruit of the trees (10:29,30). This seems almost incredibly severe, but evidence is not lacking of its probability . . . . With Seleucus IV (187-176 BC) the Jews felt for the first time, indirectly but powerfully, the pressure of Rome. This disreputable ruler had to pay tribute to Rome as well as to find means whereby to gratify his own passion for luxury, and was correspondingly rapacious in the treatment of his subjects (II Macc. 3).
>
> ISBE, Vol. V., op. cit., pp. 2919,2920

The "Seleucus IV" referred to above is the "little horn" of

Daniel 8:9-14 as well as the "contemptible person" of Daniel 11:20-45. The taxes upon the Jewish people by their own Hasmonean (Maccabean) rulers (ca. 160-60 B.C.) were nearly as exorbitant as those of their immediate predecessors, the Seleucids.

The New Testament era, from the birth of Jesus Christ to the Revelation of John to the seven churches of Asia Minor (ca. 4 B.C. — 100 A.D.). is under the Roman imperial system of taxation.

The huge "military complex" of the early Roman empire which was engaged in almost constant conquest of new territories, which, in turn, necessitated "occupation troops" to maintain its extensive sovereignty, required massive amounts of money. The incredible luxuriating, indulging, and building excesses of the Roman emperors demanded massive revenues (taxes). Most of this revenue had to come from the Roman provinces rather than the homeland. Palestine was in the Roman province of Syria. Essentially, this is what the people of Palestine (Jews and Christians) would have faced in the way of taxation:

Roman Taxes:
1. Tributum capitis — poll tax (census tax — about 1 day's ucts)
2. Tributum capitis — poll tax (census tax — about 1 days wages per census)
3. Annona — grain and cattle, (levied "in kind" for use of the Roman army)
4. Publicum — customs, sales, salt, etc. (tax on everything traded or sold)

Jewish Taxes:
1. Temple tax — half shekel (or, *didrachma*, Matt. 17:24) — every Jew over 13 years of age had to pay once each year (even those living outside of Palestine) (about 1 day's wages)
2. Tithes — 10% of everything the land produced (in-

cluding animals)
3. Synagogue Taxes — for education and local Jewish welfare
4. Herod-family taxes — to finance Herod's "public works" (remodeling the Temple, building reservoirs, sending gifts to Roman emperors, building race tracks, theaters, baths, vacation spas, etc.)

The following quotation portrays how devastating the Roman tax burden was upon its conquered peoples (this was upon Egypt):

> Taxes were laid upon every product, process, sale, export, or import, even upon graves and burials; and additional assessments were levied from time to time, in kind from the poor, in liturgies from the rich. From Augustus to Trajan the country — or its masters — prospered; after that zenith it succumbed to the discouragement and exhaustion of endless tribute and taxation and the lethargy of a regimented economy.
> *The Story of Civilization — From Caesar to Christ, III,*
> by Will Durant, pub. Simon & Schuster, p. 409

One is not left to wonder that there were so many poor people mentioned in the New Testament, nor why the just and loving Jesus showed them so much compassion and understanding.

The following quotation, at considerable length, best describes taxation as experienced by people in later Bible times (100 B.C. to 300 A.D.):

> In being excused military service, the Jews were spared the payment of the tax of blood; but the taxes that they did have to pay in money and in kind were exceedingly heavy, and they were all the heavier in that two forms of taxation ran side by side for them, civil taxes and religious taxes; and neither was light.
> The first were of great antiquity in Israel. They were at least as old as Solomon, who had ingeniously divided his realm into twelve districts, each of which in turn had to supply his needs.

This system, naturally, had been kept and improved upon. At times of great crisis there had even been capital levies, as for example under Menahem to pay the Assyrian tribute and under Jehoiakim of Judah to pay the sum required by the Pharaoh Nechoh. Yet these were still taxes raised by the government of Israel for the glory or the safety of the Chosen People. But after the return from exile the taxation became far more bitter to the people, since the taxes were to be paid to pagans, Persians, Greeks from Egypt and then from Syria, and then Romans or Roman vassals. Herod the Great particularly, made himself so unpopular by the severity of the imposititons that he laid on the people to finance his immense undertakings and his ostentatious policy, that on several occasions he was forced to grant a remission in order to prevent an outbreak of rage. His heirs the tetrarchs modestly followed his example: in direct taxes alone Archelaus raised six hundred talents (about 125 million dollars) in Judea and Samaria; and Galilee brought in two hundred for Antipas.

In that part of Palestine which was incorporated into the Roman empire after the year 6 A.D., the Roman system of taxation was established; and it was the same rapacious system that was known everywhere else. Even Tactitus, who is so hostile to the Jews, lets it be understood that it was this taxation that was the immediate cause of the great rising. There were then, as there are in our modern states, direct taxes and indirect taxes; Saint Paul refers directly to both (Rom. 13:7). The first, which were collected by agents of the imperial treasury, included on the one hand a tax on real property, affecting all producers, especially landowners, which was paid in kind and which is estimated to have amounted to between twenty and twenty-five percent of the product; and on the other hand a capitation or poll-tax, which was perhaps in proportion to the payer's wealth: it was about the lawfulness of this last tax that the Pharisees questioned Jesus one day, trying to draw Him into an embarrassing position (Matt. 22:17; etc.) The indirect taxes were more like the import duties and internal customs of some European countries than our sales-tax: they were collected at certain bridges, fords, important crossroads, the entries into towns and the market-places; and thus we find Matthew "sitting at work in the customs-house" at Capernaum.

These indirect taxes were made far heavier by their manner of collection. They were farmed, as the salt-tax and the aids were in

TAXATION

France as late as the eighteenth century. Upon the supreme control of a financial procurator, who had to be a Roman knight, the farmers-general (they might be individuals or groups) signed a contract, usually for five years by which they agreed to pay the state a fixed sum in return for being allowed to reimburse themselves by collecting the dues as they saw fit. For this they raised a whole army of tax-gatherers, with officers (Luke speaks of the small-statured Zacchaeus as "the chief publican"), gaugers and inferior minions. It need scarcely be said that under such a system every form of dishonesty was possible, and as Jesus Himself implies, the tax-gatherers would claim "more than their right" (Luke 3:13). The employees of the revenue department were therefore cordially hated and despised; partly because they stole and partly because they served the pagans. These men were the notorious publicans who are to be met with so often in the Bible Gospels, and whose very name was synonymous with public sinner, contemptible creature, outcast of society. Everywhere they were seen, with their stick in their hand and their brass plate on their chest, peering in their rasping and rapacious manner into bales and containers. The Talmud says that they formed a positive caste; and when one member of a family became a publican, all the rest followed him. The example of Zacchaeus proves that there were good and generous men among them; that excellent little Zacchaeus who gave "half of what he had to the poor, and if he had wronged anyone in any way, made restitution of it fourfold." And it is quite certain that there were admirable souls, like that publican who stood "afar off" and humbly in the Temple and prayed so well to God. But on the whole, it is comprehensible that this breed of men was not widely popular.

The civil taxes were not the only ones: the religious taxes were to be paid as well as those that the Romans collected. They went back to the remotest antiquity: had not Abraham "given the tithes of all he had won" to the Almighty? But since then the system had been much improved: the rabbis listed no less than twenty-four dues that were owing to the religious authorities, and they exhorted the faithful to pay them with the greatest care. It may be supposed, however, from the repetition of the homilies upon this theme, that the Jews were not always over-eager with their payments. These religious taxes were recognized by the Romans and they had an official character: the Temple authorities were given great facilities for the collection of the money, and its transport was protected by the imperial troops.

In a general manner, these religious taxes fell into two categories. The Temple tax, or rather the true Temple offering, was intended for the upkeep of the sanctuary and the costs of the officiating priests. It was collected everywhere, in Palestine as well as in the Jewish communities of the Diaspora, from the fifteenth day of Adar onwards, that is to say, during the month which preceded the feast of the Passover. Every adult Israelite, by which was meant every Israelite over thirteen, had to pay it, whether he was rich or poor. Traditionally it was half a shekel, as Yahweh Himself had stated to Moses that that was the amount. We know from a very exact verse in Saint Matthew (Matt. 17:23) that at the time of Christ it was a didrachma, or about seventy cents.

This was very little, in comparison with the tithes. In principle the payment of tithes meant the payment of a tenth part of everything that the soil produced, and it was the very type of religious obligation. For was not Yahweh the owner of the earth, and was it not thanks to Him that the fruits of the earth were to be had? It was therefore but right to offer a share to Him, the first-fruits of all the crops which as far back as the days of the desert were put in a basket and carried to the sanctuary "with rejoicing in all the good things that He had given His people" (Deut. 26). These first-fruits were now taken by the priests, and not returned to the producer as they had been in early times, and they had become a due which the priests insisted upon most strictly, sending out Levites to collect it and insisting that everything, however small, should be tithed. The rabbis had laid down the principle that all untithed products of the soil were unclean and that the eating of them was an exceedingly grave sin. The sheep of a flock were to be tithed just as much as the eggs from the poultry-yard or even, as we see in the Gospel (Matt. 23:23), the humblest plants used in the kitchen, such as mint, dill and cummin. It was only during the sabbatical year that the tithe was not due, for in that year, at least in theory, both the land and its workers were to rest.

However onerous the tithes may have been, particularly when they were added to all the other taxes, they were still paid more willingly than the dues that had to be given to the occupying authorities. Indeed, the getting ready of the carts that were to take the first-fruits to the Temple was something of a rural holiday. There was a proper and accepted way of preparing the carts: the barley had to be put in first, at the bottom, then the wheat and the

TAXATION

dates, then the pomegranates, the figs and the olives, and at the very top, the grapes. Properly loaded and decorated with branches and flowers the carts met at one of the twenty-four centers, then they were led off in picturesque procession to the sound of psalms as far as Jerusalem, where they were joyfully welcomed by the priestly dignitaries and by crowds of the ordinary people. It would be pleasant to think that these rejoicings made the burden of taxes, dues and payments seem less overwhelming.
  Daily Life in The Time of Jesus, by Henri Daniel Rops, pub. Mentor-Omega Book, pp. 161-165, paperback

Nobody likes to pay taxes. The less one earns, the harder it is to make ends meet after taxes. The more you earn, the greater bite the tax-collector takes from you. Taxation has been a historic root of bitterness periodically springing up through the ages. It was certainly no less so in Bible times and among Bible people. The following summary of taxation in the first century A.D. is helpful:

There were various forms of taxation, just as there are today, and some were direct, like the poll-tax, which in Syria is said to have been one percent on your assessed income, or the *tributum*, which was also a special sort of property tax, levied in time of emergency, and from which at some periods Roman citizens were exempt. Then there were duties on food, duties payable on the transfer of property, including the sale of slaves, there were land-taxes, taxes on the profits of mining, and so forth, and there were also customs dues to be paid on all exports, purchase-taxes or 1 or ½ percent on sales, death-duties, etc. The city-dwellers are said to have loathed the purchase-tax.

How were these taxes collected? There was a Roman official called Censor, and it was the business of his department to see that the revenue was collected in the cheapest manner possible. One common method was to auction the task to the lowest bidder, so that he who tendered the lowest rate of commission got made collector of taxes in a given area. This was no doubt the way that things were done in Palestine, and we know that the tax-gatherers there were unpopular with the citizens, partly because they were collaborators with an alien government, partly because they often extorted more money than they really had a right to do, and pocketed the difference. The contracts with these collectors were for five years at a time. Such a contract of course allowed them in theory a fixed scale of percentage, but they often exceeded this, and cheated the tax-payer and probably the government too, and it is very likely that they took bribes to let off rich citizens from paying their full share of the taxes. Like the unjust steward in the parable, they would say to a wealthy tax-payer: "and how much owest thou unto the government? Take thy demand-note and sit down quickly and alter it by 50 percent." It is not surprising that the *publicani* as they were called, were classed together with "sinners," which in this case means chiefly people who did not keep the Jewish law of Moses as they should.

Everyday Life in New Testament Times, by A.C. Bouquet, pub. Charles Scribner's Sons, pp. 13-15

There are three major passages in the New Testament with which we conclude our review of what the Bible says about taxes. From these three passages we shall have the final and absolute revelation of Jesus Christ the Son of God, and His Spirit speaking through anointed apostles, as to what the Christian is to believe and practice about taxation and civil government.

The first of these passages is in Matthew's (himself a former tax-collector) Gospel. Matthew is the only gospel writer to record this incident:

When they came to Capernaum, the collectors of the half-shekel tax went up to Peter and said, Does not your teacher pay the tax? He said, Yes. And when he came home, Jesus spoke to him first, saying, What do you think, Simon? From whom do kings of the earth take toll or tribute? From their sons or others? And when he said, From others, Jesus said to him, Then the sons are free. However, not to give offense to them, go to the sea and cast a hook, and take the first fish that comes up, and when you open its mouth you will find a shekel; take that and give it to them for me and for yourself (Matt. 17:24-27).

Some have used this passage to justify *not* paying taxes. But, in context, the incident teaches quite the contrary. It is altogether possible that Jesus used this incident to teach his ambitious and bickering disciples who had the wrong concept about the kingdom (see Matt. 16:13-28; Matt. 18:1-20) that servanthood is the essence of Christian discipleship. Jesus graciously paid this temple tax which he did not owe because as the Son of God he is the "reigning prince" (actually co-creator and owner) of the temple. Jesus paid taxes he did not owe to keep others who do owe from being tempted to sin by not paying them. "*Toll or tribute* is tax money for the support of the kings themselves and *their sons* as well. To tax their sons is tantamount to taxing themselves, like one hand paying the other. No, kings collect taxes, not from their own sons, but from those outside the royal family, i.e. from *strangers*." (Fowler, in *The Gospel of Matthew, Vol. III*, College Press, p. 657). The Jewish rulers would never have accepted Jesus' claim to be the Son of God and owner of the Temple and, thus, his exemption from paying the tax. Such a statement from Jesus to these tax-collectors would have, in fact, probably precipitated an untimely and violent action against Jesus.

> For our magnanimous Lord, the dilemma was easy to resolve: to refuse to pay, merely to prove a point for some, would cause others to stumble and cost the salvation of some precious souls, but to pay when under no obligation to do so, costs exactly one *didrachma* and He could teach his disciples deference! So He paid, and in so doing He did not violate either His own freedom or the conscience of others. Rather, by submitting, He demonstrated his majesty . . . . By His example He instructs all disciples not to abuse their freedom and to be sensitive to unbelievers, refraining from unnecessarily offending those who could be positively influenced to accept the Gospel . . . . To relinquish one's own undeniable, inalienable personal rights for the good of others is true self-denial and the story of Jesus' life.
>   *The Gospel of Matthew, Vol. III*, by Harold Fowler,
>   pub. College Press, p. 661

It is interesting that even after the Romans destroyed the Temple in 70 A.D., Titus Vespasian, the Roman emperor, considered the tax so practical and useful, he made the Jews continue to pay the tax and he used it to build and sustain the pagan Temple of Jupiter Capitolinus which was built by the Romans on the grounds where the Jewish Temple had previously stood!

What is most significant, however, is the fact that Jesus paid, and taught his disciples to pay, taxes into a treasury of an ungodly and apostate religion whose priests and rabbis would soon execute him! Jesus paid tax to a temple he called "a den of thieves and robbers." He taught his disciples to pay taxes to an institution that was a mockery to God, corrupt, exploiting every worshiper, and that was doomed to extinction within a few short years. Jesus paid the tax and taught believers to do so because paying taxes is ordained of God — it is right. However, Jesus clearly and demonstrably denounced the injustices and corruptions of the very institution into which he paid taxes.

So the Bible (Jesus Christ, himself) says it is right to pay taxes. And, while the institution to which those taxes are paid may be corrupt and the tax money itself may be used by corrupt people to perpetuate their wickedness, believers have no right to withhold payment of taxes to support civil order and government. Christians should feel obligated (by Jesus' example) to verbally, at least, denounce the corruption — while they continue to pay their taxes. Jesus could well have started a violent reaction over this Temple tax had he desired to do so. But rather than cause civil rioting and disorder, he humbly forfeited his right of exemption and paid the tax.

Our second passage from God's word in the New Testament concerning taxes is recorded by the three synoptic gospels, Matthew, Mark, and Luke. We shall quote here the passage as Matthew (former tax-collector) recorded it:

> Then the Pharisees went and took counsel how to entangle him in his talk. And they sent their disciples to him, along with the Herodians, saying, Teacher, we know that you are true, and teach the

TAXATION

way of God truthfully, and care for no man; for you do not regard the position of men. Tell us, then, what you think. Is it lawful to pay taxes to Caesar, or not? But Jesus aware of their malice, said, Why put me to the test, you hypocrites? Show me the money for the tax. And they brought him a coin. And Jesus said to them, Whose likeness and inscription is this? They said, Caesar's. Then he said to them, Render therefore to Caesar the things that are Caesar's and to God the things that are God's. When they heard it, they marveled; and they left him, and went away (Matt. 22:15-22).

There are three Greek words used by Matthew in this passage which are of importance to the matter of taxation. The first is *nomisma*, translated, "money" and is from the Greek root *nomos* meaning "a custom, a law" — that is the current coin of a state, legal tender. The second word is *kensou*, translated "tax" and is the word from which we get the English word *census* — it denotes a poll tax or some form of "tribute." The third word is *denarion* translated, "coin" — it was the Roman *denarius* (one day's wages for the common laborer). Matthew's expert and precise description of the coinage being used gives impact to the seriousness of the confrontation. In addition, the "likeness and inscription" (Gr. *eikon . . . epigraphe*, literally, "icon or image, and drawing") on the *denarius* was that of Tiberius Caesar. It read, *TICAESARDIVI AUGFAUGUSTUS* ("Tiberius, emperor, son of the divine Augustus, the illustrious"); and on the reverse side it read, *PONTIF MAXIMA* ("High Priest"). It shows the emperor Tiberius on a throne with someone kneeling to him pouring out a drink offering in worship to him. Some rabbis said, "Whoever pays his taxes acknowledges the truth of this" (idolatry). Thus we have this dilemma: the tax money was (1) a law, (2) a tribute to a foreign conqueror, (3) propaganda for idolatry! What is a loyal and "righteous" Pharisee to do?

To make matters worse, this "tribute" was a poll-tax to be paid to the Roman imperial treasury which had been instituted during the last days of the hated Archelaus, son of Herod the Great.

Josephus tells us that "Cyrenius" had been sent by Caesar Augustus about 6 A.D. to depose Archelaus and "to take an account of their (the Jews) substance" (that is, to take a census), and "to dispose of Archelaus's money" (i.e., the taxes Archelaus had collected for the Roman treasury) (see Josephus' *Antiquities*, Book XVIII, 1:1; 2:1; Matt. 2:22).

> More than one Jew who paid this tribute was unsure of the basis on which supporting a pagan government could be defended. Several factors contributed to this confusion:
> 1. In the Mosaic legislation God had not spelled out His will for His people when they became subjects of foreign powers, so no Old Testament text could be cited. True, various prophets had addressed themselves to specific situations, but what should Israel do in Jesus' day? THAT was the issue. The whole debate revolved around the contradiction between ideal Israel (under God alone) and actual Israel (under Caesar too), or between what seemed to be prophesied for Israel and what Israel suffered under Rome at the time. Although Mosaic legislation had decreed that Israel must establish as king over them only men of Hebrew descent, the choice must be God's appointment (Deut. 17:14f). Since the close of the Old Testament no genuine prophet had arisen to indicate the Lord's choice and anoint His appointee (cf. I Macc. 14:41; 4:46).
> 2. Before Christ's coming the Jewish people had been conquered various times by pagan peoples and had been forced to pay them tribute. Naturally, this subjugation bred its deeply-felt bitterness and fiercely proud resentment toward the occupying powers, be they Assyrian, Babylonian, Greek or Roman. As a result of these invariably heathen influences in the national life, there arose religious patriots at various intervals who fomented political revolution. They preached holy war against the pagans as God's will. Engaging in terrorist activities, they sowed terror in the land. Their war-cry was "No king but Jahve! No Law but the Torah!" (cv. Antiq. XVIII, 1,1,6; Wars, II, 8,1)
> 3. One of the great ironies of Jewish history especially in this context is that around 4 B.C. the Jews sent their best ambassadors to plead with Caesar to establish ROMAN

government over them in decided preference to semi-Jewish Herodian rule! (Antiq. XVII, 11,1,2; and again in 6 A.D., Antiq. XVII, 13,1,2,5; XVIII, 1,1). And, if they had requested it, should they not also pay for it?
The Gospel of Matthew, Vol. IV, by Harold Fowler, pub. College Press, pp. 200,201

Jesus' answer to the question posed by the disciples of the Pharisees (who would be *against* tribute to Caesar) and to the "Herodians" (those who supported the dynasty of Herod, and therefore the rule of Rome, who would be *for* tribute to Caesar) is a master-stroke of logic and truth. It is in fact, a divine exposure of a sinful enigma. The inquisitors said, "Is it lawful to *give* taxes to Caesar or not?" Matthew (as do Mark and Luke) reports the question using the word *dounai* (Gr. from *didomi*, "give, yield, grant, offer"). They looked upon taxes as that which was "yielded" — a grudging gift. Jesus replied, "*Pay* unto Caesar that which is Caesar's and unto God that which is God's!" Matthew (as do Mark and Luke) reports Jesus' reply by using the Greek word *apodote*, "restore, pay, render what is due." Taxes to government is *paid* for services received (law and order). Taxes are *dues* (Rom. 13:7), they are not gifts. Every citizen should pay taxes because every citizen receives some service from the government. *There are no free lunches*!

The outstanding analysis of this passage by Harold Fowler is quoted here at length:

A. Man's Relationship to the State
1. *Render unto Caesar.* Jesus' attackers had asked, "Shall we give tribute unto Caesar *(dounai kenson Kaisari)*?" Although *didomi*, when used in contexts involving taxes, tribute, rent and the like, should be rendered "pay," its usual meaning is "give." (Cf. Arndt-Gingrich, 191ff). Nevertheless, because Jesus Himself does not use their term in His answer, but rather the intensified form, *apodidomi*, He implies a subtle verbal contrast between their word and His. Accordingly, their question means, "Is it right to GIVE taxes to Caesar?" and He retorts, PAY BACK Caesar

and God what is their right." Your tribute is no voluntary gift as your question implies. You are paying back the Roman government money you legally and morally owe for every benefit and advantage that this regime provides its subjects.

2. *The things that are Caesar's.* What does this involve?

a. Both Jesus and Paul explain that *what is Caesar's* has been delegated to him by God in the first place. (Rom. 13:1; John 19:11; Study Ps.82:1,6 in connections with Exod. 21:6;22:8f., 28 and John 10:34f. Had the Jews forgotten Dan. 2:21, 37f.; 4:17, 24-32; 5:21,23?) The political irony of the historical situation in which the first century Hebrew nation found itself was the fact that God had not intervened to free them from Roman domination. It could be argued, therefore, that it was at least His permissive will that this domination continue to exist. Even king Agrippa argued similarly (*Wars*, II, 16,4).

> Could any Jew seriously affirm that Rome's liberal policy toward the Jewish faith interfered with its free exercise? Had not Rome rectified the controversy over the images? (*Ant.* XVIII, 3,1; *Wars*, II, 10) Had not Rome recalled and banished Archelaus? (*Ant.* XVII, 13,1-5) Was not even Jewish religion solicitous of the Emperor's good health and government by virtue of the sacrifices offered on his behalf) (*Wars*, II,10,4; 17:2) Did not even the Jewish authorities themselves distinctly admit that the acceptance and use of a sovereign's coin was tantamount to recognizing his sovereignty? (Edersheim, *Life*, II,385, cites Babha K.113a and Jer.Sanh. 20b) This was not unlikely based on earlier practice (I Macc. 15:6). In fact, Jewish independence from Rome was celebrated by coins blatantly celebrating the first Jewish revolt (66-70 A.D.) Later, Bar-Cochba's revolt spawned a new series of Jewish shekels around 132-135 A.D. (*Davis Dictionary of the Bible*, 512) Jesus too had expressed the common understanding that taxes were leveled upon subject people (Matt. 17:25f.). For Jews, therefore, to pay Casesar's head-tax meant that they there-by admitted his political lordship, an admission they later shouted to Pilate (John 19:15).

Insofar as the political government does not interfere with the activities and adoration of God and His people, there is no violation of religious liberty in the paying of revenue to the State to pay for goods and services on behalf of the taxed. Money must come from somewhere to pay for law and order, to build highways for ready access to the entire empire, to construct harbors and public buildings. God expects His people to help pay for the whole realm of governmental activity whereby the State benefits all its citizens by good laws, the protection of civil and religious rights and the general administration of justice. This is no gift to Caesar, but a legal and moral obligation. Can it be right to accept the advantages of orderly government and yet be unwilling to pay the cost of them?

b. Jesus' word is the State's charter that guaranteed its right to function. It also condemns every conniving attempt of tyrannous churchmen to usurp the State's authority. Duty to God recognizes the sphere of obedience to State law too (Rom. 13:1-10; I Tim. 2:1f.; I Peter 2:13-17).

c. But we must render *ONLY* the things that are Caesar's to him, nothing more. Jesus' second dictum demands this limitation. (Cf. the position taken by Daniel and his three friends: Dan. 1:3-16; 3:16-18, 28; 6:1-27.)

B. Man's Relationship to God

1. But the first is that we must be religious about paying our taxes! Obedience to God means to respond conscientiously and positively to His ministers who are attending to this very thing (Rom. 13:5-7). There is a direct chain of command running from God down to the common citizen, a chain which runs right through the hands of the governing authorities of the land. Recognition of this reality should take all the sting out of paying "all of them their due, taxes to whom taxes are due, revenue to whom revenue is due, respect to whom respect is due, honor to whom honor is due." From this point of view, *to render unto Casesar IS to render unto God what is God's!* There is no necessary conflict of responsibility between God and the State.

2. The crisis of conscience arises for the believer only when Caesar thinks that he is god and begins to require that we render unto Caesar the things that are God's. Despite Jehovah's Witnesses' protestations to the contrary, Christ has not established a theocracy wherein we must render unto God what is Caesar's. The Kingdom of God and the State are not essentially in competition.

At this juncture we must face the dilemma of Acts 4:19 and 5:29. The Lord does not suggest that no situations would ever arise where the choice would be the State over against God. In fact, many such occasions have arisen in Church history when wicked rulers have persecuted and slaughtered God's people for refusal to render to Caesar what belongs to God, their highest loyalty and worship. (Study Revelation 13.) Such times call for resolute refusal to submit to this pagan worship and the choice of death to compromise. God has already demonstrated His sovereign might against rulers who claimed His rights (Acts 12:10-23; Dan. 4,5; Isa. 36,37). And He will do so again (Rev. 16:6; 19:11-21; 20:7-15)!

3. The doctrine of separation of Church and State is solidly rooted in Jesus' declaration. Our Lord did not demand unquestioning submission to all tyrants whatever their requirements, because this would render it absolutely impossible to *render unto God the things that are God's*. His latter demand places the freedom of conscience and the Church above every secular claim. But only bad, wrong-headed exegesis could ever justify the conclusion that our Lord left the respective spheres of influence of God and of Caesar as so separate that God's will cannot interfere with the Christian citizen's relationship and duty to the State. ("Religion and politics do not mix"!) Rather, the State could not exist or function without God's permission and it is responsible to Him for the exercise of its proper functions. The child of God must always act in harmony with God's will therefore, even when he serves as a citizen of the State. God is ABOVE the State, not sharing equal time with it!

4. Jesus' sharp distinction between God and Caesar denounces all forms of Caesar — worship. Any godless political philosophy that would deify the State must reckon with Jesus' spiritual demand: *and to God!* Although His questioners could object that His reply evades what they considered the real issue, His word was clear and definite enough to uphold the principle of the State and civil government. His view of the abuses of the Roman state is more clearly and concretely expressed elsewhere. (See notes on 20:20-28). For Jesus, the ruthless exercise of raw power, or power for power's sake, is Satanic. In His eyes, all ambition to become great and to maintain power by arbitrary and oppressive rule is to be decisively rejected and stedfastly resisted by His disciples. Only humble, useful service is the path to true

greatness and proper dominion. (See notes on Matt. 18.)
The Gospel of Matthew, Vol. IV, by Harold Fowler,
pub. College Press, pp.206-209

Our final New Testament passage dealing with taxes is:

Let every person be subject to the governing authorities. For there is no authority except from God, and those that exist have been instituted by God. Therefore he who resists the authorities resists what God has appointed, and those who resist will incur judgment. For rulers are not a terror to good conduct, but to bad. Would you have no fear of him who is in authority? Then do what is good, and you will receive his approval, for he is God's servant for your good. But if you do wrong, be afraid, for he does not bear the sword in vain; he is the servant of God to execute his wrath on the wrongdoer. Therefore one must be subject, not only to avoid God's wrath but also for the sake of conscience. For the same reason you also pay taxes, for the authorities are ministers of God, attending to this very thing. Pay all of them their dues, taxes to whom taxes are due, revenue to whom revenue is due, respect to whom respect is due, honor to whom honor is due (Rom. 13:1-7).

In this passage the apostle uses the Greek words *phoros* and *telos* to designate, respectively, "taxes" and "revenues" (13:7) (see definitions earlier). He also uses two different Greek words, *teleite* and *apodote* both of which are translated, "pay" in 13:6 and 13:7. *Teleite* is present indicative active, meaning "keep on paying for government ends." *Apodote* is aorist imperative active, meaning "you are ordered to be making payment." Paying taxes is an apostolic command and it is a perpetual apostolic command! One more Greek word of interest in this text is *opheilas*, translated "dues" in 13:6. In I Corinthians 7:3 the same Greek words, *apodidoto* ("pay") and *opheilen* ("dues") are used concerning conjugal *rights* that are to be *paid* by one spouse to another. A wife has a God-given *right* to be *paid* conjugal dues by her husband, and vice versa. Civil government has a God-given *right* to demand that civil government reciprocate (i.e. pay) with its God-ordained ministry for citizens.

It could not be more unequivocal than when it is stated that citizens are *obligated* to pay taxes "to avoid the wrath of God, but also for the sake of conscience." The person who refuses to pay taxes or cheats on taxes will suffer the wrath of God. He has violated not only the revealed law of God, he has also violated the "natural law" of God written on every human conscience.

Consider some of the "ends" (*telos*, tribute) for which the Roman tax was used — both good and bad:

Good:
1. equal justice (theoretically) for all Roman citizens
2. maintenance of civil order through magistrates and soldiers
3. highway system (approx. 47,000 miles of it) for travelers and merchants; other public services, aqueducts, reservoir, etc.
4. passenger, freight, and express system including post-stations where riders, drivers, conductors, doctors, blacksmiths, wheelwrights, and reserve rolling-stock were always available.
5. education, schools, literature, arts
6. firefighters, police
7. banking and trade expansion and assistance

Bad:
1. war, conquest, imperialism, destruction and devastation
2. incredible extravagance of the Roman authorities (from emperors to senators, to lesser procurators, magistrates, etc.) Tiberius supported a colony of 300 homosexual boys on the island of Capri for his indulgence; Nero married a homosexual in a public ceremony; others gambled away millions of dollars in one night; drunkenness, sexual immorality, assassination, waste was the rule rather than

the exception.
3. building of pagan temples and the support of an idolatrous priesthood (involving sexual perversion and demonology)
4. building of huge, complex, expensive gladitorial arenas and payment for all expenses incurred for games at which thousands of animals and humans were slaughtered
5. a welfare "dole" in massive proportions that resulted in a huge class of citizens with nothing to do but mischief
6. foreign aid to keep in power "puppet" officials (like the Herods) who were brutal and corrupt
7. supported an empire that arbitrarily and without compassion enslaved large portions of nations and cultures it defeated in war (there were more slaves in first century Rome than free citizens).

For more detailed information on the extravagance and barbarity of the Roman empire to which Paul commanded taxes be paid see, *Twenty-Six Lessons on Revelation, Vol. I & II*, by Butler, College Press; *The Story of Civilization III, Caesar and Christ*, by Will Durant, Simon & Schuster; *Seutonius, The Twelve Caesars*, translated by Robert Graves, Penguin Classic Books; *The Greek and Roman World*, by W.G. Hardy, Schenkaman Pub. Co.

In light of the "bad" some citizens (especially Christians) might think they would be justified in refusing to pay taxes to such a government. But here are two voices from the ancient past, testimonies of Christians who lived in that barbaric empire of Rome:

> Everywhere, we, more readily than all men, endeavor to pay to those appointed by you the taxes both ordinary and extraordinary, as we have been taught by (Jesus) . . . . Whence to God alone we render worship, but in other things we gladly serve you, acknowledging you as kings, and rulers of men, and praying

that with your kingly power you be found to possess also sound judgment.

    Justin Martyr (A.D. 100-163), *First Apology*, Chapter *xvii*

Without ceasing, for all our emperors we offer prayer. We pray for life prolonged; for security to the empire; for protection to the imperial house; for brave armies, a faithful senate, a virtuous people, the world at rest — whatever, as man or Caesar, an emperor would wish.

    Tertullian (A.D. 160-230), *Apology*, chapter *XXX*

Any government, no matter how "bad" is better than *no* government at all. Government is instituted by God for the protection and preservation of basic inalienable human rights, life, liberty and property. And government must be paid for by taxes. The apostolic command is very simple: Pay your taxes! The apostle Paul warns all citizens (especially Christians) to avoid attitudes of rebellion and revolution toward civil government. Christians are obligated by their belief in Christ to avoid disorder, chaos and insurgency. They must be beacon-lights of order and peace in a world of lawlessness. In spite of hostile, persecuting, corrupt, decadent, and often unjust governments, Christians in every age are bound by their covenant of grace in the New Testament of Jesus Christ to submit to civil government and to sustain it by paying taxes.

Abuses of civil governments in the practice of taxation have caused as many violent revolutions and wars as any other matter. Rus Walton, in his book, *One Nation Under God*, has made the following suggestions for "tax reform" in the United States of America:

1. *Taxes should be used to raise revenues for legitimate government activities, period. Taxes should not be used for social control or social reform.*

   When taxation is employed to finance the proper and necessary functions of government, it is a legitimate extension of civil authority. When taxation exceeds those limitations, it becomes a license to plunder; it violates God's laws (*Thou shalt not covet, thou shalt not steal*).

There are those who see the instrument of taxation as a means to achieve their concept of "social justice" — of redistributing income and wealth . . . and forcing individual initiative and reward down to the lowest uncommon denominator. "One of the prime functions of government is continually to redistribute market incomes so that incomes are in accordance with our social or collective judgments as to what constitutes a just distribution of economic resources." (L.C. Thurow and R.E.B. Lucas, in *The American Distribution of Income: A Structural Problem*, Joint Economic Committee, March 17, 1972).

Where? Where in the Constitution is this "function" of government set forth? Where does it say that "redistribution of wealth" is a power given by the people to the government — at any level? . . .

2. *Taxes should be apportioned so that each citizen pays a fair share of the cost of government — no more and no less.*

Every citizen should help pay the cost of government — no matter how small the levy or how minute the share . . . .

Tax rates should be proportional, not progressive. If the cost of government is, for example, thirty percent of total personal income, then a flat rate of 30 percent should be applied to all incomes. At the same time all loopholes and exceptions should be eliminated . . . .

3. *The amount of taxes government collects each year should be clearly established in advance, with a cast-iron lid on that amount.*

The citizen has a right to know that government will not take more than a set amount of his wealth and that no open-ended budgets at any level can cause taxation to exceed that limit during the stated (annual) period . . . .

Such a lid would force government to set a budget within the people's means — and stay within it . . . .

4. *Property taxes should be levied at the local level only.*

"When the power to tax (property) leaves the county, tyranny will then begin in the United States . . . .The people of a county will be helpless as their property is taxed to the point of expropriation by a distant state capital . . . ."

5. *Property taxes should be levied for "property-connected" ser-*

vices only (police, fire, sewer, special districts, etc.).

Forcing property owners to pay taxes for general governmental functions (such as education, welfare, courts, etc.) is forcing them to pay twice — once through property taxation and again through taxes on income and/or purchases . . . .

6. *"People" taxes (income, sales, etc.) should be used to finance "people" services (general services such as education, public assistance, justice, etc.).*

Financing "people" services through "people" taxes would help to spread the tax burden so that it would be more equitable and easier for all citizens to bear.

Those who receive a service should foot the bill; as widely as possible, government should base its income on a fee-for-services basis and operate on a cost-price-market system . . . .

7. *Only those who are to pay a tax should be permitted to vote on the imposition and amount of that tax.*

To some this will no doubt seem to be heretical. But, fair's fair! Why is it right that someone who will not pay the tax should have the license to vote on the amount of tax others will be forced to pay?

(Even Karl Marx, "Mr. Communism" said,) "Is not private property as an idea abolished when the non-property owner becomes legislator for the owner? The property qualification for the vote is the ultimate political form of the recognition of private property" . . . .

8. *Taxes should always be visible: no more "hidden taxes" — and, no more pyramiding of taxes.*

The people have a right to know when, and how, and how much they pay out in taxes. Hidden taxes make for invisible government.

Further, hiding taxes tends to encourage pyramiding of taxes — taxing the tax on a product. A gross example of this : slapping a sales tax on gasoline that already includes in its price per gallon both state and federal excise taxes. Thus, the consumer is compelled to pay a tax on a tax . . . .

9. *Government representatives (federal, state or local) who seek to spend the taxpayers' money should be required to levy the tax necessary to raise that money. With the power to tax should go the direct responsibility to answer to the taxpayers.*

The common practice of state and local officeholders basing their spending programs on "federal" money invites ex-

TAXATION

travagances and irresponsibility. It is a shell game that permits government offices to escape accountability . . . .

10. *All tax agencies and agents should be required to abide by and uphold all Constitutional guarantees and protections (due process, restrictions on search and seizure, presumed innocence, etc.).*

In a society of freemen, all individuals stand equal before the law and every man is entitled to his full day in court. No man is beneath the law, and no man — *not even The President and certainly not tax agents* — is above the law.

One Nation Under God, by Rus Walton, pub. Third Century Publishers, June 1975, pp. 223-228.

All the above propositions are inherently biblical in *principle* because they advocate "fairness" and "justice" and lawfulness. Furthermore, these principles, because they are in harmony with the biblical doctrines of the dignity of all human beings and their inalienable rights to life, liberty and property, should be the ideal goal of all civil governments.

The Bible clearly teaches and exemplifies that all people are obligated to pay taxes in support of civil government. And that biblical obligation is not qualified by any biblically ideal form of government. In other words, citizens are to pay taxes even if their government does not follow "christian" or "biblical" principles of taxation. Both the Lord Jesus and the apostle Paul obligated believers to pay taxes to Jewish and Roman systems of civil government that misappropriated and misused tax revenues. Both systems left much to be desired in personal "liberties" considered to be fundamental and taken for granted by practically all Americans today.

The total cost of all government for the United States of America estimated in 1974 was 43 percent of the nation's total personal income and 35 percent of it gross national product. That is all government — federal, state and local. But that does not include inflation (a tax, just as certainly as other forms of taxation). Figured on the basis of *per producer* — per working men and women in the labor force, in 1974 it came to $5290 per worker per year. Most U.S. citizens would not believe they pay those amounts of taxes per year — but they do not figure the "hidden taxes." Someone has estimated that there are 502 taxes of one sort or another on a pair of shoes; each one levied at a different stage of production and distribution and sale by a different governmental agency.

It is one of the hard cold facts of life that everything civil government spends comes from the taxpayer's pockets — either now, or later. The now we call taxation, the later we know as inflation. The more *services* demanded by citizens from its government, the more the *taxpayer* has to *pay*. There are no *free* lunches! History bears witness to the spectacle of a number of "great" governments and "states" instituting enormous "social welfare" programs and taxing themselves into oblivion — the Roman empire was one! Bible believers must conscientiously pay taxes for services rendered from their civil governments. And Bible believers are equally obligated to conscientiously exert all peaceful and legal means possible to bring their civil government to the practice of a Bible-based set of principles in the appropriation and use of taxes. The Bible has a great deal to say about civil government and taxes — more than many people realize.

8

PRIVATE OWNERSHIP OF PROPERTY

God intended human beings to be social (live in societies — group). That alone would necessitate some divisional control or ownership of properties (things, objects, necessities for existence in a physical world). The fact that human beings were created with physical bodies to exist or subsist in a physical world of objects necessary to that physical subsistence proves that acquisition of "things" is imperative. The proprietorship of physical things is an inalienable right of human beings — an imperative consequence of their physical nature.

Proprietorship was mandated by Almighty God when he created humankind:

> So God created man in his own image, in the image of God he created him; male and female he created them. And God blessed them, and God said to them, Be fruitful and multiply, and fill the earth and subdue it; and have dominion over the fish of the sea

and over the birds of the air and over every living thing that moves upon the earth. And God said, Behold, I have given you every plant yielding seed which is upon the face of all the earth, and every tree with seed in its fruit; you shall have them for food (Gen. 1:28,29).

The original human beings (Adam and Eve) were given "dominion" over every part of the earth they could "subdue."

> Here is the primeval commission to man authorizing both science and technology as man's basic enterprises relative to the earth. "Science" is man's disciplined study and understanding of the phenomena of his world. "Technology" is the implementation of this knowledge in the effective ordering and development of the earth and its resources, for the greater good of all earth's inhabitants . . . .This twofold commission to subdue and have dominion, to conquer and rule, embraces all productive human activities. Science and technology, research and development, theory and application, study and practice, and so forth, are various ways of expressing these two concepts . . . .
> This command, therefore, established man as God's steward over the created world and all things therein . . . . The scientific and technological enterprises still comprise God's mandate to man relative to the earth and its inhabitants, and man would find himself immeasurably more productive and effective in such pursuits if he would only approach them in the reverent and believing attitude of an honest and good servant of his Maker.
> *The Genesis Record*, by Henry M. Morris, pub. Baker Book House, p. 77

Property rights are more than rights to things. In essence, property is an extension of the person who has acquired it for in acquiring it he has "spent" part of his life (time, energy, expertise, etc.). Thus, to take a man's "property" is to take his life. That is why the founding fathers of the United States of America were so jealous of their rights to hold *private* property.

> . . . by virtue of his power of reason, man's place in the natural order is that of lord tenant of the earth. (1) Reason has been

defined as the "spark of the Infinite" in man; it is that power which impels him to seek to penetrate the meaning of the universe and of his life within it; it is the power which qualifies him for natural dominion over all the lower orders; it is the power which has enabled him, little by little, to gain control over his natural environment (see Psa. 8:3-8) . . . . (2) According to Biblical teaching, this dominion was vested in man by the Creator Himself: (Gen. 1:27,28) . . . . After all, what is the story of man's development of his science throughout the centuries — that science by means of which he has gradually "subdued" the forces of his physical environment — but his own natural spontaneous fulfillment of this divine command? (3) "Astronomically speaking," said someone, "man is insignificant — hardly a speck on a speck of the totality of the cosmos." To which reply was made: "Yes, but astronomically speaking, man is the astronomer." Despite fulminations to the contrary, our world is definitely *anthropocentric*, that is, in the sense that every person is unavoidably the center of his own experienced world. Moreover, man apparently is the only being who strives to inquire into the mysteries of the world around him and of his own life in that world. (4) History shows that man has, from the beginning of his existence upon earth, assumed *proprietary right* over all the subhuman orders and utilized them for preserving himself in physical existence. He has done this, moreover, naturally and by natural right. For if he has, by creation, *the right to life*, then surely he has also the right to the means of sustaining life; and what other means have "Nature and Nature's God" provided for his sustenance than the plant and animal orders? Again as Aristotle has put it: "The business of nature is to furnish food to that which is born." The corresponding obligation (for with every right there is also an obligation) which has been placed upon man himself is, of course, that he shall eat his daily bread "in the sweat of his face" (Gen. 3:19), that is to say, as the fruit of honest labor, mental or physical. For a man to fail in this obligation on his part is for him to become a parasite upon society.

Commonsense Ethics, ibid, pp. 107,108

Evidently the right of proprietorship was assumed not only by Adam and Eve, but also by their first offspring:

Now Adam knew Eve his wife, and she conceived and bore Cain, saying, I have gotten a man with the help of the Lord. And again, she bore his brother Abel. Now Abel was a keeper of sheep, and Cain a tiller of the ground. In the course of time Cain brought to the Lord an offering of the fruit of the ground, and Abel brought of the firstlings of his flock and of their fat portions (Gen. 4:1-4a).

Cain "subdued" the ground and produced "fruit" for his labor. Abel "subdued" animals and also exercised proprietorship over the "fruit" of his labors. Both men clearly understood that they had some "dominion" over these "things" inasmuch as they brought a portion to the Lord as an "offering." They *offered* it. It was theirs to *offer*. The did not *have* to offer it; no one *took* it from them against their will. They had spent part of their life (energy, time and expertise) to subdue "the earth" and that which was produced became, by God's beneficence, their property to give or keep.

The same proprietorship was mandated to Noah (see Gen. 9:1-7) after the Flood. Noah became the first "tiller of the soil" after the Flood and planted a vineyard and consumed part of the fruit of his labor (Gen. 9-20ff). The formation of the nations by the descendants of Noah implies proprietorship in the phrase, "These are the sons of Japheth in *their lands* . . . . " (Gen. 10:5) etc.

Abram's faithfulness in obeying the Lord's command to migrate to Canaan was rewarded: he "took . . . their possessions which they had gathered" when he left Haran for Canaan (Gen. 12:5). The Hebrew word for "possessions" is *rekusham* which is translated in the LXX in the Greek word *huparchonta* and literally means, "property, possessions, belongings" (see Matt. 19:21; Luke 8:3; Acts 3:6; 4:37). We read further that "Abram was very rich in cattle, in silver and in gold . . . " (Gen. 13:2), and when he rescued his nephew Lot from the kings of the East, Abram "brought back his kinsman Lot with his goods . . . " (Gen. 14:16). The king of Sodom recognized Abram's right to *take possession* of the "goods" which had previously belonged to the people of Sodom because of Abram's risk and work in rescuing them from the robber-kings. But Abram declined (Gen. 14:21-24). Abram was promised that his descendants would come out of a future bondage "with great possessions" (Gen. 15:14).

The following is a partial list of statements or inferences from the pre-Mosaic era (the books of Genesis and Job) concerning property and proprietorship:

1. Abraham insisted on purchasing a burial place for his family from the Hittites (Gen. 23:8-16; 25:10; 49:28-33).
2. Abraham's family was involved in a dispute over ownership or property rights concerning certain water-wells in Canaan (Gen. 26:17-22).
3. Jacob worked for his uncle Laban and acquired possessions (Gen. 29:15-20; 30:27-43) and when God protected him from Laban's cheating, Jacob disputed with Laban over proprietorship (Gen. 31:1-55 — all through this chapter Jacob speaks of his "goods").
4. Jacob's wives lay claim to part of their father's property as *their* property and bid Jacob take it (Gen. 31:14-16).
5. Jacob claimed the things he was giving to Esau belonged to him (Jacob) (Gen. 32:17-18).
6. Esau claimed he had enough property of his own (Gen. 33:9), as did Jacob (Gen. 33:11).
7. Jacob bought land (Gen. 33:19).
8. Hamor invited Jacob and his family to "get property" in Canaan by "trading" (Gen. 34:10).
9. Jacob rebuked his sons for looting the property of others (even of Canaanites) (Gen. 34:25-31).
10. Jacob and Esau's possessions were "too great" for both clans to be supported by the land of Canaan, so Esau moved (Gen. 36:6-8).
11. Joseph's "robe" was his (Gen. 37:23).
12. Judah possessed a "signet, a cord, and a staff" (Gen. 38:18).
13. Potiphar owned much property (Gen. 39:4-6).
14. Joseph became "rich" in Egypt (Gen. 41-45).
15. Egyptians clearly exercised the right of proprietorship when they traded "their" cattle, "their" land, and "themselves" for

grain during the great famine in Joseph's day (Gen. 47:13-26). It is here we read of the first civil government "socialization" of private property.
16. Job had great possessions (Job 1:3; 42:10-12).

Private property is from God. It is important. It is to be valued. Any politico-economic systems which denies this God-mandated right of private property is under the condemnation of Almighty God. Human proprietorship of property is also clearly a right by "Natural Law":

> 1. *The right of private ownership is a natural right.* This right is founded on no other fact than the fact of man's existence: the right to life carries with it the right to the means of sustaining life and of enriching the personality. Among primitive peoples, allocation of land (real estate) was not necessary because of sparseness of population: however, as population grew, it became necessary to allocate land, and later to make a distinction even between surface and subsurface (mineral) rights. That the external goods of the world exist for man's use and benefit is evident from (1) *his absolute need of them*, and (2) *their perfect adaptability to his needs as an organism*. A natural right is one that is postulated by the needs of human life itself — individual, family, and social. The right to acquire private property is postulated by this threefold need. *Individual need* includes (a) capability and necessity of human providence, (b) the right of the individual to the fruits of his labor, and (c) the necessity of an adequate incentive to personal labor. That which belongs to everybody is never properly cared for, because it is human nature to have special interest only in what is one's own. *Family need* includes (a) duty of maintenance of home, wife, and family, (b) duty of adequate education of offspring — physical, intellectual and moral, and (c) provision for emergencies, such as births, sickness, accidents, old age, etc. The right to private ownership of a home goes along with the right to establish a family. The most stable form of civil society is that in which there is a dominant home-owning middle class. Revolutions occur only in cases in which this middle class disappears, leaving only the ultra-rich and the ultra-poor. *Social need* includes (a) the promotion of the arts and sciences, and of the amenitites of life; (b) wholesome competition arising from

private enterprise; (c) prevention of anarchy that arises from universal sloth, or of tyranny from forced conscription of labor, conditions that invariably occur if private enterprise is outlawed. Man either owns some private property, or he will be owned by the state (the ruling regime). As Aristotle pointed out long ago, (a) the great crimes of man are not due to considerations of property but to human excess (passion, lust); property, moreover, would destroy the virtue of liberality (generosity) altogether and would make man simply a ward of the state. Any governing regime that tries to eliminate private property will have to resort to brute force to do so. Complete equalization is contrary to human nature: unity is not to be confused with uniformity. A Kentucky thoroughbred and a Missouri mule can be put on the same track, and if the track is made muddy enough, the thoroughbred will not be able to move any faster than the mule. Again, a thousand dollars may be divided equally among ten persons, but it will not be long before two or three of the ten will, by superior initiative or ability or cleverness, acquire possession of the entire sum. Equalization of human talents and incentives, and equalization of property as well, goes directly against human nature itself. Paternalistic government, moreover, destroys individual initiative; citizens who must be "kept" by the state can hardly be called citizens. Finally, no evidence is forthcoming that the much-touted proletarian (from *proles*, Latin word for a father whose only property is offspring) will prove to be his own messiah; he turns out to be, rather, merely the puppet of the ruling regime.

2. *The right of private ownership, however, is not an unlimited right.* (1) The individual has the absolute right to assume those goods which are necessary to the sustenance of his own life, provided he is willing to give honest labor in return: the obligation placed upon every man is that he shall earn his daily bread in the sweat of his face, a provision which is for man's own good. The individual has the right to assume for his own use that which has not been assumed by others on the basis of the same right. (2) Other persons have rights, too: the same basic rights (to life, liberty, and the pursuit of happiness); rights to safety, order, security, integrity of limb, etc. Property right is a right which I am obligated to use *reasonably*. I do not have the right to drive my automobile at excessive speed such as to endanger the lives of others, nor do I have the right to drive anywhere, on the sidewalks as well as on the streets, etc. I have no right to use my

residence as a place for making explosives, nor as a brothel; I have no right to set fire to my property and thus endanger the property and lives of others, etc. In fact I have no right to use my property in any manner that would be injurious to others — not even to manufacture chemicals, narcotics, etc., that would destroy the minds and bodies of my fellows. (3) Nor do I have any right to the unlimited accumulation of wealth. There was a time a few years ago when a few men owned the quinine supply of the world; had they resorted to price-fixing to excess, that would have been monopoly, and the kind of monopoly that is detrimental to human welfare the world over. And therefore both immoral and illegitimate. One of the legitimate functions of government is that of outlawing such monopolistic practices. There is a moral limit even to "free enterprise." Excessive monopoly can stifle free enterprise as effectively as government control. (4) Much ado has been made in recent years about the subordination of property rights to human rights. No sane person questions the fact that human rights take precedence over everything; indeed there are no rights, property rights included, which are not human rights.

3. *That private property is a natural right is confirmed historically.* (1) The right to life carries with it the right to the means of sustaining life. The only means of sustaining life available to man are those material goods which provide for him food, shelter, clothing, etc. Hence we reason that the material goods of the earth are here for all mankind. The only ethical problem involved is that of the *just allocation of such goods*: no society can afford to allow such a maladjustment to prevail as to make it impossible for a citizen to earn a livelihood through honest toil. The world does not owe me a living, but society does owe me the opportunity of making a living. (2) History proves that private property, through relatively just allocation of material goods (and *relative justice* is all that one can expect in this present world), is the only method that has ever been found to succeed permanently and at the same time to provide for the greatest measure of individual freedom and initiative together with collective security and contentment. Hence private property has existed as a worldwide institution from the very dawn of history. (3) No other system can be correlated with the rise and spread of human initiative and freedom and with the rise and spread of democracy. The only alternative is strict regimentation under a rigid dictator-

ship; in a word, totalitarianism, in which the social, political, economic, and even the *cultural* life of a people are all placed under rigid bureaucratic control.
Commonsense Ethics, by C.C. Crawford, pub. Brown, pp. 302-304

One commentator has pointed out that the very essence of the Law of Moses is best seen in its regulations about proprietorship. The regulations and principles set forth in God's revelation to Moses in the area of property ownership and economics were (and still are to some extent) unparalleled. The laws regulating property in the Mosaic theocracy set that nation apart from all other nations on earth.

The commands of the law regarding wealth and its use are all addressed to the heart, aimed at quenching the desire for earthly riches and mammon-worship. Yet on the other hand, they were not intended to dull enthusiasm for honest industry and proper gain thereby, and certainly not to encourage sloth, waste, or indolence. If work and thrift are part of the Puritan ethic, we know where the Puritans, famous for their interest in the Scriptures, got such ideas.
Toward a Biblical View of Civil Government, by Robert D. Culver, pub. Moody Press, p. 151

The citizens of theocratic Israel began to obtain property on a national scale when they were the guests of the Egyptians in the "land of Goshen" (see Gen. 47:1,6,27; Exod. 11:1-3; 12:35,36) and from the spoils of wars against their adversaries of the "wilderness wanderings" (see Num. 31:32-54). All this "portable wealth" or "personal property" was divided among all the families (Num. 31:25-54). The "real estate" properties were acquired when Israel invaded and occupied Canaan and the land was apportioned to tribes and then to families within the tribes (see Num. 26:52-56; 33:54). And it was a rich and productive land (Deut. 8:7-10; Exod. 3:8; Lev. 26:5; Num. 13:21-24). There were many exportable natural resources for trading (see Jer. 22:6; Zech. 10:10; Jer. 8:22; 46:11; Ezra 27:17; Gen.

37;25; II Sam. 18:6-8, etc.). Real estate properties were to be held by families *in perpetuum*. They were to be passed on by inheritance within the same family "forever." Ownership of the land was by *family*. It could not be transferred from that family by any means, person, or state. It was a "trust" from the Lord to the family "forever" (see Lev. 25:23-28). Land might be temporarily "indentured" or "sold on loan" but it legally reverted to its original family proprietor when debts were paid or at the "year of jubilee" (every fifty years). The family to whom the land was originally allotted by Mosaic law could not *sell* their land in a perpetual sense.

The eighth and tenth commandments of the Decalogue (Exod. 20:1-17) unequivocally state the Almighty God holds *ownership* of *private property* inviolable. Stealing of another's property, by whatever means (robbery, forgery, cheating, embezzlement, thievery) is divinely forbidden. The human right to hold private property originates with the Sovereign God of all creation, not with any political or social entity. Sophisticated methods of stealing like moving a neighbor's property boundary marker is forbidden (Deut. 19:1). Not even a king dared to steal the property of one of his people (I Kings 21:15-19). The human law of "eminent domain" was not a part of God-approved legislation about property.

> Eminent Domain is the inherent right of a state to force a property owner to sell his property when it is needed for public use. This right is based on the legal rule that all real property is subject to the control of the state, just as all real property in England was once owned by the king . . . . The use of Eminent Domain by governments originated in the Middle Ages. It once meant the right that an overlord (ruler) had over the land farmed by his vassal (tenant).
> *World Book Encyclopedia*, Vol. 6, pp. 209,210

The Old Testament theocracy, as such, had no control of "real property." There is no inherent "eminent domain" authorized by God for the state in all the Bible, neither in the days of the patriarchs, nor in the theocracy, nor the monarchy, nor in the New Testament. "Eminent domain" may be considered by modern civil governments the only expedient way to make technological progress, but it has no basis in the Bible. To condemn a property-owner's land (or other property) by the rule of "eminent domain," against the property-owner's wishes, even though fairly appraised market-value exchange is made for it, would be classified as stealing in the Bible.

Following are some of the theocratic regulations concerning private *personal* property (Exod. 22:1-14; Deut. 5:15-21):

1. The penalty for stealing property (animals) was restitution, five fold and four fold. THAT IS COSTLY! THAT IS A LAW THAT FAVORS THE VICTIM RATHER THAN THE CRIMINAL! SOCIETY MAY WINK AT IMMORALITY (IF NO ONE IS PHYSICALLY INJURED). BUT THEFT IS NOT SO EXCUSABLE.
2. If a thief was breaking in at night, there was the possibility that he was going to harm or kill the householder — therefore the householder was exonerated if he killed the thief. But in the daytime the thief's intentions would probably be visible by his actions. He was not to be smitten without first determining his intention. The principle is that human life is greater than property. THERE IS A HIERARCHY OF ETHICS, EVEN IN GOD'S LAW!
3. The penalty for damage to another's property whether by fire or by unrestrained animals, was full restitution. AND WITHOUT INSURANCE COMPANIES, SUCH A LAW WOULD MAKE A PROPERTY OWNER VERY CAREFUL ABOUT BURNING OR LETTING HIS ANIMALS RUN LOOSE!
4. The penalty for borrowing something and then losing it or having it stolen was having to prove it was stolen or proving it was lost. The *borrower* had to prove he had not stolen it! Men must show responsibility for other's property! If a borrower and a lender both claim "This is it" (my property), when the Lord (probably through a priest's Urim and Thumim) proves who its owner is, the other claimant has to pay the true owner double the price of the object. A LOST OBJECT REMAINED THE

POSSESSION OF ITS ORIGINAL OWNER, WHO COULD CLAIM IT ON SIGHT.
5. In case of uncertainty about the loss of a beast (property) by an owner when the beast was in the care of a neighbor, an oath was sworn by both as to the keeper's innocence; and if the oath is accepted, the keeper does not pay restitution. Natural losses were not the responsibility of the keeper. BUT THE KEEPER WAS RESPONSIBLE TO PROTECT THE OTHER MAN'S BEAST AGAINST THIEVERY!
6. If a man borrows anything of his neighbors and it dies or is hurt and the borrower has neglected being with the thing borrowed, he must make restitution. Presumably he could have prevented its hurt had he been present. If the object is let out for hire by the owner, the renter is not liable if the object dies or is hurt . . . THE OWNER ASSUMED THIS RISK IN RETURN FOR THE HIRE GIVEN TO HIM. IN OUR LAWS, THE RENTER IS USUALLY LIABLE FOR ANY DEATH OR HURT OF AN OBJECT RENTED!

A few additional references to proprietorship in the Pentateuch follow:

1. Stealing prohibited (Lev. 19:11)
2. Robbery and cheating prohibited (Lev. 19:13,35)
3. Moving property lines to steal another's land prohibited (Deut. 19:14)
4. Assisting a neighbor to reclaim lost or imperiled property is enjoined (Deut.22:1-4)
5. Property crucial to another's livelihood is not to be taken as surety for a loan (Deut. 22:1-4)

References to private ownership of property in the era of the Judges and the Monarchy are indisputable. The following is listing of the most significant ones:

1. Samuel's "resignation speech" lends insight into the respect a godly judge had for individual proprietorship (I Sam. 12:1-5).
2. King Saul's father owned property (I Sam. 9:3)
3. David informs the rich man Nabal that he had respected

PRIVATE OWNERSHIP OF PROPERTY

Nabal's property even when the exigencies of David's circumstances might have made a lesser man steal (I Sam. 25:1ff) (Nabal's subsequent insult and miserliness toward David nearly precipitated an act of ungodly revenge from David)

4. David refused to accept *gratis* the threshing floor of Araunah even though the property was desired as the site of the future Temple of God (I Chron. 21:18ff) and purchased it at "full price," saying, "I will not give as an offering to the Lord something that belongs to you, something that costs me nothing." Another incident showing that the so-called "right" of eminent domain is not a biblical mandate.
5. The personal property of king David is listed (I Chron. 27:25-31; 28:1; 31:3; 32:29; 35:7).
6. Solomon's wealth was unparalleled (I Kings 4:20-28; 10:14-29) and his wisdom in all areas of commerce made the whole citizenry prosper (I Kings 4:25, etc.).
7. King Ahab and his pagan queen Jezebel coveted Naboth's property (vineyard) and wrested it from him with vicious, deceitful and criminal perjury (I Kings 21:1ff). Additional evidence against eminent domain as a biblical concept.
8. King Hezekiah's pride in his personal wealth was his undoing (II Kings 20:12-19; Isa. 39:1-8).
9. Solomon wrote many proverbs about property and wealth (Prov. 3:9; 3:16; 6:30,31; 8:18,21; 10:4; 12:11,14; 13:4-11; 14:20,23; 19:14; 20:10; 21:6,20; 22:7; 28:8,20,22,25; 29:3 etc.).
10. Solomon also philosophized about property and wealth (Eccl. 2:1-8; 2:18-23; 5:10-20; 6:1-9; Song of Solomon 8:7).
11. The people returned to the land of Canaan after the captivies with Ezra and brought their "possessions" (Ezra 8:21; 10:8).
12. The people of Israel who remained in Persia, including Queen Esther, became prosperous (Esther 8:1,2, etc.).

Direct statements and indirect inferences to individual proprietorship in the Old Testament Prophets are pervasive. Below is a sampling:

1. Isaiah condemns "plundering" of private property (Isa. 3:14; 10:2).
2. Jeremiah speaks of "their" houses (Jer. 6:13; 8:10; 22:13-17).

3. Jeremiah "bought" for himself a linen cloth (13:1-11) and a potter's flask to break to pieces (19:1ff), and a field (32:6-15).
4. There were some poor people who evidently had no real property (Isa. 58:6,7; Jer. 39:10).
5. Jeremiah told the Israelites who went into captivity to work and acquire property in a foreign land (Jer. 29:4-9).
6. Ezekiel had a "house" in Babylon (Ezek. 8:1).
7. Daniel had a "house" in Babylon (Dan. 2:17: 6:10) and wealth (6:28).
8. Condemnation of stealing the property of others is severe (Hosea 4:2; 6:9; 7:1; 12:7-9; Amos 2:6-8; 3:10; 4:11-13; 8:4-8).
9. Obadiah condemns pagan Edomites for not assisting the Israelites to protect their property from being plundered by invading pirates.
10. Other prophets speak to the issue of violation of property rights (Micah 2:1,2; 2:8,9; 3:1-3; 6:9-12; Zeph. 3:1-5).
11. Haggai teaches that spiritual priorities are more important than private property (Hab. 1:2-11).

When we turn to the New Testament we see unimpeachable evidence, in both teaching and example, that Jesus Christ and his apostles approved of the principle of the ownership of private property — real and personal:

1. John the Baptist warned soldiers not to "rob" the property of others (Luke 3:14).
2. The first disciples Jesus called were property owners and workers (Matt. 4:18-22; Mark 1:16-20; Luke 5:1-11).
3. Pharisees owned lavish homes (Luke 7:36ff) and Jesus dined with them.
4. Levi (Matthew) the tax-collector owned a home (Matt. 9:9-13; Mark 2:14-17; Luke 5:27-32).
5. Jesus spoke of laying up treasures on earth; of others taking away, begging from us or our lending to others "our goods" (Matt. 5:39-42; Luke 6:27-36; Matt. 6:19-21; 6:33).
6. Wise men build *their* houses on rock foundations (Matt. 7:24-27).
7. A centurion told Jesus of "his roof," "his servant" (Luke 7:1-10).

PRIVATE OWNERSHIP OF PROPERTY

8. Jesus told of the man who sowed good seed in "his field" (Matt. 13:2-29).
9. Jesus told the parable of the man who sold all he *had* in order to buy a field in which he had found hidden treasure (Matt. 13:44); and of a pearl merchant who sold all he *had* to buy one pearl of great price (Matt. 13:45,46).
10. Women supported Jesus' ministry from "their means" (Luke 8:1-3).
11. Jesus told of a man who "had" an hundred sheep and lost one (Matt. 18:12,13).
12. Jesus was often a guest in a house owned by two women and their brother (Luke 10:38-42) — Martha, Mary and Lazarus.
13. One of two brothers attempted to make Jesus arbitrate the family estate (Luke 12:13); then Jesus told a parable of the land belonging to a rich, foolish, farmer (Luke 12:15-21).
14. Jesus told a parable of a man who had planted a fig tree in "his vineyard" (Luke 13:6-9).
15. Jesus, dining in a Pharisee's house, referred to the hypocritical priority Pharisees placed on their property (Luke 14:5).
16. Jesus condemned those who let property keep them from the banquet of the "great man" (Luke 14:15-24).
17. Jesus told parables of property owners who lost precious property (Luke 15:1-10).
18. He told about a rich man who had an unrighteous steward (Luke 16:1-13).
19. He told about a rich man who was indifferent to the needs of a beggar (Luke 16:19-31).
20. Jesus told of those who would be so wrapped up in "their goods" they would be unprepared for the end of the world (Luke 17:25-37).
21. Jesus tried to convert a rich, young ruler from idolizing riches but the ruler rejected Jesus (Matt. 19;16-30; Mark 10;17-31; Luke 18:19-30).
22. Jesus told the parable of the man hiring workers for "his" vineyard (Matt. 20:1-16).
23. Jesus told the parable of a nobleman who owned pounds which he disbursed among his servants for investing (Luke 19:11-28).
24. The gospel writers tell of Mary who owned an alabaster jar of expensive ointment (a year's wages worth) and who anointed Jesus in anticipation of his vicarious death (Matt.26:6-13; Mark

14:3-9; John 12:1-8) and of Judas' avaricious scheming to get the money for himself.
25. Jesus told of another vineyard-owner who let "his" vineyard out to wicked tenants (Matt. 21:33-46; Mark 12:1-12; Luke 20:9-19).
26. He told another parable of those who used their property as excuses to reject a king's invitation to the prince's marriage feast (Matt. 22:1-14).
27. Jesus told another parable of an householder who had a wicked steward (Matt. 24:45-51); and of the man who had talents which he disbursed to his servants to invest (Matt. 25:14-30).
28. Jesus made certain that the disciples would explain his "borrowing" the foal of an ass upon which he would ride into the city of Jerusalem (Matt. 21:1-11; Mark 11:1-11; Luke. 19:29-44; John 12:12-19).
29. Jesus held his last Passover with his disciples in the upper room of an "householder's" house (Matt. 26:17-19; Mark 14:12-16; Luke 22:7-13).
30. Jesus told his disciples to "purchase" a sword (evidently as a precaution against mob-arrest of the disciples) (Luke 22:35-38).
31. When Jesus gave his mother into the care of "the disciple whom he loved" this disciple took her "to his own home." (John 19:25-27).

These few references clearly prove that Jesus Christ specifically and unequivocally approved of the ownership of property by individual persons. Not one word in the Gospels would give divine sanction to the ownership of property by a political state. States may commandeer property by "eminent domain" but such action is not sanctioned by Christ. While a state has divine mandate to exist by collecting taxes, it has no right to invade or confiscate private property.

Perhaps the most unambiguous statement of the divine sanction in favor of human proprietorship is that in Acts 4:32-5:6. It is the story of the first century Christians declaring their "possessions" available to any of their brethren who had need.

Those who had real estate property sold some of their holdings and made the proceeds available to the apostles for distribution to the needy. They did this on their own. There is not one word in the New Testament that indicates they were commanded to do this. We are not even told that God approved of their doing this. The judgment that came upon Ananias and Sapphira was *not* for holding back part of their property — it was for *lying* to God about what they had done in order to appear to have done differently. These are the apostle Peter's words:

> Ananias, why has Satan filled your heart to lie to the Holy Spirit and to keep back part of the proceeds of the land? While it remained unsold, did it not remain your own? And after it was sold, was it not at your disposal? How is it that you have contrived this deed in your heart? You have not lied to men but to God (Acts 5:3,4).

After this incident nothing more is said in the New Testament about this kind of alleged "communism." Besides, what the early church was practicing here in no way resembles the humanistic, socialistic dictatorship of modern Marxist communism where the wealth is controlled by an elitist hierarchy of power-brokers. The fact that the apostle Paul had to call upon other Christian churches to take up spontaneous, free-will offerings and collections to supply physical assistance to the brethren at Jerusalem (Rom. 15:25-31; I Cor. 16:1-3; II Cor. 8:1-9:15; Gal. 2:10) indicates the early church discontinued abruptly its practice of "having all things common." The following passages seem to indicate early discontinuation of a "community of goods" practice:

> But concerning love of the brethren you have no need to have anyone write to you, for you yourselves have been taught by God to love one another; and indeed you do love all the brethren throughout Macedonia. But we exhort you, brethren, to do so more and more, to aspire to live quietly, to mind your own affairs, and to work with your hands, as we charged you; so that you may

command the respect of outsiders, and be dependent on nobody (I Thess. 4:9-12).

Now we command you, brethren, in the name of our Lord Jesus Christ, that you keep away from any brother who is living in idleness and not in accord with the tradition that you received from us. For you yourselves know how you ought to imitate us; we were not idle when we were with you, we did not eat any one's bread without paying, but with toil and labor we worked night and day, that we might not burden any of you. It was not because we have not that right, but to give you in our conduct an example to imitate. For even when we were with you, we gave you this command; If anyone will not work, let him not eat. For we hear that some of you are living in idleness, mere busybodies, not doing any work. Now such persons we command and exhort in the Lord Jesus Christ to do their work in quietness and to earn their own living. Brethren, do not be weary in well-doing. If anyone refuses to obey what we say in this letter, note that man, and have nothing to do with him, that he may be ashamed. Do not look on him as an enemy, but warn him as a brother (II Thess. 3:6-15).

Paul also gave apostolic command:

Let the thief no longer steal, but rather let him labor doing honest work with his hands, so that he may be able to give to those in need (Eph. 4:28).

Paul told Timothy to exhort the "rich in this world" to "do good, to be rich in good deeds, liberal and generous . . . " (I Tim. 6:18) without one word of condemnation for the fact that they were rich. He told Titus to command servants to "be submissive to their masters and to give satisfaction in every respect; they are not to be refractory, nor to pilfer, but to show entire and true fidelity, so that in everything they may adorn the doctrine of God . . . " (Titus 2:9,10). Slaves and servants who had very little property, if any at all, were to respect the property of others and not steal! Paul even went so far as to return a slave-owner's

(Philemon's) slave (Onesimus) out of respect for "property rights" — exhorting the "owner" to treat his "slave" as a "brother" and no longer as "a slave" (Philemon).

In Hebrews 10:32-36 we are informed that certain Hebrew-Christians had *joyfully* "accepted the plundering of their property" during the persecution of Christians by their Jewish (anti-Christian) kinsmen.

James severely condemns those who own property and misuse it or refuse to share it (James 2:1-26; 5:1-6); and he warns those whose whole lives are centered in "trading and getting gain" to consider the brevity of life on this earth (James 4:13-17).

The Bible says that owning private property has divine sanction. It goes further and pronounces severe condemnation upon those who would violate the rights of proprietorship. The Bible acknowledges the reality that there will always be rich and poor in this world (Deut. 15:11; John 12:8; Matt. 26:11; Matt. 14:7). But it places no spiritual premium on either economic category, *per se*.

Dr. C.C. Crawford discusses the rationale ("natural law") of human proprietorship from the standpoint of titles to property:

> A title of ownership is a clearly evident fact by which a moral bond (of ownership) is established between a definite person and a definite thing. No definite thing can belong to a definite person (natural or juridical) without a title.
> 1. *Original titles* are those by means of which a thing formerly belonging to no one becomes the property of a particular person: these are *effective occupation, accession,* and *productive labor.*
> (1) *Effective occupation* is the action by which an unowned thing is taken as the possession of a person or persons. This country was settled in this manner: people settled on the land occupied by no one (certainly the landed area of the United States was not being effectively occupied by the aborigines); hence, effective occupation gave original title. No other original title — to land, especially — is conceivable: however, great injustices can occur in the process. Juridical prerequisites of effective occupation are

(a) that the thing is capable of exclusive ownership, (b) that there is a permanent occupancy (squatters are outside this category); and (c) that a permanent sign is set up denoting intention to occupy and thus to acquire possession. No injustice is involved in taking over a thing which belongs to no one, which is not being utilized by anyone: if someone does not come along and take possession of the thing, it will be of no use to anybody. Before injustice can occur, one has to infringe on the rights of another. (2) *Accession* is the original title to the natural increase of the thing possessed, such as new creatures of the herd, fruits of the orchard, yield of farm land, alluvial deposits, etc. (What about mineral rights?) (3) *Productive labor* is the gainform or quality to something already existing and hence makes that thing more useful and valuable. To the extent, therefore, that it makes the occupation effective, labor becomes a primordial title to ownership. (Non-productive labor takes the form of service rendered: it includes the various services and liberal professions, *e.g.*, teachers, dentists, physicians, etc. Such persons do not produce anything as a rule; they do render invaluable services, however, and hence are entitled to proper remuneration).

2. *Derivative titles* of ownership occur by transfer of ownership from one person to another: these are *prescription, inheritance,* and *contract*. (1) *Prescription* is the acquiring of ownership by fortuitously coming into possession of a thing that once belonged to another whose claim to the thing has evidently been abandoned. *E.g.*, an outlawed debt, an article which one finds with which no previous owner is identifiable, etc. Prescription is a natural title for two reasons: unless it were, many material things would be of no utility to man; ownership would be so uncertain that contests for it would be multiplied beyond reason. (2) *Inheritance* is legitimate succession to ownership of a thing upon the death of the former owner. *Intestate succession* (when an individual dies without leaving a will) is in favor of the wife and children of the deceased. *The right of inheritance is essential to democratic society*, for the following reasons; (a) right order demands the stability of family life; wife and children are clearly indicated by the Moral Law to be the natural heirs of the husband and father of the family, as the continuation of his personality; (b) heredity succession is necessary to safeguard parental authority; (c) if a person could make no such disposition of his earthly goods, and if the state took them over at his death, ob-

viously the state would own everything within a generation or two; (d) if the state did not take over the property of the deceased, then the first occupant would do so, and this would mean a fight among the relatives for the disposition of the property, and in the end would spell the destruction of the social order; (e) abandonment of inheritance would mean that all families ultimately would be thrown upon the bounty of the state: (f) abandonment of inheritance would throw upon the state the duty of subsidizing all worthy cultural and humanitarian causes, and the result would be the stamping out of altruism; (g) the right of inheritance is a positive stimulus to human initiative; (h) property right is domestic and personal in character, and therefore is by nature antecedent to civil law and even to the beginning of civil power; hence it is the duty of a society to safeguard this right and to control its use by law, in such a manner as to prevent the accumulation of vast wealth in the hands of a privileged few. While *equal* distribution of material goods is impossible and unnatural, *equitable* distribution is absolutely essential and should be maintained by governmental action if necessary. By *equitable* distribution is meant a relatively fair allocation of goods among all segments of the population, in order to prevent unemployment and to safeguard free enterprise in general. Devices that serve this general purpose are death taxes, inheritance taxes, income taxes, minimum wage laws, collective bargaining, etc. In the final analysis, private inheritance, if properly controlled, is a necessary safeguard of democratic institutions. The state has a *right* to be supported by its citizens by means of taxation of private enterprises. The state also has the *duty* of protecting its citizens from the corruptions and injustices that proceed from the "cornering" of excessive wealth in the hands of a minority, to the detriment and degradation of the many. Such a condition — that in which only two classes exist, the ultra-rich and the ultra-poor — issuses inevitably in violent revolution and the overthrow of the government. As Aristotle pointed out long ago, the stability of any social order depends on the stability of a large home-owning class. Individuals who are fortunate enough to amass great wealth — and in most cases *great* wealth comes fortuitously — are too often prone to overlook the fact that great wealth entails great responsibility to society.

I have no quarrel with men of wealth, but I must insist that responsibility to society is in proportion to the wealth accumulated. I have often made the statement that if I am to be exploited, and I know that I am exploited (by marked-up, even excessive, profits) about everytime I go to the store to purchase needed material goods, I prefer to be exploited by private industry than a government bureaucracy of some kind. It is not money, but the love of money, that is the root of all kinds of evil (I Tim. 6:10). We can — and often do — carry the profit motive to unjustifiable extremes; yet we cannot do away with it without destroying democracy and every value that is associated with it, even freedom itself. There are two fundamental human rights, lacking either of which no political order can rightly call itself democratic; these are the rights of religious freedom and private property. When these two rights are usurped by government, democracy perishes. Moreover, I have never been able to convince myself that poverty is a virtue, when, as a matter of fact, it breeds vice, crime, and all kinds of wickedness; it is about the costliest business — to all segments of the economy — that any community can engage in. Among the poor themselves it usually resolves itself into a psychological, rather than an economic, problem: hence the solution is not easy to find. Nations and communities are acting wisely, however, in seeking a solution, one that at least will reduce poverty to a minimum.

I recall walking with a friend, on one occasion, over his fertile farm land of several hundred acres in extent. In the course of the conversation, he became rather boastful. "I suppose," he said "that I could sell out tomorrow for a quarter of a million dollars. Yes, I think I am worth that much." That was about all I could take, and so I said to him, "You are mistaken. That is not what you are worth." In astonishment, he replied, "I don't understand. Just what do you mean?" "I mean," I answered, "that two hundred and fifty thousand dollars represents what you have *cost* society. What you are *worth* is to be measured by what you put back into society, for the common good." Worth is not measured by getting, but by giving. Jesus, Luke 12:15: "A man's life consists not in the abundance of the things which he possesses." This is a truth that selfish man is very reluctant to admit.

Commonsense Ethics, C.C. Crawford pp. 307-309

God judges not by how much property a person has, but by what he *thinks* about it in his heart and what he *does* with it in his life!

PRIVATE OWNERSHIP OF PROPERTY

ECONOMIC SYSTEMS

Economic systems and political structures are not necessarily one and the same. "Communism" is fundamentally an economic system — not a political one. In Biblical times there were apparently four major politico-economic systems:

1. Theocratic — a nation organized politically around a religious system of "priests" or "judges." As it is demonstrated in the theocracy of the Israelites, its economic system was somewhat "free enterprise" and *semi-laissez faire* (semi-government regulated). The Israelite economic system certainly was neither *socialistic* nor *communistic*.
2. Feudalistic — (from the word *feudum* which means a landed estate or group of estates held by a person in return for military service or political service to the recognized owner [usually called, "lord" or "king"] of the land). Politically it involved a "lord" or "king" who controlled all the economic resources including land which he "gave" to certain "knights" or "nobles" for their services to him. These "nobles, knights, princes, satraps," etc., produced economically from this granted property (called a "fiefdom") through "vassals" "serfs" (actually, slaves, or non-property-owners) who were allowed a meager living as "tenants" working the land. Even merchants and craftsmen in the feudal system were little more than slaves. Most of the ancient pagan empires were, economically, modified feudal and fascist systems.
3. Fascist — (from the word *fasces*, an object symbolizing absolute power). Politically, a dictator has absolute and rigid control over all aspects of the nation's life (extreme nationalism) — political, religious, social, and economic. Private ownership of property is allowed, but both labor and management lose their individual liberties — the economy is determined by the dictator. The ancient pagan monarchies and empires were, economically, semi-feudal-fascist systems.
4. Republican — The Greek and Roman republics were modified forms of free-enterprise economics systems. In the later Roman imperial political structure, the emperor exercised a more rigid and centralized control over the entire society (including economics) while still granting private ownership of property

(except when certain emperors *confiscated*, by deceit, the property of others to pay for their huge military debts and social indulgences). In the Roman empire there were citizens and provincials who owned properties and businesses; there was a nobility-class (senators, noblemen, etc.) who received properties by inheritance over which they exercised a "feudal" lordship; a huge class of slaves, and non-property owners who lived essentially by the "welfare" dole of their masters and "lords."

Different economic systems have developed as a result of specific political systems. Hardly any economic system is pure or absolute. All are eclectic. These systems develop and commingle because nations and cultures can not agree on how to solve their basic economic problems. Four important economic systems today are:

1. Free Enterprise: — an economic system in which private individuals or corporations of individuals own and direct the important means of production. Ideally, the more *laissez faire* (absence of government interference) the better. Adam Smith (1723-1790) proposed that governments should not interfere in economic affairs at all. He believed that the desire of businessmen to earn a profit, when regulated by competition, would work almost like "an invisible hand" to produce what consumers want and thus regulate a fair and just economy.
2. Socialism — an economic system which proposes government or "collective" ownership of resources, industries, businesses, and services to a large extent. Theoretically, some private ownership is permitted, thus the forces of supply and demand exerts some influences on production and prices. Some socialist nations have modified "democratic" (or parlimentarian-monarchial) forms of government. Ideally, socialism proposes that the citizens may protest economic policies they do not agree with, and may allegedly vote to increase or reduce the amount of governmental control over the economy.
3. Communism — (an economic system — not a political one). It is allegedly based on *government* ownership of nearly all productive resources. The government directs all economic activi-

ty — decides what shall be produced and in what quantity and what it shall sell for. It sets wages and prices. It plans the rate of economic growth (theoretically). Consumers may purchase as they wish and are able — but only what the government makes available for purchase. Politically, communism is the dictatorship of an elitist "clan" of power-holders. Historically, the elite authorities in communist governments live in much higher economic circumstances than the ordinary citizenry.
4. Fascism — already discussed above.

Some anonymous wit made the following facetious definition of basic economic systems:

Socialism: — You have two cows: you give one to your neighbor.
Communism: — You have two cows: you give both to the government, and the government gives you back as much milk as the government thinks you ought to have.
Fascism — you keep two cows, and then give the government the milk, and the government gives you as much milk as it dictates.
Nazi-ism: — The government shoots you and takes the two cows.
New Dealism — The government shoots one cow, milks the other, and then pours the milk down the sewer.
Capitalism: — You sell one cow and buy a bull.

In every civilized society of national and political structure, the government must play a role (i.e. regulation and services) to one degree or another in the economic system of its citizenry — even in a "free-enterprise" system. Some form of authority or enforcement must be delegated to regulate economic activity (by law) to assure justice and fairness — to prevent monopolistic exploitation of individuals. Further, a federalization of some form of government must exist with the authority and resources at hand to provide services for the citizenry (e.g. legislation, national defense, local law enforcement, roads, postal system, judicial system, currency, etc.) that individuals and smaller social groups cannot provide for themselves. America's founding fathers put it this way in the Preamble to the Constitution adopted September 17, 1787:

We, the people of the United States, in order to form a more perfect Union, establish justice, insure domestic tranquility, provide for the common defense, promote the general welfare, and secure the blessings of liberty to ourselves and to our posterity, do ordain and establish this Constitution for the United States of America.

Because of the imperfection and sinfulness of human beings, human political structures and economic systems must be restrained by law. Since all human laws that are just and reasonable have their source in the Law of God (both "natural" and "revealed"), it is logical to conclude that the Bible will say something about a systemization or regulation of economics. While the Bible mandates no specific politico-economic system, it does show that believers may live and serve God as citizens under varied economic arrangements. The institution of an economical scheme most in harmony with biblical principles and precepts seems to be that of modified "free-enterprise." It appears that the Bible presents an example of economics that would be strong on *laissez faire* with the federal government interfering in property ownership and private business enterprise only to guard against exploitation of individuals and providing only the basic services that individuals and corporations of citizens cannot provide for themselves. Crawford postulates the "free-enterprise" system from the standpoint of reason and conscience (the "natural law" of God):

> 4. *Any politico-economic system which denies this basic right of private property is undemocratic and therefore unacceptable,* e.g., the following: (1) *Social Positivism,* which is the doctrine that the sole source of private property right is the civil law, hence, that only such "rights" exist as are granted (created) by the state. This is simply the denial of *natural* law and *natural* right. Under such a view, obviously neither the right of individual conscience, nor minority right, exists: only the will of the ruling regime, enforced by physical power, becomes the source of laws and "rights." However, these would hardly be rights at all: rather, they

would be only gratuities doled out by the ruling authority. (2) What is called *Communism* holds that no right of private property exists and calls the exercise of that right "robbery." *Absolute Communism* would make all things positively common (including women — the doctrine of "free love") so that neither the individual person nor society as a whole could have dominion over them, but individuals could use them according to their individual desires. This is real "Communism": it seeks the overthrow of all government and hence is *anarchistic* in character. Marxist-Leninism entrusts the dominion over all goods to the society as a whole, in the final analysis, to the ruling regime set up by the society. In practice this is really *Absolute State Capitalism*. (Advocated by Fourier, Robert Owen, Marx, Engels, Lenin, Trotzky, Stalin, etc.) *Limited Communism* takes the form of what is generally called *Socialism*.

It would vest in the community as a whole, operating through a duly elected government and through "public corporations," the administration of all means of production and distribution of goods essential to the general welfare. [*Evolutionary Socialism* (also known as "Fabian" or "creeping" Socialism) proposes to bring in the socialistic order gradually by *ballot* (legal change). Marxist — Leninism contends that the rule of the prolaetariat can be achieved only by violent revolution (by bullets); hence it is known as Radical or *Revolutionary Socialism*.] (3) *Anarchism* rejects all public authority and would destroy the present social order by force. It would tolerate no other bonds than those by which workers might associate themselves in guilds and in municipalities, to which would be entrusted dominion over various kinds of goods to be produced. (Cf. Syndicalism, Guild Socialism, Industrial Workers of the World, etc.). We must conclude that any politico-economic system is inadmissible, the introduction of which and the administration of which reduces the citizenry of a given region to abject subservience to the ruling regime, otherwise known as the State, the Party, or the Cause. Totalitarian systems, moreover, are ethically unjustifiable because they can be instituted only by bloody revolutions (in no instance has what we call "Communism" today ever been introduced by a free popular election). In a democracy, however, the only justifiable instrument for effecting political change ("reform") which public sentiment may deem necessary, is the ballot-box. Certainly our Constitution is sufficiently elastic to permit any kind of change which public sentiment may demand sufficiently to bring about constitutional amendment by due process of law (as provided for, in the Constitution itself); hence there is no excuse for the existence of any movement in the United States that is committed to the doctrine of revolution by force: such a movement cannot be regarded, in the very nature of the case, as anything but a *conspiracy*, a form of treason. Totalitarianism can be achieved only by the "liquidation" of the middle class (the *bourgeoisie*), and can be maintained only by brute force, so contrary is it to human characer. The "dictatorship of the proletariat" is, in the final analysis, not a "classless" society, but a one-class society maintained by a ruling oligarchy which sees to it that there shall be one, and only one, class in the state.

Commonsense Ethics, by C.C. Crawford, pub. Brown, pp. 304-306

Dr. Crawford holds that practically all economic systems except modified "free-enterprise" are illogical and impractical. Being unreasonable and disenfranchising they are philosophically unacceptable. They go against human conscience (the "natural law" of God) and the desire for freedom. Only the "free-enterprise" system of economics, modified by a civil regulatory arrangement which conforms fundamentally to both reason and the propositional revelation of God in the Bible is acceptable for human societies. Other economic systems may be *endured* by believers but they can never be acceptable.

From the very beginning, the Bible portrays man as a proprietor operating in an exclusively free-enterprise economy. "Abel was a keeper of sheep and Cain a tiller of the ground" both earning what was "theirs" and disposing of it according to their own determination (Gen. 4:1-7). Next, acting strictly on his own initiative (free-enterprise), "Cain built a city" (Gen. 4:17) and some of Cain's early descendants, also acting on individual initiative, chose vocations and trades obviously indicating a "free" economy (Gen. 4:20-22). But since we know very little detail about pre-diluvian structures of society it is irrelevant to make comparisons between these earliest economic inferences and later ones more precisely detailed.

Immediately after the flood, Noah and his sons began the human race again as sole proprietors (Gen. 9:1-29). As the descendants of Noah's sons migrated and populated the earth, they developed political and economic structures according to the circumstances of their environments and leadership. Early post-diluvian societies were sufficiently sophisticated to build cities and massive architectural structures (Gen. 11:1-4; 11:31,32) which should require some necessity for "free-enterprise" systems of economics.

It is clear from our previous analysis of what the Bible says about property that the patriarchs who believed God (i.e. Abraham, Isaac, Jacob, and others) practiced a rigid "free-enterprise" system of economics while most of their unbelieving contemporaries lived in cultures which practiced feudal or fascist arrangements economically. There is one significant and very interesting economic case study in Genesis — that of Egypt in the days of Joseph. The economic system of Egypt was apparently "free-enterprise" (modified) until the great famine when Joseph "bought" all the privately owned land from individual landowners (Gen. 47:13-27). At that point Egypt's economy shifted, by consent of the starving populace, to a feudal or fascist system where the land was owned by the King (Pharaoh) and farmed by vassals ("tenants or share-croppers") who had indentured themselves to Pharaoh for food by which to survive.

> In contrast to the happy condition of Joseph's father and brothers in the land of Goshen, the Biblical record . . . depicts the state of privation in Egypt. In need of food, the Egyptians presented themselves to Joseph to explain their plight. On the first such occasion, Joseph purchased their cattle, allowing them "bread" in exchange for horses, flocks, herds, and asses. When the Egyptians present themselves a second time, they had nothing to exchange for food except their lands. Thereupon Joseph secured the lands of the Egyptian people for Pharaoh, because they received an allotment of food at Pharaoh's expense. This in-

troduced the feudal system into Egypt: the system of land tenure. Seed was allotted to the Egyptians on condition that one-fifth of the produce of the land would revert to Pharaoh. "Although this act of Joseph involved a measure of humiliation, including the surrender of lands to the state, it made possible a strong central government which could take measures to prevent famines. The life of Egypt depends upon the Nile, and all the inhabitants of the Nile Valley must cooperate if the water is to be used efficiently. The government was in a position to regulate the use of Nile water and also to begin a system of artificial irrigation by means of canals which could carry the waters of the river to otherwise inaccessible areas. Joseph's economic policy is described with no hint as to either approval or censure. Some have thought that Joseph drove a hard bargain and took advantage of the conditions to enhance the power of the throne. That the emergency resulted in a centralization of authority is clear. There is no hint that Joseph, personally, profited from the situation, however. On the contrary, the people said to Joseph, *Thou hast saved our lives* (47:25). Many, doubtless, resented the necessity of being moved, but in famine conditions it was necessary to bring the population to the store-cities where food was available. Convenience must be forgotten in a life-and-death situation such as Egypt faced. Joseph thus destroyed the free proprietors and made the king the lord-paramount of the soil, while the people became the hereditary tenants of their sovereign, and paid a fifth of their annual produce as rent for the soil they occupied. The priests alone retained their estates through this trying period." (Pfeiffer, *The book of Genesis*, 98,99). The "tax" of a fifth of the produce of the fields was not excessive according to ancient standards, we are told. In the time of the Maccabees the Jews paid the Syrian government one-third of the seed (I Macc. 10:30). Egyptologists inform us that large landed estates were owned by the nobility and the governors of the nomes ("states") during the Old Empire period (c. 3000-1900 B.C.). By the New Kingdom (after 1550 B.C.) power was centralized in the person of the Pharaoh. It would appear that Joseph, as Prime Minister, was instrumental in hastening this development. There is no doubt that Egypt was, during the most of the last two millennia of her existence, essentially a feudal state in which the nobility flourished and slaves did all the work. "At the end of two years (see Gen. 45:6) all the money of the Egyptians and Canaanites had passed into the Pharaoh's territory (Gen.

47:14). At this crisis we do not see how Joseph can be acquitted of raising the despotic authority of his master on the broken fortunes of the people; but yet he made a moderate settlement of the power thus acquired. First the cattle then the land of the Egyptian became the property of the Pharaoh, and the people were removed from the country to the cities. They were still permitted, however, to cultivate their lands as tenants under the crown, paying a rent of one-fifth of the produce, and this became the permanent law of the tenure of land in Egypt; but the land of the priests was left in their own possession (Gen. 47:15-26)" (OTH, 121).
Genesis, Vol. IV, by C.C. Crawford, pub. College Press, pp. 567-569

While there is no revelation from God as to heaven's acceptance or rejection of the "feudal-system" of economics instituted by Joseph, the incident does show that believers may function in such a system without violating divine revelation.

After the exodus of Israel from Egypt, the Israelites were structured into a "nation." This necessitated more regulation of individualism and privacy. The Law of Moses regulated property and business transactions with divinely revealed and codified rules. Previous detailing of Mosaic laws of property and business portray a "modified" free-enterprise system. Israelites owned their land privately and were allowed to succeed or fail by their own initiative so long as they obeyed the regulations of Moses' Law. Some became affluent, some poor. But participation in the "market place" was open to all.

Now the approach of the Mosaic law to the matter of wealth and its distribution is both novel and realistic. It envisioned no perfect utopia in which all men would be equal in ability and possessions. On the contrary, there was a frank recognition of the perennial nature of the economic problem in a sinful race, even under the beneficient rule of a kingdom of God on earth: "For the poor shall never cease out of the land" (Deut. 15:11). This is not a laissez faire form of economic fatalism, but simply one price which a society must pay for human freedom. For, if men are to enjoy any satisfactory measure of personal liberty in economic affairs — men being what they are, widely different in disposition and ability — some will gain and others will lose. Historically, no perfect way has ever been found to reconcile personal liberty with complete economic equality; the reason being that the root of the problem is in the nature of man himself, and consequently individual action is never wholly predictable. The law of the historical kingdom (i.3., Mosaic law) accepted these facts and laid down its rules accordingly. Since men could not be left wholly free and at the same time be fully protected from their own economic follies, certain provisions were established to safeguard them in the exercise of their economic rights and also to ameliorate some of the inequalities arising therefrom.

The Greatness of the Kingdom, by Alva J. McClain, p. 76

A socialist or communistic economic system has been tried in modern Israel and "found wanting":

BEIT OREN, Israel (AP) — The new kibbutzniks may not be yuppies yet, but some of Israel's socialist communes are modifying the collective life with white-collar jobs, privacy and self-fulfillment.

Beit Oren, one of the oldest communal farms, is leading the experiment with ideas that were anathema to the pioneers: private ownership, paying salaries and letting members choose their own jobs . . . .

It also has a special motivation: the need to attract new members who can help erase a $6.5 million debt that nearly forced the settlement to close in 1987 . . . .

"We are trying to make a better kibbutz by changing the role of the individual," said Zeev Shabtai, 48. "It used to be that the individual worked for the collective. This is over. People no longer want to be a tool. Let's allow the society to be the tool" . . . .

Kibbutz members will be free to spend their money as they choose, even to squander it on such capitalist luxuries as vacations abroad or stereo equipment . . . .

Under the old system all income, regardless of source, went into the kibbutz treasury to be shared by all . . . .

In exchange for the new freedom, Biet Oren plans to charge individual members for such things as electricity, water and food rather than paying the bills collectively.

Joplin Globe, 1-8-89, Joplin, MO, AP wire item

PRIVATE OWNERSHIP OF PROPERTY

During the period of the judges Israel maintained its "free-enterprise" system of economics. But individuals and their properties were in constant peril from heathen plunderers (Jdgs. 2:14). Israel was primarily an agrarian society with a scattering of tradesmen or craftsmen and merchants. But the continual harassment of pirating heathen seriously impeded their economy. At one point they had to hide themselves and the produce of their lands in caves and holes in the ground (Jdgs. 6:1-6). The book of Ruth informs us that individual Israelites owned their own farms, bought and sold land according to their own choice (Ruth 4:3), and were able to feed themselves while in Moab there was serious hunger and privation.

The institution of a monarchial political structure, at the insistence of the citizenry (I Sam. 8:1-22), did not fundamentally change the Israelite economic system. It remained free-enterprise, but government interference intensified. Encroachment upon the citizen's ownership of private property took the form of increased taxes. The "king" would "take" not only things from his subjects, he would take some of the people themselves to be his servants in the armed forces, as servants in his palace and his "fields." It is inevitable — the more a citizen demands his government "give" him, the more rights and liberties and possessions the individual has to surrender to the government!

A few references from the period of the Israelite monarchy will confirm a "modified" private enterprise system of economics:

1. David tended his father's sheep and took food to his brothers who were fighting in Saul's army (I Sam. 17:12ff).
2. Saul tried to bribe the Benjaminites for information about David by promising them "fields and vineyards" and commissions in the army (I Sam. 22:6-10).
3. Nabal, very rich, "churlish and ill behaved" (I Sam. 25:2) whose "business" was in Carmel, refused to give sustenance to David and his starving men.
4. David restored Saul's "land" to Mephibosheth (II Sam. 9:7-10).

5. Nathan's parable to David about the rich man who had many sheep and the poor man who had "one ewe lamb," (II Sam. 12:1-6) confirms the free-enterprise system.
6. Judah dwelt safely in Solomon's days, "every man under his vine and under his fig tree . . . " (I Kings 4:25).
7. Omri "bought" the hill of Samaria from Shemer for two talents of silver and built a fortified capital city there (the king did not exercise any so-called right of "eminent domain," even though he was not the "best" king Israel ever had!) (I Kings 16:24).

A free-enterprise system of economics is clearly apparent in the literary prophets (Isaiah through Malachi) and has already been documented in our listing of references to proprietorship during the days of the prophets. As in the days of the judges, however, so in the days of the prophets, apostasy from the law of Moses and idolatry which led to gross immorality and wickedness resulted in widespread civil injustices. Theoretically, the nation's economic system was capitalism, but the power which accrued to the rich allowed many of them to exploit the poor. Severe condemnation of pervasive economic injustice is a fundamental theme of all the literary prophets.

We know that many of the Jews prospered during their exile in Babylon, Persia, and under Greek rule. In exile in these foreign lands and under imperial, monarchial and fascist politico-economic systems (with their varying degrees of private ownership of property granted) the Jewish culture took on a more mercantile, professional, and tradesman character. In fascist economic systems private property is often confiscated with suddenness at the caprice or whim of the ruling monarch or one of his subordinates (see Dan. 2:5; Esther 8:1ff).

Free-enterprise economics were reinstituted in the new Jewish commonwealth upon the return of some fifty thousand with Ezra, Nehemiah and Zerubbabel. However, the system was always regulated by the Law of Moses (as interpreted later by the rabbinic traditions). And that is essentially the system of economics we find among the Jews at the time of Jesus Christ and the New Testament. Israel was, for all practical purposes, under the rule of the Roman Empire at the birth of Christ. Thus, if we wish to know the economic arrangements under which people lived from the time of Christ to the end of the New Testament, a resume of the Roman economic system is in order:

THE LAW OF PROPERTY — Problems of ownership, obligation, exchange, contract, and debt took up by far the largest part of Roman law. Material possession was the very life of Rome, and the increase of wealth and the expansion of trade demanded a body of law immeasurably more complex than the simple code of the Decemvirs . . . .

Ownership (*dominium*) came by inheritance or acquisition . . . . Every testator was compelled to leave a specified portion of his estate to his children, another part to a wife who had borne him three children, and (in some cases) parts to his brothers, sister, and ascendants. No heir might take any part of an estate without assuming all the debts and other legal obligations of the deceased . . . . Where an owner died without children and without a will, his property and his debts passed automatically to the nearest "agnate," or relative descended from a common ancestor exclusively through males . . . .

Acquisition came by transfer, or by legal conveyance resulting from a suit at law. Transfer (*mancipatio*, "taking in hand") was a formal gift or sale before witnesses and with scales struck by a copper ingot as token of a sale . . . . An intermediate or potential ownership was recognized under the name of *possessio* — the right to hold or use property; e.g. tenants on state lands were *possessores* ("sitters," squatters), not *domini*; but their prescriptive right (*usucapio*, "taking by use") became *dominium*, and could no longer be questioned after two years of unchallenged occupancy . . . .

Delicts or torts — noncontractual wrongs committed against a person or his property — were in many cases punished by an obligation to pay the injured person a sum of money in compensation. A contract was an agreement enforceable at law. It did not have to be written; indeed, until the second century A.D. the verbal agreement made by uttering the word *spondeo* — "I promise" — before a witness was considered more sacred than any written compact . . . . Any seller of slaves or cattle . . . was required by law to disclose their physical defects to the purchaser and was held accountable despite a plea of ignorance . . . .

Commercial defaults were mitigated by a law of bankruptcy which sold the bankrupt's property to pay his debts, but permitted him to keep as much of his later acquisitions as his subsistence required . . . .

The chief crimes against property were damage, theft, and rapine — theft with violence. The Twelve Tables had condemned a detected thief to be flogged and then delivered as a bondsman to his victim; if the thief was a slave he was to be scourged and flung from the Tarpeian rock. Increased social security permitted praetorian law to soften these severities to a twofold, threefold, or fourfold restitution. In its final form the law of property was the most perfect part of the Roman code.

Caesar and Christ, by Will Durant, pub. Simon and Schuster, pp. 399,400

These are the laws of economics and property that structured and regulated the economic life of the Roman empire. The similarity of these laws to those of the Mosaic code strongly imply that the economic system of the New Testament (under which the people of the Gospel history and the first century church functioned) was a modified, government-regulated, free-enterprise arrangement.

A partial listing of New Testament references indicates that the free-enterprise system of economics was what Christians experienced in the first century A.D.:

1. Jews were selling sheep and oxen in the Jewish Temple (John 2:13ff; Matt. 21:12-17; Mark 11:15-19; Luke 19:45-48). The Lord abhorred it and drove them out — but the incidents do show a capitalistic system.
2. Jesus called men who had a fishing business to be part of his band of apostles (Matt. 4:18-22; Mark 1:16-20; Luke 5:1-11).
3. Jesus said in his Sermon on the Mount, "Do not lay up for yourselves treasures on earth" (Matt. 6:19) which would indicate at least an economic system in which what is forbidden would be possible.
4. Jesus told parables which gave tacit approval to investing

capital for profit (Matt. 25:14-30; Luke 19:11-27).
5. The New Testament does not condemn wealth, only the abuse and misuse of wealth (James 5:1ff; I Tim. 6:17-19).
6. Jesus told a parable of a rich farmer, fool though he was, who was a capitalist.
7. Jesus had an opportunity to renounce capitalism and private proprietorship and embrace or urge economic socialism (redistribution or equalization of wealth) had he been inclined to do so when the man asked him to "probate" an estate and arbitrarily redistribute it (Luke 12:13ff).
8. The classic incident proving free-enterprise in the New Testament is that of Christians selling privately owned property and being told that even after it was sold the proceeds remained theirs to disburse or keep as they wished (Acts 4:32-5:6).
9. Lydia, a female entrepreneur, a business-woman, was a free-enterprising "seller of purple" (Acts 16:11-15).
10. Paul, Aquila and Priscilla his wife, were "tent-makers" who sold their productions to support themselves (Acts 18:1-4).
11. There were "silversmiths" in Ephesus who were free-enterprising craftsmen (Acts 19:23-27).
12. Revelation 18:11-24 confirms an international economy of the first century (and later) that was capitalistic.
13. James speaks of people going from city to city to trade and get gain (James 4:13ff).

Robert Culver summarizes his view of what the Bible says about civil government and economic systems:

> The doctrine that personal property is a sacred right is clearly evident in Scripture .... Furthermore, wealth is proclaimed by the Old Testament prophets, by Jesus, and by the New Testament writers to be a sacred trust, a stewardship for God .... Yet there is nothing doctrinaire about all this. Many features of capitalism are there ... but not capitalism per se, for much that seems contrary to the formal theory is also there. Many of the criticisms against capitalism (e.g., that it is morally wrong to buy and sell with profit as motive) are specifically rejected by Scripture. Yet it is perfectly possible for a Christian man to live in a socialist country and submit to the socialist economic system. I dare say, the same man will be freer to invest his life and substance in Christian mis-

sions, evangelism, and benevolences as features of private enterprise and free competition are reintroduced into the socialist system. The problem is that until the individual is able to gather to himself some monetary or other substantial surplus not allowed in a strict socialism, he has nothing at all to give away on a personal basis. Thus, though the system of private enterprise and free competition (which is what most of us really mean when we speak of capitalism) is in certain respects more congenial to Christianty than is strict socialism, one does not find the Bible forbidding him to practice socialism. Furthermore, the Bible itself furnishes examples of limitation on private enterprise and furnishes a number of examples of voluntary poverty and even of voluntary communism, mixed with wealth and private property holding . . . .
Toward a Biblical View of Civil Government, by Robert D. Culver, pub. Moody Press, pp. 281,282

9

PUBLIC WELFARE

The Bible says a great deal about social welfare, but very little *per se* about the involvement of civil government in it. The Bible focuses almost entirely on the responsibility of the individual to provide for the social welfare of the needy. Moses codified a number of laws as to how the Israelites were to care for the poor in their theocracy, but the caring was to be done by individuals who had the means to do so, and not by any form of civil bureaucracy. The only biblical instance of civil government providing social welfare for its citizenry through government regulations and structures is that of Pharaoh and Joseph in Genesis, chapters 41 through 47 (elaborated upon in previous chapters). We do know from extra-biblical sources, however, that believers of Bible times did live under civil governments (mostly pagan) which had varying forms of government-regulated social welfare programs. It is certain that first century Christians lived in a Roman empire which administered a "dole" system (see *Caesar and*

Christ, by Will Durant, p. 333).

It is a reality of history that humankind has always consisted of a wide spectrum of economic classes from the very rich to the extremely poor (with an occasional "middle-class" which has usually been taxed to provide economic relief to the extremely poor). The Bible is realistic about life. Man's sin and rebellion against the law of God is, according to the Bible, the cause of poverty. God told Israel that if they would keep covenant with him by keeping his laws there would be no poor among them (Deut. 15:4,5). However, God knew Israel would *not* obey his law perfectly and there *would be poor always* (Deut. 15:7-11) among even his theocratic people. Jesus Christ also acknowledged that, even after the messianic age had been ushered in, "you always have the poor with you . . . " (John 12:8). As long as there is sin, there will be poverty. As long as this present world exists there will be sin. Man, this side of heaven, will never find an economic Shangri-La, a utopian society where poverty is eliminated. Some poverty is inevitable because of physical circumstances beyond human control (drought, floods, or human physical limitations and defects). Some poverty results from human sin and depravity (greed, war, laziness, exploitation, injustice). The Bible is almost completely silent about any responsibility of civil governments from becoming involved in social welfare. The Bible clearly lays obligation for assisting the poverty stricken on the conscience of the individual who has been blessed with economic means.

There are twelve Hebrew words sometimes translated "poor." They are:

1. *dal* — exhausted, poor
2. *'aniy* — afflicted, oppressed, poor
3. *miseken* — honest poor
4. *eveyun* — needy, poor
5. *muk* — bankrupt, poor
6. *rashash* — one who has impoverished himself, poor
7. *rash* — an impoverished person, poverty stricken
8. *chelekah* — dejected, wounded in spirit

9. *'enaviym* — meek, poor in spirit
10. *machesor* — in want, be deficient
11. *chelekkaiym* — very miserable, cast down, dejected
12. *dallath* — the poorest

The Hebrew word most often translated "poor" is *'aniy* (no. 2 above), but it does not necessarily mean impoverished or financially destitute. It usually means "humbled, afflicted, oppressed, powerless." As may be seen from above there are three Hebrew words which have to do specifically with economic impoverishment (*dal*, or *dallath*; *muk*; and *rash* or *rashash*). The word *muk* is used in Leviticus 25:35-55. The word *dal* is used in Genesis 41:19; Exodus 23:3; 30:15; Leviticus 14:21; 19:15; Judges 6:15; Ruth 3:10; I Samuel 2:8; II Kings 25:12; Job 5:16; 20:10,19; 31:16,19; 34:19,28; Psalms 41:1; 72:13: 82:3,4; 113:7; Proverbs 10:15; 14:31; 19:4; 21:13; 22:9,16,22; 28:8,11,15; 29:7; 30:14; Isaiah 11:4; 14:30; 25:4; Jeremiah 5:4; 39:10; 40:7; 52:15,16; Amos 2:7; 4:1; 5:11; 8:6; Zephaniah 3:12, and the word *dallath* ("the poorest") is used only once in II Kings 24:14.

The Hebrew word *rash* is used in I Samuel 18:23; II Samuel 12:1,3,4; and in the following listing of scriptures from Proverbs indicated with an asterisk:

Care for the Poor	Condemnation of Laziness or Extravagance
Proverbs 10:3	Proverbs 10:4
Proverbs 10:15	Proverbs 10:5
Proverbs 13:8*	Proverbs 12:24
Proverbs 13:23*	Proverbs 12:27
Proverbs 14:20*	Proverbs 13:4
Proverbs 14:21	Proverbs 13:11
Proverbs 14:31	Proverbs 13:18*
Proverbs 15:15	Proverbs 13:22
Proverbs 17:5*	Proverbs 15:14
Proverbs 18:23*	Proverbs 18:9

Proverbs 19:1*	Proverbs 19:15
Proverbs 19:7*	Proverbs 19:24
Proverbs 19:17	Proverbs 20:4
Proverbs 19:22*	Proverbs 20:13*
Proverbs 21:13	Proverbs 21:17
Proverbs 22:2*	Proverbs 22:13
Proverbs 22:7*	Proverbs 23:21*
Proverbs 22:9	Proverbs 24:30
Proverbs 22:22	Proverbs 24:31
Proverbs 28:3*	Proverbs 24:32
Proverbs 28:6*	Proverbs 24:33
Proverbs 28:27*	Proverbs 24:34*
Proverbs 29:7	Proverbs 26:13
Proverbs 29:14	Proverbs 26:14
Proverbs 30:14	Proverbs 26:16
Proverbs 31:20	Proverbs 28:13*
	Proverbs 28:19*
	Proverbs 28:22

In Proverbs 10:15; 13:18 and 23:21, the word *rush* (a derivative of *rash*) is translated "poverty." The word *rash* is also used in Ecclestiastes 4:14 and 5:8. In practically all other cases where the English word "poor" appears in the Old Testament it is a translation of the Hebrew word *'aniy* or *eveyun* and speaks of the "oppressed" (not necessarily, economically destitute).

Specific laws were codified in the Law of Moses concerning the poor:

1. Every third year ten percent was to be given to the Levite, to the sojourner, and the fatherless and widow (Deut. 14:28,29; 26:12ff).
2. The poor were to have free use of all that grew "volunteer" in the fields or vineyards during the Sabbatic year (Exod. 23:10ff; Lev. 25:5,6).
3. Each year "gleanings" and the "corners of the fields" were to be left for the poor, and if a sheaf was forgotten at harvest, it too, was to be left for the poor (Lev. 19:9,10; 23:22; Deut. 24:19).
4. Hungry traveling through a field or vineyard or orchard were permitted to eat what they could but none was to be carried

away (Deut. 23:24,25).
5. The poor were to be subsidized as participants in the Feast of Weeks (Deut. 16:9-12).
6. Every seventh year there was to be a "writing-off" or "release" of debts owed (Deut. 15:1ff) and indentured servants were to be set free (Exod. 21:2), and every fiftieth year indentured property was to be returned to its owner (Lev. 25:8-17).
7. Israelites were to lend to their poor brethren and take no interest (Exod. 22:25; Lev. 25:35-37; Deut. 15:7ff); no widow's cloak was to be taken as surety for a loan (Deut. 24:17) nor handmill nor millstone.
8. The Mosaic law was categorically insistent that justice be done for the poor (Exod. 23:6; Deut. 27:19).
9. The poor were extended leniencies concerning the offerings they had to make for sin and purification (Lev. 5:7; 12:8, etc.).

Oppression, exploitation and abuse of any kind against the "poor" was severely denounced by the prophets (e.g. Isa. 1:23; 10:1,2; Ezek. 34:1ff; Amos 2:6; 5:7; 8:6; Micah 2:1,2; Hab. 3:14; Mal. 3:5). Isaiah has an especially pertinent passage (58:3-9) showing that God desires "mercy and not sacrifice" — love and goodness to those in need before ritualism.

But there is not one word of command that the individual is to leave caring for the poor to a civil government or organization. The welfare of the poverty stricken and helpless is the responsibility of every "neighbor" who has enough for his own needs (not his extravagances). That is God's ideal. And if all individuals would pay heed to God's law concerning the poor, that is one area civil government would not need to administrate. However, even as God knows, the ideal will never be reached as long as there are people who reject God. Therefore, laws and regulations have to be enacted for the care of the poor. And when society has to be moved to do good through law, there has to be a law-enforcer. That is the role of civil government — "God's servant for . . . good" (Rom. 13:4). And when government has to administrate good on behalf of the poor, those who are not poverty stricken have to support such administration with their taxes

(Rom. 13:6,7). It is evident from Daniel's exhortation to Nebuchadnezzar that he must "break off . . . sins by practicing righteousness, and . . . iniquities by showing mercy to the oppressed" (Dan. 4:27). The ancient pagan societies administered welfare to the poor. Nehemiah, governor of Judah, ordered the poor cared for (Neh. 8:10). The Jews living within the land of Persia, instituted a Jewish national holiday (Purim) upon which they made a feast, "sending choice portions to one another and gifts to the poor" (Esther 9:22). King Herod the Great in the thirteenth year of his reign, used his government powers to extend famine relief to the poor (Josephus, Antiq. XV:9:1,2), and Queen Helena, of Adiabene, employed her government's resources to send famine relief to Judea (Josephus, XX:2:1,2,3). When catastrophic poverty descends upon a whole culture or civilization, it is essential that human beings pool their resources and offer them through a government administered program to those in need. In catastrophic and pervasive poverty it is practically impossible that such needs could be met by individual enterprise alone.

The Greek word *ptochos* is used almost exclusively in the New Testament for "poor" or "poverty" in the sense of economic impoverishment. The Greek words *penichros* and *penes* are sometimes translated "poor" but they mean more precisely, "the person who labors for his daily bread" — a peasant (see II Cor. 9:9; and in the LXX, Exod. 22:25; Prov. 28:15; 29:7).

The New Testament, in total agreement with the Old Testament, expects that believers will, on an individual basis, be especially sensitive and beneficent toward those in need — the "poor." Believers are expected to so care for their families, young and old, that none of their "own" would need financial assistance from other sources (Matt. 15:3-6; Mark 7:6-13; Eph. 6:1-4; I Tim. 5:8). The commandment to "honor" is *tima* which means "to page wages to" (see I Tim. 5:17,18). "If anyone (a believer) does not provide for his relatives, and especially for his own family, he has disowned the faith and is worse than an unbeliever" (I

Tim. 5:8). This is more than a suggestion! This is a warning, a commandment, an obligation. Believers should not expect the civil government to care for their relatives.

In the New Testament, believers are emphatically instructed to "work with their hands" so that they should be dependent on nobody (see I Thess. 4:9-12; II Thess. 3:6-15; I Pet. 4:15; Eph. 4:28; Acts 20:34,35; I Cor. 4:12; II Cor. 12:13-17; Phil. 4:10-17; I Thess. 2:9). Those who can and will not work, shall not eat! That seems harsh to some, but it is an *apostolic command*. The command of God from the beginning has been, "In the sweat of your face you shall eat bread" (Gen. 3:19; II Thess. 3:10-13). Those who cannot work, or those who would work but are hungry and naked due to circumstances beyond their control are to be fed and clothed by those who have anything to give. Any believer who has anything at all, regardless of how little, must have a conscience to share with those who have nothing (see Matt. 5:42; 25:31-46; Mark 14:7; Luke 14:13; Mark 12:41-44; Luke 21:1-4; Rom. 15:26; II Cor. 8:1-9:15; Gal. 2:10; I Tim. 6:17-19; James 2:1-7; 2:14-17; I John 3:15-18).

However, our world is populated by millions of people who do not ascribe to God's biblical ideals. They are, in fact, in rebellion against God's "kingdom" standards. That is why God "ordained" civil government. In a world where a massive majority of people are unbelievers it is essential that civil governments become the source and regulators of social welfare for that segment of citizenry found to be legitimately impoverished (starving, naked, and shelterless). That being the biblical principle (Rom. 13:1-7), it is also imperative that civil governments be guided by Bible principles in administering social welfare:

1. Those who are able to work should be forced by law to do so (I Thess. 4:9-12; II Thess. 3:6-15). If the tax-payers are to feed the hungry through government administered money, the government should see that the recipients work. Service in the nation's military forces; cleaning up the nation's littered cities and highways; working in conservation corps; any number of

millions of jobs for minimum wage could be engaged in. Work is a fundamental and insistent biblical doctrine. All work that edifies is dignified in the Bible, no matter the job and no matter the pay (see Eph. 6:5-8; Col. 3:22-25, etc.) — even that of servants (see Eccl. 2:24; 3:13; 6:12; 9:10).
2. Those claiming to be unable to work must be legitimately unable to do so. Legislation must be enacted and enforced to eliminate laziness (Prov. 12:24; 13:18; 18:9). Those who resist a law against laziness should not be fed (II Thess. 3:6-15; Prov. 20:4).
3. Civil legislation must make the family unit the first line of social security (I Tim. 5:8; Eph. 6:1,2, etc.). Laws must be made and enforced to make those who produce children out of wedlock (both man and woman) work to support them. Legislation should be enacted that makes the nearest relative responsible to support family members who cannot or will not provide for themselves.
4. Civil government administered social welfare should be strictly and constantly "policed" to minimize fraud and waste. We hardly need to cite scriptures condemning fraud and cheating (which is nothing more than stealing and robbing). The Bible condemns wastefulness and extravagance (Luke 15:11-16; 16:1-3; John 6:12,13).
5. Tax-payers must insist that their governments, in providing social welfare to those in legitimate need, are not thereby given a mandate to provide luxuries — only necessities (I Tim. 6:6-10: Luke 12:15).

PUBLIC WORKS

Strictly speaking, the Bible makes no specific assignment of public works to the domain of civil government. The generic statement in Romans 13:1-7, and precisely the phrase, " . . . would you have no fear of him who is in authority? Then do what is good, and you will receive his approval, for he is God's servant for your good . . . " may be understood to include any number of "good" services, including public works and social welfare. Undoubtedly the Bible is silent concerning the details of

PUBLIC WELFARE

civil government's "good" services so that enough latitude may be granted for the exegencies of varying cultures, socio-economic systems, historical circumstances and political structures. It appears that the biblical writers simply assumed public works (roads, buildings, fortifications, communications, general education, commerce, and other works especially necessary to urban life and international commerce) would generate through the auspices of a central government and be paid for by taxing the citizenry.

The Bible documents a number of "public works" engaged in by civil authorities and "governments":

1. Cain, a tribal patriarch, "built" a city and named it Enoch (Gen. 4:17).
2. Egyptian Pharaohs built public storehouses in which grain was stored for public consumption (Gen. 41:56).
3. Nimrod "built" cities in the land of Assyria (Gen. 10:11,12).
4. Those of the "land of Shinar" "built" a city and a tower (Gen. 11:4).
5. Pharaoh forced the Hebrews to build "store cities" at Pithom and Raamses (Exod. 1:11).
6. Moses as leader of the nation of Israel built the nation's most "public" edifice — the Tabernacle (Exod. 25:1ff).
7. Joshua "rebuilt" the city of Timnathserah for his clan (Josh. 19:50).
8. Danites "rebuilt" the city of Bethrehob (Jdgs. 18:28).
9. David "built" the city of Jebus (Jerusalem) "round about from the Millo in complete circuit . . . . " (I Chron. 11:8).
10 Solomon employed nearly 200,000 workers and took 20 years to build the first Temple in Israel (I Kings 5:1-9:14).
11. Solomon also "built" walls, palaces, cities, government storehouses, war-horse stables, a national maritime fleet, and did public landscaping in Jerusalem (I Kings 9:15-28; see Eccl. 2:4; II Chron. 8:2). All this was done with tax money and the spoils of war in the national treasury.
12. Rehoboam, son of Solomon, built cities, fortifications, storehouse (II Chron. 11:5-12).
13. Asa built fortifications and cities (I Kings 15:22-24; II Chron. 14:6,7).

14. Jehoshaphat built cities, fortifications and storehouses (II Chron. 17:12,13).
15. Joash (boy king) taxed the people and restored the Temple (II Chron. 24:8-14).
16. Uzziah built towers, cisterns and weapons of war (II Chron. 26:1-15).
17. Jotham built gates, walls, towers, cities, and forts (II Chron. 27:3,4).
18. Hezekiah built up the walls of Jerusalem (II Chron. 32:5) and treasure houses, storehouses, cattle barns, cities, aqueducts (II Chron. 32:27-31).
19. Manasseh (after repenting) built a wall and increased Jerusalem's fortifications (II Cor. 33:14).
20. Omri built Samaria and fortified it (I Kings 16:24). Ahab built cities (I Kings 22:39).
21. Nebuchadnezzar built Babylon (Dan. 4:28-30).
22. Ezra began the work of rebuilding the Temple (Ezra 3:7ff).
23. The king of Persia ordered and assisted in rebuilding the Jewish cities and its Temple (II Chron. 36:22,23; Ezra 1:1-4; 6:1-5; 7:21-24).
24. Nehemiah rebuilt the wall of Jerusalem (Neh. 2:17ff).
25. Zerubbabel carried on the rebuilding of the Temple (Zech. 6:12).

Very little, if anything, is said by the Old Testament prophets about public works. The focus of their messages was primarily on the *destruction* of many of these "public works" (including the glorious Temple of Solomon) by heathen empires as they took the Israelites into exile.

There are no explicit references to public works by civil government in the New Testament with the exception of the notation in John 2:20 that the Temple in Jesus' day had been "forty-six years" under construction (actually, remodeling) and the notation in Luke 7:5 about an individual civil officer (a Roman centurion) who "built" a synagogue in Capernaum for the Jews of that city. We do know that a tremendous amount of public works construction was generated by Herod the Great (and his successors):

PUBLIC WELFARE

He (Herod) furthered the emperor's cultural policy by his vast building enterprises. Old cities were refounded and new cities were built; temples, hippodromes and amphitheatres were constructed — not only in his own realm but in foreign cities as well, in Athens for example. In his own kingdom he rebuilt Samaria and renamed it Sebaste, after the emperor (*Sebastos* is the Greek equivalent of the Latin *Augustus*, the title by which Octavian was known from 27 B.C. onwards). He also rebuilt Strato's Tower on the Mediterranean coast and equipped it with a large artificial harbour, calling the new foundation Caesarea, also in the emperor's honour. The work occupied some twelve years, from 22 to 10 B.C. Other settlements and strongholds were constructed here and there throughout the land, many of them bearing names in honour of members of his own family, such as Antipatris (on the road from Jerusalem to Caesarea), Cypros (at Jericho), and Phasaelis (west of the Jordan). At Jerusalem he built a royal palace for himself adjoining the western wall (c. 24 B.C.). Northwest of the temple area he had already rebuilt the Hasmonaean fortress of Baris and renamed it (after Antony) Antonia. But the greatest of all his building enterprises was the reconstruction of the Jerusalem temple. This grandiose project was begun early in 19 B.C. A thousand Levites were trained as builders, and they carried out their work in such a way that the sacred offices of the holy place were never interrupted while it was going on. The great outer court was enclosed, and surrounded by colonnades; the whole area was beautified with splendid gateways and other architectural structures until the temple became renowned throughout the world for its magnificence . . . . The main work of reconstruction was completed within Herod's lifetime, but the finishing touches were not put to it until A.D. 63, only seven years before its destruction.

Israel and The Nations, by F.F. Bruce,
pub. Eerdmans, pp. 194,195

We also know from Josephus that Pilate, Roman procurator of Judea in the days of Jesus' manhood, built an aqueduct to bring outside water into the city of Jerusalem (Josephus, Antiq. XVIII:3:2) but caused a near riot among the Jews because he used money from their Temple treasury to build it. What an individual or a small group of individuals cannot do for themselves, they must seek from either a much larger group of individuals engaged in private enterprise (corporations) or from a common and centralized treasury administered by a government which has been granted the authority to generate resources (from taxes) and enact legislation ordering the (public) work to be done. History has demonstrated that corporations engaged in private enterprise will seldom produce "public works" affordable to individuals or small groups of individuals. Thus the much larger public treasury (government) becomes necessary for certain exegencies (national defense, law enforcement, roads, communications, etc.). Reason (the "natural law" of God) justifies government initiative in these necessities. In addition, citations from the Bible are sufficiently abundant to confirm that civil authorities did, in fact, assume responsibilities for necessary public works without divine censure for doing so. We may thus conclude that public works (with some qualifications) are a part of the mandate from God that civil authorities are man's servants for the good of man. Public works produced through the civil government should be expected to conform to the following principles — all of which may be found in the Bible:

1. They should not contribute to depravity or be detrimental to the public welfare.
2. They must be "policed" to insure against fraud or waste.
3. They should be only such as are necessary to carry on the functions of the nation's defense, commerce, communication, or cultural edification.
4. They should be submitted to a public referendum either through a general election or through a polling of legislative representatives. Those who pay for public works (tax-payers) should have a decisive voice in approving their creation.
5. All citizens should have access to all public works, if such access does not impair national security.
6. Civil government should not generate any public work that might be done more efficiently, with greater expertise, and that is sufficient to meet the need, by private enterprise. This is simply the principle of wise stewardship. God will call civil governments to account for their stewardship of his creation!

PUBLIC WELFARE

The Bible does have something to say about social welfare and public works. It does not give extensive and categorical direction but it does reveal unequivocal principles by which any individual or group of individuals (civil governments) may be guided in what is right and just. God has kept his Word silent on the details to allow man latitude in working out the mechanics of social welfare and public works himself. In exercising this latitude, however, the wisest of civil governments will mold its service to man according to the divine principles revealed in God's Word.

10

CIVIL DISOBEDIENCE

The question of obedience or disobedience to civil government is an issue as constant as the sunrise! All crime is violent civil disobedience and essentially revolutionary in intent. But what about non-violent civil disobedience? Is it criminal, or is it christian? Or, is it neither? Does the Bible ever sanction disobedience toward civil authority? If so, when? And to what extent — overthrowing the incumbent regime by revolution or only verbal activism? While the Bible is silent about some of these questions, it does have something to say about others.

Fundamentally, as discussed in earlier chapters, the Bible clearly stands for obedience to civil government:

> Scripture regards the laws of any community as binding on the people of God unless they command or imply disobedience to God's revealed will (Dan. 1:6; Acts 4:18-20; 5:27-29; I Pet. 4:15,16). The validity of civil legislation in no way depends on the

cnaracter of the legislator(s), but rather upon the providential ordering of society, in which all authority is ultimately of God (John 19:10,11); Rom. 13:1-7; I Pet. 2:13,14), despite the fact that the rulers of this world are generally spiritually unenlightened (I Cor. 2:8).

Baker's Dictionary of Theology, pub. Baker, p. 319

There are a number of scriptures that are emphatic about obedience to civil government:

1. Let every person be subject to the governing authorities. For there is no authority except from God, and those that exist have been instituted by God. Therefore he who resists the authorities resists what God has appointed, and those who resist will incur judgment (Rom. 13:1,2). There are no qualifications or extenuations to this apostolic demand in this context. Qualifications are to be found in other scriptures, of course.
2. Be subject for the Lord's sake to every human institution, whether it be to the emperor as supreme, or to governors as sent by him to punish those who do wrong and to praise those who do right (I Pet. 2:13,14). Again, no mitigation of the demand in this context.
3. Have reverence for the Lord, my son, and honor the king. Have nothing to do with people who rebel against them; such men could be ruined in a moment. Do you not realize the disaster that God or the king can cause? (Prov. 24:21,22, TEV).
4. When a nation sins, it will have one ruler after another. But a nation will be strong and endure when it has intelligent, sensible leaders (Prov. 28:2, TEV). The Hebrew word *pesha* is translated "sin" but may also be translated "rebellion." Saul accused Jonathan of "rebelling" against his own father (I Sam. 20:30). Civil disobedience and rebellion against their civil rulers brought the ten northern tribes (Israel) to a state of anarchy in its last days (see Hosea 13:9-11; Isa. 3:6-8, etc.).
5. People with no regard for others can throw whole cities into turmoil. Those who are wise keep things calm (Prov. 29:8, TEV). Rabble-rousing and civil unrest creates turmoil for everybody.

6. If any of you suffers, it must not be because he is a murderer or a thief or a criminal or meddles in other people's affairs (I Pet. 4:15, TEV). The Greek word *allotrioepiskopos*, translated "meddler" or "busybody" was a legal term used by the first century heathen courts to charge Christians with "being hostile to civilized society," in other words, "revolutionaries" "seditionists." Peter says Christians should not be guilty of this.
7. Each one should go on living according to the Lord's gift to him, and as he was when God called him. This is the rule I teach in all the churches . . . . Everyone should remain as he was when he accepted God's call. Were you a slave when God called you? Well, never mind; but if you have a chance to become a free man, use it. For a slave who has been called by the Lord is the Lord's free man; in the same way a free man who has been called by Christ is his slave . . . . My brothers, each one should remain in fellowship with God in the same condition that he was when he was called (I Cor. 7:17-24 TEV). While the apostle Paul urged slaves to become "free men" should the opportunity present itself (non-violent) to do so, at the same time he emphasized over and over that people who were slaves when they became Christians should not, because of the exegencies of the times in which Corinthians was written, resist civil government in any violent or seditious manner to change their status. Paul practiced what he preached. When he was unjustly accused of a crime and arrested, he did not react violently or even resist the authorities physically. He verbally asserted his rights, and his innocence, but he did not resist civil authorities.
8. Declare these things; exhort and reprove with all authority. Let no one disregard you. Remind them to be submissive to rulers and authorities, to be obedient, to be ready for any honest work . . . (Titus 2:15-3:1).
9. Philemon v. 1-25 — Philemon was a prominent Christian, probably a member of the church at Colossae and the owner of a slave named Onesimus. This slave had run away from his master, and then somehow he had come in contact with Paul who was then in prison. Through Paul, Onesimus became a Christian. Paul's letter to Philemon is an appeal to be reconciled to his slave, whom Paul is sending back to him, and to welcome him not only as a forgiven slave but as a Christian brother. Paul did not put Onesimus on any "underground

railroad" that would take the slave to "freedom" — he sent him back.
10. Slaves, obey your human masters with fear and trembling, and do it with a sincere heart, as though you were serving Christ. Do this not only when they are watching you, because you want to gain their approval; but with all your heart do what God wants, as slaves of Christ. Do your work as slaves cheerfully, as though you served the Lord, and not merely men. Remember that the Lord will reward everyone, whether slave or free, for the good work he does (Eph. 6:5-8, TEV). This verse would seem to disapprove of all social revolutions, economic revolutions, and political revolutions. It certainly does not offer justification to modern "social revolutionaries" whose economic and political circumstances are a far cry from "slavery."

Dr. Carl F.H. Henry, in his book, *Aspects of Christian Social Ethics*, writes at length on this matter:

While under some conditions Christian conscience may indeed approve certain *consequences* of revolution, Christian social theory neither promotes nor approves revolution itself as a method of social transformation . . . .

Since government's function is to preserve order as well as to promote justice, Christian social theory opposes social change by anarchic methods. When revolution is regarded as a self-sufficient objective (and hence is represented as itself a panacea for social evil) it becomes insupportable and intolerable. Moreover, when revolution is detached from spiritual and moral obligations and proffers exemption from social responsibility it breeds irresponsibility and bestiality and must therefore invite Christian condemnation. Christianity's interest in social change always carries with it the demand for inner renewal, and not simply external readjustment. But contemporary revolutions, advancing anti-christian concepts of life and society, seem usually to promote social disorder and to displace one form of political injustice by another . . . .

Nonetheless, Christian social theory is free to approve certain results of revolution, including the abolition of tryanny. Social resentment thrives wherever and whenever citizens are deprived of elemental human rights. Totalitarian demands for behavior that violates biblical imperatives arouse indignation and resistance. Such resistance in turn may contribute to a counter-revolution that tries to restore authority to the side of law and justice. The objective of such Christian action is not merely to overthrow one revolutionary form of government in favor of another, but rather to restore government to its proper concerns . . . .

Revolution can hope for Christian sympathy only where it actually protests against an established government's persistent abuse of the norms of government (maintenance of law and order, protection of the innocent, repression of bad works) and where it openly purposes to re-establish these norms. At its worst . . . the State may become almost a demonic power whose organization gives new and terrible strength to the world's hostility to God . . . . Every form either of rebellion or of passive resistance to the government must justify itself as a protest made in the name of the state as it might and ought to be — it seeks the reorganization of the State itself on a juster model (pp. 176-179).

Citing several examples, Dr. Henry offers them as New Testament perspectives on the subject of civil disobedience:

During the three hundred years when the Roman emperors declared Christianity an illegal religion, Christians were marked as criminals by civil law simply because they were Christians. Against such government the Christian movement generated no revolutionary temper, and to such government Christian believers pledged their prayers and paid their taxes. The Christian does not promote the cause of anarchy, since he knows that government has a biblical role. Even if a government now and then exceeds its proper authority, the Christian's hope of a better tomorrow is sustained by a firm reliance on divine providence more than by enthusiasm for human revolution. The Book of Revelation (ch.13) depicts the saints as preparing for martyrdom rather than for revolution.

While Jesus did not regard the State "as in any sense a final, divine institution," he nonetheless "accepts the state and radically renounces every attempt to overthrow it . . . . This double attitude is characteristic of the entire New Testament" . . . (p. 180).

However, Henry clearly acknowledges that the civil state must be resisted, and that Christians are biblically obligated to do so, when the state goes beyond the biblical mandate with which it is charged:

> Yet the Christian need not always "suffer injustice." Obedience and silence are not forever the only course open to him in the face of unlawfully constituted authority. Under some circumstances, in fact, disobedience to government becomes a Christian duty. In Cullmann's words: "It is not our business to take the sword, to wage war as the fellowship of Christians against this (totalitarian) State in order to destroy its existence." Our obligation, rather, is "positively, perseverance in our Christian preaching; negatively, perseverance in our refusal of the idolatry demanded by the State." The Acts of the Apostles leaves no doubt that rulers are to be disobeyed when they forbid the proclamation of the gospel. Christians then resist the ruler not in opposition to civil law but in obedience to God's command. "As soon as the State demands more than is necessary to its existence," observes Cullman, "as soon as it demands what is God's — thus transgressing its limits — the disciple of Jesus is relieved of all obligation to this requirement of a totalitarian State."
>
> The Christian approach to government differs from the anarchist concept in several ways. It gladly obeys where government observes its proper limits, protests where it exceeds those limits, and actively resists where a totalitarian demand requires disobedience to the revealed will of God. "In the Roman State emperor worship is the point at which the State exceeds its proper bounds . . . . For the rest, the Roman State was a legitimate State, knowing how to distinguish between good and evil." The German national-socialistic state (Nazi government of Adolph Hitler), however, fell away "from the order in which every State is placed; for here the distinction between good and evil, right and wrong, no longer prevailed: on the contrary, right was whatever the State required."
>
> Yet the Christian does not then face totalitarian forces in the human spirit of counter-revolution. The New Testament does not approve renouncing the State as an instituion, and limits the resistance shown even to a totalitarian state . . . .
>
> The Christian Church is not anarchistic. The Christian Church

CIVIL DISOBEDIENCE

is not revolutionary. The Christian Church does not initiate movements for political independence . . . the Church remains ready to proclaim and ready to be martyred for proclaiming those abiding truths and ultimate loyalties whose surrender reduces every revolution to lawlessness and whose loss casts even a free people into subjection and nihilism (pp. 181-186).

The Bible strongly insists that violent revolution which is aimed at destroying the very concept of civil government (anarchy or nihilism), or any kind of revolution that would destroy one oppressive form of government simply to install an equally oppressive form, is forbidden. The Bible insists (by historical examples) that believers may live, prosper, and even participate in civil governments which are godless and relatively oppressive (Daniel, Esther, Joseph, Christ and his apostles and the first century church). To instigate the overthrow of civil government for *any* reason is to jeopardize social order, freedom, human life, and destroys all opportunity for the truth of God to be disseminated. That is why Paul urges believers to pray for the stability of civil governments (I Tim. 2:1-4).

John MacArthur writes:

> Other than instructing us to be model citizens, Scripture says nothing at all about Christians engaging in politics. It says nothing about Christians engaging in civil change. Those things are not our priority . . . . We are to be the conscience of the nation through godly living and faithful preaching. We do not confront the nation through political pressure but through the Word of God . . . .
> *The Christian and Government*, Moody Press, p.5

MacArthur illustrates his proposition by pointing to the example of Jesus Christ who came into a world of slavery, dictatorship, exorbitant taxes, and religious persecution:

> . . . but he did not come with power and force to overthrow Roman tyranny. He did not seek social change. He did not at-

tempt to eliminate slavery. He did not come with political or economic issues at stake. He did not come to bring a new government or to wave a flag of Judaism . . . . Jesus did not participate in civil rights or crusade to abolish injustice; He preached the gospel of salvation. Once a man's or woman's soul is right with God, it matters very little what the externals are. Jesus was not interested in a new social order, but in a new spiritual order — the church. And he mandated the church to carry on the same kind of ministry.

ibid, pp. 6-8

The conclusion Dr. MacArthur reaches from his study of biblical examples of civil disobedience is:

The one time we have a right to disobey the government is when it commands us not to do something God has commanded us to do, or when it commands us to do something God has commanded us not to do . . . .
If our government changes its form, as governments often do, we are still called to submit and be model citizens. We are called not only to obey but to obey with a spirit of obedience. We are to give honor to those who are in authority over us so that evil might not be spoken about the name of Christ. If there are critics who are looking for ways to condemn Christians, please let them condemn us for our faith and not our political viewpoints.

ibid, pp. 15-17

MacArthur cites the testimony of a former Christian citizen of Russia:

George Vins is a Christian who lived for many years in the Soviet Union. He met with our staff one day, and we asked him what it was like to live under tyranny and repression in a communist country. He told us that Christians can't pursue an education or a career. They have no say in the government and no freedoms to speak of. The question was then posed to him: How do you respond to that kind of government? He said, "We obey every law in our nation, whether it appears to us to be just or unjust, except when we are told that we cannot worship God or obey the Scripture. But if we are persecuted, put into prison, or killed, it will be a result of our faith in Jesus Christ, not because we violated some law in our nation.

ibid, pp. 12,13

The Bible reveals that God, by supernatural interventions or by ordering human agencies, has overthrown certain civil governments. The flood (Gen. 6), the thwarting of the tower of Babel (Gen. 10-11), Sodom and Gomorrah (Gen. 19), the exodus of Israel from Egypt (Exod. 1-15), all involved destructions of civil governments. Through Samuel, God anointed David to kingship while Saul was still on the throne (I Sam. 16:1-23); God commanded Jehu to kill Jezebel and overthrow her government (II Sam. 9:1-10); Isaiah, Jeremiah and Daniel all declared that God used the pagan empires of Assyria (Isa. 10:5ff), Babylon (Jer. 25:8-14; 27: 5-15), Persia (Isa. 13:17; 21:2; Jer. 51:11; Dan. 5:28; 7:1ff; 8:1ff; 9:24-27) and others to overthrow and replace existing civil governments.

However, there is no biblical sanction whatever for individuals, believers or not, who have no direct revelation from God, to assume such prerogatives. The terms "rebellion, rebelled," etc., found some one hundred times in the Bible, are almost without exception used disapprovingly:

1. The rebellion of Korah, Dathan and Abiram so displeased the Lord he opened up the earth and swallowed thousands of the rebels (Num. 16:1-34).
2. The rebellion of Abner and Ishbosheth against David resulted in eventual disaster (II Sam. 15:3ff).
3. Absalom's violent revolution against his father, David, had a tragic ending (II Sam. 15:3ff).
4. Sheba, who also attempted a violent *coup d'etat* against David, brought about his ignominious death (II Sam. 20:22).
5. The rebellion of Jeroboam divided the nation of Israel into two hostile, warring nations and eventuated in a long history of idolatry, social depravity, political anarchy and exile for both nations (I Kings 12:1ff).

6. Zimri's violence toward civil government was eventually repaid to him in kind at his assassination (I Kings 16:8-20).
7. Athaliah, queen of Judah, imitating the violence and wickedness of her mother and father, Jezebel and Ahab, attempted to murder all her grandsons to keep the throne for herself (II Kings 11:1ff).
8. Those who plotted to overthrow the Persian monarch were exposed by Mordecai and hanged (Esther 2:21-23).

It is a serious matter for an individual to disobey civil authority and civil law. And it is extremely so for individuals to presume to destroy civil government by revolution, violent or otherwise. At all costs, except denial of faith in God and Christ, civil order and government must be preserved.

Yet, in spite of the extreme gravity of "resisting the authorities," the Bible clearly, by precept, by principle, and by example, declares there are limits to civil obedience for the believer at least. Francis Schaeffer writes:

> Has God set up an authority in the state that is autonomous from Himself? Are we to obey the state no matter what? Are we? In this one area is indeed Man the measure of all things? And I would answer, not at all, not at all.
> When Jesus says in Matthew 22:21, "Give to Caesar what is Caesar's, and to God what is God's," it is not:
> GOD and CAESAR
> It was, is, and always will be:
> GOD
> and
> CAESAR
> The civil government, as all of life, stands under the Law of God. In this fallen world God has given us certain offices to protect us from the chaos which is the natural result of that fallenness. But when *any office* commands that which is contrary to the Word of God, those who hold that office abrogate their authority and they are not to be obeyed. And that includes the state . . . .
> God has ordained the state as a *delegated* authority; it is not autonomous. The state is to be an agent of justice, to restrain evil by punishing the wrongdoer, and to protect the good in society.

When it does the reverse, *it has no proper authority*. It is then a usurped authority and as such it becomes lawless and is tryanny . . . .

Why were the Christians in the Roman Empire thrown to the lions? From the Christian's viewpoint it was for a religious reason. But from the viewpoint of the Roman State they were in civil disobedience, they were civil rebels. The Roman State did not care what anybody believed religiously; you could believe anything, or you could be an atheist. But you had to worship Caesar as a sign of your loyalty to the state. The Christians said they would not worship Caesar, anybody, or anything, but the living God. Thus to the Roman Empire they were rebels, and it was civil disobedience. That is why they were thrown to the lions.

A Christian Manifesto, by Francis A. Schaeffer, pub. IVP, pp. 90-92

The statement of Jesus Christ, quoted above, is the quintessential proclamation for civil disobedience. There are spheres that belong to "Caesar" and spheres that belong to God. God, because he is the Sovereign Creator of all, including "Caesar," forever takes priority. When "Caesar" presumes to legislate what God has forbidden, or to forbid what God has legislated, Caesar must be disobeyed. Following are some biblical examples and/or principles which provide guidelines for believers in the matter of civil disobedience:

1. The Egyptian Pharaoh's edict that the Hebrew midwives must murder every new-born Hebrew male-child (Exod. 1:15-22). While we believe "abortion on demand" in every case except where the mother's life is unquestionably jeopardized is murder, the instance of the Hebrew midwives does not fall into the category of abortion, but unequivocal murder! The Hebrew midwives were right in disobeying the civil ruler, for the civil ruler had ordered them to disobey God. Civil authorities of the United States have not *ordered* any woman to have an abortion — they have "legalized" individuals to *choose* murder. While we believe civil authorities have no right to make such a law, and believers should make every orderly action possible to overturn such a law, there is a difference between abortion "on

demand" and a civil edict that babies *must* be killed.
2. The exodus of the Israelites from Egypt (see Exod. 5:1ff). The exodus (civil disobedience) was not because of physical oppression, primarily, but because Pharaoh would not let the Israelites go worship God as God had commanded (Exod. 5:1-4; 8:25-32; 10:24-29; etc.). It must be noted that while the Israelites insisted that Pharaoh let them leave Egypt, they did not attempt any *coup d'etat* — they did not overthrow the Egyptian government. God, of course, used "violent" means as a "last resort" to convince Pharaoh to let them go worship, but the Israelites attempted no violence against Egypt on their own.
3. Jonathan's disobedience of King Saul, his own father, was nonviolent and proper (I Sam. 20:1ff). Saul wanted his son to become an accomplice to murder.
4. David would not raise his hand against Saul, although he had personal provocation to do so plus the knowledge that God wanted him to be king in Saul's place. David was engaged in non-revolutionary disobedience to the civil government then in power (I Sam. 24:1-7; 26:7-12).
5. Isaiah made no overt attempt to overthrow the rule of the wicked Ahaz, who among other things sacrificed children to death by fire; yet Isaiah did not always obey everything the kings of his day commanded (Isa. 7:1ff).
6. Jeremiah disobeyed orders of civil rulers (26:1ff; 37:1ff; 38:1ff) and was severely persecuted and threatened, but made no effort physically or verbally to incite the overthrow of the governments.
7. Amos, likewise, disobeyed orders from the government of Israel to stop preaching (Amos 7:10-17), but did not become a political activist.
8. Jehosheba (II Kings 11:1-3), at the risk of her life, disobeyed queen Athaliah and hid the boy prince Joash from assassination.
9. Daniel, taken to Babylon as a prisoner of war, and commanded to eat food forbidden an Israelite by the Law of Moses, disobeyed the emperor's edict (Dan. 1:1-21).
10. Shadrach, Meshach and Abednego disobeyed the Babylonian emperor's edict to bow down before an idolatrous image of the emperor (Dan. 3:1-15), declaring: "Your Majesty, we will not try to defend ouselves. If the God whom we serve is able to

save us from the blazing furnace and from your power, then he will. But even if he doesn't, Your Majesty may be sure that we will not worship your god, and we will not bow down to the gold statue you have set up (Dan. 3:16-18, TEV).
11. Daniel refused to obey the order of the Persian emperor that no one in Persia might pray to any god except the king of Persia (Dan. 6:6-28), was thrown into the lion's den, but rescued by God and became a high-ranking official in the Persian government.
12. Vashti, queen of Persia, resisted the emperor's command to appear before the emperor to apparently be disrespectfully and lewdly exhibited to his drunken officials (Esther 1:1-22). She was deposed from her throne.
13. Jesus is the perfect example of non-violent disobedience toward civil government demanding an individual disobey God (Luke 22:66-71; 23:1-25).
14. The classic example of believer's non-violent disobedience toward civil government is that of Peter and John when ordered to cease preaching the gospel of Christ (Acts 4:18-22; 5:27-32). They knew what the consequences of their disobedience would be, having been forewarned by Jesus (Matt. 10:16-25; John 15:18-27; 16:1-4, etc.). They were willing to suffer the consequences, counting it an honor to do so (I Pet. 3:18-22). They told all Christians to expect the same (I Pet. 4:12-19).
15. Paul, the Jewish apostle to the Gentiles, gives all Christians an example of personal civil disobedience to civil authority when it has demanded what only God may demand (Acts 16:16-24; 16:35-40; 18:12-17; 21:33).
16. And last, but probably most significant, is the prediction in the book of Revelation that Christians of the early centuries would be called upon to disobey the Roman emperor's orders to worship him and do other things forbidden by God (Rev. 13:1-18) and suffer imprisonment and death for refusing to do so.

Clearly, a crucial element of gospel proclamation is to exhort the world of mankind to be obedient to civil government. But when any civil ruler or authority of any kind demands that we do anything to disobey God, our reply must always be:

WHAT THE BIBLE SAYS ABOUT CIVIL GOVERNMENT

Whether it is right in the sight of God to listen to you rather than to God, you must judge . . . we must obey God rather than men . . . (Acts 4:19: 5:29).

John Eidsmoe cites five principles which are clearly discernable from Bible examples of civil disobedience:

1. Normally we should obey, respect, and do our best to please those in authority over us in civil government.
2. We should resist and disobey government only when that government commands us to do something the Word of God forbids, or forbids us to do something the Word of God commands — either directly or by clear implication.
3. Even when government and the Word of God conflict, we should not disobey government unless and until we have done everything possible to try to work out the conflict and effect a suitable accommodation of our religious beliefs. In a system of representative government like ours, we have a great responsibility to use the courts and the political process to try to get the law changed.
4. When it is necesary to disobey government, we should be willing to suffer the necessary civil or criminal punishment for our act. If the principle is not worth being punished for, it is not enough of a principle to justify civil disobedience.
5. Even while disobeying government, and even while being punished for our disobedience, we should at all times be respectful to the civil authorities. Even though they have misconstrued God's will, they are still God's ministers — whether they know it or not!

God and Caesar, by John Eidsmoe, pub. Crossway, p. 32

Any consideration of what the Bible says about civil disobedience for an American Christian inevitably raises the question, "What about the American Revolution of 1776?" The question will always be problematic, and there will always be Bible-believing Christians taking both sides of the issue, just as they did in 1776. Many "Tories" (those who remained loyal to the English crown in 1776) were opposed to the war by their Christian principles, just as there were many others who fought in, or otherwise supported, the war by their Christian convictions. The issue divided many families in 1776, notably among them, Benjamin Franklin and his son William. William Franklin was arrested as an enemy of America and eventually moved to England, never to see his father again. It is our opinion that the American "Revolution" was justified. Other Christians must study the history as thoroughly as possible and form their own conclusion. Here are our reasons:

1. First, consider the American Declaration of Independence:
    A Declaration: By the Representatives of the United States of America, in Congress Assembled:
        When, in the course of human events, it becomes necessary for one people to dissolve the political bands which have connected them with another, and to assume among the powers of the earth the separate and equal station to which the laws of nature and of nature's God entitle them, a decent respect for the opinions of mankind requires that they should declare the causes which impel them to the separation.
    We hold these truths to be self-evident: that all men are created equal; that they are endowed by their Creator with certain inalienable rights; that among these are life, liberty, and the pursuit of happiness. That, to secure these rights, governments are instituted among men, deriving their just powers from the consent of the governed; that, whenever any form of government becomes destructive of these ends, it is the right of the people to alter or to abolish it, and to institute a new government, laying its foundation on such principles, and organizing its powers in such form, as to them shall seem most likely to effect their safety and happiness. Prudence, indeed, will dictate that governments long established should not be changed for light and transient causes; and, accordingly, all experience hath shown that mankind are more disposed to suffer, while evils are sufferable, than to right themselves by abolishing the forms to which they are accustomed. But, when a long train of abuses and usurpations, pursuing invariably the same object, evinces a design to reduce them under absolute despotism, it is their right, it is their duty, to throw off such government, and to provide new guards for their future

security. Such has been the patient sufferance of these colonies, and such is now the necessity which constrains them to alter their former systems of government. The history of the present King of Great Britain is a history of repeated injuries and usurpations, all having, in direct object, the establishment of an absolute tyranny over these States. To prove this, let facts be submitted to a candid world . . . .

We have condensed the original "facts" as follows:)

Great Britain refused the colonies laws for the public good.
Refused to let colonial governments pass such needed laws.
Demanded people relinquish rights of representation in legislation.
Made legislative meetings unavailable to local citizens.
Arbitrarily dissolved representative legislative bodies in some areas.
Refused to reinstitute dissolved legislatures for long periods, leaving such areas open to anarchy and disorder.
Refused immigration to frontier areas and thus hindered economy.
Obstructed justice, refusing to let States establish judiciary powers.
Installed judges dependent entirely upon the Crown, independent of any restraint from the colonies.
Multiplied the bureaucratic system administering the Crown's control.
Posted huge numbers of soldiers in a time of peace in America.
Granted the British military immunity from the civilian governments.
Made and enforced laws contrary to the laws already enacted by the colonies.
Quartered large numbers of troops in private residences against owner's will.
Allowed soldiers to be exempt from civil law (even law against murder).
Cut off the colonies' trade with other nations.
Taxation without representation or consent.
Deprived many in colonies of trial by jury.
Transported many colonials to England for trial in "pretended offenses."
Revoked charters of the colonies (which granted self-government).

368

Suspended colonial Congress.
The Crown abdicated its governing of the colonies and declared war upon them.
Plundered ships of colonies, burned and looted cities, and killed citizens.
Brought large armies of mercenaries to subjugate American citizens.

Consider further:

2. When the English monarchs granted "charters" to groups of individuals to colonize the North American continent, they granted these colonies complete authority of self-government. The Charter of Maryland of 1632 is an example:

> . . . free, full and absolute Power . . . to ordaine, Make and Enact LAWS of what kind soever, according to their sound discretion.

Charters of other colonies such as Plymouth, Massachusetts Bay Colony, etc., were granted similar self-governing authority. Thus, the coercive measures taken by Great Britain against the American colonies were, in effect, an invasion attempting to overthrow their legally established governments. Americans did not "revolt" they merely took up arms in defense of, not only "inalienable rights" but of legal rights. Americans fought against the aggression of a "foreign" power. Had the Crown acknowledged their right of self-government there would have been no war.

3. The British Crown and Parliament was usurping rights granted to Englishmen as far back as the Magna Charta (1215 A.D.). Rights such as legislative and judicial representation of the governed, trial by jury, protection of life and property, and many others which are listed in the American Declaration of Independence. American statesmen were not "revolutionaries" or "anarchists."

4. British civil authority over the colonies was repudiated by the British themselves when, on December 22, 1775, Parliament passed the Prohibitory Act which removed the colonies from the king's protection and declared that the colonies were to be treated

as foreign enemies. When British protection was removed, the duty of allegiance was removed, and Parliament in effect, declared war upon the colonies. Many people in England, including the famous statesman Edmund Burke, acknowledged the American declaration of independence to be legally and morally justifiable.

Impressed American seamen into British navy and forced them to fight their own American countrymen.

Incited domestic insurrections among American Indians against the frontiers.

American petitions to King George unheeded for many years.

We, therefore, the representatives of the UNITED STATES OF AMERICA, in GENERAL CONGRESS assembled, appealing to the Supreme Judge of the World for the rectitude of our intentions, do, in the name, and by the authority of the good people of these colonies, solemnly publish and declare, That these United Colonies are, and of right ought to be, FREE AND INDEPENDENT STATES, they have full power to levy war, conclude peace, contract alliances, establish commerce, and to do all other acts and things which INDEPENDENT STATES may of right do. And for the support of this Declaration, with a firm reliance on the protection of DIVINE PROVIDENCE, we mutually pledge to each other, our lives, our fortunes, and our sacred honor.

Note that those who made this Declaration did so believing that King George's government had "become destructive" of "certain inalienable rights" which are fundamental rights granted to man by his Creator and not by any government; that human governments are established to "secure" these rights, and when any government makes these "certain inalienable" rights *insecure* it is the duty of human beings to "alter or abolish" such a government and "institute a new government" as will "effect" these "inalienable rights." These were the "inalienable rights," "life, liberty and property (property is what the phrase "pursuit of happiness" means; see George Mason's draft of the Virginia Bill of Rights)" being destroyed by the Egyptians when God gave Israel exodus and mandate to establish their own government. Note also the caution and reluctance ("Prudence . . . will dictate . . . ") with which this Declaration was made. These men were not nihilists, nor did they enter into this over "light and transient" causes. They had petitioned for redress for over one hundred years receiving only intensified usurpation of rights.

Human beings have inalienable rights. These rights are granted by the Creator and not to be usurped by any other human being or group (government) of human beings. Any government, duly established by the consent of the governed, and securing inalienable human rights for its citizens, has the God-given right to defend itself against the insurrection of a minority or the invasion of an alien aggressor. When any government takes it upon itself to destroy *inalienable* human rights or usurp another nation's duly constituted government, it ought to be resisted by force or non-violent disobedience, according to the circumstances and the abilities of the victims. Such action, in our opinion, is implied in what the Bible says about civil government.

In Biblical times, in pagan and Jewish cultures alike, especially during the days of the Roman empire, ordinary citizens suffered extreme political and social oppressions:

1. There was racial discrimination much more pervasive and malicious than is found anywhere in today's world!
2. No ordinary citizen had the right to vote for political leadership or laws of governance.
3. Millions were slaves — bought and sold and treated like animals.
4. There was no freedom of the press or criticism of the social order as is enjoyed in democratic countries today.
5. There were no "women's rights" or "equalities."
6. Educational opportunities were available only to the rich and powerful.
7. There were no labor unions — no "social securities."
8. There were no representative systems of government.
9. Children had absolutely no rights until their majority (fathers had the power of life or death over their children). Abortion and abandonment were widely practiced.

10. Exorbitant taxation was by extortion.
11. Tax money was embezzled by corrupt political officials whose lives were profligate and shameful.

In spite of these and many other diabolical abuses of human rights, we find *no biblical advocacy* of massive marches, "sit-downs," lobbyings, civil disobediences or civil rioting. The Bible does not approve of civil disobedience as an answer to injustice unless there is abuse of "unalienable" human rights or a direct commandment of God.

11

INTERNATIONAL RELATIONS

The Bible, the divine revelation of the Creator of all mankind, cuts across all cultural and national peculiarities and deals with mankind universally. It was written by individuals and initially addressed to nations, communities or individuals within their historical times. However, because the Bible is a supernatural revelation from the Author and Sustainer of all history, its time-oriented-specifics may also be eternally-principled-universals.

Foreign policies or international relations practiced by nations many centuries ago may be technologically or technique-wise inapplicable to our modern world, but the principles are as valid today as they were 3000 years ago. Truth and values do not change. God is the author of all truth and all morality. In fact, God *is* truth and God *is* morality. Truth and righteousness have their source in the Divine Person — that is where they reside. Since he does not change, they do not change. They are his nature.

The Creator made man in his own image, a person whose worth is determined by the truth, righteousness, love and justice that resides in him. Man, this creature of the Divine Father, is procreative and social. Man has communalized himself into social structures, in response to Divine fiat and providential circumstances. The larger of these social structures are called "nations." Because God scattered his creatures, confounding human language into many diverse tongues, men have adapted themselves to many different "cultures," climates, circumstances and political contingencies. Huge masses of individuals with the same languages and cultures have come together to cooperate in political, economic and other structures to form nations. But nations are still simply massive concentrations of individuals.

Therefore, what is called "international relations" must be fundamentally approached from the perspective of individual, personal relations. Practically all the biblical truths which reveal the mind of God for individual relations may be extrapolated to the national level:

1. So whatever you wish that men would do to you, do so to them; for this is the law and the prophets (Matt. 7:12).
2. Everyone to whom much is given, of him will much be required (Luke 12:48).
3. Take heed and beware of all covetousness; for a man's life does not consist in the abundance of his possessions (Luke 12:15).
4. Which of these three, do you think, proved neighbor to the man who fell among the robbers? . . . The one who showed mercy on him . . . . Go and do likewise (Luke 10:36).
5. He has showed you, O man, what is good; and what does the Lord require of you but to do justice, and to love kindness, and to walk humbly with your God (Micah 6:8).
6. Live in harmony with one another . . . . If possible, so far as it depends upon you, live peaceably with all (Rom. 12:16,18).
7. Owe no one anything, except to love one another; for he who loves his neighbor has fulfilled the law (Rom. 13:8).
8. . . . aspire to live quietly, to mind your own affairs, and to work with your hands, as we charged you; so that you may

INTERNATIONAL RELATIONS

command the respect of outsiders, and be dependent on nobody (I Thess. 4:11,12).

9. What causes wars, and what causes fighting among you? Is it not your passions that are at war in your members? You desire and do not have; so you kill. And you covet and cannot obtain; so you fight and wage war. You do not have, because you do not ask. You ask and do not receive, because you ask wrongly, to spend it on your passions (James 4:1-3).

10. If a brother or sister is ill-clad and in lack of daily food, and one of you says to them, Go in peace, be warmed and filled, without giving them the things needed for the body, what does it profit? (James 2:15,16).

Scores of other principles concerning human relations could be cited from the Bible which apply universally and internationally. But there are also principles and illustrations in the Bible that have something to say more specifically about God's will for international relations. Some of these are as follows:

1. The world is a "community of nations" — all men are brothers in the sense that they are God's creatures and "sons." We *are* "our brother's keeper" (Gen. 4:9) because we have all descended from one father and mother (Adam and Eve). Furthermore, Jesus dictated this principle of the "brotherhood of man" and its implications for international relations in his parable of the Good Samaritan (Luke 10:29-37). Peter further amplified the principle in his statement, "Truly I perceive that God shows no partiality, but in every nation any one who fears him and does what is right is acceptable to him" (Acts 10:34). Nations should conduct their relations with other nations on the principle that God is not partial to any nation, but that people are, as far as this world is concerned, brothers — especially when any are in need of succor (see Job 31:13-15).

2. Jehovah God in the person of his Son, Jesus Christ, is Sovereign Lord of lords, and King of kings. His will rules the universe and the affairs of men. He sets up kings and deposes them (Dan. 2:21,47, 4:1-3; 4:17; 4:34-37; 6:25-27). "Man proposes and God disposes." Kings and rulers make their choices and act, and God uses all to his glory and the fulfill-

ment of his redemptive program in history (e.g. Isa. 10:5-27; Jer. 27:1-11; John 19:10,11). God expects nations to conduct their international relations through an acknowledgment, to some degree, of his sovereignty. This is clearly demonstrated by the fact that Amos held pagan nations morally responsible to Jehovah for their relations with other nations (Amos 1:3-2:16). Others uncompromisingly reinforce this principle (Isaiah ch. 13-23; Jonah; Jeremiah ch. 46-51; Ezekiel ch. 26-39). And the book of Revelation portrays the once Incarnate Lamb (Jesus) as the Glorified and Enthroned ruler of nations who "puts it into their hearts to carry out his purpose . . ." (Rev. 17:15-18; compare Dan. 7:13ff).

There has been only one theocratic nation, it is true (Israel). However, the law of God by which all nations are to conduct their affairs has been written on men's hearts (Rom. 2:12-16) innately, it has been written in "nature" (Rom. 1:18ff) objectively, personified in Jesus Christ, historically (John 1:1ff, I John 1:1-4), and revealed to mankind in human language (I Cor. 1:18-25; 2:10-13), propositionally. So that all men (and nations) are without excuse! All men of every nation have been given minds with which to think and laws of logic by which to think. Therefore, they "ought not to think" that God is nonexistent or that he is a piece of wood or stone (Acts 17:26-31). "Oughtness" implies moral responsibility. It is a self-evident truth, that all men are created, and endowed by their Creator with certain inalienable rights.

While no nation, including the one theocratic one, has ever conducted its international relations whole-heartedly from this principle — they are not guiltless, even though heathen, for having failed to do so. Nations are warned to give "homage" to God's Son (Psa. 2:1-12). Only the very naive unbeliever and the uninformed Christian will ever expect this principle to be made a primary factor in the foreign policies of human governments. Human governments by nature and necessity are coercive and materialistically oriented. Even the best of them are never completely surrendered to the sovereignty of God spiritually or ideologically. Some are by degrees; some not at all. But there is a plateau of relative acknowledgment of Divine sovereignty for nations that is acceptable to God. The Bible expects it! It is upon this principle, for the first time in history (except the Israelite theocracy) that the founding fathers (from the "plantation" at Plymouth to the framers of the Constitution) established the United States of America. While more and more atheistic minority groups try to undermine this as a principle of American civil government, the vigilance of Americans who still believe strongly in this principle must remain ever alert and passionate to insure that it is continued.

3. Another principle of international relations enunciated in the Bible is that there must be *no* "one-world government." The principle is first stated in Genesis 10:5ff and is revealed to be the will of God in Genesis 11:1-9. Man has been resisting this principle from Genesis 11 to this day. The great Mesopotamian civilizations (Assyria, Babylon and Persia) attempted to conquer the world and amalgamate all peoples into one Mesopotamian culture. The expected result would be peace, prosperity and a humanistic "utopia." Nebuchadnezzar dreamed of himself as the magnificent, powerful, and beneficent "tree" whose "top reached to heaven, and . . . was visible to the end of the whole earth . . . its leaves were fair and its fruit abundant, and in it was food for all . . . the beasts of the field found shade under it, and the birds of the air dwelt in its branches, and all flesh was fed from it . . . " (Dan. 4:11,12). Alexander the Great, emperor of Greece took with him on his crusade to conquer the world philosophers, scientists, poets, artisans, and the trappings of Western culture fully intending to "Hellenize" (Greekize) all of civilization. Remnants of Greek culture may be seen as far east as India, as far west as the Balkans, and as far south as Egypt to this day. Alexander's thrust was the most far-reaching and the shortest-lived. It lasted only eleven years and was divided up, never to fulfill its utopian ambitions, when Alexander died at the prime age of thirty-two. Then came the Roman empire with its aspirations of creating on earth the "golden age of man." Daniel predicted that these four attempts at "one-world government" would temporarily succeed (Daniel, ch. 2,7) but would eventually collapse and in the days of the "fourth" world-domination by man, God would establish his spiritual kingdom which would be the only truly universal kingdom (the church of Jesus Christ) to last forever (Dan. 2:44,45). "One-world government" does not work — it never has and it never will. History has proven that time and again. The "Holy Roman Empire," Napoleon, Kaiser, the

British Empire, Hitler, Communism, none of them have produced "Shangri-La." At the end of World War I, the victorious allies (U.S., England, France, et al.) formed "The League of Nations" as a "one-world" government structure but in 20 short years World War II ensued. In 1945, at San Francisco, California, the "United Nations" was born. Since that time there have been scores of wars (hot and cold), economic depressions, famines, and other world-wide catastrophies to which the "United Nations" is demonstrably incapable of responding with a solution. It has proven to be almost totally impotent! "One-world government" will *never* work while this sinful world lasts. Furthermore, the Bible rejects it (see Deut. 32:8; Acts 17:26).

4. A fourth principle by which international relations should be conducted is the inviolability of national sovereignty. A nation has the right to borders or territories which have been established by cultural and language difference, by topographical circumstances, and by long generations of occupancy. This has seldom been honored by any civil government or by any people. The history of the world is one of constant movements of national borders through treaties, purchases, migrations, coercive annexations (wars), and sundry other sociological changes. The Bible is silent about most of these, except "coercive annexations." "And he made from one every nation of men to live on all the face of the earth, having determined allotted periods and the boundaries of their habitation . . . " (Acts 17:26). "When the Most High gave to the nations their inheritance, when he separated the sons of men, he fixed the bounds of the people according to the number of the sons of God" (Deut. 32:8).

   a. Isaiah predicted that the Assyrian emperor would violate the national sovereignty of Israel, as he had that of others, but God would punish the arrogance of Assyria in due time (Isa. 10:5ff). The prophet Nahum especially brings God's accusation against "Nineveh" (Assyria) for "preying" upon other nations and "plundering" them (Nahum 2:9-13; 3:1-12). When Assyria threatened the national sovereignty of Judah in the reign of Hezekiah, God brought judgment upon Sennacherib (Isa. 37:22ff).

   b. The same condemnation falls upon Babylon for violating the national sovereignty of many peoples and nations (see

Isa. 13,14; Jer. 50,51). Habakkuk had difficulty understanding how God, it seemed to him, could allow the king of Babylon to sweep nations into his "net" like a great fisherman (Hab. 1:14-17). God answered Habakkuk by showing him the future destruction of Babylon for violating the sovereignty of other nations (Hab. 2:6-17).

    c. Amos condemns Syria, Gaza, Edom, Ammon, and Moab for invasions and violations of other nations' sovereignty (Amos 1:3-2:3).

    d. Daniel prophetically condemns the aggressive and violent invasions of other nations' sovereignty by the "kings of the north and the kings of the south" (Syria and Ptolemies) (Dan. 11:1-45).

The principle of inviolable individual sovereignty is clearly upheld in the Bible. No individual has the right to invade another individual's domain or take his property by coercion or stealth. Unquestionably the same principle would apply nationally. God is not man that he would change. As for the land of Canaan, first, God had the right of "divine domain." He had the right to give it to whomever he chose (see Jer. 27:5ff), so in his sovereign wisdom, he "gave" it to Abraham and his descendants. Second, the many nomadic clans "squatting" in Canaan, could claim no more "squatter's rights" to it than Abraham, a clan from Ur of Chaldea, who migrated and "squatted" there just as the others had done. Third, Abraham and his descendants brought righteousness, justice, and physical improvement (relatively speaking) to the land where other "squatters" had not. Technically, Israel violated no "nation's" sovereignty when they occupied Canaan. In God's sovereign justness, the despicable clans "squatting" in Canaan had forfeited any claims they might have to any portion of the land by defiling the land with their inhuman and atrocious behavior.

5. A fifth fundamental for international relations between civil governments found in the Bible is that of national integrity (especially in the keeping of treaties and upholding basic human rights or humaneness). ". . . I will not revoke the punishment; because . . . they . . . did not remember the covenant of brotherhood . . . " (Amos 1:9). God promises to punish Tyre because she violated a treaty ("covenant of

brotherhood").

In Romans 1:32, "covenant breakers" (or the "faithless" are severely condemned.

God expects vows by individuals to be kept (Num. 30:2; Deut. 23:21; Eccl. 5:4-6) and that would apply equally to nations.

The prophet Obadiah commiserated about the tragedy befalling Edom due to the fact that "All your allies have deceived you, they have driven you to the border; your confederates have prevailed against you; your trusted friends have set a trap under you — there is no understanding of it" (Obadiah v. 7).

The same tragic failure of international integrity befalls Judah, according to Jeremiah (Jer. 30:14) and Ezekiel (Ezek. 16:39ff; see also Jer. 38:22).

Nahum accuses Nineveh of "countless harlotries . . . graceful and deadly charms, who betrays nations with her harlotries, and peoples with her charms . . . " (Nah. 3:4).

Amos charges certain nations with inhumanity: " . . . they threshed Gilead with threshing sledges of iron . . . they carried into exile a whole people . . . cast off all pity, and his anger tore perpetually . . . they have ripped up women with child . . . and burned to lime the bones of the king of Edom (Amos 1:3ff).

Isaiah condemns Egypt, calling her, "Rahab who sits still" (Isa. 30:7). "Rahab" is a Hebrew word meaning, "big mouth, braggart, vain-talker"; and the words "sits still" are from the Hebrew word *shabath*, or "resting, inert, unmoving." Egypt's word was worthless — she could not and would not keep it.

The empire of Rome is represented as having "deceived" all nations (Rev. 18:23). In her latter years, Rome lost her integrity. She would not keep her word.

At the end of his second term as President, which would be his last public service to America, George Washington, in his Farewell Address, said: "Of all the dispositions and habits which lead to political prosperity, religion and morality are indispensable supports . . . . In vain would that man claim the tribute of patriotism, who should labor to subvert these great pillars of human happiness, these firmest props of the duties of men and citizens . . . reason and experience both forbid us to expect that national morality can prevail in exclusion of religious principles . . . . It is substantially true, that virtue or morality is a necessary spring of popular government . . . . Observe good faith and justice toward all nations; cultivate peace and harmony with all; religion and morality enjoin this conduct . . . . It will be worthy of a free, enlightened and . . . a great nation, to give to mankind the magnanimous . . . example of a people always guided by an exalted justice and benevolence . . . . Can it be that Providence has not connected the permanent felicity of a nation with its virtue?"

The Bible says that nations must maintain moral integrity. They must, to the best of their ability, keep their word; they must not deceive for wicked purposes; they must make every effort toward international peace and harmony; and they must do good whenever and wherever they are able.

6. The Bible appears to give a sixth principle of international relations as a caution against naivete or foolishness. It is very unwise for a nation to make an alliance with another nation when their ideologies are diametrically opposed to one another. It would seem to be clear logic that a nation whose political ideology is basically theistic should not expect a nation whose ideology is overtly atheistic to keep its treaties except when it is forced to do so by powers greater than its own. Atheism's motives are those of the jungle. In nearly all acounts of international relations in the Old Testament, alliances between governments of different ideologies wrought only evil and destruction:
   a. God's theocratic people were warned not to "return" to Egypt for military assistance (Deut. 17:16).
   b. Joshua and the Israelites were deceived into making a treaty with some of the Canaanites (Josh. 9:1-27) and it resulted in the oppressive days of the Judges (see also Josh. 10:5,33; 11:5, Judges 3:13, etc.).
   c. Menahem of Israel made an alliance with the Assyrian Tiglath Pileser (II Kings 15:19) and the Assyrian quickly violated it invading Israel (II Kings 15:29).
   d. Ahaz of Judah, for fear of the coalition of Israel and Syria (II Kings 16:5-20; Isa. 7:1-25) made an alliance with Tiglath Pileser of Assyria. But Assyria soon forgot this

alliance and at the invasion of Israel kept marching southward, invading Judah and devastating over 40 cities of Judah also (II Kings 18:13ff).
e. Hosea made a treaty with Shalmaneser of Assyria (II Kings 17:1-6), but in a few years violated it which resulted in the Assyrians taking the ten northern tribes into exile.
f. Hezekiah treatied with the emperor of Assyria, paid tribute, but woke up one morning to find Jerusalem under Assyrian siege (II Kings 18:14-19:37).
g. Hezekiah "showed" his treasury and armory to the Babylonians (apparently in a treaty-making session against the Assyrians) (II Kings 20:12-19; Isa. 39:1-8), which precipitated a later siege of Jerusalem by the Babylonians and exile for Judah.
h. Asa treatied with Benhadad of Syria (II Chron. 16:3-10) which resulted in perpetual war during his reign.
i. Jehoshaphat of Judah entered into a semi-treaty relationship with Ahab of Israel through the marriage of Jehoshaphat's son to the daughter of Ahab and Jezebel (Athaliah) (II Chron. 18:1ff). This led to Baalism in Judah and murder of the royal family.
j. Jehoshaphat made an alliance with king Ahaziah of Israel (he did not seem to learn anything from his relationship with Ahab) and it resulted in failure (II Chron. 20:35-37).
k. Even the "sweet singer of Israel" was wise enough to recognize that most international alliances usually pit the "bad" against the "good" (Psa. 83:1-18).
l. The Old Testament prophets severely rebuked the theistic nation of Israel (and Judah) for attempted alliances with idolatrous nations (Isa. 30:1-7; 31:1-3; 28:15-18; 36:6; Jer. 2:14-18; 2:36,37; Ezek. 17:15; Hosea 7:11; 8:8-10; 12:1).
m. Daniel (11:1ff) depicted the idolatrous Seleucids and Ptolemies ("kings of the north and kings of the south") as inveterate treaty-breakers. Daniel especially points out that nations with such ideologies deliberately make treaties to deceive other nations (Dan. 11:23).

It is unequivocally true that there is no civil society which is to be equated in any way with Israel of the Old Testament or the Church of the New Testament. God has no "chosen people" now according to race, nationality, or culture. At the same time, the Bible clearly reveals that God expects all civil governments to conduct their "ministries" (Rom. 13:1-7; I Pet. 2:13-17) though basic "natural laws" (Rom. 1:18ff; 2:12-16) of goodness, integrity, and logic. That being so, the statement of Paul to the Corinthians (II Cor. 6:14-18) should be a part of that generic law of God which would apply to civil international relations — "Do not be mismated with unbelievers. For what partnership have righteousness and iniquity?" The fact that the majority of civil governments do not see their powers as "ministries" of God does not invalidate the Biblical expectation that they should do so!

The sagacious and godly "father of our country," George Washington, said: "In the execution of such a plan (a government observing good faith and justice toward all nations . . .), nothing is more essential than that permanent inveterate antipathies against particular nations, and passionate attachment for others, should be excluded; and that in place of them, just and amicable feelings toward all should be cultivated . . . . As avenues to foreign influence, in innumerable ways, such attachments are particularly alarming to the truly enlightened and independent patriot. How many opportunities do they afford to tamper with domestic factions, to practice the art of seduction, to mislead public opinion, to influence or awe the public councils! Such an attachment of a small or weak, toward a great and powerful nation, dooms the former to be the satellite of the latter . . . . Against the insidious wiles of foreign influence . . . the jealousy of a free people ought to be *constantly* awake; since history and experience prove that foreign influence is one of the most baneful foes of Republican Government . . . . There can be no greater error than to expect . . . real favors from nation to nation. It is an illusion which experience must cure, which a just pride ought to discard."

Farewell Address, September 17, 1796)

In a world whose modern technology (communications, weapons, transportation) has made all nations "next door neighbors, does George Washington's warning about "foreign entanglements" still hold true? Are the biblical principles we have been enumerating still valid for international relations? We believe they are. The Bible does not prohibit all relations between sovereign nations. George Washington advised an "amicable" balance between cooperation and non-cooperation. Biblical principles of Divine sovereignty, national sovereignty, and national integrity do not have to be compromised to promote a diplomacy of "balance" in international relations. Ronald Kirkemo, Associate Professor of International Relations at Point Loma College in San Diego, California, former employee of the U.S. Government and candidate for the California State Legislature, expounds a philosophy of "balance":

> What, then, brings peace? How is peace attained and preserved? How can the world be made safe *with* international diversity and safe *for* international diversity?
>
> Peace does not come because nations are friendly and generous with each other since then it would be gone whenever some nation wanted to be unfriendly or covetous and had the power to have its own way. To have peace requires more than just being peaceful and hoping all the other nations will be peaceful too. To have peace the nations must create the conditions that will protect it.
>
> Peace among nations has to be built. Natural peace does not exist. But a constructed one is possible. It results from the conscious fashioning and maintaining of certain international and domestic conditions. Foreign policy, then, must not direct its efforts toward peace itself but toward the creation of balance of power, moderation in policy, legitimacy and acceptance of these by public opinion.
>
> Balance, the first pillar of a constructed peace, is important to prevent any one nation from becoming powerful enough that it can successfully insure (through the use or threat of military and economic power) that its specific demands are met by other nations. Balance comes when nations align and realign themselves in such a way that the sum of their combined power equals or surpasses the power of the threatening nation. In this way its power and demands are either scaled down or neutralized altogether.
>
> This process of maintaining an international balance among nations requires leaders who are adept at manipulating their countries' alignments with each other. They must be flexible, able

to shift their relationships when necessary. Such manipulation means that a nation will have no or few permanent friends and enemies. As America has experienced with Germany, Japan, China, Russia, Turkey and others, enmities and friendships do not last forever. The leaders must also be willing and able to work and cooperate with nations they disapprove of, nations whose internal activities are open to criticism but whose support is necesary to prevent a general war. That can be very uncomfortable for nations and their people, but the preservation of peace usually involves neither simplicity nor an easy and permanent division of countries into good and bad.

Lastly, the balancing process may involve conflict, and nations must be willing and able to engage in limited conflict to prevent the balance from being over thrown. If this balance can be preserved, then the ambitions of nations can be resisted. Conflicts that do occur can be kept limited, or they can be isolated and contained within a geographic region before they become global and catastrophic.

The successful operation of an international balance over a long period can lead to the second element of a constructed peace, moderation. Moderation is the absence of grandiose ambitions, and intemperate actions, the presence of restraint and toleration. A nation can be induced to be moderate when other nations act together to contain and frustrate its ambitious design, and to accommodate its aspirations whenever reconciliation is both possible and safe. The process of balancing can lead to moderation but it must be coupled with efforts to bring some relative satisfaction to all the nations so that all will find it worthwhile to be moderate. An international balance itself is too fragile, too mechanical. Without the leaven of reconciliation and relative satisfaction, ambitious nations will simply bide their time until they can move and catch the others off guard.

This accommodation and reconciliation comes from negotiations and mutual compromises. We cannot expect the world to be changeless, and we cannot expect nations to be talked out of their historical aspirations and ideological convictions. But if these nations with aspirations and convictions can be balanced and contained, they can be given the choice of no satisfaction by mutual compromise. It is then in their interest to moderate their goals. That in turn makes it in the interest of the other nations to be tolerant.

This reconciliation process is not appeasement. The deals and agreements that are worked out must not be based on personal friendships or friendly atmospheres. Rather, the bargains made must be deeply analyzed and thought through to insure that all concerned are protected. This means that the first round of negotiations may not be successful because the goals have not been moderated enough for it to be safe to accommodate. But if the nations can negotiate a mutually beneficial agreement, then the factors of moderation and tolerance will be strengthened and international relationships made more stable.

The two elements of balance and moderation can construct a peace among the nations. But both are fragile and may not survive changes of leadership in key nations or the development of new issues of crucial importance to some. New leaders may not be skillful in handling the balancing process. The advantages of moderation and mutual compromise may not be self-evident to those facing important new issues. What is needed is a concept of cooperation that will transcend immediate problems and justify commitment to an international system of relative equality of nations (balance) and relative satisfaction of needs and goals (moderation). In other words, the nations need a concept of world affairs that will lead them to see a stable world as a legitimate world, a world they feel obliged to protect from disruption. With such a concept of legitimacy, mediocre leaders can be tolerated and new issues resolved without conflict. The great legitimizing principle of the second half of the twentieth century is the commitment to avoid nuclear war. What is needed now is another legitimizing principle to join it, one which would take nations beyond a commitment to avoid nuclear war to a commitment to establish conditions of greater humaneness and justice among the peoples of the world.

The fourth element in a constructed and lasting peace relates to domestic public opinion. The leaders must convey to the people how the legitimacy of world cooperation makes sense in light of their historical heritage and aspirations. They must explain why shifting national alignments and a balance of power are necessary. The importance of participation in world cooperation must be made clear. This is difficult to achieve because the need to compromise is dimly understood by a public that believes its values and policies are right and just. There is also the danger of apathy by citizens who consider shifting alignments to be too intricate or too political (and thus disgusting) to pay close attention. On the other end of the spectrum is the danger that the public will become infected with utopianism and expect far more than its leader can deliver by participation in international cooperation.

If any of these conditions occur, the regime may find its policies emasculated in an unsympathetic Congress. Or it may find itself voted out of office in the next election and replaced by a regime which promises either more "hard-headed realism" and less association with international conferences and disagreeable nations, or more grand and utopian goals. Long-term, patient domestic support is a necessity for the establishment of an international order that provides moderation and stability as well as benefits, all without loss of sovereignty and independence.

Between the Eagle & the Dove, by Ronald Kirkemo, pub. IVP, pp. 50-53

Would this philosophy of "balance" in international diplomacy compromise biblical principle? We do not believe it would. There appears to be biblical precedent for some political cooperation between nations with quite opposite ideological bases. David, the "man after God's own heart", entered into some international commerce with Hiram, king of Tyre (Phoenicia) (II Sam. 5:11f) without any disapproval from God and with no disastrous results. This international cooperation continued into the reign of Solomon (I Kings 5:1-18). Solomon and the Queen of Sheba were on friendly terms (I Kings 10:1ff). But even earlier, Abraham cooperated with the king of Sodom in an international effort without compromising his faith in God (Gen. 14). The Egyptians in Joseph's time sold grain to people from all over the world (Gen. 42:5-7), and offered asylum to thousands (Gen. 47:1ff). Jacob and Esau entered into amicable "international" relations (Gen. 33). Israel tried diplomacy with Edom as she marched toward Canaan (Num. 20:14-21) but Edom would not negotiate. David, fleeing from his own king Saul, took his family to the king of Moab for his protection (I Sam. 22:3,4). Both Ezra and Nehemiah tell of the cooperativeness of the Persians in the restoration of the Jewish commonwealth.

Many acts of international diplomacy are recorded in these two books of the Bible. Finally, the book of Esther chronicles a series of "international relations" transpiring between a nation-within-a-nation (Israel) and that nation itself (Persia).

The New Testament takes no historical note of international relations of the first century, except for the prophetic ones concerning the Roman empire (Rev. 17-18). The very silence of the Gospels and the Epistles indicates divine latitude in international relations anticipating that the fundamental moral principles of "natural law" will prevail. The New Testament (the book of Revelation, specifically), like the Old (Daniel, especially), is revelationally realistic about human, civil government — calling it "beastly." All human governments are predatory — some more than others. It is not without significance that most nations symbolize themselves as wild animals (lion, bear, eagle, tiger, etc.). The Bible does not portray any human civil government as a paragon of godly virtue; none of them will ever be the "kingdom of God." But the Bible does expect civil governments to serve God as "ministers" to enforce the virtues of logic and natural law. On that basis, international diplomacy and commerce can be conducted from a base of "balance of power" and biblical integrity maintained. Perhaps the statement of the apostle Paul to Christians at Corinth concerning necessary relations with non-christians would help believers resolve the pragmatics of international relations:

> I wrote to you in my letter not to associate with immoral men; not at all meaning the immoral of this world, or the greedy and robbers, or idolaters, since then you would need to go out of the world (I Cor. 5:9,10).

Christians are in the world; Christians are subject to civil governments; civil governments are not "Christian" *per se*. The best a Christian can expect of his civil government is that it see itself as a "minister" of God to punish evil doers and reward good doers, guided by the will of God demonstrated in the natural and propositional revelation, as impartially as possible in a highly pluralistic world.

7. Finally, the Bible's highest expectation for international relations would be that of humaneness — international relief, especially when unavoidable human suffering occurs on a massive and unexpected scale.
   Several biblical examples of this may be cited:
   a. Abraham and the people of Sodom (Gen. 14).
   b. The Egyptians and the nations (Gen. 42-47).
   c. Moab offered political asylum to David's family (I Sam. 22:3,4).
   d. Isaiah exhorts his own nation to "be a refuge" to suffering Moabites (Isa. 15:5-16:5).
   e. God expected Edom to lend assistance to the people of Jerusalem when they were ravaged by foreign invaders (Obadiah).
   f. Surely the Parable of the Good Samaritan (Luke 10) could be applied on a national scale.
   g. While Paul's collection of money to help feed the famine-stricken saints in Judea was not taken through the auspices of any civil government — but from individual Christians — it was, nevertheless, an "international" relief fund (Rom. 15:22-29; II Cor. 8-9; Acts 24:17).
   h. The principle of "cast your bread upon the waters . . . " (Eccl. 11:1,2) could be applied internationally.
   i. The call for international compassion, as well as for individual mercy, is in the words of Jesus, "Love your enemies . . . " (Matt. 5:43-48).
   j. The same call is in Paul's words: " . . . if your enemy is hungry, feed him; if he is thirsty, give him drink . . . " (Rom. 12:14-21).

Compassion is a most God-like virtue. But no one nation should be expected to feed the whole world of starving people. No one nation should be expected to arm all the defenseless nations or fight all their battles for them. Nations must be self-centered to the extent that their first responsibility is to their own citizens. That is the primary purpose for which God ordained civil governments. The principle enunciated by Paul that those who "do not provide for their own" has disowned the faith (I Tim. 5:7,8) is applicable here. Certainly, another principle, "Unto whomsoever much is given, of him shall much be required" (Luke 12:48) should also apply internationally. America has certainly been "given much." She should be expected to extend a compassionate hand to those less fortunate. But she must not jeopardize her own economy or her own national security to do so. America's biblical mandate is to so govern her own affairs that she is "Gods servant for your (America's) good" (Rom. 13:4). She must, in the words of George Washington, "avoid passionate attachments" to any other nation. She must act in her own self interest. That is what civil governments are for. They are not the kingdom of God — they are not the church of Christ. They are servants of God in the secular world to insure a "quiet and peaceable life" for their citizens so that men may come to the knowledge of the truth (I Tim. 2:1-4). Let us pray for our nation and all the nations of the world to that end.

12

CHURCH AND STATE

There is no such thing as a Christian State, either in fact or in the Bible. Nor should there be! The New Testament, especially the statement of Jesus Christ:

> Render to Caesar the things that are Caesar's, and to God the things that are God's (Matt. 22:21; Luke 20:25)

is the generic statement concerning church and state. It is fundamental and authoritative. Clearly, there are two spheres of human existence — "Caesar" (the state) and "God" (the church). Man owes allegiance to both but as is pointed out in chapter ten ("Civil Disobedience"), there is a definite limit to man's allegiance to the state. Ultimate allegiance must be to God — it is his by right of creation and redemption. God has ordained the state for a definitive ministry (punish evil doers and reward right doers, Rom. 13:1-7 et al.). Its function is physical and transient. Its method is coercion. Inasmuch as the function of the state is declared to be a "ministry" by God, we must admit that when it is carrying out its mission in accordance with the will of God it is assisting the church to carry out its mission (see I Tim. 2:1-4, etc.). The function of the church is primarily spiritual. Its method is love and persuasion. The church is also charged with doing as much as it can to minister to people's physical needs (except for administering civil justice). When the church is redeeming people by the Spirit of Christ and ministering to the physical needs of people, it may be assisting the state to carry out its mission.

The state is not redemptive. It cannot forgive sins, relieve guilt, reconcile man to God, impute perfect righteousness, or promise eternal blessedness. The state can only maintain social order and protect human life and property. Insofar as it does this it fulfills its divinely ordained ministry. When it attempts to produce spiritual redemption it has overstepped its sphere.

Ideally, God would have the state and the church cooperating (not consolidated or combined) each acting within its own ordained sphere according to the will of God which he has revealed in conscience, reason and the Bible. C.C. Crawford writes:

> *Church and State.* (Cf. the words of Jesus, Matt. 22:21, "Render unto Caesar the things that are Caesar's, and unto God the things that are God's.") (1) Personal religion, if at all vital, necessarily affects personal attitudes and shapes personal conduct: one naturally translates his religious convictions into all activities of life, including those of his duties as a citizen. Hence any complete "separation" of personal religious conviction and personal political decisions is impossible. It must be remembered also that practically all members of the church (or any other religious institution) are also citizens of the state. (2) The norms explicitly set down in the Constitution regarding the separation of state and church are those of (a) *non-establishment* and (b) *non-interference* (Amendment I: "Congress shall make no law respecting an establishment of religion or prohibiting the free exercise thereof"), and (c) *non-qualification* (Article VI: "No religious test shall ever

be required as a qualification to any office or public trust under the United States.") It should be noted that the Constitution thus explicitly bans any *institutional* union of state and church (or any other religious institution). (Institutional union tends to secularize the church and thus to vitiate its mission and influence.)

(3) However, since it obviously was never the intention of the Founding Fathers to put the state in a position of hostility to any form of religion, the policy of the United States has always been that of what is called "a union of minimum essentials." That is to say, the church is recognized by the state as a complementary and therefore privileged society; the state acknowledges the good that is done by the church (or synagogue) and gives the latter recognition and encouragement. This recognition takes several forms, as follows: (a) the church is granted competence in marriage and in the education of the young; (b) church property is exempt from taxation; (c) the church is granted various other immunities; (d) the government manifests the state's interest in religion by providing chapels and chaplains for the armed forces; (e) all citizens are guaranteed the right to worship according to their private convictions and are protected in the exercise of such rights. This is the type of relationship between state and church that prevails in the United States.

(4) The most recent decision of the United States Supreme Court invalidating an officially formulated and prescribed prayer for use in the public schools of New York state has caused a great deal of confusion in the public mind. This decision disallowed "official prayers." It is not prayer in itself, but *officialism*, which is the nub of this particular decision: a fact which has been all too generally overlooked. Moreover, a prayer of the kind involved in this Court decision is bound to be so innocuous as to bring discredit on religion in general. However, it must be admitted that a precedent has been set here which could have serious consequences in the future, especially at the hand of a Court made up largely of legal postivists. One wonders how the Court would rule if any agency of government should order the periodic singing of the national anthem in the classroom ("Then conquer we must, when our cause it is just, And this be our motto, "In God is our trust"), or the periodic recitation of the first two paragraphs of the Declaration of Independence (with the phrase, "the Laws of Nature and of Nature's God"), or the periodic singing of "My Country, 'Tis of Thee" (the last verse of which is a prayer, "Our Father's God, to

Thee, Author of liberty, To Thee we sing," etc.). Is it not true that we may be catering too much to insignificant minorities of "fastidious atheists and agnostics" and allowing these groups to become the tail that wags the dog? . . . . These apparently insignificant trends in our democratic system could have disastrous consequences, especially, I repeat, if our juridical system falls into the hands of legal positivists. Is minority "bigotry" any less bigoted than majority "bigotry"? *Eternal vigilance is always the price of liberty.*

Commonsense Ethics, by C.C. Crawford,
pub. Brown pp. 365-367

In the Old Testament the separate spheres of ministry for church and state are not incisively delineated. However, the division is there, by implication if not by commandment. The era of the patriarchs (Noah through Jacob) shows that the "fathers" did not expect the functions of civil government to fulfill the functions of religion. Abraham's civil action to rescue his nephew Lot (and others) from the kings of the east (Gen. 14) is a case in point. Abraham used coercion (force) to carry out the civil function of protecting physical life and property. But when it came to spiritual matters Abraham turned from coercion to worship and prayer (Gen. 14:17-24). He would not use force to try to redeem Lot from Sodom (Gen. 18:22-33). In ancient times as well as in the New Testament church and state are clearly and permanently separated, because one's relationship to God must be strictly a matter of free choice and privacy. Religion, because it comes from the inner-man must not, and ultimately cannot, be dictated, distorted or repressed by a civil state of any kind. This is the approach taken by godly patriarchs in the Old Testament.

In the pagan cultures of Bible times (both Old and New Testaments), church and state were usually consolidated. The king or emperor was not only the head of the civil government; he was also the high priest of the national religion. There was little ideological or practical distinction between the two. Ordinarily in such cultures, the survival of the state was thought to depend on the enforcement of the national religion (almost always polytheistic and iconic). To refuse to worship according to the dictates of the government was considered seditious and treasonable. Often, the head of the civil government was deified and worshiped as the chief god of the nation. This was true of the ancient cultures of Egypt, Assyria, Babylonia, Persia, Greece and Rome. It is significant, however, that the Jews who so often lived under the civil suzerainty of these cultures were usually allowed to worship according to their own consciences and customs. In the Bible, all attempts by pagan civil governments (e.g. Daniel) to force the Jews to abandon their own religion and worship according to that of the heathen state (polytheism) ended eventually in the providential deliverance of the Jews.

When Israel became a nation, she became a theocracy. Still, it was not a society where the religion and civil government functioned entirely as one unit. Israel practiced neither complete separation nor complete consolidation of church and state. Sometimes priests acted as judges in civil matters (Moses and Aaron) and sometimes judges acted as priests in religious matters (Samuel). But the concept of separation of church and state, each with its limited sphere, has its basis in the Old Testament as well as in the New. Priests came only from the tribe of Levi. Judges and kings (except for Moses and Samuel) came from other tribes. And even in the case of Moses and Samuel, the offices were clearly separated. And in the theocracy, while (*some*) legislation and punishment was directed toward religious matters (e.g. idolatry, blasphemy, ritual uncleanness), no Israelite was driven by sword or spear to the Tabernacle to worship. It is true, Israelites were forbidden, on the threat of death, to worship gods other than Jehovah; at the same time, they were not *forced* to worship Jehovah. The word *theocracy* does not mean the church rules society; it literally means, "God rules" society. There is a difference! In a theocracy where God's word is law, there is necessarily a closer *cooperation* between church and state. A theocracy is possible only in a theologically-monolithic culture.

Theocracy is impossible in an ideologically-plural society. In the world of the twentieth century the nearest any cultures come to being theocratic are the Islamic ones. Not even modern Israel is theocratic. The separation of church and state, each assigned a definite sphere in which to minister, with limited powers granted to both, is uniquely a biblical (Judaeo-Christian) concept. History makes it transparently clear that separation of church and state never originated in atheism, polytheism or idolatry of any kind. History further shows that any culture or nation slipping from a Bible-believing ideology toward an atheistic or humanistic ideology drifts inevitably from limited government to totalitarianism and the consolidation of church with state.

The Old Testament monarchial system differentiated even more distinctly between church and state. Kings came from the tribe of Judah; priests came from the tribe of Levi. Kings could not be priests, and priests were not to be kings. At least two kings tried to perform the functions of the priest (Saul in I Sam. 13:1ff; Uzziah in II Chron. 26:16-21) and God punished both of them. The message in both cases is that civil government is not to presumptuously invade the sphere delegated to the church! In the ninth century B.C. (ca. 841 B.C.) Athaliah tried to murder all her grandchildren in order to get the throne for herself (II Kings 11:1ff; II Chron. 22:10ff). But the infant Joash was saved by one of his sisters. She and a priest named Jehoiada kept the boy safe for six years until the people could be aroused against the wicked queen-mother to slay her. Then Joash, a mere boy of seven years, was anointed king of Judah (II Chron. 23:1ff; II Kings 11:4ff). This is further proof that the Israelites understood a clear separation of church and state. Jehoiada might have attempted to take the throne, at least until Joash had grown to young manhood, but the priest refused the opportunity to unite church and state under himself and anointed a seven-year-old boy as civil ruler. In the exile, Daniel, Shadrach, Meschach, Abednego, Esther, Mordecai (and many other Jews in pagan government positions) had no difficulty keeping church and state separated although they were all employees of the state!

When the Jews returned from their exile to reconstruct their national identity under Ezra, Nehemiah, and Zerubbabel, church and state, priesthood and civil leadership, were essentially separated. However, close cooperation between religion and civil government continued as a practice among the Jews until the destruction of Jerusalem in 70 A.D. In the era of the Gospels and Acts of the Apostles, Jewish synagogues and Jewish rabbis exerted strong influence in political affairs of state and had more than a little impact upon the conduct of specific rulers at various times. However, the Herods and the Romans made it perfectly clear that in civil affairs, the government was the ultimate authority. At the same time both the Herods and the Roman procurators meddled in religious affairs at great risk to their own careers and with disastrous results the few times they did so.

As has been pointed out, the categorical statement concerning separation of church and state is that of Jesus (Matt. 22:21; Luke 20:25). The apostle Paul confirmed it as Christian doctrine and practice when he said:

> . . . I am standing before Caesar's tribunal, where I ought to be tried; to the Jews I have done no wrong, as you know very well. If then I am a wrongdoer, and have committed anything for which I deserve to die, I do not seek to escape death; but if there is nothing in their charges against me, no one can give me up to them. I appeal to Caesar (Acts 25:10,11).

The Jews had charged Paul with civil "agitation" (Acts 24:5) and with being a member of a revolutionary group. These were not church matters. The Jewish priests and elders were trespassing civil authority by attempting to execute him (Acts 23:12ff). But he also challenged any attempt by a civil ruler to limit his spiritual ministry (Acts 16:19-39). Paul makes a significant contribution to the principle that believers have not only a right, but an obligation, to use the powers of persuasion and love to influence civil rulers in favor of Christ and the Scriptures. He did so in the presence of many rulers and civil authorities (see Acts 13:4-12; 16:19-39; 19:23-41; 24:10ff; 25:1-12; 26:1ff; 27:21ff).

Finally, the book of Revelation warned the churches of Asia Minor in the first century that the Roman empire was soon to amalgamate civil authority and pagan religion as one powerful, seemingly invincible dictatorship (Rev. 13:1ff). This wicked and mighty force would demand that all its civil subjects worship its civil ruler as god. Those who did not do so would suffer death, imprisonment and persecution. But the book of Revelation stands adamantly against such an idolatrous amalgamation and bids its believers resist even unto death.

Manifestly, it is the Bible, God's Word, that stands for separation of church and state. All secular governments, without strong biblical influence from their constituents, inexorably move toward uniting religion and the state. Nazi Germany and Communist Russia are classic examples where biblical religion had lost its impact in the lives of individuals which, in turn, made room for power-hungry atheists and humanists to take over the government and turn civic ideology into a state religion. History keeps repeating itself in this matter. It is for this reason Christians in the United State must elect Christian civil authorities. They alone truly stand for separation of church and state. Secularists, by the very nature of their ideology, inevitably turn the state into the religion.

> Sectarian doctrines cannot be taught in our state-supported schools, to be sure; this, I believe, is as it should be. However, it happens that the courts of the United States have established fairly well-defined procedures to govern various aspects of this problem of church-state-relationship. They have ruled uniformly against the teaching of religious doctrines, and especially of sectarian dogmas, on public school property. On the other hand, they have validated the following procedures: (1) the reading of the Bible as literature; (2) the teaching of the role of religion in

life, and (3) The teaching of religious thought as history. Moreover, in a decision handed down in 1951, the United States Supreme Court validated the "released time" program of religious education. According to this procedure, public school pupils may be released from classes, at their own request, to receive religious instruction away from school property. Justice W.O. Douglas, in delivering the majority opinion in this case, held that the Constitutional provision (the ban against any "establishment" of religion) does not mean that "in every and all aspects there shall be a separation of church and state." If it did, Justice Douglas went on to say, "the state and religion would be aliens to each other — hostile, suspicious and even unfriendly" — to such an extent that prayers in legislative halls, and even police protection for worshiping assemblies, would be forbidden.

. . . *After all is said and done, the fact remains that the restraints upon the teaching of religion do not confer upon any instructor the license to propagate irreligion.*
Commonsense Ethics, by C.C. Crawford, p. xii

The Bible does not present the church and the state, ideally, as hostile to one another. If the state carries out its ministry (Rom. 13:1-7; I Pet. 2:13-17) it will protect the church's right to be left alone in spiritual matters and allowed to teach its doctrines, evangelize the world, and produce a redeemed society. That redeemed society will, in turn, leave the civil government alone to legislate, adjudicate, and enforce order. The redeemed people will lend the government its spiritual influence by infiltrating the ranks of civil authorities with Christian people and by acting as the conscience of government through preaching and living the doctrines of the Bible. This was the light by which the Founding Fathers of the United States of America saw the issue.

Our laws and our institutions must necessarily be based upon and embody the teachings of The Redeemer of mankind. It is impossible that it should be otherwise; and in this sense and to this extent our civilization and our institutions are emphatically Christian . . . . This is a religious people. This is historically true. From the discovery of this continent to the present hour, there is a single voice making this affirmation . . . we find everywhere a

clear recognition of the same truth . . . . These, and many other matters which might be noticed, add a volume of unofficial declarations to the mass of organic utterances that this is a Christian nation.
> *Supreme Court Decision, 1892*, Church of the Holy Trinity vs. United States

Thomas Jefferson once said, "Can the liberties of a nation be secure, when we have removed the conviction that these liberties are the gift of God?" George Washington said: "No people can be bound to acknowledge and adore the invisible hand which conducts the affairs of men more than the people of the United States. Every step by which they have advanced to the character of an independent nation seems to have been distinguished by some token of providential agency . . . . We ought to be no less persuaded that the propitious smiles of heaven cannot be expected on a nation that disregards the eternal rules of order and right, which heaven itself has ordained." And Noah Webster wrote: "The moral principles and precepts contained in the Scriptures ought to form the basis of all our civil constitutions and laws. All the miseries and evils which men suffer from vice, crime, ambition, injustice, oppression, slavery, and war proceed from their despising or neglecting the precepts contained in the Bible."

The principles of God's Word guided the decisions on which this nation built its foundation. This was the discovery of Alex DeTocqueville, the noted French political philosopher of the nineteenth century. He visited America in her infancy to find the secret of her greatness. As he traveled from town to town, he talked with people and asked questions. He examined our young national government, our schools and centers of business, but could not find in them the reason for our strength. Not until he visited the churches of America and witnessed the pulpits of this land "aflame with righteousness" did he find the secret of our greatness. Returning to France, he summarized his findings: "America is great because America is good; and if America ever ceases to be good, America will cease to be great." Abraham

Lincoln said: "It is the duty of nations, as well as of men, to own their dependence upon the overruling power of God and to recognize the sublime truth announced in the Holy Scriptures and proven by all history, that those nations only are blessed whose God is the Lord." Calvin Coolidge wrote: "The foundation of our society and our government rest so much on the teachings of the Bible that it would be difficult to support them if faith in these teachings would cease to be practically universal in our country." The following story illustrates how closely connected our Founding fathers saw the Bible and civil government:

> The American Revolution was in full swing. The Bible, through more than one hundred fifty years of early settlement in America, remained the base of her people's religious devotion, her education, her colonial government. These Bibles had been shipped in from England.
>
> Now, suddenly the American Revolution cut off this supply, and the stock dwindled.
>
> Here was America in its greatest crisis yet — and without Bibles! Patrick Allison, Chaplain of congress, placed before that body in 1777 a petition praying for immediate relief. It was assigned to a special committee which weighed the matter with great care, and reported: " . . . that the use of the Bible is so universal and its importance so great that your committee refer the above to the consideration of Congress, and if Congress shall not think it expedient to order the importation of types and paper, the Committee recommended that Congress will order the Committee of Congress to import 20,000 Bibles from Holland, Scotland, or elsewhere, into the different parts of the States of the Union.
>
> Whereupon it was resolved accordingly to direct said Committee to import 20,000 copies of the Bible. During the session on the fall of 1780 the need arose once more.
>
> Robert Aitken, who had set up in Philadelphia as a bookseller and publisher of *The Pennsylvania Magazine*, saw the need and set about quietly to do something about it.
>
> In early 1781 he petitioned Congress and received from them a green light to print the Bibles needed. The Book came off the press late next year, and Congress approved it.
>
> So originated the "Bible of the Revolution," now one of the

world's rarest books — the first American printing.
>> *The Rebirth of America*, pub. by the Arthur S.
>> DeMoss Foundation, p. 39

While the Bible stands for separation of church and state, it also stands for civil government acknowledging its subservience to Almighty God and for civil government to carry out its divinely ordained mission in adherence to the guidelines of divine revelation ("Natural" and Biblical). The phrase so often quoted, and thought by many uninformed Americans to be part of the U.S. Constitution, "a wall of separation" between church and state, is *not* in the Constitution at all. It is a statement from a speech by Thomas Jefferson (who was *not* one of the drafters of the Constitution) to the Danbury Baptists in 1802, thirteen years after the passage of the First Amendment. In no way should this phrase of Jefferson be considered the definitive interpretation of the First Amendment.

> It was Thomas Jefferson who used this phrase in a letter written to a group of Baptist pastors in Danbury, Connecticut in 1802. The purpose of the letter was to assure those Baptist pastors that Jefferson's somewhat unorthodox view of Christianity would not be pressed on the church in the United States during his presidency.
> President Jefferson assured them that there was a wall of separation that supposedly protects the Church from any undue meddling by the State. The irony is that the phrase never implied that the State needed to be protected from the Church; Jefferson was guaranteeing the church the benefit of the wall.
> The contemporary anti-Christian religious establishment has turned the issue completely on its head by redefining the phrase. This trick is called "historical revisionism" Historical revisionism twists history and interprets it for one's own purposes.
>> *The Forerunner*, "Separation of Church and State,
>> Clearing Up the Misconceptions", by Dennis
>> Peacocke, April 1988, p. 13

Indeed, it is not the United States government that needs to be protected from religion, for the U.S. Constitution institutes a government that is functionally secular. Religion cannot, by the very nature of the Constitution, pose any danger to the government. The government has protected itself by its Constitution. It was the church that needed protection from the government that gave impetus to the First Amendment.

> The unique American doctrine of separation of church and state is not a by-product of the First Amendment's religious clauses. Those clauses were intended to guarantee the religious liberty already implicit in the Constitution's provision for a wholly secular government. The historian, Charles A. Beard, wrote that the Constitution "does not confer upon the Federal Government any power whatever to deal with religion in any form or manner" (The Republic). James Madison called it "a bill of powers" which "are enumerated, and it follows that all that are not granted by the Constitution are retained" by the people (Annals of Congress of the United States).
> *Phi Kappa Phi Journal, Winter 1988*, "Education in Religious Schools, The Conflict over Funding," by John M. Swomley, p.12

While government must be protected against domination by the church, it must be constant in acknowledging its need of a moral influence from the Bible and Bible-believing constituents. Rulers of this world's governments are vulnerable to moral darkness and apt to commit the most heinous crimes against God and man without the wisdom of divine revelation:

> Yet among the mature we (apostles) impart wisdom, although it is not a wisdom of this age or of the rulers of this age, who are doomed to pass away. But we impart a secret and hidden wisdom of God, which God decreed before the ages for our glorification. None of the rulers of this age understood this; for if they had, they would not have crucified the Lord of glory (I Cor. 2:6-8).

Even humanists have acknowledged that the state cannot

fulfill its mission to protect inalienable human rights without God. Will Durant wrote in the *Humanist* magazine of February 1977: "Moreover, we shall find it no easy task to mold a natural ethic strong enough to maintain moral restraint and social order without the support of supernatural consolations, hopes and fears." Mr. Durant, in his book, *The Lessons of History*, quoted the famous agnostic Renan: "If Rationalism wishes to govern the world without regard to the religious needs of the soul, the experience of the French Revolution is there to teach us the consequences of such a blunder." And Durant, himself, says in the same book, "There is no significant example in history, before our time, of a society successfully maintaining moral life without the aid of religion."

The Bible stands for separation of ministries of church and state. The two have distinctly different functions and dominions in this world. But the Bible clearly indicates that God and his Son, Jesus Christ, are sovereign over both and that both should embrace that sovereignty by fulfilling their ministries according to God's revealed will:

> Why do the nations conspire, and the people plot in vain? The kings of the earth set themselves, and the rulers take counsel together against the Lord and his anointed, saying, Let us burst their bonds asunder, and cast their cords from us. He who sits in the heavens laughs; the Lord has them in derision. Then he will speak to them in his wrath, and terrify them in his fury, saying, I have set my king on Zion, my holy hill. I will tell of the decree of the Lord: He said to me, You are my son, today I have begotten you. Ask of me, and I will make the nations your heritage, and the ends of the earth your possession. You shall break them with a rod of iron, and dash them in pieces like a potter's vessel. Now therefore, O kings, be wise; be warned, O rulers of the earth. Serve the Lord with fear, with trembling kiss his feet, lest he be angry, and you perish in the way; for his wrath is quickly kindled. Blessed are all who take refuge in him (Psa. 2:1-12).

A brief comparison of church and state in their biblically mandated dominions shows the necessity for separation:

The Church (and/or Bible)	The State
1. Is a universal, spiritual "kingdom" (Matt. 28:18-20, Rev. 7:9-12).	1. Is a cultural, provincial "kingdom" (and transient) (I Cor. 15:24-28).
2. Majors in ministering the Bread of Life (the Word of God) (John 6:25-26; Acts 20:32, etc.).	2. Ministers strictly the physical through protecting inalienable human rights (Rom. 13:1-7, etc.).
3. Is redemptive, not retributive (I Cor. 5:3-5; Matt. 5:38-48; Eph. 6:10ff).	3. Renders retributive justice in this life (Rom. 13:1-7; I Pet. 2:13-17; I Tim. 1:8,9).
4. Has a mandate to control thoughts and motives (II Cor. 5:14-21; II Cor. 10:3-5).	4. Forbidden to control thoughts (Acts 4:19,20; 5:29).
5. Proceeds from a philosophical base of absolutism: a. sovereignty of God, (Psa. 2). b. infallibility of the Word of God (Psa. 119:89,90).	5. Proceeds from a philosophical base of relativism and pragmatism: a. "natural law" (Rom. 1:18ff). b. reason and conscience (Rom. 2:14ff).

John Eidsmoe, in his book, *God & Caesar, Christian Faith & Political Action*, pages 12-16, points to at least four different historical perspectives of the church-state relationship. Mr. Eidsmoe calls them, "The 'Two Kingdoms' Concept in Church History." The first concept he lists is the Roman Catholic view:

> Catholic theologians have generally recognized the two kingdoms and the distinct role played by each. But they have usually considered the church to be the greater kingdom and the state to be the lesser, because the church is eternal while the state is only temporary (Augustine's explanation), and because the church must answer to God for the conduct of the state (the explanation of Pope Gelasius I). Some have argued that the power of the keys given to Peter in Matthew 16:19 gave the church the authority to control the state. Many medieval theologians saw the church's

authority in the two swords of Luke 22:38. One of these swords is the sword of the church to be wielded by the church, and the other is the sword of the state, to be given by the church to the state. As Pope Boniface VIII decreed in his papal bull, Unam Sanctum, in 1302 . . . .

This view would be conceptualized by the following diagram:

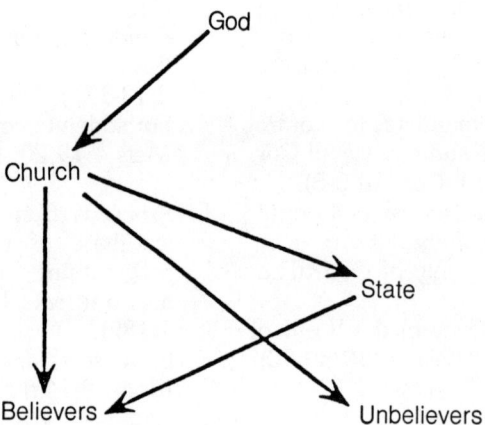

The next concept is that of the Anabaptists led by Menno Simons (ca. 1536 A.D.), from whom modern Mennonites get their name:

> Many . . . believed that the state was part of the evil world-system from which believers were to separate themselves. If Satan were not actually the founder of the state, he had at least taken control of it. Consequently believers were to separate themselves from the state as much as possible; they were not to vote, hold public office, serve in the armed forces, or involve themselves with government in any other way. They were to obey the state generally, but the state had no real authority over believers, nor did the church have any authority over unbelievers . . . .

CHURCH AND STATE

This view would be conceptualized by the following diagram:

The next view is the "Calvinist view." John Calvin was a Frenchman who was trained for the profession of law. He published his "Institutes" in 1536 A.D. at Basel, Switzerland. His training in law made it quite natural for him to connect religion with the law. His attempts to form a sort of "theocracy" in Geneva, Switzerland, aroused opposition and he was driven into exile. Shortly later he was asked to return to Geneva and did fulfill his ambition to set up a church-controlled civil society. While he verbally advocated religious liberty, he consented to the execution of "heretics." Calvin argued that the church has the right and calling to exercise discipline not simply moral but also physical. He said the civil administration exists only for the defense of the church, and it is the duty of the state to carry out the regulations of the church. He insisted that the state has no right to enact laws concerning religion nor to interfere in matters purely ecclesiastical. Calvin virtually made every sin a crime, and so did not hesitate to make use of the civil power for the execution of church discipline. Calvin believed the mission of the church is to redeem the world, including civil governments, in harmony with Christian doctrine, and the state is God's instrument to assist the church in converting the world to Christ. Calvin's view would be conceptualized by the following diagram:

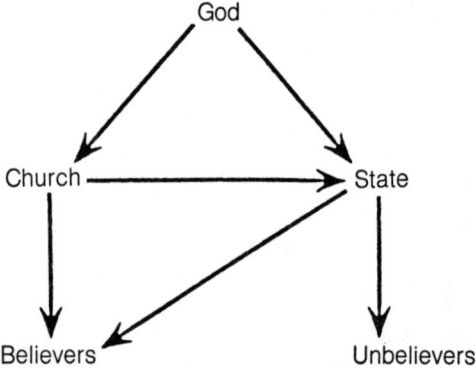

Eidsmoe cites Martin Luther's view of church-state relationship as his last presentation:

> Like Calvin, he (Luther) recognized that the church and state are each ordained by God. Like Calvin, he recognized that believers belong to both kingdoms, the church and the state, and have responsibilities to each. Unlike Calvin, he hesitated to impose Christian precepts upon an unbelieving world. Luther . . . believed that Christians relate to the first kingdom (the church) primarily by means of faith in divine revelation, and to the second kingdom (the state) primarily by means of reason . . . . Luther even went so far as to say that if he were faced with the choice between a ruler who was prudent and bad and another who was good but imprudent, he would choose the prudent and bad, because the good by his imprudence would throw everything into disorder, whereas the prudent, however bad, would have enough sense to restrain evil. This does not mean Luther wanted immoral rulers. He would have preferred a ruler who was both prudent and good . . . . Luther's primary difference with Calvin . . . would be that he did not believe Christians had the right to use the state to promote Christianity and to Christianize the world. Christians in government could invoke Christian principles in the affairs of state, only to the extent that those Christian principles could be defended and justified by natural reason.

Luthers view would be conceptualized by the following diagram:

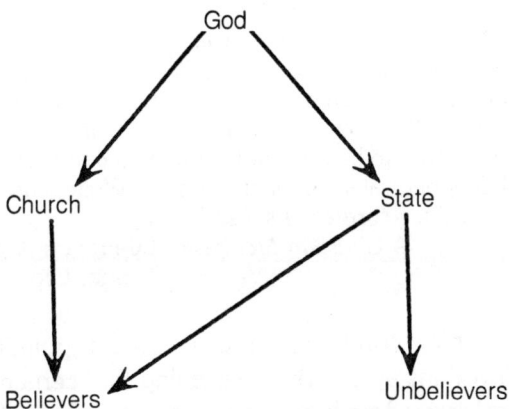

We believe a fifth view of the church-state relationship, as conceptualized in the final diagram, is a more biblical view. Church and state are clearly both under the sovereignty of God. Church and state are both assigned distinctive "ministries" to fulfill for God in this present world. Church and state are clearly to be separated so that each has its God-ordained dominion protected from the other. Christians are under biblical commandment to render allegiance to both — with allegiance to God and his word first, when there is a clear conflict between the two. Finally, as documented from the patriarchs to the apostles, the Bible strongly advocates that individual believers be involved in and exert an influence over the civil government to the fullest extent possible so long as the revealed word of God is not compromised. Civil government is ordained by God to execute his justice on earth, maintain civil order, and protect inalienable human rights. This "ministry" has its origin and revealed guidance from God. Human rulers would be ignorant of that without the constant proclamation of God's word by believers and other forms of Christian influence on civil government. As Francis Schaeffer writes:

> Most fundamentally, our culture, society, government, and law are in the condition they are in, *not because of a conspiracy, but*

because the church has forsaken its duty to be the salt of the culture. It is the church's duty (as well as its privilege) to do now what it should have been doing all the time — to use the freedom we do have to be that *salt* of the culture. If the slide toward authoritarianism is to be reversed we need a committed Christian church that is dedicated to what John W. Whitehead calls "total revolution in the reformative sense."
A Christian Manifesto, by Francis A. Schaeffer, pub. Crossway, p. 56

Dr. Schaeffer continues in this context pointing out that whether Christians agree with everything that certain fundamentalist political crusaders have done or not, many of them have "certainly done one thing right: they have used the freedom we still have in the political arena to stand against the other total entity (humanism). They have carried the fact that law is king, that law is above the lawmakers, and God is above the law into this area of life where it always should have been. And this is true spirituality." Unless every Christian is in some way exerting a biblical influence upon civil government, he is not showing the Lordship of Christ in the totality of life. So, we believe the church, through its individual members, should exert an active, biblically contained, impact upon the civil state. The following diagram is our view of what the Bible says about church and state:

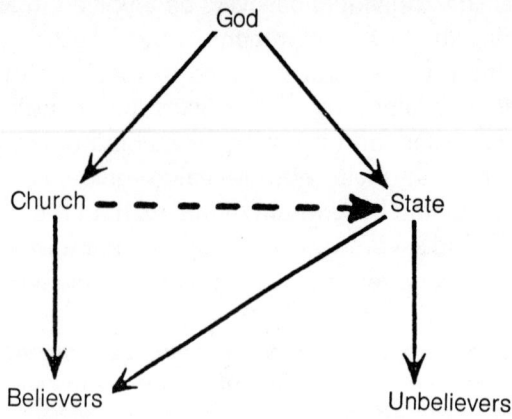

CHURCH AND STATE

Christians should not expect or condone the state to exert its powers to the advancement of any religion — neither Christianity nor Humanism (and Humanism is a religion!). The church should accept neither finances or political advocacy from civil authority. Should the church depend on government for either, she will find herself inevitably state-controlled. The church does have the right to expect civil government not to be hostile to it, but to protect its rights to exist, to evangelize, and to worship freely according to its conscience so long as it does not infringe upon anyone's civil rights or advocate disorder or subversion of civil authority. Christians have a right to expect civil government to act justly, fairly, decently, and orderly. They have the right to expect treatment under law equal to that granted any other citizen or religious person. What the government does for one religion it should do for all religions willing to exist and function within the laws of reason and for the common good. For the civil government to allow one metaphysical view (Humanism or Evolutionism) to be taught in taxpayer-supported institutions (public schools) and not another (Creationism) is unreasonable, unconscionable, and unconstitutional in the United States of America. America's foundation is on equal rights and civil responsibility to the Divine Sovereign:

> June 25, 1960. The Supreme Court had just declared prayer in the schools unconstitutional. Senator Robert Byrd of West Virginia, a Bible teacher and respected member of the U.S. Legislature, was so moved by the disastrous decision that two days later he delivered an address to his colleagues in Congress reminding them of the Christian symbolism throughout their own city.
>
> "In no other place in the United States are there so many, and such varied official evidences of deep and abiding faith in God on the part of Governments as there are in Washington."
>
> He verbally escorted them to the Library of Congress, the Washington Monument, the Lincoln Memorial, the Jefferson Memorial, the Supreme Court, and other landmarks. Then he concluded: "Inasmuch as our greatest leaders have shown no doubt about God's proper place in the American birthright, can

we in our day, dare do less?"

The Capitol

Every session of the House and the Senate begins with prayer. Each house has its own chaplain.

The Eighty-third Congress set aside a small room in the Capitol, just off the rotunda, for the private prayer and meditation of members of Congress. The room is always open when Congress is in session, but it is not open to the public. The room's focal point is a stained glass window showing George Washington kneeling in prayer. Behind him is etched these words from Psalm 16:1: "Preserve me, O God, for in Thee do I put my trust."

Inside the rotunda is a picture of the Pilgrims about to embark from Holland on the sister ship of the Mayflower, the Speedwell. The ship's revered chaplain, Brewster, who later joined the Mayflower, has open on his lap the Bible. Very clear are the words, "the New Testament according to our Lord and Savior, Jesus Christ." On the sail is the motto of the Pilgrims, "In God We Trust, God With Us."

The phrase, "In God We Trust," appears opposite the President of the Senate, who is the Vice President of the United States. The same phrase, in large words inscribed in the marble, backdrops the Speaker of the House of Representatives.

The Supreme Court

Above the head of the Chief Justice of the Supreme Court are the Ten Commandments, with the great American eagle protecting them. Moses is included among the great lawgivers in Herman A. MacNeil's marble sculpture group on the east front. The crier who opens each session closes with the words, "God save the United States and the Honorable Court."

The Washington Monument

Engraved on the metal cap on the top of the Washington Monument are the words: "Praise be to God." Lining the walls of the stairwell are such biblical phrases as "Search the Scriptures," "Holiness to the Lord," "Train up a child in the way he should go, and when he is old he will not depart from it."

The Library of Congress

Numerous quotations from Scripture can be found within its walls. One reminds each American of his responsibility to his Maker: "What doth the Lord require of thee, but to do justly and love mercy and walk humbly with thy God" (Micah 6:8).

Another in the lawmaker's library preserves the Psalmist's

CHURCH AND STATE

acknowledgment that all nature reflects the order and beauty of the Creator. "The heavens declare the glory of God, and the firmament showeth His handiwork" (Psalm 19:1).

And still another reference: "The light shineth in darkness, and the darkness comprehendeth it not" (John 1:5).

Lincoln Memorial

Millions have stood in the Lincoln Memorial and gazed up at the statue of the great Abraham Lincoln. The sculptor who chiseled the features of Lincoln in granite all but seems to make Lincoln speak his own words inscribed into the walls.

". . . That this Nation, under God, shall have a new birth of freedom, and that government of the people, by the people, for the people, shall not perish from the earth."

At the opposite end, on the north wall, his Second Inaugural address alludes to "God," the "Bible," "providence," "the Almighty," and "divine attributes,"

It then continues: "As was said 3000 years ago, so it still must be said, The judgments of the Lord are true and righteous altogether."

Jefferson Memorial

On the south banks of Washington's Tidal Basin, Thomas Jefferson still speaks:

"God who gave us life gave us liberty. Can the liberties of a nation be secure when we have removed a conviction that these liberties are the gift of God? Indeed I tremble for my country when I reflect that God is just, that his justice cannot sleep forever."

Senator Byrd cites these words of Jefferson as "a forceful and explicit warning that to remove God from this country will destroy it."

The Rebirth of America, by The Arthur S. DeMoss Foundation, pp. 66-69

EPILOGUE

Civil government is of God. God is its mentor and his will is its *raison d'etre*. Almighty God orders civil governments and he sustains them. Their mandate is a "ministry" (Rom. 13:1-7; I Pet. 2:13-17) of justice and goodness. Civil rulers are servants of God to enforce social order so that the gospel truth of Christ may be made available to all mankind (I Tim. 2:1-4). In order to fulfill that stewardship they may often be called upon to punish criminals and wage wars. The Creator has endowed all men with certain inalienable rights; the same Creator has charged civil governments with the responsibility to ensure those rights.

The Bible teaches that citizens enjoy the protection of their inalienable rights by civil government only at certain costs to the individual. It is clear biblical commandment that citizens are to pay taxes, obey laws, and lend support to their governments — including military or other constabulary service when defense of the government is necessary. The Bible offers numerous historical examples of godly believers serving directly in structured civil governments. Many of these (David, Daniel, Esther, Mordecai, Nehemiah et al.) are held up in Scripture as heroes of faith whose lives and service are worthy of emulation.

Human governments are important, but they are not *all* important. The people of God are citizens of two kingdoms — the church and the state. The two are, by divine fiat, separate; the "things of God" always take precedence over "the things of Caesar" (Acts 4:19,20; 5:29). Ideally, God would have the two, church and state, acknowledging and practicing their distinctive ministries, but cooperating to work the Divine will in the world where they may do so without compromising his Word.

God ordained man to "have dominion" (Gen. 1:28. Man is ordered to serve God, in part, by exercising that "dominion" through human government (Gen. 9:6; Rom. 13:1-7). God reveals his law in creation, conscience, reason (Rom. 1:18ff; 2:14ff) and in the Bible. His law is good if it is used lawfully (I Tim. 1:8-11). But man is a sinner at heart (Jer. 17:9,10). He does not always use God's law in a lawful way. When man exercises his dominion in rebellion against the laws of God he is actually cooperating with Satan's attempt to thwart the redemption of mankind. Human rulers who do not seek the guidance of divine revelation are not servants of God but enemies of God (I Cor. 2:6-9).

Many forms of human government have been tried. Some in rebellion, some in harmony with God's will. Because man is a sinner even a theocratic form of government like that administered by Moses may find itself less than perfect. God may, himself, choose a "man after his own heart" (king David), but it takes more than one good man to govern a nation. Cultural pluralism, widespread human migration, and highly advanced technologies demand alternative forms of human goverance. Governments more complex and yet much more flexible have developed from necessity. More than all else, however, the spread of Christianity has forced cultures and nations to turn toward governments that emphasize inalienable human rights and every-citizen participation.

No matter the form of human government, the church will never perish. It is God's eternal kingdom. It has existed, and will continue to exist, in the midst of many different forms of human government. However, when human governments acknowledge their subservience to God and build themselves on his eternal principles, freedom, human dignity, and justice exist and flourish. This serves God. When inalienable human rights are ensured, the gospel of Christ is preached and men and women are redeemed. While the government of the United States of America is not prefect, millions may thank God that they have come to know the truth of God because this government was founded upon the eternal principles of God in the Bible.

>In his stirring anthem to the solidity of the Christian faith, George Chapman penned the now-familiar words, "How firm a foundation, ye saints of the Lord, is laid for your faith in His excellent Word!" And how appropriate are these words when correlated to America's glorious heritage.
>
>This nation, without reasonable doubt, was established on the firm foundation of Scripture. Our forefathers, brilliant as they were, openly acknowledged the true genius behind the new system to be the eternal principles of God's Word. The most fundamental concepts of the republic find their roots in the Bible. From the beginning, the basis for law and government in American society was decidedly biblical. What's more, the new land was forged through the energy of the Judeo-Christian work ethic.
>
>The United States in her first century of existence knew the stinging reality of conflict. There were wars, assassinations, injustices, catastrophes, and plagues of disease. But the young nation endured, for its moral fabric had been woven with the durable threads of Scriptural truth. Societal ills, like slavery, were ultimately recognized for what they were: violations of God's standard.
>
>The record of the establishment of America bears the clear stamp of Christian influence. The impact of the Gospel is evident in the leaders chosen, the laws written, and the sweeping changes brought about through the transforming power of Christ in in-

dividual lives and corporate experience. America was not formed a nation apart from God, but a nation under God.
The Rebirth of America, by The Arthur S. DeMoss Foundation, p. 70

The reader may have expected many other subjects to be treated in this work because civil government reaches into many more areas than those with which we have dealt. Such may be the areas of freedom of speech, education, ecology, racial discrimination, euthanasia, abortion, organized labor, and a multitude of others. We believe the Bible has divine guidance in every one of these areas, and more. God has granted to us all things that pertain to life and godliness through his precious promises (II Pet. 1:3,4). There are both precepts and principles in the Scriptures that will provide the answers to these questions. These latter subjects are more properly treated in works on biblical ethics. We choose to leave them there.

APPENDIX

The Providence of God in the Colonization of America!
by Paul T. Butler

Much of today's liberal press is up in arms over recent Supreme Court rulings having to do with religion and civil liberties. While no certain religious group or bloc of groups should be allowed to control or dictate civil law or policy, it is one of the first duties of the civil government to protect every man's right to openly worship as his own conscience moves him, or not to worship as he chooses. God holds all civil governments responsible to protect and promote civil liberties for all human beings equally.

And, while it is the responsibility of civil leaders to protect the sovereignty of human conscience, they are, at the same time, obligated to exercise their civic duties under the guidance of the precepts and principles in the Bible. That is because the Bible claims (and proves) itself to be the exclusive and all-inclusive revelation of God to man for the conduct of every facet of human life here on earth. God speaks in the Bible clearly and imperatively about the duties of the civil state. All human beings, judges and journalists, politicians and preachers, congressmen and carpenters are obligated by the same Bible and by conscience to be "subject to, pay taxes to, respect and honor" such God-guided government. Those who would resist such government will incur the judgment of God (see Rom. 13:1-7).

But the humanistic, atheistic element in our beloved land advocating the total divorce of all levels of government and civil structure from God and the Bible are not only theologically ignorant, they are ignorant of history. It is extremely difficult today to find any history textbook, used by our public schools from elementary to college, that does not portray the God-fearing discoverers and founders of America as scheming, exploiting, religious bigots; at the same time applauding the few agnostics and humanists involved in America's origins as the true patriots and founders of democracy. Besides this, most modern American history textbooks openly declare that the democratic-republic our forefathers founded must, and is, inevitably moving toward humanistic socialism or some "democratic" form of communism.

In years past some of our compatriots have, at great personal sacrifice, fought the subversion of American history in public textbooks. Judge Wallace McCamant, President General, National Society, Sons of the American Revolution, 1921, conducted an exhaustive research and published a brochure severely critical of inaccurate and subversive books being used as history textbooks. His brochure on this subject was responsible for extensive revision of certain books. He gave liberally of his talents, finances and abilities to crusade against the destructive sabotage being done to true American history. While we probably will not reach those heights, we must take every opportunity to make whatever contribution we can to the struggle against a constant, subversive, historical revisionism. Errors honestly made are excusable, but the revisionism of which we speak is not innocent — it has a socialistic oligarchy or elitism as its ultimate goal.

To this end let us now remind you of a few points of American history you already know, and perhaps a few you have never read simply because they just recently became available.

A. *Christopher Columbus*: Most of us read years ago in our history texts that he discovered the New World by accident, while seeking a trade route to the Indies. No mention was ever made of Columbus' faith in God, let alone that he felt he had been given his life's mission directly by God.

We were never taught that he felt called to bear the light of Christ to undiscovered lands in fulfillment of Biblical principles, nor were we taught that he believed he had been guided by the Spirit of God every mile of his journey.

Here, in the words of Christopher (means, "Christ-bearer") Columbus himself, from Columbus' *Book of Prophecy* never published in this country (a compilation of his in Spanish of Biblical teachings on the earth's distant lands, population movements and undiscovered tribes) are the reasons Columbus searched for the New World:

> It was the Lord who put into my mind (I could feel his hand upon me) the fact that it would be possible to sail from here to the Indies. All who heard of my project rejected it with laughter, ridiculing me. There is no question that the inspiration was from the Holy Spirit, because He comforted me with rays of marvelous inspiration from the Holy Sciptures . . . .
>
> I am a most unworthy sinner, but I have cried out to the Lord for grace and mercy, and they have covered me completely. I have found the sweetest consolation since I made it my whole purpose to enjoy His marvelous presence. For the execution of the journey to the Indies, I did not make use of intelligence, mathematics or maps. It is simply the fulfillment of what Isaiah had prophesied . . . .
>
> No one should fear to undertake any task in the name of our Savior, if it is just and if the intention is purely for His holy service. The working out of all things has been assigned to each person by our Lord, but it all happens according to His sovereign will, even

though He gives advice. He lacks nothing that it is in the power of men to give Him. Oh, what a gracious Lord, who desires that people should perform for Him those things for which he holds Himself responsible! Day and night, moment by moment, everyone should express their most devoted gratitude to Him.

Bishop Las Casas, 16th century historian, who was with Columbus in Espanola on his third journey, relates an incident which took place on his fourth and final voyage. After he had been made Governor of Espanola and had then been relieved of that command for mismanagement, sick with a fever and in the depths of despair, Columbus had a half-waking dream in which he heard a stern voice strongly rebuke him for self-pity. The voice reminded him that the almighty had singled out him, of all the men in his age, for the honor of bearing the Light of Christ to a new world, had given him all that he had asked for, and was recording in heaven every event of his life! Whether this was a direct divine revelation or whether it was simply a dream like you or I have, it still indicates that deep in the recesses of his thinking, he believed his had been a God-appointed mission. Fame and greed later seduced Columbus and he did not fulfill in action what he professed to be in his original purpose. But his later failures do not invalidate the fact that impetus for discovery of the New World came from Columbus' knowledge and love for the Bible and his faith in God.

B. *The Conquistadors*: Every junior high school student knows the era of the Conquistadors. They have been told rosy tales about the contributions of these soldiers to the establishment of the New World. But the actual story of Cortez, Pizzaro and Coronado is one of rape, murder, and plunder. If God had a hand in the new nation upon this continent, it was not there. But wait, the Conquistadors all brought monks with them, possibly to salve their consciences, or to boost the morale of the men who were so far from home. But these Franciscan and Dominican friars were not straw men; they loved God — deeply and totally. The first white man to explore territory in what is now the USA was the Franciscan friar Marcos De Niza in 1539 on a journey into what is now New Mexico. With these men of God came orphanages, schools and refuges for the destitute. It was a priest, Bartolome de Las Casas (the same who traveled with Columbus) who was instrumental in the overthrow of the Spanish system called *encomienda*, a system whereby the Indians were enslaved by Spanish colonists. A group of French Huguenots seeking haven from religious persecution landed in 1562 at what would soon be named Saint Augustine and settled at what is now Beaufort, South Carolina. Jesuits Jacques Cartier, Samuel de Champlain, Jacques Marquette, Louis Joilet, served Christ by trying to help the Indians and exploring the vast wildernesses and rivers of this great land. Many of them were martyred for their faith that God wanted the gospel brought here. The Jesuit missionary Jean de Brebeuf, worked for 19 years with the Hurons, enlarging the influence of Christ among them. Captured in 1649 by an Iroquois war party, he was subjected to the most horrible tortures and finally martyred; first they poured boiling water over his naked body in mockery of Christian baptism; when he refused to cry out in agony, they tied a collar of metal hatchets heated red-hot around his neck. Still he would not cry out, and they fastened a belt of birchbark, filled with pitch and resin, around his waist and set it afire. Still he remained silent. Enraged, the Indians cut off his lips and tongue and rammed a hot iron down his throat. Then they cut strips of flesh from his arms and legs and devoured them before his eyes. He died expressing his faith in God. In the end, they cut his heart out and ate it and drank of his blood, in the hope that they could thus gain the spirit power that had given him more courage than any man they had ever seen.

And what of these martyrs? Other than the tremendous example of their selflessness and sacrifice, did their deaths play a part in God's unfolding plan for America? In terms of mass numbers of Indians being converted to Christ, their impact on the continent as a whole may not at first seem to have been that significant. But God does not take the measure of men's lives by the sum of their accomplishments. Rather, in the case of the founding of America, He seems to have been more concerned with the quality and depth of commitment. Jesus said, "Unless a grain of wheat falls into the earth and dies, it remains alone; but if it dies, it bears much fruit, John 12:24. These French and Spanish martyrs were willing to be the grains of wheat which fell into the earth and died. In soil watered with the blood of their sacrifice, God could now plant the seeds of the nation which was to become the New World.

C. *Jamestown, Virginia*: Before this New World is born, however, the classic example of horrible failure when God's will is not primary in human endeavor will be forever etched in the Jamestown debacle. Selfishness, avarice, laziness, immorality and arrogance resulted in murder, starvation, mutiny, and cannibalism. When the ships, *Deliverance* and *Patience* came with food supplies May 1610, there were only 60 stickfigured zombies remaining alive out of the 480 who had been there the previous August. It had finally come to the time known forever after as "the starving time." All the livestock had been consumed — hogs, sheep, goats, and a few horses — every bit, even the hides themselves. Next went the dogs and cats, and the rats that had once thrived on their corn, and any field mice they could find, or little snakes. But the hunger continued unabated and now became ravenous. They dug up the roots of trees and bushes and gnawed on them, and every bit of shoe leather on the plantation — every book cover, every leather hinge or strap or fitting was boiled and eaten. The colonists grew so weak that many, lacking the strength to move, froze to death in their beds. And still the hunger raged on. Here, the nicer histories leave off, for a number of the settlers who were still alive began digging up the fresher corpses. These they cut up into stew meat and boiled. There is only a single (recorded) instance of one person nudging another into the stew-meat stage a little more quickly. This is the case of the man who had become "unhinged" and killed his wife, salted her down, and had already begun to partake of her, when he was discovered. He was executed.

The settlement of Jamestown was undertaken without God and His word. But the next settlers to cross the Atlantic knew better than to attempt it without Him. They knew that they had no choice but to put *all* their trust in Him.

D. *The Pilgrims*: There were 102 Pilgrims (including a few "strangers") crammed into a space about equal to that of a modern volleyball court. Compound that misery by the lack of light and fresh air. Add to it a diet of dried pork, dried peas, and dried fish, and the stench of an ever-foul bilge, and multiply it all by 66 days at sea. Exiles from their homeland, England, they indentured themselves indefinitely to a financial sponsor. But they paid this enormous price cheerfully. Their own writings and the writings of independent contemporaries show them to be humble, just, compassionate, unprejudiced, wise and completely committed to making the will of God as revealed in the Bible the controlling factor in every experience of life. Seeking religious asylum in Holland, as near-penniless foreign immigrants, they found themselves reduced to near slavery there. They finally decided they must move to another place for their own survival as well as for carrying out their avowed mission to restore the Lord's church in its "ancient purity and recover its primitive order, *liberty* and beauty." Notice that word *liberty*. They were deeply God-fearing and fiercely freedom-loving. Humankind cannot have one without the other!

Increasingly, the Pilgrims (known as Separatists) came to believe America was the place to which God intended them to go, despite the horrors of Virginia's "starving time," which had reached their ears, and the well known savagery of some of the Indians. Even at this late date, the death rate at Jamestown was still well over 50 percent. The Pilgrims prayed. All circumstances seemed to point to America. But getting there was another question. The Virginia Company was on the brink of bankruptcy. But that closed door was providential, for they would probably have been sent to Jamestown.

A private investor had heard of their problem and came, unsolicited and unexpectedly, to offer his services. They sold all their homes and immovable possessions, drew up a contract with him, and prepared to set sail. Their sponsor had secretly pressured one of their leaders to certain changes in their contract. They refused to sign the altered contract, the sponsor refused to come through with the money for their supplies as he had agreed upon at first, so to keep their consciences clear before God, they sold off emergency food stores (for which they would suffer much later) and promised to indenture themselves to their suppliers beyond the original contract — indefinitely. They were admonished by their pastor, John Robinson, just before setting sail, to be "earnest in repentance . . . eagerly practice brotherly forebearance . . . choose leaders among equals . . . and yield unto these leaders all due honor and obedience in their lawful administrations, for the image of the Lord's power and authority, which the magistrate beareth, is honorable, in how mean persons soever . . . ."

In complete contrast to the Jamestown situation, the Pilgrims sought the will of God in almost every step of their planning. Three days out of port the *Speedwell*, the old freighter they had purchased to carry them to America, was reported by the captain to be severely leaking and needing to return to port. They returned for repairs, set sail, and again they returned — this time to Plymouth, England. Some of the Pilgrims themselves scrutinized the hull of the *Speedwell*, with candles, but found no evidence of loose seams. Frustrated, they decided to sell the *Speedwell* and book passage with those on board the *Mayflower*, also headed for the New World. The *Speedwell* was rerigged and used for many years afterward. Some historians have found hints that the captain, anxious to get out of his contract to spend a year wherever the Pilgrims landed, had deliberately crowded on sail to make the seams work loose.

But this also had the hand of Providence in it. It helped separate the wheat from the chaff. Some who began to lose faith and courage (about 20) willingly dropped out. One of the drop-outs later wrote a friend, ". . . if ever these people make a plantation, God works a miracle . . . ." Though he spoke from despair, he spoke what actually was to happen — for in spite of the tremendous faith and courage of those who finally sailed, they would reach their destination and "make their plantation" only after many clear acts of heavenly providence.

In addition to the terrible living conditions which put terrific strains on their Christian brotherliness, they had to endure unmerciful mocking and harassment from the crew of the *Mayflower*. One particular crew member continually sneered threats and predictions that they would all be buried at sea and fed to the fish. He called them the "puniest assortment of psalm-singing puke-stockings" he had ever seen. But just at the peak of his tormenting, he suddenly took gravely ill of an unknown fever and died within a single day! No one else caught this mysterious disease, and his was the first shrouded body to go over the side in burial. No more mocking from the crew was heard.

A huge cross-beam supporting the main mast cracked in a storm putting the ship in imminent danger of sinking and providentially, the only contraption that could have fixed it was the great iron screw of William Brewster's printing press. Now, even the sailors joined the Pilgrims in praising God for His providence.

They had started for America, intending to land at the mouth of the Hudson River. Their journey from start to finish seemed to be under one continuous storm. In spite of the most unlikely sailing conditions, when they finally landed at Cape Cod, they had been blown only about 100 miles off their course. They concluded, after much deliberation and prayer, that they would accept this landing as the will of God and they could put ashore to "make their plantation" here. Now a new question arose: if they were to settle here, they would no longer be under the jurisdiction of the king's Virginia Company. And since they obviously had no patent from the New England Company, they would be under . . . NO ONE! At this thought, rebellion began to stir in the hearts of some of the "strangers" of the group. The Pilgrim leaders realized they had to act quickly and decisively to forestall the possibility of mutiny and all its consequences. Their solution was pragmatic, realistic and expedient, and it took into consideration the basic sinfulness of human nature as they had experienced it under the temptations and stresses of their recent voyage. They drafted a compact (constitution) which embodied the principles of equality and government by consent of the governed which would become the *cornerstone* of the American Republic. The Pilgrims had no idea how significant this document was to be. *It marked the first time in recorded history that free and equal men had voluntarily covenanted together to create their own new civil government.*

This *Mayflower Compact* was the preface to the ringing affirmations a century later, such as: "We hold these truths to be self-evident, that all men are created equal and are endowed by their Creator with certain unalienable rights . . . ." This is the *Mayflower Compact:*

> In the name of God, amen. We whose names are underwritten, the loyal subjects of our dread Sovereign Lord King James by the Grace of God of Great Britain, France, Ireland, King, Defender of Faith, etc.
> Having undertaken, for the glory of God and advancement of the Christian Faith and honor of our King and country, a voyage to plant the first colony in the northern parts of Virginia, do by these presents solemnly and mutually in the presence of God and one of another, covenant and combine ourselves together into a civil body politic, for our better ordering and preservation and furtherance of the ends aforesaid, and by virtue hereof to enact, constitute and frame such just and equal laws, ordinances, acts, constitutions and offices from time to time, as shall be thought most meet and convenient for the general good of the colony. Unto which we promise all due submission and obedience. In witness whereof we have hereunder subscribed our names at Cape Cod, the 11th of November, in the year of the reign of our Sovereign King James . . . Anno Domini 1620.

William Bradford's diary, entitled *Of Plimoth Plantation* (which by the way, in at least one modern edition has edited out of it certain "irrelevant theological meditations"), says of the day the Compact was signed: "Being thus arrived in a good harbor and brought safe to land, they fell upon their knees and blessed the God of heaven, who had brought them over the vast and furious ocean, and delivered them from all the perils and miseries thereof, again to set their feet on the firm and stable earth, their proper element. And no marvel if they were thus joyful . . . for we marvel at this poor people's present condition . . . no friends to welcome them, nor inns to entertain or refresh their weatherbeaten bodies, no houses, or much less towns to repair to, to seek for succor . . . . If they looked behind them, there was the mighty ocean which they had passed, and was now as a main bar and gulf to separate them from all the civil parts of the world . . . . What could now sustain them but the Spirit of God and His grace?"

Sixteen Pilgrims went ashore first to reconnoiter. The first evidence of God's providential care was their finding an abandoned cache of buried

THE PROVIDENCE OF GOD IN THE COLONIZATION OF AMERICA

corn, 36 ears in a large iron pot. This was the Pilgrim's first taste of a food that would later save their lives. Next they were attacked by hostile Indians but not one of the Pilgrims was even wounded. Then the Pilgrims started dying. At one time there were only five men well enough to care for over 100 sick and dying. When the worst was finally over they had lost 47 people, nearly half their original number. Thirteen out of 18 wives died; only 3 families remained unbroken. But compared with Jamestown's mortality rate of 80-90 percent, they came through remarkably well. Through it all their hearts remained soft toward God. And all went gladly to worship services every Sunday (by the way they did not wear the somber browns and blacks of the pictures that hang in schoolrooms around Thanksgiving).

If any one event may be singled out to mark the turning point of their fortunes, it would be what happened on a sunlit Friday in the middle of March, 1620. Someone shouted "Indian coming!" Surely he meant, "Indians coming" — but no, here came a solitary Indian swaggering up main street of the little compound. "Welcome," he suddenly boomed in a deep resonant voice. The Pilgrims were to startled to speak. Finally, they replied, "Welcome." The strange Indian fixed his piercing stare upon them, and said, in clear, flawless English, "Have you got any beer?" Now they were astounded! You see, the liquid of survival on every long ocean voyage in those days was beer — water became too quickly contaminated. The Pilgrims drank beer all the way over from England. They looked at one another, then turned back to the Indian, "Our beer is gone. Would you like some brandy?" The Indian nodded. They brought him some brandy, and a biscuit with butter and cheese, and then some pudding and a piece of roast duck. Finishing his meal, he introduced himself as Samoset, chief of the Algonquins in Maine, visiting in Massachusetts for the past eight months, sent to explore the coast for the Council for New England, the very company to whom the Pilgrims would now be applying for a patent. The Indian loved to travel and he had learned his English from various fishing captains who had put into the Maine shore.

The next story he told filled the hearts of the Pilgrims with gratitude to God. The area which they had occupied had formerly been the territory of the Patuxets, a large, hostile tribe who had barbarously murdered every white man who had landed on their shores. But 4 years prior to the Pilgrims' arrival, a mysterious plague had broken out among them, killing every man, woman and child. So complete was the devastation that the neighboring tribes had destroyed the Patuxets. Hence the *cleaned* land on which Pilgrims had settled literally belonged to no one! Their nearest neighbors were the Wampanoags, 50 miles to the southwest, numbering about 60 warriors, whose chief was Massasoit.

Samoset slept with the Pilgrims that night and departed the next morning with gifts from the Pilgrims to Massasoit. The following Thursday Samoset returned accompanied by another Indian who also spoke English and who, of all things, was a Patuxet! This was Squanto, and was to be, according to William Bradford, "a special instrument of God for their good, beyond their expectation." His Indian name was Tisquantum. He had been captured by George Weymouth, taken to England, taught English, and spent nine years there, where he met Captain John Smith who promised to take him back to his people. On Smith's 1614 voyage he took Squanto back. Captured again, along with other Patuxets, Squanto was bought (for 20 pounds — $1400) by Spanish friars who introduced him to the Christian faith. Thus did God begin Squanto's preparation for the role he would play at Plymouth. Squanto left the monastery in Spain with an Englishman bound for London where he lived another four years and returned to the place of his people on Cape Cod in 1619! When Squanto stepped ashore, only six months before the Pilgrims, he received the most tragic blow of his life: not a man, woman or child of his tribe was left alive . . . nothing but skulls and bones and ruined dwellings remained. In despair he wandered southwest into Massasoit's tribe where this chief took pity on him. Hearing Samoset's news to Massasoit of the Englishmen forming a colony at New Plymouth on Cape Cod where his people had lived, he accompanied Samoset and Massasoit there and that is where the Pilgrims met him. Out of their meeting with Massasoit came a peace treaty of mutual aid and assistance which would last for 40 years, and be a model for many such treaties that would be later made. Massasoit was God's providence, too, for he was probably the only Indian chief on the northeast coast of America who would have welcomed the white man as a friend.

Squanto stayed with the Pilgims. He taught them how to squash edible eels out of the Cape Cod mud with their bare feet and catch them with their hands. But what he showed them next was the most important thing they would learn — for it saved every one of their lives. He showed them how to plant corn in six-foot squares, fertilizing the corn with fish. He taught them how to stalk deer, plant pumpkins, refine maple syrup, gather medicinal and edible herbs and berries, and introduced them to trapping and trading beaver pelts. The harvest of 1621 was so bountiful the Pilgrim leader, Governor Bradford, declared

THE PROVIDENCE OF GOD IN THE COLONIZATION OF AMERICA

a day of public Thanksgiving to be held in October. Massasoit was invited and arrived unexpectedly a day early with 90 Indians! The Pilgrims had to pray hard to keep from giving in to despair. To feed such a crowd would cut deeply into their food supply supposed to get them through the winter. But they had learned to trust God implicitly. As it turned out the Indians did not come empty handed. They had brought no less than 5 dressed deer, and more than a dozen fat wild turkeys. The Indians taught the Pilgrim ladies how to make hoecakes, tasty pudding out of cornmeal and maple syrup, and finally, showed them an Indian delicacy — how to roast corn kernels in an earthen pot until they popped, fluffy and white — popcorn! Things went so well, and Massasoit showed no inclination to leave — that first Thanksgiving lasted three days.

In November, 1621, a full year after the *Mayflower's* arrival, the first ship from home dropped anchor in the harbor. It was the *Fortune*, off of which stepped one of my lineal ancestors, Stephen Deane, whose wife Elizabeth Ring, after Stephen had died, married Josiah Cooke, a *Mayflower* passenger. Along with him were 35 other colonists and the Plymouth colony's royal charter granted through the New England Company. Stephen Deane built the first mill of the colony. While the Pilgrims were celebrating these new arrivals, they suddenly realized the 35 new colonists would force the whole community to go on half-rations through the coming winter in order to survive. In addition to this they were pressured to enter into an agreement with their old nemesis, Weston, which would see them struggle for more than 20 years to get out from under it. They were mercilessly taken advantage of during those years, at times having to borrow money at interest rates of 30 to 50 percent. The Pilgrims paid every bill, no matter how fraudulent, and were finally able in 1645, to buy themselves clear of Weston's group — at a fearful cost for it took some 20,000 pounds to retire a debt of only 1800 pounds, and to do it many sold their farms and homes.

During that winter (1621-1622), with all the extra people to feed, exploitation by their creditors, the Pilgrims entered into their own "starving time." They were reduced to a daily ration of five kernels of corn per person. It is almost inconceivable how life could be supported on this. But, in contrast to what happened at Jamestown, not one of them died of starvation. The merciful God sustained them once again. Unexpectedly a ship put into their harbor on its way back to England from Virginia. There was no extra food on board but they did have beads and trinkets with which they could trade for corn. So the captain traded his trinkets for their beaver hides for 3 shillings per pound — he would take them back to England and get six times as much for them. But the Pilgrims had no choice and they thanked God for seeing them through that winter.

You are wondering whatever happened to their old exploiter, Weston? He wound up on America's shore, humiliated, penniless, and wandered into the Pilgrim colony with only the shirt on his back, begging them for mercy and the loan of a load of beaver skins to get him back on his feet. He promised to pay later for the skins with a shipment of supplies. They took pity on him and agreed. He finally found his way back to England where he did repay the Pilgrims — with scorn and vicious slander, and not a penny in interest for the loan.

In the spring of 1624 they planted their corn but a severe drought appeared ready to totally destroy the crop. Not even the oldest Indians could remember anything like it. The Pilgrims entered into fasting, repentance and prayer, and God sent 14 days of gentle, soaking stormless rain which saved their crop. The yield that year was so abundant they wound up with a surplus of corn. A second day of Thanksgiving was planned, and Massasoit was again the guest of honor, and this time he brought his principal wife, three other chiefs, and 120 braves. Fortunately he again brought venison and wild turkey as well. One of the white men describes the feast in a letter to his brother in England:

> After our arrival in New England, we found all our plantation in good health, and neither man, woman or child sick . . . in this plantation is about twenty houses, four or five of which are very pleasant, and the rest (as time will serve) shall be made better . . . the fishing that is in this country, indeed it is beyond belief . . . in one hour we got 100 cod . . . .
>
> And now to say somewhat of the great cheer we had at the Governor's feast. We had about twelve tasty venisons, besides others, pieces of roasted venison and other such good cheer in such quantities that I wish you some of our share. For here we have the best grapes that ever you saw, and the biggest, and divers sorts of plums and nuts . . . six goats, about fifty hogs and pigs, also divers hens . . . . A better country was never seen nor heard of, for here are a multitude of God's blessings.

What this letter fails to mention, however, was the first course that was served: on an empty plate in front of each person were five kernels of corn — lest anyone should forget.

These Pilgrims were a mere handful of Light-bearers, on the edge of a vast and dark continent. But the Light of God was penetrating further into the heart of America. William Bradford would write with remarkable discernment: "As one small candle may light a thousand, so the light kindled here has shown unto many, yea in some sort to our whole nation . . . . We have noted these things so that you might see their worth and not negligently lose what your fathers have obtained with so much hardship."

Bible Preachers — Forerunners of Freedom
by Paul T. Butler

Over six hundred Separatists fled England after trying to reform the Church of England had resulted in severe persecution. They took up residence in Leyden, Holland. Bradford wrote they had "as the Lord's free people, joined themselves by a covenant to the Lord into a church estate, in the fellowship of the Gospel, to walk in all His ways made known . . . ." They could not fulfill their ambitions for a Biblically-based civil society in Holland so they made arrangements to migrate to "the New World" (America). One of the most significant leaders of these "Puritans" was Reverend John Robinson, minister of the congregation. He could not join the "Pilgrims" bound for America on the *Mayflower*. There was room for only 120 persons from a congregation of 600, but he prayed for them at their departure and wrote a letter of warnings and instructions which William Brewster read to the "saints and strangers" as they began that epochal journey — it ended: ". . . whereas you are to become a body politic, using amongst yourselves civil government, and are not furnished with any persons of special eminency above the rest . . ." (no "lords," "earls" or "barons" on board), they would have to choose their leaders from among equals. Rev. Robinson continued: "Let your wisdom and godliness appear not only in choosing such persons as do entirely love and will promote the common good, but also in yielding unto them all due honor and obedience in their lawful administrations . . . for the image of the Lord's power and authority, which the magistrate beareth, is honorable, in how mean persons soever . . . ."

Bible-believing preachers have always been in the forefront for civil government as ordained by God and structured on the principles for civil society as revealed in the Bible. The "Mayflower Compact," dated November 11th, 1620, the first time in recorded history that free and equal men voluntarily covenanted together to create their own new civil government, was drafted by ministers and other church leaders among the "Pilgrims." In the "Pilgrim" colony of Plymouth and the ever-expanding colonies of all New England, Puritan preachers like John Cotton, Cotton Mather, Roger Williams, and Thomas Hooker were singularly instrumental in forming the structures of the earliest democratic civil governments of America.

Thomas Hooker left the Bay Colony and settled with his congregation on the Connecticut River. Hooker's concept of civil government was that it should parallel the "covenant" structure of the church of Christ as he saw it in the Bible: "There must of necessity be a mutual engagement, each of the other, by their free consent, before by any rule of God they have any right or power, or can exercise either, each toward the other . . . ." *The Fundamental Orders of Connecticut*, principles for civil governance of Hooker's community were constituted: (a) religious qualification or affiliation in order to vote was not required; (b) clear, definitive restraints were enjoined regarding the authority of the magistrates; (c) non-landholders (servants, etc.), not allowed to vote for executive civil officers, could elect deputies to the governing council; (d) the chief executive's powers (the governor's) were closely circumscribed and he was prohibited from immediate re-election. It was not yet the great American republic, but it was on its way — thanks to a preacher!

Slowly, gradually, however, the obsession for civil freedom and human rights begain to subside. The colonies were growing in population, territory and resources. Ships were docking daily, disembarking hundreds and hundreds of "old world" immigrants. These were from every class, vocation and religious or non-religious persuasion of Europe (as well as slaves from Africa). Secular historians would say that the mania for "making a fortune" smothered the Pilgrim dream for a free civil republic founded on the principles of the Bible. The truth of the matter is, however, that with economic prosperity came a suffocating complacency toward spiritual matters. Sermons about justice, righteousness, human rights and truth fell on increasingly deaf ears. The majority of immigrants were no longer interested primarily in civil and religious reformation but in economic advancement. A prolonged and disinterested civic and religious complacency seemed to settle over America between the end of the seventeenth century and the first three decades of the eighteenth century. Between the "Puritan era" and the first stirrings for independence, Americans seemed content with the subtle, but ever-increasing, encroachments upon their civil rights as "Englishmen" so long as profits continued.

> The only significant spiritual development in this span of more than half a century was that sunburst of light in the middle of this period, which historians call the Great Awakening . . . actually a *re*-awakening of a deep national desire for the Covenant Way of life. This yearning did not die with the passing of the Puritan era, but only went dormant. It was a desire which would produce a new generation of clergymen who would help to prepare America to fight for her life.
> *The Light and the Glory*, by Peter Marshall and David Manuel, pub. Revell, 1977, p. 240

The most eminent figure of the Great Awakening was George Whitefield. Whitefield went to Oxford in 1733 and was ordained to the ministry in 1736 at the age of 22. After extraordinary evangelistic success in England, he was convinced of a mission to evangelize the Indians of America.

> Thus began the ministry of the greatest evangelist of the eighteenth century, one of the handful of men in the history of Christendom to be used by God to change the course of nations through the power of His Spirit . . . he dared to trust that his preaching might help create one nation under God — thirteen scattered colonies united with each other . . . .
> *ibid*, pp. 244,246

It is recorded that Benjamin Franklin was deeply impressed by the preaching of Whitefield. Listening to Whitefield preach one evening on the steps of the Philadelphia courthouse, Franklin was amazed and intrigued, of course, at the carrying power of his voice. Like the scientist he always was, Franklin retraced his steps backward down Market Street until he could at last no longer hear Whitefield. The amazed Franklin computed that in an open space, Whitefield's words could be distinctly heard by 30,000 people.

It was George Whitefield's passion to convert all of New England and arouse believers and non-believers alike to personal faith and righteous living. Horseback, through rain, snow, blistering heat and dust he rode the highways and byways of New England covering nearly 2000 miles in a five-month period. He often preached four times per day, sometimes for two hours per sermon.

> The Lord, through the preaching of this covenanted man was uniting the thirteen colonies — on a level so deep that few people even realized at first what was happening . . . . They were beginning to discover a basic truth which would be a major foundation stone of God's new nation, and which by 1776 would be declared self-evident: that in the eyes of their Creator, all men were of equal value . . . .
> *ibid*, p. 251

Altogether, Whitefield preached more than 18,000 sermons between 1736 and 1770. Whitefield proclaimed that men are reconciled to God by grace, that God is no respecter of persons, that denominational divisions should disappear and all should be known simply as Christians. Singlehandedly, Whitefield inoculated the American mentality with the divine concepts of human rights which would fan the spark of freedom into a burning flame again. And that flame burned brightest in the hearts of Bible-believing preachers.

As the great Biblical principles of civil government (i.e. that all civil rulers are subject to the divine laws of social contract the same as all citizens, that there are unalienable rights belonging to all human beings equally such as life, liberty and proprietorship, that government's singular reason for existence is to protect these rights) were emphasized more and more in American pulpits. It was inevitable that colonial political "philosophers" (many of them faithful Christians) would rise to libertarian activism. Men like Samuel Adams, John Adams, Patrick Henry, George Washington, George Mason, James Madison, and a host of others were convinced that Almighty God had moved providentially in the colonization of America. God was continuing His providential work with America thrusting her toward the "great experiment" — a democratic-republic. America would be the first civil society where the citizenry would have a voice in its governmental structure. That government would be so constituted as to guarantee, as much as humanly possible, man's basic unalienable rights. It would be so because it would be constituted on the revealed will of Almighty God for civil social structure in the Bible.

> Here then, was the seed of that democracy which would be embodied in the Constitution of the United States: of the political understanding that all men were equally entitled to the vote, and that, in the sight of God, a farmer was as good as King George. For God was no respecter of persons: His laws applied equally to all men . . . . It is difficult for us, with ten generations of democracy behind us to appreciate just how radical were the words of the Declaration of Independence that "all men are created equal." Never before in history had the world actually *believed* in the equality of man. That is why, beginning with the Mayflower Compact, a century and a half earlier, the American system of government under God had been so unique. *Under God* — that was the key. Democracy would be subsequently tried in many places through the next two centuries, but only in nations where the one true God was worshiped would it succeed. For the study of man's history shows that equality without the unifying hand of Almighty God, inevitably breeds chaos and anarchy.
>
> *ibid*, p. 255

BIBLE PREACHERS — FORERUNNERS OF FREEDOM

The British Parliament and Crown increasingly imposed arbitrary civil restraints and taxes upon the colonies. Subtle, but ever increasing abridgments of Englishmen's constitutional and natural civil rights were exacted. The colonial citizenry was being denied the basic right of the Englishman's civil contract (Magna Charta), representation in the government enacting its laws and levying its taxes. For the King and Parliament to suspend this right meant that they were putting themselves above the law (constitution) and that was contrary to God's word and to reason (the natural law).

During this ominous erosion of basic human rights, an "army" of American preachers were continuing to proclaim Biblical principles and precepts antithetical to these infringements and demanding reformation of the "mother government" in England. Thanks to the Great Awakening, there was now a new generation of committed preachers spread throughout the American colonies, and out to their frontiers, many of them men of considerable mental and spiritual depth and maturity.

It is in the so-called "Election Sermons" of New England ministers that we find some of the most fluent expressions on the subject of civil government. "Election Sermons" were preached annually on "general election day" (the last Wednesday in May when colonial legislatures met according to their "charters" to elect representatives for the coming year). Such sermons were also preached later when officers of the militia were elected. On these occasions political subjects were considered very proper. Usually the sermons were printed so that they could be distributed among the civil and military nominees. Many of the sermons most zealous about human rights and most apt to spread the thirst for liberty were often printed far and wide in patriot newspapers. Many an agitated Loyalist or Tory admonished these preachers to ". . . confine themselves to gospel truths" instead of mixing religion with politics. But for the Puritan ministers the cornerstone of liberty was the Bible. Favorite texts were: "Where the Spirit of the Lord is there is liberty" (II Cor. 3:17); and "Ye shall know the truth and the truth shall make you free . . ." (John 8:32). Upon such Biblical truths New England preachers fed their own souls and those of their congregations. Charles Turner, preacher at Duxbury, Massachusetts, expressed the point of view of many ministers: "The scriptures cannot rightly be expounded without explaining them in a manner friendly to the cause of freedom."

Because of their education these preachers were well grounded in Greek and Roman philosophers and historians. From these ancients they became aware of the fruits of both liberty and tyranny. They also studied in their colleges the writings of John Locke, Baron Montesquieu, Hugo Grotius, Samuel Pufendorf, Emmerich de Vattel, Sir Edward Coke, and John Milton (theologians and philosophers). From these and political philosophers contemporary with themselves they formed clear conclusions about civil government which they shared unequivocally with their parishioners and others through the printed page. Their Biblically based political conclusions may be summarized as follows.

a. The powers of civil government and everyone of its officials is derived from Almighty God and His word. Jonathan Mayhew said: "Rulers derive their power from God, and are ordained to be his ministers for good." Their study of Biblical texts concerning civil governance indicated a number of fundamental divine guidelines intended for all civil governments to follow. Puritan preachers believed strongly that no King or Parliament could claim to rule by divine right unless they had the covenantal (constitutional) consent of the governed unto whose welfare civil government owed its ordination.

b. Government was to be structured according to a compact or constitution. If God condescends to rule by law, if the Absolute Sovereign rules through covenant or constitution (laws), it is clearly reasonable and essential for imperfect human rulers to rule through covenants and constitutions rather than by tyrannical edict. Rule by constitution provides limitations and obligations upon ruling officials, established by Biblical precept (Deut. 17:14-17; I Sam. 10:25). Thomas Barnard said in 1763: "All power has its foundation in compact and mutual consent or else it proceeds from fraud or violence."

c. Liberty is grounded in Scripture and reason and is always requisite. It is necessary, therefore, that all citizens proclaim it verbally and promote it by personal involvement. Liberty can never be taken for granted. It is always tenuous, never to be equated with economic prosperity or military superiority alone. Economic fortune or misfortune should not determine political convictions.

d. Preachers before and during the Revolution were, for the most part, politically centrists. They were not extremists and anarchists, nor were they for the status quo and passive pragmatism. They were not nihilists, but they believed government as they were experiencing it had to be changed. They were "constitutionalists" who believed in reasonable laws imposing obligations upon both governors and the governed. If rulers violated their constitution with the people, they must be ousted. If they honored their compact with the people, they should be obeyed. Andrew Eliot, minister in Boston, said in 1765: " . . . when rulers are wise and good, opposition is a high crime." In the opinion of the Puritan preachers, the real radicals were those in the British government who were disregarding the rights of Englishmen guaranteed by the Magna Charta.

The intent of this paper is to give a minuscule biographical sampling of preachers whose ideas gave birth to American independence. There were hundreds of others, (especially on the frontiers of the colonies), besides these mentioned, equally fervent in preaching liberty and independence. But their sermons were not printed so their legacy was not preserved.

First, there is Jonathan Mayhew (1720-1766), of Boston. His contribution was one of the most significant:

> It is regrettable that Jonathan Mayhew is not better known and more rightfully honored by our generation. He was an inspired courageous pioneer, not only in his theological thought, but also in his convictions regarding civil and religious liberties. Robert Treat Paine, a signer of the Declaration of Independence and one-time attorney general of the United States called Mayhew, "The Father of Civil and Religious Liberty in Massachusetts and America." John Adams not only ranked him along with Otis and Samuel Adams as a patriot-statesman, but also said of him, "To draw the character of Mayhew would be to transcribe a dozen volumes."
>
> *They Preached Liberty*, by Franklin P. Cole, pub. Liberty Press, p. 26

Jonathan Mayhew was born on Martha's Vineyard in 1720, the son of Reverend Experience Mayhew and his wife, named Remember. His parents had bravely evangelized the Indian tribes of New England. Jonathan graduated from Harvard with honors in 1744. He reported that his university training had initiated him in the doctrines of civil liberty as taught by such men as Plato, Demosthenes, Cicero, and other ancients, along with Milton, Locke and Hoadley. Mayhew said, "I liked them; they seemed rational . . . . And having learned from the Holy Scriptures that wise, brave and virtuous men were always friends to liberty . . . because where the Spirit of the Lord is, there is liberty —

this made me conclude that freedom was a great blessing." He advocated the right of private judgment and the reality of the free human will. Ignoring the creeds of both Catholicism and Calvinism, Mayhew went directly to the Bible for his religious authortiy. He was a New Testament Church "Restorationist" a hundred years ahead of the times.

In 1750 a quarter of a century before the Declaration of Independence, Jonathan Mayhew preached his famous sermon entitled, "A Discourse Concerning Unlimited Submission and Non-Resistance to the Higher Powers." It was preached on January 30, 1750, and heard by a young lad of 15 named Paul Revere, in the West Church of Boston. John Adams said later that this sermon "fired the opening gun of the Revolution." In this sermon Mayhew expounded the people's right to resist, even to the "chopping off of kings' heads" to resist tyranny. This sermon was widely read and quoted throughout the colonies and in Great Britain. Mayhew said:

> It is blasphemy to call tyrants and oppressors God's ministers . . . .When (magistrates) rob and ruin the public, instead of being guardians of its peace and welfare, they immediately cease to be the ordinance and ministers of God, and no more deserve that glorious character than common pirates and highwaymen . . . .

Fifteen years later he responded to the hated Stamp Act:

> The king is as much bound by his oath not to infringe the legal rights of the people, as the people are bound to yield subjection to him. From whence it follows that as soon as the prince sets himself up above the law, he loses the king in the tyrant. He does to all intents and purposes un-king himself by acting out of and beyond that sphere which the constitution allows him to move in, and in such cases he has no more right to be obeyed than any inferior officer who acts beyond his commission. The subject's obligation to allegiance then ceases, of course, and to resist him is no more rebellion than to resist any foreign invader . . . it is making use of the means, and the only means, which God has put into their power for mutual and self-defense.
> *The Light and The Glory*, by Marshall and
Manuel, pub. Revell, pp. 264,265

It is enlightening to compare parts of Mayhew's sermons with the Declaration of Independence. The Declaration says: "We hold these truths to be self-evident, that all men are created equal, that they are endowed . . ." etc. Twenty-six years earlier, Mayhew preached: "Nothing can . . . be imagined more directly contrary to common sense than to suppose that millions of people should be subjected to the arbitrary, precarious pleasure of a single man — who has naturally no superiority over them in point of authority — so that their estates and everything that is valuable in life, and even their lives also, shall be absolutely at his disposal, if he happens to be wanton and capricious enough to demand them."

The Declaration says: "But when a long train of abuses and usurpations . . . evinces a design to reduce them under absolute Despotism, it is their right, it is their duty, to throw off such a Government, and to provide new Guards for their future Security . . . ." Mayhew said: "Those in authority may abuse their trust and power to such a degree that neither the law of reason nor of religion requires that any obedience . . . be paid them; but . . . they should be totally discarded, and the authority which they were before vested with transferred to others, who may exercise more to those good purposes for which it is given."

The Declaration closes by a lengthy listing of constitutional violations and usurpations of King George III — Jonathan Mayhew constructed a case against the King and Parliament very similar to Jefferson's (Mayhew's was directed against King Charles I). Great minds may run in the same channel, but preacher Mayhew's ran there before Jefferson's.

A generation before 1776, the congregation of New England had heard and read many "declarations of independence." Sermon after sermon referred to the "natural rights of life, liberty, and property." But to Jonathan Mayhew belongs the distinction of being the first of the Revolutionary preacher-patriots. Mayhew was an intimate of James Otis, John Adams, and Samuel Adams. It was Mayhew who suggested to Otis, in a letter dated June 8, 1766, the idea of Committees of Correspondence, which later rendered invaluable service to the patriot cause:

Would it not be proper and decorous for our assembly to send circulars to all the rest . . . . Pursuing this course, or never losing sight of it, may be of greatest importance to the colonies, perhaps the only means of perpetuating their liberties.

They Preached Liberty, p. 33

Six weeks later, on July 19, 1766, at the prime age of 46, Jonathan Mayhew, preacher of the gospel and father of American liberty, died of a "nervous fever," probably stroke or heart attack due to stress and overwork.

Next, we give you Samuel Cooper, one of the half-dozen most influential men of Boston during America's struggle for independence. Born in Boston in 1725, graduated from Harvard in 1743, he became the minister of the Brattle Street Church in Boston and remained there 40 years until he died in 1783. He was elected President of Harvard in 1774 but declined the position. His father before him was elected and also declined. Both considered their life's work to be the ministry of the Brattle Street Church.

Samuel Cooper was a vigorous preacher in behalf of the patriot cause, and a stirring writer as well. He dared to protest the Stamp Act and other "intolerable acts" in Boston Gazette articles bearing his signature. This made him a target of abuse by officers of the Crown in and around Boston. In 1775 the British contemptuously quartered troops in his church building. He was a close friend of Benjamin Franklin, John and Samuel Adams, and John Hancock was one of his faithful parishioners. Generals George Washington and Henry Lee along with Franklin and Hancock were guests at his table and recipients of his correspondence.

Samuel Cooper preached: "We want not, indeed, a special revelation from Heaven to teach us that men are born equal and free; that no man has a natural claim of dominion over his neighbors, nor any one nation any such claim upon another; and as government is only the administration of the affairs of a number of men combined for their own security and happiness, such a society has a right freely to determine by whom and in what manner their own affairs shall be administered. These are the plain dictates with which the Common Parent of men has informed the human bosom."

Cooper pled for peace, but not without liberty: "Peace, peace we ardently wish; but not upon terms dishonorable to ourselves, or dangerous to our liberties; and our enemies seem not yet prepared to allow it upon any other. At present the voice of Providence, the call of our still invaded country, and the cry of everything dear to us, all unite to rouse us to prosecute the war with redoubled vigor . . . ."

Foreign policy was also a topic for Reverend Cooper: "Conquest is not indeed the aim of these rising states; sound policy must ever forbid it. We have before us an object more truly great and honorable. We seem called by heaven to make a large portion of this globe a seat of knowledge and liberty, of agriculture, commerce, and arts, and what is more important than all, of Christian piety and virtue . . . . May our conduct correspond to the face of our country . . . ."

Finally, one of the most colorful and versatile of the patriot-preachers of Revolutionary New England was Jonas Clark. He graduated from Harvard in 1752 and settled in Lexington, Massachusetts, for a ministry that lasted 50 years. he supplemented his meager income as a minister by farming. His salary of 80 English pounds per year plus 20 cords of wood, was never enough to support a family of six girls and six boys. He made his home a meeting place for many of the patriot leaders. The very night Paul Revere made his famous ride to warn that the British were coming, April 18, 1775, the two "rebels" for whom the British were "coming," Samuel Adams and John Hancock, were being entertained in Jonas Clark's home! When Adams and Hancock asked Jonas Clark if the Lexington people would fight, Clark replied, "I have trained them for this very hour." It was just a few strides from the Clark parsonage that the first blood of the Revolution was shed on the following day, April 19, 1775, when the "shot was fired heard round the world." Many of the men who fell slain or wounded that day were members of Clark's congregation. Upon viewing the aftermath of the Lexington-Concord engagement and his slain parishioners, Clark said: "From this day will be dated the liberty of the world."

Jonas Clark had these words to say about Lexington and Concord: "And this is the place where the fatal scene begins! . . . without provocation, without warning, when no war was proclaimed, they draw the sword of violence, upon the inhabitants of this town, and with a cruelty and barbarity, which would have made the most hardened savage blush, they shed INNOCENT BLOOD . . . . They have not bled, they shall not bleed in vain . . . ." In the same sermon he said: "Injustice, oppression, and violence (much less the shedding of innocent blood) shall not pass unnoticed by the just Governor of the world. Sooner or later, a just recompense will be made upon such workers of iniquity."

Striking statements from a few more American patriot-preachers are worthy of quotation here:

> All power is originally from God, and civil government his institution, and is designed to advance the happiness of his creatures. Civil power ought therefore ever to be employed agreeable to the nature and will of the Supreme Sovereign and Guardian of all our rights.
>
> Benjamin Stevens, of Kittery, Mass., 1761

WHAT THE BIBLE SAYS ABOUT CIVIL GOVERNMENT

... I cannot help hoping, and even believing, that Providence has designed this continent for to be the asylum of liberty and true religion.
Samuel West, of Salisbury, Mass., 1776

... They left their native land with the strongest assurances that they and their posterity should enjoy the privileges of free natural-born English subjects, which they supposed fully comprehended in their charter. The powers of government therein confirmed to them they considered as including English liberty in its full extent . . . .
Samuel Cooke, of Cambridge, Mass., 1770

As no body on earth had any title to this land but the original inhabitants — our fathers got leave of them to settle, and made peace with them, and fairly purchased their lands of them. The king has no right to give it, nor the people of England, for it is not theirs to give. But God gave our fathers favor in the eyes of the people of the land; and they obtained their title to these lands; which was as good as the people of England have to theirs, or any other people under heaven. All pretenses to the contrary are vain and frivolous to the last degree.
Samuel Webster, of Salisbury, Mass., 1774

The practice of religion and virtue tends, above all things, to promote the public welfare and happiness of mankind, and to secure the ends of civil government; therefore rulers should be nursing fathers to it. Civil government was originally instituted to protect and defend men's lives and liberties, to guard and secure their properties, and promote their temporal interests and advantages . . . . Now the practice of religion and virtue, tends, above all other things, to promote those very ends, for which men entered into society.
Edward Dorr, of Hartford, Conn., 1765

Laws may be said to be good . . . when they tend to the securing and establishing the liberties and privileges of men; which they are entitled unto, by the constitution of the government they have voluntarily engaged to submit to; and which are confirmed to them by the revealed will of God . . . . And I will add here, that only such laws as these, are fit for the government of rational, in-

telligent, moral agents, all equal and upon a par, antecedent to any political combinations among men; and after all, entitled to certain immunities and benefits, as members of the body politic.
     Ebenezer Bridge, of Chelmsford, Mass., 1767

My . . . brethren in the ministry will remember that it is part of the work and business of a gospel minister to teach his hearers the duty they owe to magistrates . . . . In order to the right and faithful discharge of this part of our ministry, it is necessary that we should thoroughly study the law of nature, the rights of mankind, and the reciprocal duties of governors and governed. By this means we shall be able to guard them against the extremes of slavish submission to tyrants on the onehand, and of sedition and licentiousness on the other.
     Samuel West, of Dartmouth, Mass., 1776

On the free exercise of their natural religious rights the present as well as future happiness of mankind greatly depends.
     Daniel Shute, of Hingham, Mass., 1768

Religious liberty is so blended with civil, that if one falls it is not to be expected that the other will continue.
     Charles Turner, of Duxbury, Mass., 1773

The greatest restraints, the noblest motives, and the best supports arise from our holy religion. The pious ruler is by far the most likely to promote the public good . . . . Superior to base passions and little resentments, undismayed by danger, not awed by threatenings, he guides the helm in storm and tempest, and is ready, if called in providence, to sacrifice his life for his country's good. Most of all concerned to approve himself to his God, he avoids the subtle arts of chicanery, which are productive of so much mischief in a state; exercising a conscience void of offense, he has food to eat that the world knows not of.
     Phillips Payson, of Chelsea, Mass., 1778

During the War for Independence many ministers descended from the pulpit in order to engage actively in the fighting:

When the news of Lexington and Bunker Hill arrived, parson after parson left his parish and marched hastily toward Boston.

Before daylight on the morning of April 30, 1775, Stephen Farrar, of New Ipswich, New Hampshire, left with ninety-seven of his parishioners. Joseph Willard, of Beverly marched with two companies from his town, raised in no small part through his own exertion. David Avery, of Windsor, Vermont, after hearing the news of Lexington, preached a farewell sermon, then, outside the meeting-house door, called his people to arms, and marched with twenty men. On his way he served as captain, preached, and collected more troops. David Grosvenor, of Grafton, left his pulpit and musket in hand, joined the minute-men who marched to Cambridge. Phillips Payson, of Chelsea, is given credit for leading a group of his parishioners to attack a band of English Soldiery that nineteenth day of April. Benjamin Balch, of Danvers, Lieutenant of the third-alarm list of his town, was present at Lexington and later, as chaplain in army and navy, won the title of the "fighting parson." Jonathan French, of Andover, Massachusetts, left his pulpit on the Sabbath morning, when the news of Bunker Hill arrived, and with surgical case in one hand and musket in the other started for Boston.
New England Clergy and the American Revolution,
by Baldwin, pp. 154-167

Many who did not join in the actual fighting rendered invaluable service to the cause for independence through preaching and writing, encouraging boycotting of English imports, giving of their small salaries to the cause of liberty, feeding soldiers, nursing wounded, caring for husbandless families, and serving as recruiting agents in towns and villages.

Peter Muhlenberg, having delivered a passionate sermon on the text "For everything there is a season, and a time for every matter under heaven" climaxed the message by saying, "In the language of the Holy Writ, there is a time for all things. There is a time to preach and a time to fight." Throwing off his clerical robe he revealed to his startled congregation the uniform of a colonel in the Continental Army, and cried, "*And now is the time to fight* . . . roll the drums for recruits!" He went off to war and his 8th Virginia Regiment distinguished itself in battle and he rose to the rank of brigadier general.

One story which is filled with both pathos and irony for preachers would be that of a battle in New Jersey, just across the river from Staten Island·

BIBLE PREACHERS — FORERUNNERS OF FREEDOM

> Early in June of 1780, in support of a British advance, Hessian General Wilhelm von Knyphausen crossed from Staten Island to New Jersey with five thousand men. At the little village of Springfield, just west of Union, he encountered unexpected resistance and was forced to withdraw. In the course of this action, the wife of the Reverend James Caldwell, a mother of nine, was shot in her home, while her husband was away. Whether or not it was intentional (Caldwell had a price on his head and later that same day his house was burned to the ground), the incident inflamed the townspeople. When Knyphausen's force returned two weeks later, even though reinforced by British General Clinton himself, he was again stopped, this time in furious action. At the height of the shooting, the Patriots, taking cover behind a fence that was adjacent to Caldwell's church, ran out of the paper wadding needed to hold powder and ball in place in their muskets. Caldwell gathered up all the copies of *Watts Psalms and Hymns* he could carry, and rushed out to the crouching riflemen. Tearing pages out of the hymnal, he passed them out, shouting, "Put Watts into 'em boys! Give 'em Watts!"
>
> *The Light and The Glory*, p. 291

Scores of Quaker preachers (and church members) gave physical support, as well as verbal, in the form of food and clothing to the soldiers. Some of the Quakers even bore arms in the war. The contributions of preachers on America's frontiers (Georgia, southwest Virginia, western North Carolina, east Tennessee, Kentucky, western Pennsylvania, etc.) is a story by itself. The impact that the "over-the-mountain" people had on the Revolution, led and empowered by their preachers, is immeasurable!

> There is probably no group of men in history, living in a particular area at a given time, who can speak as forcibly on the subject of liberty as the Congregational ministers of New England between 1750 and 1785.
>
> *They Preached Liberty*, p. 43

In a day when our liberties are threatened by pressure groups at home and by totalitarian philosophies and wars from abroad, we may well hearken to these preachers of liberty. Although their wisdom has been ignored by our generation, they can tell us much about the nature of liberty which is relevant for our day. They can tell us from sacrificial experience of the cost of liberty. But, perhaps most important of all, they can help us root our passion for liberty deep in the soil of American tradition, as well as Providential creation. Their age taught them, as our age teaches us, that democracy and the religion of Jesus are closely allied; when one falls the other is likely to follow. "Where the spirit of the Lord is, there is liberty" — a favorite text of the Revolutionary ministers — may well be the watchword of freedom in every age.

An Assembly of Demigods
(A few of the signatories of the U.S. Constitution)
by Paul T. Butler

Benjamin Franklin looked over the roster of delegates at the start of the Constitutional Convention of 1787 and said, "We have here at present what the French call 'an assembly of notables,' a convention composed of some of the principal people from the several states of our Confederation." Thomas Jefferson, examining the same roster in Paris, proclaimed the convention, "an assembly of demigods (half-gods)."

Most prominent among the "demigods" was *George Washington*. Early on the morning of May 9, 1787, he left Mount Vernon in his carriage. He wanted to bring Martha but she had "become too domestic and attentive to her two little grandchildren to leave home" said the General in his diary. The retired general received almost hysterical cheers and applause from huge crowds all along his route to Philadelphia, often delaying him for hours during his trip. He arrived in Philadelphia on May 13 and senior officers of the Continental Army greeted him at the outskirts of the city and formed an escort. Guns fired a salute and the bells of Christ Church pealed as the great man rode into the city.

Washington was 55 years old. His once-powerful physique was wracked with rheumatism. He was not convinced that the Philadelphia convention would find a solution to the nation's political problems and was hesitant to get involved in an effort that might be doomed to failure. When he resigned his military commission in December 1783, he clearly state his intention of spending the rest of his days in private life. Friends urged him to reconsider and lend his commanding influence and prestige to the Philadelphia assembly.

Washington was still an impressive looking man. He had huge hands and feet; he wore size 13 shoes and always ordered "extra large" gloves. He stood 6 ft. 2 in. tall and weighed between 190 and 210 pounds, at a period when the average American male was approximately 5 ft. 7 in. and 140 pounds. He had deeply set blue-grey eyes, a prominent nose, and a well-defined and firm jawline. His auburn hair had turned to white by 1787, and he wore reading glasses and suffered from poor hearing. His mouth was bulged by ill-fitting upper and lower dentures (not made of wood, incidentally, but of hippopotamus, elephant and walrus tusks and cattle and human teeth; weighing about 4 ounces, held together by gold springs; talking was very difficult). Though beset by rheumatism, his posture remained erect; his countenance was somber and serious; his manner reserved, dignified and aloof.

He wrote in his diary for May 25, 1787, ". . . by unanimous vote I was called up to the Chair as President of the body . . ." and later wrote Henry Knox, "I was, much against my wish, unanimously placed in the Chair." Douglas Southall Freeman writes, "Parliamentary argument had never been among Washington's skills; his value (as President of the Convention) would rest more in presence than in active participation." The assembly surely knew this. They must have anticipated times when this convention could be held together *only* by the sheer prestige of his presence.

As President, Washington believed his main task was to keep the deliberations focused always on the central objective — the establishment of a workable government. He, along with all the others, were very nearly overwhelmed with the awesomeness of free men (for the first time in history) determining what form of government should rule them. He writes, "The establishment of our new government seems to be the last great experiment for promoting human happiness by reasonable compact in civil society."

Washington deliberately refused to participate in the committee work, in the floor debates, in making any speeches or offering his opinions on any matter lest his great prestige should influence the paths of discussion or decision. He did vote as a delegate from Virginia. He voted on the losing side of more debates than on the winning side. He voted that a ¾ majority be required to override a Presidential veto, but lost to the majority who voted for ⅔. He preferred a strong Chief Executive.

He was not bereft of all humor. When the Convention got around to discussing the power of Congress to raise an army, one of the delegates moved "that the standing army be restricted to 5000 men at any time." Washington was amused by the motion, but as chairman would not offer a motion himself. Instead, he whispered to one of the delegates sitting near him that they had better amend the motion to provide that "no foreign army should invade the United States at any time with more than 3000 troops."

Washington became depressed over the long, long, debates. He was used to quick decisions and immediate action. He was afraid the nation would soon disintegrate. He wrote in his diary, ". . . procedures which take the shortest course, in my opinion will, under present circumstances be found best. Otherwise, like a house on fire, whilst the most regular modes of extinguishing the flames is contended for, the building is reduced to ashes . . . ." He wrote to Thomas Jefferson on May 30, 1787, that it was far too soon to anticipate what was going to come out of the Convention, but that something must soon come, ". . . for the situation of the General Government (if it can be called a government) is shaken to its foundation and liable to be overset by every blast. In a word, it is at an end, and unless a remedy is soon applied, anarchy and confusion will inevitably ensue."

Washington was a very social person. Most people do not know that. During the four months he was in the Philadelphia convention, his evenings and Sundays, when not resting or studying political matters, were spent socializing. He had tea and dinner with a host of different friends; attended a wedding dinner; attended religious services; went to a musical concert; inspected the gardens of botanist William Bartram; visited farms; sat for two portraits; dined with Ben Franklin; dined with the members of the Society of Cincinnati; twice went to plays in a theater; attended a gathering of the "Sons of Saint Patrick"; went to a grist mill; inspected vineyards and beehives; went trout fishing; toured Valley Forge and other former battle sites; and inspected a "new fangled" invention of Ben Franklin's called a "Mangle" for pressing clothes.

He could also be stern and strict when the occasion demanded it. When the Convention first opened, each delegate was given a copy of several propositions concerning the kind of government to form. They were cautioned to keep the copy in strict secrecy. A few days later, a copy that had been dropped on the floor was picked up and handed to Washington who put it in his pocket. Hours later, just before adjourning for the day, the President spoke to the members: "Gentlemen, I am sorry to find that some member of this body has been so neglectful as to drop in the State House a copy of their proceedings, which was picked up and delivered to me this morning. I must entreat the gentleman to be more careful, lest our transactions get into the newspapers and disturb the public repose by premature speculation. I know not whose paper it is, but there it is (throwing it down on the table). Let him who owns it take it." Then Washington, according to the Georgia delegate who recalled this story, "bowed, took his hat, and left the room with a dignity so severe every person seemed alarmed."

As presiding officer, Washington firmly ruled out all motions to adjourn before the scheduled 4:00 p.m. closing hour. He was determined to have the delegates keep at the job, full-time. They worked from 5 to 7 hours every day (except for Sundays and 10 days of adjournment for committee work) for more than 4 months. Each delegate was given a printed copy of the final document; they went over it line-by-line, word-by-word. Washington made hand-written notations on his copy, inserting changes agreed to verbally. On September 15th, for instance, there were at least 25 separate motions made for changes and alterations that were put before the Convention for decision.

At the final session on Monday, September 17, 1787, George Washington stood by the table, pen in hand, and said, "Should the states reject this excellent Constitution, the probability is that opportunity will never be offered to cancel another in peace; the next will be drawn in blood."

Both Patrick Henry and Thomas Jefferson had declared that George Washington had the soundest judgment of any person in colonial America. And Jefferson expressed the opinion that the key to his effectiveness as a leader was not only his honesty and integrity but also the soundness of his judgment. Washington himself, however, said he was merely "a humble agent of a favoring heaven" and God had marked the path "so plainly that I cannot mistake the way."

Clearly, we, and generations yet to come, are indebted to this singular individual, greatest of the great, not only for leading the physical struggle of war for human freedom, but for leading the philosophical struggle for preserving it in our Constitution. Had it not been for Washington's influence our Constitution would never have been born, nor ratified. Throughout the stormy and doubtful ratification process he continued, in the words of congressman Henry Lee, "firm as a rock." And Washington maintained his unshakable faith that God would shed His special light on the efforts. He wrote about his anticipation of the acceptance of the Constitution by the people, "A few short weeks will determine the political fate of America for the present generation and probably produce no small influence on the happiness of society through a long succession of ages to come." The importance of George Washington's leadership was summarized by James Monroe to Thomas Jefferson: "Be assured that George Washington's influence carried this government."

Perhaps the second greatest influence in the formation of our Constitution was that of *Benjamin Franklin*. He was 81 and beset by infirmities (gout and gall stones). His illnesses made it all but impossible for him to even walk. But his mind was bright and alert, and he had continued to play an active role in the affairs of Pennsylvania government right up to this date. He had recently served as America's minister to France. Wishing to retire after that, he had been prevailed upon to accept election as governor of Pennsylvania, and then delegate to this Convention. Because horse-drawn carriages jostled his aching, 81 year old, gout-afflicted body, Franklin rode in an imported sedan chair. He was carried in it almost daily to and from the State House by prisoners from the Walnut Street Jail. Legend has it that on days when Franklin suffered severe attacks of gout, both he and the chair were taken directly into the assembly room where the delegates were meeting.

It was Franklin, when with the stifling heat, the endless, tedious, wrangling debates became rancorous, who suggested inviting clergymen to attend their sessions and offer daily prayer. He said, in part:

> In the beginning of the contest with Britain, when we were sensible of danger, we had daily prayers in this room for Divine protection. Our prayers, Sir, were heard, and they were graciously answered . . . do we imagine we no longer need His assistance? . . . We have been assured, Sir, in the Sacred Writings that except the Lord build the house, they labor in vain that build it. I firmly believe this . . . I therefore beg leave to move that, henceforth, prayers imploring the assistance of Heaven and its blessing on our deliberation be held in this assembly every morning before we proceed to business.

Franklin's motion was defeated because, in those days, it was expected that ministers be paid for such services, and the Convention had no authority to acquire or disburse such funds.

Rumor was circulating in Philadelphia that Ben Franklin objected to the Constitution the convention was writing and that it was doomed to failure. Franklin, on the final day, asked permission to speak. He had a speech written out. He could not stand to speak so he asked James Wilson to read his speech for him. Briefly, these were Franklin's words:

> I confess that there are several parts of this constitution which I do not at present approve, but I am not sure I shall never approve them: For having lived long, I have experienced many instances of being obliged by better information or fuller consideration, to change opinions on important subjects, which I once thought right, but found to be otherwise . . . Thus I consent, Sir, to this Constitution because I expect no better, and because I am not sure, that it is not the best.

Printer, scientist, inventor, philosopher, diplomat, politican, and leader of the fight for independence, Franklin's mere presence at the Convention became one of the primary factors in the formation of our

Constitution as we have it today.

Something hurting Ben Franklin more than his gout, however, was a broken heart over the estrangement of his only son, William. William who was 47 had been a Tory during the Revolution and had exiled himself in London. He had been born in 1730 out of wedlock (some think by a servant girl named Barbara who later died). Ben took another woman in common law marriage (she had been abandoned by her former husband) — the marriage was a happy one and William was cherished and cared for. But William, unhappy, ran away from home at the age of 16 and fought in King George's War against the French and then joined a "privateer" shipping out of Philadelphia. Ben searched him out and brought him home. William always thought of himself as an Englishman. At a later date William went to England and studied law; there he sired an illegitimate child, married an English aristocrat, and was appointed royal governor of New Jersey.

Ben and his son became political antagonists during the hectic years that fomented the Revolution. After Lexington and Concord, William began to pass on to London such information as he could glean concerning rebel activities.

In June, 1776, William was declared an enemy of the people and his arrest was ordered. He was eventually in jail in Litchfield, CT. While there his wife died before Congress could act to grant him special permission to go to her bedside. After 3 years of confinement he was exchanged and took up residence in British-occupied NY City. In the Autumn of 1782 William Franklin left America for the last time. He would see his father only once more before Ben died in 1790. William's son, Temple Franklin, returned to America to live with his grandfather Ben. For Ben Franklin, the chasm that had come between him and William proved too wide to cross. Separated in heart as well as miles from his only surviving son, Ben spent his last years attended by his daughter, Sarah. Ben left William only a pittance in his will. Benjamin Franklin wrote, ". . . nothing has ever hurt me so much and affected me with such keen sensations, as to find myself deserted in my old age by my only son."

Gouverneur Morris was 35 years old. He was not related to the esteemed Robert Morris, although their politics were much the same (federalists). He was born just outside NY City in 1752, graduated from King's College (later Columbia University) and became one of NY's prominent lawyers. He assisted John Jay and Robert Livingston in drafting the NY state constitution in 1777. He served for about a year in Congress and had been a signer of the Articles of Confederation. He moved to Philadelphia in 1779 to practice law and served as Asst. Superintendent of Finance under Robert Morris. Suave and witty, with a wooden leg he looked the part of a pirate. Talkative, aristocratic, cynical, reputed to be a woman-chaser (even in those days!), he effectively advocated a stronger union among the states. During his convention speeches, Morris would thump his wooden leg against the Assembly floor for emphasis. A gifted writer as well as speaker, he served on the five-man Committee of Style and was chosen to do the *actual drafting* of the Constitution. Although James Madison had provided much of the Constitution's substance, Morris supplied its literary form and style. Years later he would write proudly that the U.S. Constitution "was written by the fingers, which write this letter." Madison even admitted "the finish given to the style and arrangement of the Constitution fairly belongs to the pen of Mr. Morris." One of the last sections he composed was the Preamble. As originally drafted by the Committee of Detail, the Preamble read: "We the People of the States of New Hampshire, Massachusetts (listing all the 13 states) . . . do ordain, declare and establish the following Constitution for the Government of Ourselves and our Posterity." The Committee of Style rewrote the same passage to read: "We the People of the United States, in order to form a more perfect Union, to establish Justice, insure domestic Tranquility, provide for the common defence, promote the general Welfare, and secure the Blessings of Liberty to ourselves and our Posterity, do ordain and establish this Constitution for the United States of America." The change from "We the People of named states" to "We the People of the United States" did not seem particularly significant to the delegates when they read and considered Morris' draft. *To history, however, it became one of the single most important acts of the Constitutional Convention.* It would signify that the Union was the product, not of thirteen states, but of more than 3 million citizens. It was not a compact between sovereign governments, but a contract to which the *citizens* were parties.

Thirty-six year old *James Madison* of Montpelier, VA, arrived in Philadelphia on May 3, 1787 (first one there), from NY, where he had been serving in Congress. A slight man, barely 5 ft. 6 in. tall, Madison was shy and studious. What he lacked in extroversion and gregariousness, the little Virginian more than made up in wisdom, clear thinking, and scholarship. After graduating from the College of New Jersey (later Princeton), he had returned to his home state to take an active interest in public affairs. He served in the Virginia House of Delegates and Council of State and was elected to the Continental Congress twice. A close friend of Thomas Jefferson, Madison came to the convention with well developed ideas about republican forms of government and democratic processes. James Madison is often referred to as "the father of the Constitution" because during the 3 weeks before the Convention he wrote the guidelines for a strong central government that later became known as "the Virginia Plan" from which the Constitution was ultimately developed. Madison never missed a day of the convention (unlike many of his colleagues who had poor attendance records). He sat toward the front of the Assembly Room and took notes in code on the speeches and debates; today these notes form the single best record of the proceedings.

Madison was born in 1751, eldest of 12 children, from a family who had settled in VA in the 1600s. Dozens of slaves worked on Madison's plantation. He was a frail, sickly child — studied with private tutors. In Princeton, he studied intensely, sometimes sleeping only 5 hours a night, and completed the regular course for graduation in 2 years. He studied Hebrew language, philosophy and theology, but a weak speaking voice kept him from taking up a career as a preacher. Madison was one of the moving forces most responsible in building a strong federal government in America. At the Convention he argued vehemently for national union of the states. He spoke fearlessly for nationalism when most Americans (including his friend Jefferson) put state's rights ahead of national interests. He was by nature a mediator, not an agitator. He vigorously opposed Hamilton's tendency to strip the states of all their powers, but also softened Jefferson's views favoring state's rights. His support of the strong federalist constitution angered many Virginians and his own constituency defeated him in his bid for a seat in the first U.S. Senate in 1788. He later became a Representative and then President.

Madison spoke on 71 days of the whole 86. He got so excited at times that he finally asked a friend to tug on his coat-tails if he became too emotional during a speech. Once, after talking himself to the point of exhaustion, he reproved his friend: "Why did you not pull on my coat-tails when you heard me going on like that?" Said the Friend: "I would rather have laid a finger on the lightning."

George Mason, 67, was a trained lawyer who had consistently refused to accept public office, preferring to stay home with his 4 daughters and 5 sons to tend his 5000-acre plantation, Gunston Hall, on the south bank of the Potomac, not far from Mount Vernon. A life-long student of public institutions and political theories, Mason drafted the Virginia Declaration of Human Rights in 1776, a charter of individual freedom that was to become a model for similar pronouncements of individual rights around the world, including ours. Washington frequently sought his neighbor's counsel, while Jefferson described him as "the wisest man of his generation."

Most Americans do not know the name of this Virginia farmer-lawyer. Yet they owe this forgotten man, who helped write the Constitution (but refused to sign it without a guarantee of basic individual freedoms in the first draft), a large measure of thanks for the Bill of Rights adopted four years later! His personal notes of objections to the Constitution were printed by friends and became a handbook of ratification-opponents throughout the land until the Bill of Rights was added. He paid the price for insisting on the Bill of Rights — belittlement then and obscurity now.

Mason was a complex man — aristocrat who battled for popular rule; slave-holder who vehemently denounced slavery; farmer whose legal advice was sought by lawyers; legislator who distrusted legislatures; a philosopher who mastered the practical details of managing a large estate; a man who preferred his own fireside to national office.

Mason stood almost alone among his fellow-citizens in the southern states favoring and advocating freeing of the slaves. His greatest objection to the Constitution was that it compromised on the slavery question.

In 1776 George Mason wrote these words: "All men are by nature equally free and independent and have certain inherent rights . . . the enjoyment of life and liberty, with the means of acquiring and possessing property, and pursuing and obtaining happiness and safety . . ." A month later, Thomas Jefferson paraphrased these words in our famous American Declaration of Independence.

Mason said in one of his speeches at the Convention that a nation which practices slavery invites "the judgment of heaven." It has been reported that his objections to the Constitution for not guaranteeing individual liberties led to threats on his life. Announcing one day that he would speak against the Constitution on the courthouse steps of Alexandria, VA, he so aroused the anger of Virginians they gathered a mob around the courthouse to do him bodily harm. He calmly proceeded with his speech, using such wisdom and logic, that at the conclusion he simply stepped down into the throng, mounted his horse and rode away unharmed. James Madison at first saw no need for a Bill of Rights, but four years later conceded that he had been mistaken and Mason had been right.

By his crucial decision to oppose the Constitution, Mason set in motion the demand for freedom-guarding amendments which eventually forced adoption of the Bill of Rights — the most *precious* part of the Constitution to the individual American. Even though others opposed ratification — it was George Mason who initiated the fight and crystallized the issue!

As a delegate to the Annapolis convention in 1786, *Alexander Hamilton* had taken the lead in calling for the Philadelphia convention, and had pled with Washington to attend as a Virginia delegate. Hamilton was clearly one of the most brilliant delegates in Philadelphia. He was a delegate from NY. When he was in his late teens he became an officer in the Revolution. In his early 20's he served as Washington's aide and secretary. Later he would serve as George Washington's Secretary of the Treasury. Hamilton was born in the British West Indies, left an orphan as a boy. His employer helped him come to America to get an education.

Just 32 years old at the Constitutional Convention, he had already distinguished himself as a soldier, lawyer, writer, speaker and financier. But most of the people of NY had little enthusiasm for the Constitutional Convention, and Hamilton found it difficult to arouse any strong support for his state's delegation.

When Hamilton was a teenager in the Revolution, a fellow officer remembered him as "a mere boy of small slender and delicate frame, with his cocked hat pulled down over his eyes, marching beside a cannon and patting it every now and then as if it were a favorite play-thing." He won General Washington's admiration as a commander of a NY artillery company, for coolness under fire and his handling of his men. After the war he was admitted to practice law after only three months of intensive study and mastery of the subject!

Hamilton and John Adams were inveterate political enemies. Since there was mystery surrounding his birth and parentage, John Adams referred to Hamilton as "that Creole bastard," and Hamilton publicly accused Adams of incompetency, insensitivity and inertia.

Hamilton was the author of the proposal to hold a Constitutional convention to "increase central government's powers" and thus he was primarily responsible for what resulted — our U.S. Constitution. While at the Constitutional Convention he argued vehemently for the strongest possible central government — even going so far as advocating a "king" to head such a government. He later wrote 51 of the Federalist Papers (85 articles in favor of ratification) and made many political enemies, including Thomas Jefferson and other southern "state's righters." Hamilton was slain by Vice President Aaron Burr in a duel where his own son had been killed just three years before! As Hamilton lay dying he called his beloved Elizabeth to his side and said, "Eliza, remember we are Christians." According to some historical sources Hamilton had decided prior to the duel that he would not seek to take Burr's life but would aim and fire above his head. The fledgling experiment in republican democracy lost a brilliant administrator at the expense of Aaron Burr's dubious "honor."

Roger Sherman of Connecticut had been born in MA but had moved to CT as a young man and had become a lawyer, legislator and judge. A Puritan who dressed plainly, spoke simply, though clearly, Sherman was 66 years old but still vigorous. John Adams called him "that old Puritan, honest as an angel." Jefferson described him "Mr. Sherman of Connecticut, who never said a foolish thing in his life." Sherman was the only man among the delegates who signed all four of the great American document (1) Articles of Association, 1774; (2) Declaration of Independence, 1776; (3) Articles of Confederation, 1777; (4) U.S. Constitution, 1787.

John Adams said of Sherman's influence in the old Continental Congress, "He was as firm in the cause of American independence as Mount Atlas."

As a boy he learned the cobbler trade. He had no formal education except what he received from his home and what he taught himself. He became a voracious reader and self-taught himself business and law; he was both a successful merchant and lawyer.

Sherman presented the famous "Connecticut Compromise" that resolved the most crucial difference between the large and small states on representation in the national legislature calling for two lawmaking groups; one based on population (the House), the other based on the equal number of members from each state (the Senate).

He had seven children by his first wife and eight by his second. He served in the House of Representatives and the Senate until his death in 1793 at the age of 72.

Robert Morris, a delegate from PA was 54, and had the reputation of wisdom (especially in finances) and integrity. He was called "the richest man in America." He had signed the Declaration of Independence and the Articles of Confederation and had served in the PA Assembly and the Continental Congress. He was U.S. Superintendent of Finance in 1781 and during the Revolution was responsible for providing large sums of money (often out of his own private estate) to carry on the war. His experience in the financial office had convinced him that the Confederation was incapable of meeting the monetary needs of the young country, and so he resigned the position in 1783. He was a close friend and warm admirer of General Washington and kept Washington as his house guest all during the Convention. Morris was born in England and came to this country at the age of 14. He made some bad investments in his last years, and lost his fortune. He was sent to prison because he could not pay his debts (this man who had borrowed against his own estate to finance the Revolution) and died bankrupt a pauper at the age of 72!

William Livingston, a delegate from New Jersey, had been reared by his grandmother because of the early and untimely death of both his parents. He spent a year with Moravian missionaries teaching the Bible to Mohawk Indians. He was a Yale graduate, a lawyer, and author of anti-Anglican verses, essays and satirical pieces. He became a brigadier general in the New Jersey militia, and later was governor of the State of New Jersey which office he kept until his death. At the convention he fought issuing of paper money as "cheating according to the law."

Each one of these delegates is a story. More than half of all the delegates were lawyers. That is as it should have been, for members of the legal profession had long led the struggle for independence. Many present at the Convention were present or former public office holders. Four-fifths of them were serving in or had been members of the Continental Congress. Almost half of them had served in the military or assisted the military. Many had helped draft their state's constitutions. There were merchants, farmers ("planters"), and one or two men who described themselves as "bankers." Three of the delegates were physicians, two (Hugh Williamson from NC, and Abraham Baldwin from GA) were preachers, and one, Franklin, was a printer.

On the whole, the delegates were remarkably young. The average age was 43. *Jonathan Dayton* of NJ was, at 26, the youngest; Franklin at 81 was the eldest. Many had humble origins. Franklin had come to America as an indentured servant, Jacob Broom from Delaware, was the son of a blacksmith. Some of them were teachers; George Wythe of VA was a professor at William and Mary. Most delegates had acquired comfortable positions in life. A few ranked among the richest men in the country. Most of them were deeply religious and Christians. Twenty-five of them were graduates of American colleges (Princeton the leader); another ten were from English universities.

In a letter to Jefferson, Franklin expressed cautious optimism about the convention. The delegates were "men of character and ability," Franklin said, "so I hope good from their meeting." "Indeed," he added, "if it does not do good it must do harm, as it will show that we have not wisdom enough among us to govern ourselves; and will strengthen the opinion of some political writers, that popular governments cannot long support themselves."

On the morning of May 14, 1787, George Washington entered the central hall of the Pennsylvania State House, walked through the panelled doors that led from the hall into the east chamber, and took his seat in one of the chairs arranged about the low speaker's platform. "Let us raise a standard to which the wise and honest can repair," he told his fellow-delegates. Then he added, "The event is in the hand of God."

Some delegates left the convention before the final copy of the Constitution was prepared. Other remained but only to express their opposition to the final version. George Mason obstinate on the point of a Bill of Rights announced that he "would sooner chop off his right hand than put it to this Constitution." Edmund Randolph now doubted whether the people of his state would approve the document and announced that he could not sign it. Elbridge Gerry thought that the members of the Senate would hold their offices too long and that MA would not be fairly represented, and that a Supreme Court without juries would be a "Star Chamber" (kangaroo court). He announced he would not sign.

But, proceeding in the traditional order of states from north to south, the delegates walked to the front of the room, bent over the table in front of the President's Chair and, with quill pen dipped in iron gall ink, signed their names on the last page of the document. Only 5000 words, and four pages long, but one of the profoundest documents of human history! There were 38 delegates present but 40 signatures (George Read of DL, who had overcome his earlier opposition to the document, signed both for himself and for John Dickinson, who was feeling ill and had gone home — so there is a "forged" signature on the Constitution of the United States of America!). Thirteen delegates had left the convention before the final day and three had abstained. The 40th signature was that of Mr. William Jackson, not a delegate, but Secretary to the Convention, (ironically, his notes were not as complete as those of James Madison's).

This Constitution, written mostly by lawyers and planters, is a charter well suited to the needs of a great industrial nation. *Yet it has never been fundamentally revised.* In many other countries, constitutions come and go like the leaves of the trees. Ours is the result of wise and studious sages like James Madison who said, "In framing a system which we wish to last for ages, we should not lose sight of the changes which ages will produce." The framers of our constitution believed strongly in the rule of the majority. They guaranteed that no majority would have its way, however, unless it could prove itself "persistent and undoubted." They achieved this goal by separating and balancing the power of government, and by calling for a system of staggered elections, so that all elected officials would not be up for re-election at the same time.

The Constitution has continued to develop in response to the demands of an ever-growing society through amendments, congressional legislation, court decisions, presidential action, customs, state and political party actions. Yet the spirit and wording of the constitution have remained constant. Men of each generation have been able to apply its provision to their own problems in ways that protect their liberties.

James Madison, looking back on his experience at the Constitutional Convention, wrote: "It is impossible for the man of pious reflection not to perceive in the creation of the Constitution a finger of that Almighty Hand which has been so frequently and signally extended to our relief in the critical stages of the revolution." George Washington called it "a miracle." The British statesman, William E. Gladstone, described the U.S. Constitution as "the most wonderful work ever struck off at a given time by the brain and purpose of man." Others have said that it is the greatest single document, excepting the Bible, in all the history of the earth. And the greatest legal minds of two centuries have continued to marvel at it, as being almost beyond the scope and dimension of human wisdom. When one stops to consider the enormous problems the Constitution has somehow anticipated and the challenges and testing it foresaw and endured, that statement appears more understated than exaggerated. It does, indeed have the stamp of Divine wisdom upon it!

In a world of oppression and tyranny, the American people have no more precious possession (other than the Bible) than this great document. The story of how the framers wrote the Constitution and how it has met the challenges of American democracy and freedom through times of grave national testing is one that people should be proud of and never tire of hearing.

> Abraham Lincoln said: "Let every American, every lover of liberty, every well-wisher to his posterity swear by the blood of the Revolution never to violate in the least particular the laws of the country, and never to tolerate this violation by others. As the patriots of '76 did to the support of the Declaration of Independence, so to the support of the Constitution and law let

every American pledge his life, his property and his sacred honor. Let every man remember that to violate the law is to trample on the blood of his father, and to tear the charter of his own and his children's liberty . . . . Let it be taught in schools, in seminaries, and in colleges, let it be written in primers, in spelling books, and in almanacs, let it be preached from the pulpit, proclaimed in legislative halls, and enforced in courts of justice. And in short, let it become the political religion of the nation, and in particular, a reverence for the Constitution.

Over forty years ago, I raised my right hand and swore to defend my country and its Constitution against all enemies, foreign and domestic, with my life if need be. That was when I was sworn into the U.S. Navy. I still pledge my life in allegiance to the United States of America and to her Constitution today.